FOR GOD OR EMPIRE

FOR GOD OR EMPIRE

Sayyid Fadl and the Indian Ocean World

Wilson Chacko Jacob

Stanford University Press
Stanford, California

STANFORD UNIVERSITY PRESS
Stanford, California

A generous grant from the Shastri Indo-Canadian Institute has aided the publication of this book.

Printed in the United States of America on acid-free, archival-quality paper

Library of Congress Cataloging-in-Publication Data
Names: Jacob, Wilson Chacko, 1972– author.
Title: For God or empire : Sayyid Fadl and the Indian Ocean world / Wilson Chacko Jacob.
Description: Stanford, California : Stanford University Press, 2019. | Includes bibliographical references and index.
Identifiers: LCCN 2018053007 | ISBN 9780804793186 (cloth : alk. paper) | ISBN 9781503609631 (pbk. : alk. paper)
Subjects: LCSH: Faḍl ibn ʿAlawī, Amir of Ẓafaār, 1825–1900. | Sufis—India—Malabar—Biography. | Moplahs—India—Malabar—Biography. | Political activists—India—Malabar—Biography. | Sovereignty—Religious aspects—Islam. | Islam and politics—Indian Ocean Region—History. | Turkey—History—Ottoman Empire, 1288–1918. | India—History—British occupation, 1765–1947.
Classification: LCC BP80.F245 J33 2019 | DDC 297.4092 [B] —dc23
LC record available at https://lccn.loc.gov/2018053007

ISBN 978-1-5036-0964-8 (electronic)

Cover design by Susan Zucker

Typeset by Kevin Barrett Kane in 10/14 Minion Pro

To my parents, Aleyamma Jacob and Kochuputhen Jacob, again.

For a life I cannot repay in words or even deeds.

Contents

Illustrations

Preface

The original idea for this book, conceived over a decade ago as an even larger research project, was to bring the figures of the *sayyid* and the *futuwwa* into the same analytical frame. I wanted to know whether they could be regarded as loci of embodied sovereignty, and if so, what were its terms and how did they change—or not—with the emergence of the modern state in its imperial and national guises. After ending my first book on the question of the futuwwa as repressed other, in a narrative centered on the quintessential modernist subject of Egyptian history, the *effendi*, it seemed I had to follow the thread that I had just begun to weave into something whose final shape remained unclear. The last chapter of *Working Out Egypt* raised the specter of the futuwwa transformed, from a classical Islamic model of masculinity into an antimodern savage, as a problem of effendi masculinity rather than a subject in its own right.[1]

The new project was born in the wake of the 9/11 attacks on the US; I was perplexed by the new dispensation that seemed to follow, in which old laws of war and the principle of sovereignty, among others, seemed on the verge of being overwritten. In September 2001, I was in Egypt for research away from my then home of New York City—a home transformed by the time I returned a year later to be greeted by armed National Guardsmen at my neighborhood subway station. My research seeking to reimagine nationalism in terms of masculinity was suddenly rendered somewhat strange in a present that was witnessing the onset of a permanent war on transnational terrorism, or some said, on Islam. As Engseng Ho put it in recounting a similar experience, "My train of thought jumped tracks." In its flouting of state sovereignty in the war on al-Qaida, the US, as an oddly anticolonial imperial state, may have given birth to a particularly odd species of "the jihadi" as brutal, anti-imperialist colonizers, that is, ISIS.[2] In the face of these global developments, the nation-state for which I had mapped what I thought was an alternative history underwent its own transmutations.

In the years that followed, the prospects of researching the futuwwa and the sayyid began to seem overly daunting, however pressing the retrieval of their histories seemed. Blessed with a two-year sabbatical, I sat once again in a sunny yet now sad postrevolutionary Cairo in the spring of 2014, having forlornly reached a decision to abandon the futuwwa, and I began to prepare an initial draft of *For God or Empire* focusing exclusively on the *sufi-sayyid* as a specific formation of power and occasionally sovereignty. Though my inquiry into the transformation of futuwwa into *fitiwwa/baltagi*, or thuggish outlaw, was sidelined, I had plenty to deal with in the story of one particular ocean-hopping sayyid, Fadl Ibn Alawi, as sovereign, outlaw, and window onto a particular conception of life. Actually, the insight that a historical life might reveal something about a "unity of life" that was not historical per se only came later, after "the incident."

The writing was going quite well; the sources were rich. Then I experienced what might be described unexaggeratedly as a run-in with the return of the repressed. The futuwwa, or *fitiwwa* as Egyptians would say, seemed to leap out at me as if from the pages of a Naguib Mahfouz story (or a forsaken history, perhaps), and into real life. One evening, as the sun began to set, a band of four men pierced my self-satisfied writing bubble and merrily made off with my treasures: most preciously, my computer—*and* the backup drive. There is no silver lining where there is no "cloud."[3] As I struggled to recoup what had been lost and to start writing again about sovereignty, the law, and its frontiers, the terrible encounter with present-day *fitiwwat/baltagiyya* haunted the new process.

The men who came that night claimed to be Egyptian state security, though their rapid flashing of IDs and subsequent words and actions quickly cast doubt on their claim. I recall feeling comparatively relieved when I concluded they were modern-day bandits and not agents of the state. It can't be known for sure whether they were in fact official agents of the state or baltagiyya or a blend of both. The baltagiyya catapulted back into public consciousness during the Egyptian state's prolonged crisis that began in 2011, when making distinctions between thug and state seemed impossible and the "thug state" seemed quite real.[4]

Ironically, my early research was guided by the theoretical insight that the existence of a zone of indistinction at the heart of modern sovereignty between law and outlaw (life as other, naked) was constitutive and that as long as sovereignty remained meaningful for conceptualizing order, there was always already a state of exception. This seemed especially true when politics was thought historically and theoretically as developing not along a straight line in terms of interest and right but in a field of power that targeted the preservation, regulation, and improvement of life, which increasingly seemed to justify declarations of emergency. In the latter conception, of biopolitics, life's inclusion into sovereignty as a biological form and object of governmental ministrations was also its exclusion. This inclusive exclusion made life both manageable and disposable. A paradox perhaps, but also an irony?

I say irony because I realized after my face-to-face encounter with the exception that was the norm that such philosophically clever accounts of sovereignty could not account for the power of futuwwa or sayyid. In other words, ironically, I did not suddenly wish to appeal to state legitimacy as an antidote to the chaotic and dangerous forces swirling about me in local and global spheres of life. Surely the modern Egyptian state, like other states in the Middle East and across the Indian Ocean world, already fit the terms of sovereignty as put forward by Schmitt and elaborated by Agamben and others. Many of these polities inherited a state of exception from their prior histories as colonies, protectorates, mandates, or otherwise controlled political communities with very minor projects of liberal institution building in some. Thus, what better example of the topological figure of *homo sacer* or the camp than entire populations existing in a precarious relation to sovereignty, that is, their abandonment by state and their simultaneous inclusion in machineries of state violence?

Hence, who would seek more of the state? Likely, the majority of people—particularly when transnational terrorist groups threaten social peace and political stability in spectacular fashion, causing the exercise of state security to begin to appear more innocuous. The modern state's sovereignty in various degrees of perfection may be *the* global story of the long twentieth century, but it can't be the whole story. Other stories become legible when "the Middle East" and its constituent states, for example, are spun outward, as historical formations along longer timelines and broader spatial grids, and forward into a future after ISIS, after empire, and after state.[5]

Though reproducing some key tropes of modernity that historians have problematized, sociologist Armando Salvatore's reappraisal of the long routes by which liberal states in the Christian West and more-or-less authoritarian states in the Islamic East emerged as seemingly discrete civilizational blocs reveals the interconnectedness of the narratives of privatized religion and individual rights, on the one hand, and their failure or self-conscious, mostly rhetorical refusal, on the other. Famously, one side became powerful and had political sovereignty, ostensibly as a result of creating a dynamic, human-centered order, while the other became weak and struggled to mimic the Westphalian dispensation in an anticolonial register. However stark and ahistorical these comparisons may seem, rereading Marshall Hodgson for the present, Salvatore makes a valuable contribution in recuperating the Islamic "transcivilizational ecumene" and dislodging its plural transnational or supranational form from its reduction to a jihadist singularity. He offers an opening to think more critically about what the Islamic historical, ethical, political, and cultural (civilizational in Salvatore) formation (Islamdom in Hodgson) that did not mesh well with modern sovereignty might offer for thinking a shared future.[6]

It is, then, due to the troubling present and through the opening that Salvatore and other scholars of Islam, modernity, and transregional spaces have created that I chart in the following pages the course of Sayyid Fadl and others searching for meaning, reaching for more of life, while living in an oppositional or ambivalent relation to changing terms of sovereignty on a global scale.[7] It was no coincidence that futuwwa and sufi-sayyid overlapped in their historical developments and rose to prominence as urban and frontier modes of organizing life and as a perspective from which to think life in general when the universal Muslim caliphate faced its greatest and eventually fatal threats in the thirteenth century. The locations of their rise and expansion also suggest that it was no accident that they became conceptually capacious and linked categories, capable of deep and broad discourses of peace, compassion, charity, and love as well as war, cruelty, self-interest, and violence.

When facing the return of the repressed in its monstrous form on that day in Cairo, as light faded to dark, it was not the law or the state that I conjured as potential savior, nor was it God or a divine being of some other kind. Rather, in the thuggish life facing me I wondered where the real futuwwa had gone: Where might I find the futuwwa of compassion, charity, and protection that might redress this wrong for me? In which body or bodies does the life-form of al-futuwwa and the sufi-sayyid reside today? I found an answer in the aftermath of the incident that killed the first version of this book: in fact it is all around us, and in far greater numbers than the always highlighted barbaric life-forms versus compliant subjects of juridico-political bodies beholden to sovereignty and capable of repression just as readily as they are often repressed.

The presence that I have struggled to identify in this work, as resisting or exceeding the terms of sovereignty and for which I have used the shorthand "unity of life," was after all an absence in a double sense. The solitary secular scholarly enterprise in which I had become deeply enmeshed involved a gradual forgetting of this absence, and only in the aftermath of the incident did it slowly make its way back to my consciousness as being not there. The *solidarity* that binds together stranger and host, the unseen and the seen, all that has come and that which is yet to come, faith to some—this was the absence that I forgot or learned to ignore. The care and kindness of friends and strangers reminded me of the absent, leading to the book's rebirth. Thus, I owe a profound debt of gratitude to all those who helped restore my faith in our capacity to live life in terms that exceed our bounds and our boundedness.

Acknowledgments

I feel I have lived a long time, longer than may be proper, with Sayyid Fadl Ibn Alawi, having first "met" him in the marvelous Public Records Office of the UK nearly a decade and a half ago. In a strange way, then, my first thanks is owed to the meticulous record keepers of the British Empire and to their heirs at The National Archives and the British Library's India Office Records. I'm sure Fadl of all people would appreciate the irony. Though it was in the imperial archive that my discovery of Fadl's remarkable history began, it was in the remote hamlet of Mampuram and in other locations in Malabar that I learned the meaning of the "life" I would end up narrating. Thus, I owe the deepest gratitude to the Mampuram Maqam of Sayyid Alawi and to the many who sought its blessing, for opening my eyes again to a power I had lost sight of.

There were specific individuals and institutions in Malabar that offered assistance in gathering materials, serving as guides, and sharing memories, information, and food who should be thanked by name: Dr. M. Gangadharan, Sayyid Ahmad Jifri, Mujeeburrahman Kinalur, Mahmood Kooria, Abdurahman Mangad, Faris K. Muhammed, Rathish I, Rathish II, Dr. K. K. Mohammed Abdul Sathar, Darul Huda, and Other Books. This project also allowed me to reconnect with members of my own "mappila" clan—uncles, aunts, cousins of various remove—who are too numerous to thank individually but for whose warmth, hospitality, and always bountiful amounts of the most delicious food in the world I am truly grateful. My parents' homes in Punaveli and Puthuppally were welcome retreats from the solitary pursuits of the scholarly life; there is nothing like enjoying a Kingfisher while watching the monsoon rains from the verandah. And for teaching me to read my first language after decades of being illiterate, as the Communist Party official (responsible for "tribal literacy") described us students of the AIIS Malayalam School in Thiruvananthapuram, I am grateful to Dr. V. K. Bindu and Mr. Arun. I thank Dr. Jose Abraham for sharing his list of contacts before I left Montreal. And if I have missed anyone in Kerala, it has been a long journey and I hope they will forgive me.

In Istanbul, Paris, and Cairo, I benefited from the long reach of the NYU Middle East Studies program. Without Zeynep Turkyilmaz's assistance in locating sources on or by Fadl in the Ottoman archive and Zehra Gulbahar Cuneillera's translations, the story would be far less complex. Khaled Fahmy, Hanan Kholoussy, and Sherene Seikaly offered material and spiritual support during a difficult time. Beyond the NYU canopy, in Cairo, many other generous friends offered shelter and support in numerous ways. Maha Abdel-Rahman, Waleed Asfour, Neil Hewison, Nancy Mahmoud, and Nefertiti Takla were heroic; I am not sure Neil realizes how restorative the beauty of his farm in Fayyum was for me that spring of 2014. An ARCE Fellowship enabled that time in Egypt. Sinan Antoon, Waleed Asfour, Maurice Pomerantz, and Najat Rahman may have felt too often that they were being used as *qamus*-es of the Arabic language; all errors of translation are my own.

This book would not have been possible without the generous support by way of funds and time off to do research provided by Concordia University, an FQRSC Nouveau Chercheur Grant, an SSHRC Standard Research Grant, and the Shastri Indo-Canadian Institute's Publication Grant. I was also the proud recipient of a EURIAS Fellowship, which enabled me to spend a memorable year at Cambridge University as a Fellow of Clare Hall and the Center for Research in the Arts, Social Sciences, and Humanities run by the indomitable Simon Goldhill. To the shock of class-conscious Brits and to my own pleasant surprise, I found that rowing in an eight-person boat on the River Cam was an exhilarating way to start the day! Thanks to the CRASSH fellows who made the culture of pubs accessible, especially Brian Murray, who valiantly strived to help me appreciate classic ales; Eleonora Rosati, who brought an Italian flair to the English countryside; and Anders Ekström, who, with Marika and Sara, showed that Swedish ways are not as exotic as I had imagined them. In that year, I was also fortunate to be able to attend one of Chris Bayly's final seminars, though our exchange in the wine store across from King's on a Friday afternoon will remain my fondest memory of him. I thank Shruti Kapila for her fierceness, for making sure that my location at the heart of empire was interrogated properly. And I owe a special thanks to Faisal Devji at Oxford for being kind enough to write letters before seeing the project in its final form, but more important, for inviting me to lunch.

An SSHRC Connection Grant and the EURIAS Fellowship funded an engaging international workshop on sovereignty in a transregional frame, which I convened at CRASSH with the extraordinary support of Catherine Hurley and Michelle Maciejewska. I am grateful to the participants who helped me to broaden and deepen my understanding of this elusive concept. Michael Gilsenan's shift in research focus to the Indian Ocean has been an inspiration, and I am deeply grateful for his participation in the workshop and continued support. My first attempt to formulate a thesis about sovereignty, Islam, and empire could not have been delivered in a more ideal setting than on the once resort island of Bornholm in the Baltic Sea, at a conference on "Religion, Law and Regimes of Control around the Indian Ocean," convened in 2010 by Preben Kaarsholm and Bodil Frederiksen, including participants Anne Bang, Fahad Bishara, Pamela Gupta, and Jeremy Prestholdt, who all offered much fodder for thought. In the same year, I was fortunate to have the opportunity to refine my thoughts in the context of the SSRC Inter-Asian Connections Conference in Singapore. I went with the sole intention of learning from the brilliant Engseng Ho, whose work on the Alawis in the Indian Ocean world is a must-read for every historian aspiring to the global. The codirector of my workshop, Lakshmi Subramaniam, offered encouragement and indicated I was on the right path. Since then, I have presented different parts of this project as it developed in various venues around the world, and I thank all of the organizers and participants of those events for their engagements: at Concordia, UCLA, UCSB, NYU, Tufts, Berkeley, AUC, Cambridge, the Swedish Collegium, and Darul Huda. Amal Ghazal of Simon Fraser University has graciously included me in Indian Ocean world activities, allowing me to keep abreast of the latest scholarship. I especially wish to thank Gwyn Campbell, director of the Indian Ocean World Center at McGill University, for bringing together a lively group of students and researchers every week. My research has benefited from two talks I delivered in that forum and from the advice and assistance of Veysel Simsek and Zozan Pehlivan in navigating Ottoman sources online. Zozan went the extra mile of tracking down sources and reading them with me; every researcher knows that such generosity is rare and worthy of commendation.

Also from the Montreal crew of amazing friends, Aslihan Gurbuzel and Elena Razlogova took a side trip when in Istanbul to photograph the gravesite of Sayyid Fadl. Claudia Fabbricatore and Setrag and Vahagn Manoukian have always left open their door to delicious Italian food and warm company; I only wish I had walked through it more often. Setrag and Andrew Ivaska read through very rough drafts of most chapters and offered sharp critiques and comments that have made this a better work. Ted McCormick has proven himself as a fierce defender of truth and right against zealots of various stripes. At a particularly low period, Carolyn Fick gave me the best advice ever. Michelle Hartman (and Tameem), Jeehee Hong, Khalid Medani, Najat Rahman, Gavin Taylor, and Anya Zilberstein have provided many hours of fun and companionship over the years. Najat literally put a roof over my head more than once. Meanwhile, through it all, my sanity was maintained by regular runs on the mountain and watching zombies while eating Singh's with Lara Braitstein, who, I'm convinced, knows the secret of living life well. Also cherished for replenishing the spirit were the all too rare rendezvous with my old *shilla* from Brooklyn. I am humbled by the continued encouragement and support of my work shown by Zachary Lockman and Arang Keshavarzian.

The last push to finish would have been far less pleasurable if I did not have the lovely balcony of my lovely home from which to work, and for this I must thank the generous Vassilio Tzortzis. I thank the copyeditor for SUP who pushed me to be a clearer writer, the charming production manager Carolyn Brown who made the process as painless as possible (flecked with stories of Calcutta and Minnesota!), my immensely patient and compassionate editor Kate Wahl at Stanford who saw the value in Fadl's life from the very beginning, and finally, the anonymous reviewers for their penetrating critiques. It is a better book because of their generosity.

Sadly, a season of loss attended the final stretch. Saba Mahmood's radical re-visioning of agency and freedom inspire every page of this book. The body may have betrayed this powerful life, but her light continues to shine bright; I only wish we had had more time so that I could reiterate my appreciation and respect. Two people who once cared for me in the first years of my life in Kerala, Ponnamma Auntie and the Kollad Appachen, as I remember them, also passed. And though I cannot remember those years, I was fortunate to get to know them again in the time I was working on the book. Death is at the heart of this work; it is a generative force rather than the opposite of life. It is, as I have been taught, a coming home.

Note on Transliteration

This book uses an extremely simplified method of transliteration in order to keep the text as accessible as possible to nonspecialists; specialists should be able to decode the intended word. Words such as *ulama* that have entered English lexicons will not be transliterated or italicized. Generally, words from other languages will only be italicized when they first appear in the text. Also, since the source languages are many (Arabic, Malayalam, and Ottoman Turkish), the use of multiple special characters and diacritics that indicate different effects seems excessively burdensome. Only in the case of the Arabic letters ʿ*ayn* and ʾ*hamza* have the standard rules for transliteration been employed, and even then, only when the letters appear in the middle or at the end of a word.

FOR GOD OR EMPIRE

Introduction

Life In-Between

The present would appear to be one of those instances not uncommon in the East, where a man of worldly experiences and force of character, whose descent gives a kind of claim to religious sanctity, imposes by falsehood and boasted human and divine influence upon the simple minds of people of the country. The Arab character is peculiarly adapted to receive such impressions,—witness the origin and growth of Islam.

—*Loch to Jardine, 20 November 1877*

Prelude: Intimacy and Distance

For God or Empire is an experiment in writing global Indian Ocean history through biography, as well as being an effort to rethink the genealogy of the concepts of "sovereignty" and "life" through that history. It makes four interlinked arguments that marshal the aid of history, anthropology, religion, and philosophy. First, the life story narrated herein, of the peripatetic *sufi-sayyid* Fadl Ibn Alawi (22 Rajab 1240 / March 12, 1825–2 Rajab 1318 / October 26, 1900), is local, transregional, and global at once: both multiscalar and multivectored, it can only be told in terms of many places, many times, and many communities. Second, Fadl's membership in an Indian Ocean Sufi Way with a Prophetic lineage—the Tariqa al-Alawiyya—and his entanglements with empires—British, Ottoman, Omani—mean the life story must also necessarily braid together Islamic and imperial history in and between South Asia and the Middle East.[1] Third, those entanglements were conceptually and historically specific, because they were centered on the problem of modern sovereignty accompanying the history of state formation around the Indian Ocean. Fourth, since modern sovereignty was globalized as universal yet remains an unresolved problem in the present, by supplementing the historical with the genealogical in a consideration of returns—of lineages to their rightful places, of places to their rightful lineages, of the repressed other—we are able to view a politics of life confronting a philosophy of life.

Evidently, a book titled *For God or Empire* could start in a number of different places and times, in a number of different registers. Given such an overwhelming range of possibilities, let us begin with what may seem the least relevant bit: a brief conversation I had with an uncle on the verandah of my parents' pocket-sized rubber plantation in the foothills of the magical Western Ghats, on the monsoon-blessed, spectacularly green Kerala side of the border with Tamil Nadu in South India.[2] On a typical, mind-numbingly hot day in May before the June rains began, my father's eldest brother, who was born in the late 1920s, dropped in for a visit. The conversation veered toward the improprieties of the "colony" just beyond our land. I asked why he chose to use that English word over any number of Malayalam words. He deployed the word, as others of a similar landed class might, to refer to the closely built houses inhabited by a land-poor group of Christians—who were, he explained, quite unlike us *mappila*s. I was thrown now by his use of the word "mappila," since I had come to understand it differently in the course of my research. "Mappilas" in his use marked a historical and racial difference from latter-day lower-caste Hindu converts, whose Christian roots go back "only" to colonial and American missionary activities of the twentieth century. As such, they did not enjoy the gifts of land and accompanying status that Hindu rajas had bestowed on the first Syrian Christian men to arrive on the shores of historic Malabar (present-day Kerala) in the third or fourth century CE. Those men eventually took local wives, which in effect, and legally, made them mappilas (husbands), reproducing a parallel caste structure over time.[3]

Aside from the persistent class/caste chauvinism that no longer shocked me (even in a man of modest means), my uncle's words were nonetheless surprising, as they unwittingly evoked this ancient history. He was echoing a certain elite history that connected Hindu-Jewish-Christian-Muslim pasts through what might be called an originary principle of the Indian Ocean world, if there was such a world: that of hospitality. This is a history, however elite, that is often buried or written over by other narratives according to political expediency.[4] Such writing over was enabled by the institutionalization of colonial archives that were collected and housed in central repositories and are accessed today by historians. And if "the archive" is conceived more broadly, we might find it imprinted on the tongues of even the remotest of village dwellers, its words displacing others.

In the single word "mappila," the vast geography, history, and language of modern empire were evoked, though in whispers of an older generation it bespoke other forms of connected life not always discernible to geography, history, or even language—"disciplines" reborn in empire. "Mappila," as remembered and used by my uncle, evoked mobile formations, waves of wanderers bearing multiple spatial, temporal, and linguistic codes grafted onto local forms of kinship, caste, and power—without the aid of gunboats or soldiers. There was certainly room for interpretation here extending beyond crude elitism or equally crude romanticism or essentialism.

As one of the disciplined, I first encountered the Mappila (or "Moplah") through the empire's archive in London. I found this label and another, the "Outlaw," stamped onto the life and career of Sayyid Fadl Ibn Alawi, the subject I began to research over a decade ago.[5] At the time, "Moplah" was only a vaguely familiar term lodged in the recesses of my inchoate cultural memory as a Malayali born in central Kerala but raised almost entirely in the US. It was only years later sitting on that verandah in the sleepy hamlet of Punaveli that I began to suspect from my uncle's hushed tones that the term "mappila" contained many layers of meaning beyond a superficial indexing of difference. "Mappila" was clearly not a native term exclusively denoting Muslim, as was authoritatively asserted by colonial officials in the nineteenth century and has become quite widely accepted today. It is a general term that—in addition to meaning "husband," which I had always known—in ancient times signified a stranger to the land received as an honored guest, as the Syrian Christians were, as Jews were before them, and as Muslims were after. Accordingly, a global Indian Ocean history that ignores the vernacular in expressions of hospitality and attends instead to capitalist cosmopolitanism or colonial epistemes is not only inadequate—it is also often inaccurate.[6]

Another place I could have more obviously begun the book is with Sayyid Fadl, the central character of the narrative, though in fact we must first hear about his father, Sayyid Alawi (ca. 1750–January 28, 1844), because in some important ways it was this other traveler, more than the colonial official, who gave shape to the synonymous Mappila-Muslim identity in Malabar. In the middle of the eighteenth century, two interrelated things happened that set our global Indian Ocean history in motion: one, a peculiar outfit's military victory; and two, the voyage outward of a holy man and saint in the making. The peculiar outfit (though it was less peculiar after roughly a century and a half) was the English East India Company (EIC), granted Elizabethan royal charter in 1600; the victory was its defeat of the Nawab of Bengal at the Battle of Plassey in 1757. The voyage outward was the departure of Sayyid Alawi for India; his heading was the opposite end of the subcontinent, where the EIC had not yet penetrated. The former event is often said to have established the basis of British domination over South Asia. The revenue of Bengal at its command a decade or so after Plassey, the alliances it formed with local rulers, and international developments allowed the EIC to move into a preeminent position in India by the close of the century.

By comparison, Sayyid Alawi's migration from his home in Tarim in the southern Hadhramawt region of the Arabian Peninsula (or the "Arab subcontinent," as Sayyid Fadl would see it later when he journeyed in the opposite direction) across the Indian Ocean to the southwest Malabar Coast of India, ca. 1766, would seem far less significant and utterly mismatched. Certainly if our eyes are set solely on stories of conquest, organized resistance, wealth, and empire, the story of Sayyid Alawi's life may pale in comparison and fade from view. The movement of Alawi *sayyid*s, descendants of the Prophet Muhammad, through space and time may assume greater significance in an investigation that seeks to establish historically and theoretically the limits of capital, state, and secular ideologies in the determination of life's possibilities. In other words, for god *or* empire was always a question for many, and it remains a question that matters.

That said, the mid- to late 1700s witnessed upheavals so transformative of life in the century to follow that typically historians locate the beginning of the modern era in those years, and many have identified the empires that had come to span the globe as the major vectors, crucibles, or engines of change.[7] Revolutionary forces operating globally and in the overlapping domains of politics, economy, and science in turn demystified the world and made it properly ours, a kingdom of men. As our story progresses, we will have reason to reconsider the nature of change and the process of disenchantment that ostensibly marked this moment. For now, it suffices to note that grounding sovereignty in divine—mysterious and mystical—sources was deemed no longer sufficient to advance mutually recognized claims of political authority over territories or subjects. Through the course of the nineteenth century, so the story goes, this ungrounded yet ever more absolute or indivisible form of sovereignty became the universal global dispensation. This particular shift famously undergirding the rise of the modern nation-state and its evolution politically—an old mystery in a new bottle, some argue—entailed a repositioning of the ends of life such that the ministrations of pastors, sayyids, and other men of religion were relegated to increasingly narrow, private domains.

Sayyid Alawi and Sayyid Fadl encountered this state in its formative period. The EIC was not by name or constitution a state; yet its edifice and practices of rule, which were by both necessity and design a hybrid of English, British, Mughal, and other Indian institutions, illuminate in stark relief the formation of the modern state through a confluence of war-making, market relations, and ideas of economy.[8] The Battle of Plassey was one instance and outcome of the alliance politics of the long eighteenth century, through which the British and French empires vied for global supremacy, in turn forcing and fostering rapid innovations in military and administrative technologies. Another instance was the Mysore wars in southern India, which by 1799 ended in a total EIC victory and the acquisition of lands on the Malabar Coast, placing the fate of the Alawis in the hands of British magistrates.

Sayyid Alawi's route from Arabia in the mid-eighteenth century was an ancient one, as were the terms of exchange he would have encountered along the way and upon arrival in India, or al-Hind, as the (sub)continent was known to Arabic speakers and others. His son's forced departure from India nearly a century later and return to his "homeland in Arabia," as the British considered it, encompassed routes and terms of exchange that were vastly different. It was not simply the introduction of rail and steamship technology or communication by telegraph that reshaped the circuits of travel and the experience of crossing the Indian Ocean. The "sea-change in sovereignty" that swept across all shores and spaces in between, as Sugata Bose evocatively maps in his Indian Ocean history, ensured that Sayyid Fadl's movements would never be the same as his father's.[9] His "passport" to travel was issued by the EIC magistrate of Calicut and was not a letter of introduction penned by a famous scholar, long-distance merchant, sultan, or amir.[10]

In Sayyid Alawi's case, he had family members waiting for him in India, as well as the prospect of marriage. He made his way from Tarim in Wadi Hadhramawt, the home base of the Alawi sayyids and Sufi Way, to the southern coast of the Arab subcontinent. He likely found passage to India on a "dhow" sailing out of the port of al-Shihr or al-Mukalla, both of which are roughly four to five days on foot from Tarim.[11] He disembarked at the port of Calicut, which had risen to prominence in the thirteenth century as a major entrepôt—aided in part by Mongol conquests across continental Eurasia—for merchants sailing from Southeast Asia and China, on the one hand, and Western India and the Middle East, on the other.[12]

So Tarim, Shihr, and Calicut were points along an extensive transoceanic network of exchange whose "progressive intensification of contact" since the

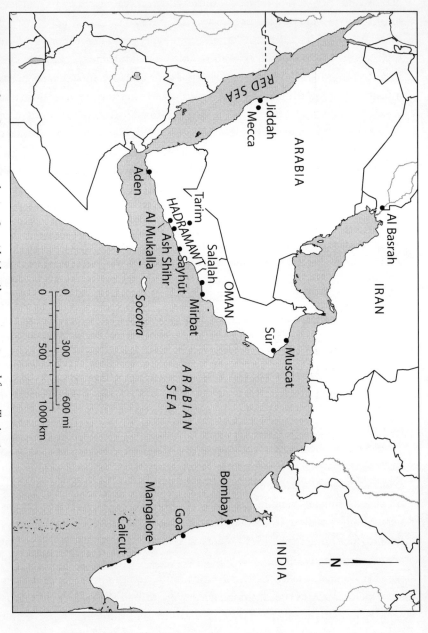

The primary Indian Ocean ports during Sayyid Alawi's voyage outward from Tarim to Calicut in the mid-eighteenth century.

thirteenth century virtually constituted the ground of a "new world" with recognizable Islamic forms of trade, culture, and politics.[13] The centuries after the Mongol destruction of Baghdad saw not the demise of "Islam" as once portrayed but quite the contrary: Islam, without an Abbasid caliph, in fact expanded further into new domains after 1258, especially across maritime spaces, and aided in the founding of Muslim polities in South and Southeast Asia. Moreover, the recovery and reticulation of trade routes and new alliances between Turkic dynasties and Sufi lineages led to the reinvigoration of old Muslim societies, laying the groundwork for the rise of the great territorial empires of the Ottomans, Safavids, and Mughals in the fifteenth and sixteenth centuries.[14]

Some attribute these globally significant shifts—especially the impact of nonsedentary peoples moving over greater distances but also the demise of once-great trading ports—to the waning of the Medieval Warm Period and the onset of the Little Ice Age that would last until the eighteenth century, wreaking most of its havoc during the cooling of the seventeenth century. Historians with a nearly religious commitment to causal explanations and an aversion to environmental explanations continue to debate whether the dramatic events of the seventeenth century throughout Eurasia (relating to wild fluctuations of price, population, and taxes) were products of a general economic crisis, separate regional developments, an exclusively European phenomenon, or in fact the growth pangs of a capitalist world system that began with sixteenth-century globalization.[15] Yet most seem to agree that a mix of good fortune, good government, and the effective use of violence decided who came out on top, who moved down in the rankings, and who was erased from the map. The latter would be the fate of the Safavids, the Mughals, and the Ming.

As we will see in the following chapters, the survival of the Ottomans in a weakened position throughout the long nineteenth century would figure significantly in the life trajectory of Sayyid Fadl, whereas in the life of his father it was the expansion and strengthening of the British at the expense of the Mughals and regional contenders, namely, the Mysoreans, that formed the backdrop to his ascension to sainthood in Malabar. The burial place of Sayyid Alawi in turn became a holy site that was enshrined by the Mappilas in the form of the Mampuram Maqam. And though the shrine only makes marginal appearances, it is a major figure in the larger picture this book attempts to draw.

Through the grave (*qabr*) that becomes a shrine (*maqam, dargah*), life becomes death becomes life again, an equation repeated around the Indian Ocean world for centuries.[16] However, in the endeavor to weigh the significance of

Fadl's inheritance from his father-friend (*wali*) for his subsequent religious and political life in exile, the methods of any one discipline proved inadequate for relating his biography to transoceanic histories of empires; the particulars and universals proper to that life tended to be swept up by the waves of modern sovereignty, becoming merely submerged background noise to ostensibly more significant or intelligible stories. For example, the usual translation of *wali* as "saint" radically recontextualizes the life story of the Alawis within a Christian theological and historical framework, missing the terms of sovereignty that were properly Islamic, wherein al-Wali is also one of the names of God, from which are derived the cognates *wilaya* (sovereignty, sanctity) and *walaya* (friendship, guardianship).[17] The conceptual relations that constitute divine sovereignty for Muslims, and particularly for the sufi-sayyid, link intimacy and unbridgeable distance in ways quite distinct from Christian-derived political theology. In the Islamic lexicon, life and death, wali and maqam, were microcosms or terrestrial signs of all existence (*wujud*) on a permanent recursive and impossible return to God (al-Wahid, al-Wajid, al-Wali): the One-Unity, Finder-Realizer, and Friend-Protector.

While journeying through history, anthropology, religion, and philosophy in search of a method, I hypothesized that the power of life that Fadl contemplated was not in the "death complex" per se. The force of this paradoxical formation of material and organic life that transmutes death to life/force/energy/power in a recursive series of returns was located in imperceptible spaces between a multiplicity of beings and things—walls, relics, sounds (of *dhikr*: prayers remembering the wali/Wali), and so forth—and not in any one body or thing. In the space between the touch and the touched, where language is held in abeyance, meaning is momentarily reconstructed in terms of a "unity of life" wherein the force of nonliving things (corpses, shrines, relics, images) is channeled to the living and vice versa, creating a paradox that might be captured in Ibn Arabi's *maqam la maqam* (the place of no place). The moment is fleeting: method, grammar, and discipline dissolve along with other rational conventions that divide life and nonlife. Life's unity, power, force, vitality, and potentiality are constituted and reconstituted in this space in between of every gathering of souls, every reaching out, every shrine's erection, every friend's birth and death. Intuition, instinct, faith—these are the "methods" for accessing and affirming that in the presence that is an absence is power.

Philosophers and theologians have long contemplated the nature of life and its connectivity, its purpose, and its power. An interesting work in comparative political theory that reveals much about the mid-twentieth-century moment of thinking life and sovereignty is Ahmad Ilyas's quest to identify the Islamic contribution to the conceptualization and right exercise of sovereignty, an inquiry that seems to map onto his preoccupation with absolutism and the Islamic state. He defines sovereignty as the exclusive property of God: "[Allah's] authority is undivided and indivisible and therefore, it is a unity. Sovereignty thus is unity and Unity is Sovereignty."[18] For a medieval Sufi scholar, Ilyas's definition only begs the question of life in relation to a sovereignty that demands its absolute distance from creation in order to be absolute, thus opening up possibilities for the soul closed off in more orthodox theology.

In the Sufi tradition of Ibn Arabi (d. 1240), which was tremendously influential to the Alawiyya, the unity of life (*wahdat al-wujud*), though never a term used by the Master, became an explicitly elaborated concept associated with him.[19] It walked the fine line between the radical monotheistic separation of God and creation and the pantheistic play of divine absence and presence(ing), of a permanently deferred finding/being (*wujud*) of the only One (al-Wahid) who can be the Finder (al-Wajid).[20] In my translation and usage of "unity of life," the focus is on the implied in-betweenness of all life (including nonlife) in relation to God and to sovereignty of any kind, a site of power that is at once in place, and not maqam la maqam. Through the death of God's friends (pl. *awliya'*) and their enshrinement, any person could potentially possess this knowledge, and not only disciples on paths dedicated to perfection. This conceptualization of life views in-betweenness as more than a way station following the end of biological life, the Sufi *barzakh*, an isthmus between the oceans of this life and the next; rather, it is a remarkably open, permanent, and powerful condition of life perpetually unfolding. The unity of life conceived as a critical category (not identical to Sufi usage) expresses a paradoxical moment of being tied to all and to nothing, temporarily suspending sovereignty's claim over (non)life.

The historian, even one who traverses disciplinary boundaries, can only ever view this power in life in glimpses of the in between of emergences and extinctions, of the touch and the touched, of departures and returns. As Fadl was compelled to leave India in 1852, the book follows his peregrinations and increasing entanglement in the politics of empires. The repercussions of his involvement in the affairs of the Hijaz soon after his arrival there seemed to drive him away from politics to a life of meditation and spiritual exercises. In the 1870s, he was again active in worldly matters, to the point of taking up the mantle of the amir of Dhofar in 1876. A mere three years later, a perfect storm involving an unprecedented drought, tribal rebellion, and imperial machinations (British and Omani) unseated him from his position and drove him into the welcoming arms of the Ottoman sultan Abdulhamid II.[21] He remained in Istanbul, in a veritable golden cage, for the remainder of his life, though he repeatedly sought to return to Dhofar and to Malabar. He became associated with the pan-Islamists, was awarded a ministerial rank, and engaged in intelligence gathering on southern Arabian affairs. He devoted the last years of his life to writing Sufi treatises on the Alawiyya.

This brief biography will be expanded upon in the chapters to follow. The preponderance of extant evidence makes clear Fadl's relationship to imperial contexts, in which sovereignty was being retooled and rooted in state through the application of new administrative and disciplinary technologies. This was no longer the sovereignty of the king's two bodies or of the sultan as God's shadow on earth.[22] Its breadth could not be explained only in terms of the secularization of theological concepts.[23] Rather, modern sovereignty worked by drawing all life closer to the ends of political considerations and social engineering, while sidelining an ever more narrowly conceived religion. Meanwhile, other evidence, namely, Sufi texts and hagiographies, makes possible readings of this historical life that reveal the ongoing significance of Islamic conceptions of sovereignty/life at the time of his death and into the present.[24]

Biographical methods help map the changing contours of historical life as conceived in relation to both divine sovereignty and modern sovereignty, giving us a rich picture of the transformations in state and society during the long nineteenth century. Biography can open a window onto global histories of Islam and imperial competition in the Indian Ocean worlds of South Asia and the Middle East. However, I argue that the very picture we shall draw here must be supplemented by a speculative inquiry, following what we shall call the methodology of the glimpse, in order to view the transhistorical yet space-time-cancelling unity of life that was and is believed to be beyond the veil, between God and creation. What sense of life is this? This question animates our study of empire and the problem of sovereignty but will be approached tangentially through two other, interrelated questions: How did Fadl's consciousness of the role of the Alawis in the making of a global Indian

Ocean world compel and structure his political activism in relation to God and in relation to imperial powers? What futures or cosmic timescapes formed his horizon of thought and insight?

Fugue: Global, Universal, Eternal

As alluded to above, answers to these two questions require, on the one hand, interdisciplinarity of method and, on the other hand, speculation as to the very validity and value of inquiring about something that is not, an absent presence. In this section I shall lay out the book's arguments, showing what proceeding on both tracks may yield in terms of writing a global Indian Ocean history and what that in turn may yield for our understandings of sovereignty and life.

Interdisciplinary Approach

At one level, all of the arguments in the book proceed from a simple premise: one cannot do a global history of the Indian Ocean without better histories of fundamental concepts that organize that world, such as life and sovereignty, the meanings of which cannot simply be assumed to be self-evident. In a recent *American Historical Review* forum, "Vernacular Ways of Knowing," Nile Green argues against a tendency to write global intellectual history in the Indian Ocean in terms of a presupposition of cosmopolitanism, understood loosely as a celebration of difference, unity, and universalism. It is not, in his view, an empirically verified characteristic but more a founding myth of Indian Ocean "world" studies, wherein "world" became romanticized shorthand for a conflict- and contradiction-free zone shattered by colonial intrusions and needing anticolonial rescue. Flattened out were the unpredictable vectors of the "waves of heterotopia" that bespoke a variety of experiences and reactions ranging from chauvinism to universalism.[25] My opening anecdote, with its moral that hospitality was a marker of this "interregional arena," is intended to offer a more qualified view of the vernacular.[26]

What Green misses in his application of the vernacular as a method to demonstrate the limits of cosmopolitanism and the colonial episteme is how in the very period he considers (1850–1930s), a hegemony was indeed realized on a global scale. That hegemony, however, was not of some reified Enlightenment subject that is easily dismissed by means of texts in the vernacular (which he starkly distinguishes from "learned colonial second languages").[27] Rather, in the preceding decades, what Reinhart Koselleck has called the "saddle period" (1750–1850), hospitality became one of the many casualties of European mercantilist policies applied in the Indian Ocean. Meanwhile, challenges to mercantilism at home and abroad engendered new claims on and about the earth and its people in various idioms—legal, economic, cultural, and political—that eventually led to radical reformations of life. This was a route to the hegemony of the modern state, an idea that washed up on all shores on the waves of the sea change in sovereignty. The revised history of modern sovereignty that we seek to unearth—as a product of shared global encounters, new conceptions of state and society, and the concomitant narrowing, or territorialization and secularization, of subjective possibilities—cannot be reduced to terms such as "de-cosmopolitanization" (a process that assumes a prior cosmopolitanization, which Green adeptly problematizes).

The empirical verification of the hegemonic conceptions of sovereignty and of life—as organized into moral and political communities protected and represented by states—would seem unnecessary if we consider the implications of being a stateless subject in the modern world by the end of Green's period. Nonetheless, the intellectual and political impoverishment that ensues from taking for granted that such (re)organization was tantamount to the subjugation of all life on the planet under a single (colonial) episteme is what I take to be the lesson of the cautionary tales excavated through the vernacular method. Both in the fantasy and imperial hubris of the long nineteenth century and in postcolonial modernization theories and nationalist developmentalism, all planetary life was destined to become the object of technologically advanced regimes. In history, the living of life, life's conceptualizations, and life's power were never quite so streamlined or reducible.

However, the work of recuperating those histories requires thinking simultaneously along historical and theoretical lines, as well as interdisciplinarily. This is especially the case since this book is concerned with how historical life, of the Alawis, reveals something about both sovereignty's transformation and a philosophy of life that is not reducible to it.[28]

Multiscalar and Multivectored Life

How can life exist on multiple planes simultaneously and in constant motion? The biography of Sayyid Fadl aims to answer this question in terms of his historical life of peregrinations and his changing conceptual framework. To appreciate the full significance of both movements, of body and mind, the investigation must track life in two registers: as lived in the past and as an implosion of past, present, and future. In doing so, then Fadl's life and concepts of life may appear in a new light.

If Fadl was simultaneously heir to a noble Muslim Sufi tradition and a student as well as subject of modern colonialism and imperialism, one might expect his religious and political horizons to be anything but simple, given, or predictable. His upbringing in India, his exile to and adventures in Arabia, his detention in Istanbul were but one trajectory, the one most legible from the records that remain. They provide us with a view onto local, transregional, and global Indian Ocean history in the nineteenth century. One's choice of archive, source, and method reveals the local, the transregional, and the global in different lights. In other words, these geographical labels that loosely represent degrees of proximity and distance as seemingly fixed points also evoke motion, mobility, and relationships, which were understood and experienced by different groups of people differently over time. In Chapter 6, Fadl's descriptive map of Dhofar illustrates this point very well; his engagement with the terms of imperial sovereignty therein was markedly different from Sayyid Alawi's assumptions about the space of Dar al-Islam and divine sovereignty, as we will see in the fatwas treated in Chapter 2.

In the interval between Sayyid Alawi's death (1844) and Sayyid Fadl's (1900), the sovereignty of Muslims, and of all others on the planet, surely changed, but life's reconceptualization in relation to that change has often been understood in the unidimensional and unidirectional terms of modernization, secularization, alienation, colonization, Westernization, and so on. As postcolonial scholars and other have shown, the subject of that life was very much human, male, and white. While the deconstruction of philosophical universals as Eurocentric was necessary, however, it has only minimally advanced our understanding of the relationship between sovereignty and life, wherein life everywhere became subject through and object of state sovereignty. Fadl's departures from his father's path, as well as his fidelity to it, illuminates the (non-)relation between sovereignty and life on scales smaller and larger, as well as multidimensionally, and in turn the limits and dangers of life's aggressively human-centered history.[29]

Islamic and Imperial History
Until recently, Islamic and imperial history were written by different sets of scholars distinguished by different training, concerns, and archives. The renewal of Ottoman studies, signaled, let us say, by the 1977 publication of Huri Islamoğlu and Çağlar Keyder's "Agenda for Ottoman History" in none other than the first issue of the Fernand Braudel Center's journal, has radically revised the Sick-Man-of-Europe declension narrative, while also encouraging a revision

of "world history" along more interconnected global lines.[30] Similar revisions were also undertaken for the other major Muslim empires, the Safavids and the Mughals.[31]

The eighteenth- and nineteenth-century adventures of Sayyid Alawi and Sayyid Fadl were connected to a revised history of the early modern world becoming smaller and more interconnected through the agencies of Islam and Christian empires of trade. One of our challenges is to determine how much of that world remained by the end of Fadl's life and in what forms, in the face of the victorious, genuinely global dispensation that was projected not only from cities such as London, Paris, St. Petersburg, Berlin, and Washington but from Istanbul, Cairo, Bombay, and Tokyo as well.[32] Beginning in the middle of the nineteenth century, the form of absolute sovereignty we associate with modern states was a juggernaut, making irrelevant distinctions between colonizer and colonized even as its putative truth was enunciated and repeated in every language into the mid-twentieth century (and even now) through the very same breach, that is, in differences of race and nation. The story I wish to tell must compete with others; indeed, it must be written over the others, which have drowned out or buried trajectories such as Fadl's. The narratives of Islamic decline and the rise of Christendom or "the West" during the period historians designate as early modern were scientifically elaborated in the nineteenth century and have had much purchase since.

The need to explain the dramatic shifts in fortune experienced by the states and societies of northwestern Europe—the once backwaters of inter-Asian systems—in an age following "Enlightenment" made providential narratives obsolete and androcentric yet teleological ones fashionable. Recently, debunking the conventional Rise-of-the-West narrative has yielded more sophisticated histories of the early modern period and the "transition" to modernity, privileging interconnected webs, networks, and polyvalent flows over stark East/West dichotomies and unidirectional movements of people, ideas, and things.[33] Nonetheless, a current of presentism runs through some of the revisionist narratives as anxieties about the reversal of old, comforting hierarchies loom on the horizon.[34]

With notable exceptions, histories of the nineteenth century tend to reflect less of the subtlety and experimentation with conceptual lenses one finds in recent early modern historiography. Instead, a more perfect overlap between state and intellectual production stubbornly persists, wherein the imaginative horizon is delimited by a certain kind of compulsion to explain the new, ever more decisive telos of all struggles.[35] It is more understandable that there would be this difference between early modern and modern historiography when we consider a factor that did not obtain in any other period of human history: the unassailable ascendancy of one part of the world over the rest by the 1830s or, at the latest, by the 1850s, together with its accompanying state form. That relative yet decisive shift in the world balance of power was the culmination of three centuries of globalization, whose end, however, was not predetermined or inevitable—even given the tremendous significance of New World discoveries.

That open-endedness may help explain the early modern historian's creativity, while the nineteenth-century resolution of the early modern "fuzziness," marked politically and militarily by the domination of the self-identified "West," narrowed the interpretive field. In other words, much of the epistemological baggage accompanying Europe's global political, economic, and military might traveled comfortably into the present via its archives, its disciplines, and its subjects, however global or interactive they were in their formation.[36] The fact that one could write the story of Fadl—even a good one—based exclusively on the British colonial archive is testament to this hegemonic outcome.[37]

However one defines and delimits it, by the end of Fadl's life in 1900 the West had overrun Muslim lands, leaving significantly diminished Ottoman and Qajar Iranian buffer states between its interests and the expanding Russian Empire. The French occupied Algiers (1830) and Tunis (1881); the British seized Aden (1839), declared India a formal part of its empire (1858), invaded Egypt (1882), and established protectorates along the Arabian coast (1891–92); the Dutch expanded their control over Java and Sumatra (nineteenth century); and the Americans, never to be left out, took over from the Spanish in a nearly perpetual war against the Muslims of Mindanao and the Sulu Archipelago in the present-day Philippines (1899 onward). From the last two decades of the nineteenth century, as interstate rivalries intensified in the wake of the first global depression, the French, British, Portuguese, Belgians, Germans, and Italians pushed further into Africa, seizing territories with significant Muslim populations. The Berlin Conference (1884–85) was convened to regulate this "Scramble for Africa" and avoid war at home. Not only had power balances shifted; the very nature, legality, and intensity of connections were transformed under the new order.

Ironically, explanations of the change experienced by societies around the globe by the end of the nineteenth century—a moment of unprecedented connectivity—have relied heavily on notions of disconnect and divergence. The economic and technological gaps between peoples were defined far more minutely and emphasized. These were then often translated into cultural differences organized on a descending scale or in terms of essential racial failings.[38] The Berlin Conference, for example, marshaled a civilizational discourse and humanitarian concerns about the persistence of slavery to legitimize the land grab in Africa. Against the backdrop of accumulating anthropological knowledge, explanations of global change assumed two basic forms, positive and negative. On the one hand, change was conceived as occurring progressively and linearly through civilizing missions and modernization projects; on the other hand, the very same change was shown to involve conflict and to result in exploitation and domination. In both cases, however, change flowed from West to East.

That this was the indisputable flow of events is in a sense true, if we assume that there is no prediscursive reality and agree on which discourses are germane in framing the global. Michel Foucault has taught us to think beyond the self-referential terms of a liberal discourse of rights to view sovereignty as also a politics of life at the planetary level. The government of life, a multivalent biopolitics, whose technologies secured the subject to power, is in some states a mere dream even today, while in others it appears to be an ever-expanding reality.[39] That the two (West/East, colonizer/colonized, Global North / Global South) remain intertwined despite asymmetries of all kinds is brought home today in the camps erected and the laws passed to contain the (problem of) refugees fleeing wars and natural disasters and migrants seeking better economic opportunities. While people seem to move in one direction, ideas continue to flow in the other.

For example, Andrew Sartori, in an inaugural attempt to stake out the terms of a global intellectual history, demonstrates that the development of the discipline of political economy was focused on the economic changes taking place in Europe that affected Europeans, no matter the interconnected transnational commercial prehistory. This science of abstraction was historically unique, referring back to European social practices that had themselves become a novel series of abstractions. The Marxian version of political economy attempted to make legible the nature of that change—of capitalism—without simply reproducing its own liberal terms. "Far from being an economistic explanation of history, Marx's critical theory sought to grasp the historicity of the economic as a peculiarly capitalist form of social interdependence." As insightful as this recuperation of Marx is for writing a global history of capitalism, which inevitably touched every corner of the planet, it is one of the stories that must be muted to make space for a fuller account of Fadl's life, which in turn provides a glimpse of the unity of life buried in or by modern ideologies and disciplinary apparatuses tethered to state and capital.[40]

Sovereignty and Life

Running against the grain of political economy, which sought a global view, the uncomfortable truth of this moment in time, when "the people" of the world and their destinies became intertwined in ways unimaginable before, was an epistemological fragmentation reorganizing that totality or the very connected reality and the people inhabiting it into increasingly discrete and ostensibly incommensurable units.[41] The attendant political and economic form, a "world system" of nation-states, followed suit.[42] The disciplines and their particular forms of storytelling that accompanied the rise of the modern state constituted objects along various lines of distance and propinquity; thus it became possible in the nineteenth century to differentiate among peoples while simultaneously declaring commonality between local groups who were, or might otherwise be, "class enemies" or engaged in a war of the genders. The political ramifications of this paradoxical order of disconnected connectivity have been legion, with the nineteenth century serving as a rehearsal of the horrors yet to come in the twentieth.[43] Understandably, the social sciences have as a result focused on explaining our differences even in the recent more self-reflexive mode, or even when the subject is ostensibly as universal as the human, humanity, and its various permutations.[44]

The story of Sayyid Fadl demonstrates how the emphasis on the divergence and difference of life-forms was politicized and codified in law as part of a colonial state project. Fadl himself eventually flirted with a governmentalizing project predicated on difference that was informed by both contemporary geo-techno-politics and an Islamic tradition of geographical description and theorizing improvement—of territory, self, umma (community/nation). Politicization and codification were fundamental to the decoupling of sovereignty and the sovereign, substituting state or nation-state in the latter's place. Nevertheless, Fadl's life tells a complex story of "connection" as the central feature of the global nineteenth century, wherein sovereignty did not simply get transferred as a complete package from Westphalia across a vast chasm of time and space. Connection engendered repeated encounters both in the "colonial laboratory" and in noncolonial spaces, between various claims to authority that ultimately renewed and resignified an old mystery: absolute sovereignty without the absolute. In other words, modern sovereignty was a joint collaboration, albeit uneven, of imperial actors, peasants, tribesmen, holy men, and others who inhabited various points along the axis between the religious and the secular, the docile and the rebellious. The devil is in the details as much as in the abstractions.[45]

Fadl's life story reconnects us to a distinctively Islamic tradition of thought and spiritual practices that questions this passage away from divine sovereignty and illuminates what we are calling the unity of life, which endures across multiple spatial and temporal dimensions, including our present, and reintroduces the mystical and the mysterious to a disenchanted world. Therein, the soul's relationship to an ultimately unreachable God predicates life and nonlife in a unity that is because it is not (*wahdat al-wujud*). Glimpsing the meaning of this paradox may compel us to reimagine the relatively sober global histories of secular scholarship by infusing it with revitalized concepts of life and sovereignty. Along the way we learn who Fadl was, and perhaps more so, who he wasn't or couldn't be.[46]

I shall close with a clarification of my use of "sovereignty" in this book.[47] I have qualified it above with the adjectives "modern," "imperial," "divine," "Islamic," and "Muslim." It should be clear that I find inadequate static and putatively objective definitions that either (1) draw from (ostensibly irreconcilable and superseded) Christian and Muslim theologies, or (2) merely reflect the current division of global power into territorial nation-states.[48] On the one hand, though God as sovereign does not resonate in the world in the same way today as once it did, theology cannot undo the relationship without being undone. On the other hand, the secular normative assumptions of the state as fundamentally essential for order are rarely challenged in political theory; therefore, modern sovereignty's natural domain is almost always, unquestioningly, the state.[49] This dilemma often makes conversations drawing on Fadl's life an occasion for miscommunication or a failure to communicate altogether about the times and faces of sovereignty.

Historians contribute to this conceptual confusion by being faithful disciplinarians, writing histories loyal to the sources. Sometimes disobedience and disloyalty are needed to see beyond the long shadow cast by the sovereign/state. The period of modern state formation in the Indian Ocean world, starting in the 1830s and extending to the 1960s (arguably continuing to the present in some places), is also the period of modern colonialism and anticolonialism. Thus, it becomes doubly difficult for historians to disentangle life and state, since the two were becoming one on a global scale.

Returning to the idea of the mappila to illustrate the intimacy between historiography and sovereignty, we note that like other products of empire it became a synonym for Muslims in Malabar through repeated inscriptions of the word in colonial records of the nineteenth century, which mainly reported on this one "troublesome" community and its representatives.[50] In these colonial records, Sayyid Fadl, willingly or not, carried this moniker of communal identity with him beyond Indian shores, taking "Mappila" to Hadhramawt, the Hijaz, Egypt, and all the way to the Ottoman capital. Indeed, even in places he never visited, such as Madras, Simla, Bushir, Basra, Muscat, and London, officials and agents invoked his name and his affiliation to the Mappilas as their "priest." This trajectory of the Mappila tracks with the evolving history of imperial sovereignty that Lauren Benton has mapped across the variegated geographies of empires in her many works, which will be discussed in subsequent chapters.[51]

The "Moplah Outlaw" I encountered in the Public Record Office all those years ago had quite the layered, interconnected, and transregional life, which was indeed a perfect example of the jurisdictional jockeying that marked this moment in the history of sovereignty—as a concept that was *not* prepackaged and exported to the extra-European world but rather was shaped in and through these kinds of encounters in and between imperial spaces. Yet as rich as the sources may be in the imperial archive, and as conducive to the new kind of global history when approached from a certain perspective, the life it wrote and made possible for future historians to write again was not Sayyid Fadl's life. It was the life of the Moplah Outlaw—a life figured in relation to imperial sovereignty.

One certainly catches glimpses of the life that was Fadl's through some of the sources in the colonial archive, but glimpses is all they are. Consider, for example, what may be learned about the last portion of his life from a missive written by an intimate associate: "Son long séjour dans la capitale Ottomane et l'expérience acquise de près sur les affaires de l'Empire l'ont entièrement désillusionné."[52] From this French translation of an Arabic letter one of his unnamed "friends" ostensibly sent to the British ambassador at Constantinople, Philip Currie, in 1894, we learn that Sayyid Fadl had grown utterly disillusioned with the Ottomans after his long stay in the capital observing the workings of imperial politics up close. In this letter, the friend essentially suggests that the sayyid was ready to betray the Ottomans and to use his influence to secure the submission of Muslims in southern Arabia, Africa, and India to the British Empire, for they were sure to benefit from its protection. Moreover, Fadl, owing to his status as a sayyid ("l'origine extra-noble du Saïd") recognized by Muslims in all of those places for his virtue and as a titled Ottoman perceived to possess political influence, was well placed to assist the British in their "mission civilisatrice." In particular, he and his sons would take it upon themselves to put an end to the slave trade and to enlighten "all the Muslims of southern

Arabia and Eastern Africa" about "l'abomination de ce trafic humain." If they were allowed to return to Dhofar and resume their rule there, they would also ensure that all its "commerce with the English and English possessions would be open and free."[53]

Ultimately, according to the letter in translation, which rendered the author anonymous, Fadl regarded the stakes in this desperate bid to gain British support as nothing short of the political and religious future of Arabs and Turks specifically and of Muslims and Islam in general.[54] The sultan-caliph had become in his mind nothing but a title, whose chosen course was bound to be "fateful" (*funeste*), unable to save the Ottoman Empire or the religion of Muhammad. Thus, to Sayyid Fadl, after fourteen years of living at the heart of the most powerful and most sovereign Muslim-ruled polity, under the given conditions of global politics in the last years of the nineteenth century, the future seemed bleak.

Though she does not cite this source, Seema Alavi spends a good deal of time in her recent book *Muslim Cosmopolitanism* sketching out the implications of Fadl's apparent double dealings, which she views as part of a general pattern found among Muslim scholars and activists whom the British designated "outlaws" after the Indian Mutiny of 1857. This choice of starting point for her narrative is tremendously consequential as far as the potential for writing life goes. It is the life of real persons inevitably bound up with imperial and later national sovereignty. I argue that, while this is an eminently historical and defensible position, a vantage point from which to regard certain political, economic, and cultural shifts taking place on a global scale, there is another story of life it effectively buries by sidelining what remained a relationship to divine sovereignty, however difficult and changing, for many like Fadl. In one sense, the burial of this other life in fact took place—and historians faithfully if not always critically record and reproduce the "event" in their choice of topoi—whose purpose was for the sake of posterity: for a future of life becoming subject to/of power in entirely new ways.[55]

Whether consciously or not, modern history writing often tracks that process of life's becoming closer to sovereignty and ultimately being possessed by / possessing it—understandably so, since this movement of life underwrites the most spectacular human dramas unfolding since the late seventeenth century, whether they be revolutions or genocides. Anthropocentric historiography, then, necessarily participates in a narration true to the celebrated and epochal becoming-sovereign of Man himself, an event that engenders the recursive burying of other stories and conceptions of life, particularly a life irreducible to the biological or historical. A straightforward excavation in turn becomes impossible.[56]

Road Map

The chapters of this book are loosely organized in chronological order, proceeding from the eighteenth century through the 1930s, then jumping to the present, then back again to the turn of the twentieth century. The broad timeframe and mixed chronology are a function of the interdisciplinary approach and the types of sources, which include traditional archival documents, Sufi treatises, hagiographies, social media, and ethnographic notes from the shrine complex at Mampuram. Moreover, time hopping emerged as a "sensible" corollary to the methodology of the glimpse, through which the very possibility of a linear narrative of life as unity was problematized. In short, we have one foot in the realm of "history as sorcery."[57]

Chapter 1 narrates the first encounter between the Alawis and the EIC in Malabar, examining the possibility of yet another form of sovereignty, sayyid sovereignty, and its relationship to Malabar's reconstitution as the land of Mappila Muslims. The question of colonial state formation is also addressed in relation to a prior history of mercantile relations that had become untenable in the face of Indian regional state experiments and the growing sophistication and standardization of imperial administrative and legal mechanisms after a period of hybrid and ad hoc institutions.

Chapter 2 continues the thread of sayyid and imperial sovereignty competing for souls at the time of Fadl's expulsion from India in the mid-nineteenth century. It first recounts a foundational myth that establishes the Indian Ocean link between Mappila Muslims, sayyids, and the Prophet Muhammad via a Hindu sovereign who converted to Islam. The chapter then elaborates in more detail how the Alawiyya, one particular, Sufi strand of the capacious Islamic tradition, developed its own distinctive conceptual apparatus for confronting and containing the fallout from the global shift in power relations that relegated Islamic polities to a subordinate position. The Indian Ocean appears here as relevant yet fading backdrop, whereas in the following chapters it reappears as Fadl's own canvas for drawing a new plan of engagement.

In Chapter 3, the conceptual shift attending imperial sovereignty's struggle to renew and reassert itself in different contexts in the second half of the nineteenth century is traced in terms of government and its role in reconstituting the relationship between state and subject along lines other than vague claims of protection or transcendental claims of salvation. We witness Fadl's own experiment in the government of men as he becomes the amir of Dhofar; at this point, the potential of renewing sayyid sovereignty was nested within Ottoman imperial restructuring (the Tanzimat). The chapter ends by examining the increasingly effective British attempts to track Fadl's movements after exile, showing the growth of an imperial surveillance net in the Indian Ocean world, which acted as another limit on sayyid sovereignty.

Chapter 4 in turn examines the limits of modern sovereignty at the end of the nineteenth century by following Fadl into the Sufi cosmos and gaining a better glimpse through him of the unity of life. This view of Fadl viewing the unity of life is contingent on the assumption that he possessed a certain future "insight," which I try to show through a reading of Malayalam hagiographies of him and his father.[58] In closing, the Fadl of Indian Ocean Sufism is contrasted to the (impossible) Fadl of the Arab Nahda, the cultural renaissance that presumably had no patience for the enchanted; we hear echoes of British efforts to identify and fix him within the horizon of modern sovereignty.

Chapters 5 and 6 are experimental chapters that blend times past, present, and future in an attempt to represent the temporality of glimpsing the unity of life. Chapter 5 begins with the 2005 return of a descendant of Fadl, the first successful return since Fadl's exile in 1852 and an occasion for the collective remembrance of the Alawi role in Malabar. The chapter then shifts gears dramatically to provide an account of the contemporary Wahhabi Salafi presence on the internet, examining how communications technology and genomics are mobilized in the rationalization of religious life and in opposition to Sufi mysticism. The section serves to illustrate the strands of life that entwine with modern sovereignty and actively block the unity of life. The chapter then resumes the history of Alawi attempts to return to Malabar to illustrate two other linked points about modern sovereignty. First, the growing sophistication of the imperial surveillance net could by the beginning of the twentieth century effectively regulate the movement of people, especially persons of interest, across once very porous borders. Second, this regulatory apparatus contributed to recasting the temporality of the return in terms of discrete and fixed periods of past-present-future times moving in an exclusively linear direction, permanently casting aside, burying in the earth, or burning to ashes the always prior, and thus making returns of dead ancestors, spirits, and others impossible, while consolidating the terms of modern sovereignty.

The return that was envisioned and that mattered most by the end of the Alawi quest in the 1930s was to the state—its recognition and rewards—aligning the act of return with a biopolitical order presupposing a radically reconfigured conception of life.

Bookended by brief ethnographic vignettes of my last visit to the Mampuram Maqam, Chapter 6 fittingly returns to Sayyid Fadl. It draws together the various threads crisscrossing spatial and temporal boundaries in a last push to gain a glimpse of the unity of life as he may have glimpsed it himself. Probing more deeply into Fadl's attachment to imperial sovereignty in relation to sayyid sovereignty, the chapter revisits the Muslim oath. Through this ancient form of covenant between tribes and holy men we are, on the one hand, afforded a view onto a particular history of territorialization in the Arab subcontinent. On the other hand, when the worldly forms of power and authority are read against Fadl's final effort to elaborate the Way of the Alawis, something else comes into view, something that does not register in the binary times of sovereignty, something we are calling the unity of life. Finally, anchored by my visit to Oman in search of an ancient figure (Cheruman Perumal) who connected the various communities of Malabar to each other and to the Indian Ocean, the Conclusion gives a last tug to the threads that have entwined life and sovereignty in the making of global history. While they do not easily unravel, the phenomenon and the history of Alawi sufi-sayyids will hopefully present again an opening to the enchanted and the mystical as not mere fancies but the real stuff of life.

1   Remaking the Indian Ocean World

Sufis, Sovereigns, and the Mappilas of Malabar

> *Your number 79 of 6th January. Sultan Muscat sent troops to Dhofar but failed*
> *in recovering forts. Emissaries of Moplah Outlaws [sic] said to be there with flags.*
> *Sultan asks us to check Outlaw's designs. Political agent Muscat proceeding*
> *to Dhofar in Brisk to effect settlement. Please instruct Resident Aden to watch*
> *any movements by outlaws. Consul General Cairo and Consul Jedda informed*
> *through Secretary of State*

THESE WORDS WERE TELEGRAPHED on March 1, 1896, from the
Calcutta Foreign Office of the British Raj in India to its Bombay Political Office,
which at the time was responsible for Near Eastern affairs. The "Outlaw" in
question is Sayyid Fadl Ibn Alawi. The various signs and geographical markers strewn throughout this telegram evoke the breadth of the story we are
embarking on. We will return to the deep context of this specific alert issued
by Calcutta in later chapters.[1] For now it suffices to take in the vastness of the
space in which the life history of a single nineteenth-century Muslim preacher
unfolded. Take in the view quickly, though, because a good map of this life must
plot a much larger, multidimensional space than the coordinates provided by
the imperial information web.[2]

In terms of empire's knowledge, the ports of Muscat, Dhofar, Shihr, Mukalla,
Aden, Cairo, and Jedda became relevant to this specific story once the British
exiled Fadl in 1852 from India. The designation "Moplah" (Mappila) evoked the
ancient connection to Malabar even as colonial officials described his expulsion
as returning him to his "home country" in Arabia. The Muslim communities
threaded around the Indian Ocean through port cities and their hinterlands
and linked in some way to the Hadhrami Alawi diaspora had maps both similar
to and radically different from the imperial map projected in the telegraphic

intelligence earlier. The sameness and difference of spatial imagination and organization is one of the themes that a history of Sayyid Fadl helps illuminate.[3] In the process, a clearer picture appears of sovereignty's reconfiguration and its implications for life, death, and more uniform—more global—conceptions of law, politics, and religion.

The life of Sayyid Fadl that I trace is not a standard biography. Rather, as Linda Colley does with the intrepid eighteenth-century world traveler Elizabeth Marsh, we may regard his life as a window onto globally significant historical changes affecting the nature of state, religion, and political subjectivity.[4] This is not simply because the kinds of sources available make it impossible to provide a sustained account of the development of an internal self, but also because the life Fadl sought to live, however (un)successfully, conformed to rules, laws, and norms that defy the limits of biography.[5] By the same token, and *pace* historical treatment of globe-trotting figures such as Marsh, an account of Fadl must also trace life's genealogy through anthropology, theology, and philosophy. A proper history of Sayyid Fadl's paradoxical life, as both his and not his, cannot be written if the discipline of history's temporal terms and conditions are accepted *tout court*. For the unity of life we seek to glimpse along with Fadl was not fashioned by humans, encompassed life and nonlife, and transcended historical time, existing before and after us. Giving a full account of the historical subject thus requires an (im)possible cartography of life as the subject's excess.

Returning to the Calcutta telegram—a technology developed during Fadl's lifetime and intimately tied to far-flung imperial projects—we find juxtaposed to territorial markers signs of sovereignty as we understand it today: flags, troops, warships, sovereigns, residents, agents, and consuls.[6] These signs recommend an examination of the state form, to which we will have recourse as we consider its expansion and transformation in the nineteenth century, though it is the looming presence of the "outlaw" that will be our primary focus. This label was applied to Fadl at a time when the terms of sovereignty around the Indian Ocean were moving out of a state of flux and settling into the governmentalized state. Probing the distance between the colonial label and the person, between the person and the state, reveals a remarkable picture of the nineteenth century and of our present, in which unresolved problems of sovereignty return as recurring nightmares for many and as an opening to life for some.

In this chapter, roughly coinciding with Koselleck's saddle period (1750–1850), we see Sayyid Alawi and son Sayyid Fadl take the stage alongside the East India Company on the Malabar Coast of India. Each represents a vector of sovereignty in a changing Indian Ocean world wherein the fraught terms of encounter when they meet, or fail to meet as it were, index a moment of global transformation in relations among peoples and between peoples and territories. Accordingly, the formation of Mappila-as-Muslim might be regarded as a product of struggles for the souls of Malabar between two transoceanic bodies representing formidable traditions of thinking life in relation to sovereignty. This chapter begins to pose the question of imperial and Islamic sovereignty's collision as constitutive of a vector of modern state formation.

Before the Fall: Sovereigns and Sufis in Eighteenth-Century Malabar

When Sayyid Alawi, Fadl's father, arrived in Calicut from Tarim around 1766, the fabled seat of the prosperous Zamorins (Samudri rajas, meaning "Lords of the Sea") had fallen on harder times.[7] Historically, the rise of Calicut was closely linked to the activities of large Muslim merchant communities from across the seas. Indeed, upon arrival Sayyid Alawi was met by his uncle Hasan al-Jifri, who had established himself in Malabar a decade or more earlier.[8] He helped set up his nephew and acclimated him to a starkly different world from that which he had left. According to one source, Sayyid Alawi was summoned to Malabar in order to marry the daughter of Hasan al-Jifri. Adaptation to local climes by Alawi and other Hadhrami men who had moved and settled around the Indian Ocean since the sixteenth century was facilitated by marriage. Marrying into a local family eased many of the difficulties of adapting to a new world. Sayyid Alawi married the daughter from such a marriage, between al-Jifri and a Malayali woman. Literally from its birth this was a hybrid diaspora.[9]

However, the ancient practice of forging local alliances proved inadequate for meeting the new challenges presented by the changing balance of power in India and the world at large. Regionally, the vicissitudes of transoceanic trade and the relatively successful state-building projects to the north and south of Calicut had lessened its fortunes in the second half of the century, with the rise of competing ports and the increasingly restricted access to its own hinterlands. Calicut was caught between two state-building projects, that of the more ambitious and aggressive rulers of Mysore (Hydar Ali, r. 1761–82, and his son Tipu Sultan, r. 1782–99) to the north and the Travancore rajas (Marthanda Varma, r. 1729–58, and Rama Varma, r. 1758–98, being the most able of them) to the south. The ambitions of Mysore and its alliance with the French led to a series of wars with the English East India Company (EIC) between the 1760s and 1790s. During this period Mysore occupied Malabar twice and effectively began the process of redrawing jurisdictions to reflect a new form of absolute sovereignty.

The change of fortune and lessened enthusiasm among Calicut's Hindu rulers for their historic courting of Arab merchants might partially explain why Jifri moved his family into the interior.[10] Such a move, though, was also consonant with a long tradition of Alawi sayyids entering "frontier" regions and opening these to religion, to merchant networks, and often to agricultural improvement.[11] Sayyid Alawi, who settled along the Kadalundi River, helped establish the first mosque and quickly attracted converts and a following of Mappilas from the surrounding area and even further afield. Mampuram was the birthplace and in one sense the site of Sayyid Fadl's patrimony—material and spiritual. The stories that were written about them in various genres, during their lifetimes and after, confirm the Alawis' importance to Malabar's history. Hagiographies of Sayyid Alawi in Malayalam attest to the miraculous powers that he possessed and passed on to his son, while the colonial sources record the same, as well as the efforts of Fadl and his heirs to regain their lands and other property in Malabar after they were exiled in 1852 into the interwar period.

Although that consummate analyst of power, Michel Foucault, did not discuss European colonial projects at any length, the EIC's inaugural step in the conquest of India, with its victory at the Battle of Plassey in 1757, times perfectly with the moment he gives as the turning point between a logic of *raison d'état* and the art of government. A hundred years of Company rule in India might exemplify, with a "colonial difference," the force he attempted to capture in his characterization of the triumph of the market as a "site of veridiction."[12] The Company, guided by its profit margin and increasingly superior intelligence, moved from victory to victory.

The EIC's conquest and rule of the northern region of Malabar on the southwestern coast of India after the defeat of Tipu Sultan in 1792 is of interest to us, for it is through this addition to British real estate in India that a protracted engagement with the Alawis began. As a geographical term designating the new administrative region under the Bombay Presidency until 1800 and thereafter under the Madras Presidency, "Malabar" would no longer refer to the entire coastal region of present-day Kerala and further north. Its constitution as a new "province" with its capital at Calicut was announced in a 1793 letter from the governor of Bombay, General Abercromby, to "all the Rajas and principal

Landholders."[13] The transfer of control to Madras entailed a change of officials and a streamlining of rule that emphasized security first—"the establishment of the Judicial authority must be postponed until the Military power of the Company shall have subjugated the refractory people of the province; and until it shall have disposed them to cultivate the arts of peace by disarming them of their habitual weapons of offence."[14] The shift in policy was predicated on the grounds of good government not having been established by Bombay, but was in fact a decision reached upon review of reports commissioned by Madras "regarding the principles and detailed system of the . . . administration of the revenue in Malabar."[15]

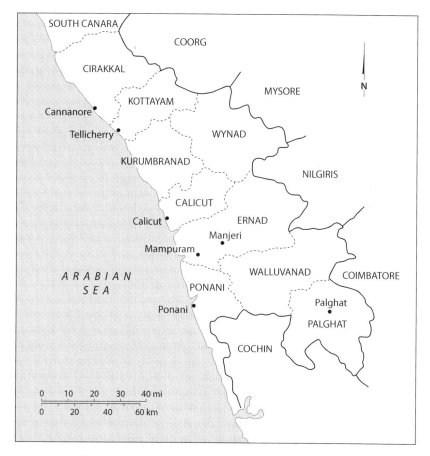

The Malabar District after its conquest by the British East India Company in 1792.

The very first mention of the Alawis in the colonial record for Malabar dates from 1817.[16] In a letter to Madras regarding an attack against government property, the Malabar magistrate James Vaughan named Sayyid Alawi as its leader.[17] The interactions of the EIC and the Alawis amply illustrate a formative moment of state (colonial), saint (sufi-sayyid), and society (Mappila), reflecting imperial and Islamic sovereignty's slow reconfiguration across the Indian Ocean world; hence, they merit careful analysis.

The incident that provoked Vaughan's response had a prior history in Malabar's long resistance to the new dispensation brought by the EIC, which its officials recorded variously in terms of rebellion, disorder, outbreaks, and eventually outrage.[18] From the arrival of the first British commissioners to assess the revenue potential of Malabar and establish a provisional government, the EIC faced a series of refusals and revolts of many hues.[19] The variety of resistance was in itself a testament to and map of the different layers of sovereignty that characterized the nature of power and authority throughout India. Although Mysore's interventions in Malabar in the 1760s, 1770s, and 1780s had also provoked local rajas and others with significant landholdings to resist, a wholesale (Nair and Mappila) rejection of its rule came at the point when it began to act in unfamiliar ways, attempting to collect taxes directly from cultivators.[20] There were political means by which Mysore could be and was accommodated in Malabar as long as it remained within the universe of layered sovereignty. However, its state experiment—informed by "revolutionary" political-economic models that began circulating globally in the 1770s from the Americas to Asia and that augured the doom of ancient fiscal regimes, mercantilist trade policies, and layered sovereignty—was not to last.[21] The once novel but now anachronistic Company made sure of that.

It is one of many historical ironies that Lord Cornwallis, who was given his walking papers by the Americans at Yorktown in what was arguably the first instance of a new kind of sovereign claim, became a hired gun for the EIC in India as governor general immediately thereafter.[22] The ancient practice of moving into "private" service after a military career, however (un)successful, continues into the present, when the line between the state and the business of "security" seems blurrier than ever—which should throw into question the dominant historical narrative of sovereignty's transformation. The stark line between premodern and modern conceptions of sovereignty, or the distinction between the theories and the performances, begs reexamination.

Although successful in relegating the upstart Kingdom of Mysore to the dustbin of history and poised to reach the zenith of its territorial expansion in India, the global transformation in conceptions of sovereignty threatened to unravel the EIC's claim to and hold on power. Its presence in Malabar was longer-lived than Mysore's, and its fiscal interventions also came with new claims of sovereignty, which similarly were incompatible with the elaborate traditions of highly localized yet interconnected forms of self-rule that were centuries in the making.[23] Those traditions were intertwined with the geographical and religious specificities of Malabar, as scholars from Ibn Battuta in the fourteenth century to Bernard Cohn and Dilip Menon more recently have observed. Nineteenth-century colonial officials also noted a distinctive order:

> To understand Malabar and the Malayalis aright it is above all things necessary therefore that this central fact—this distribution of authority—this "Parliament" as it was called so long ago as 28th May 1746 by one who was settled in the country and watching its working—this chastiser of the unwarrantable acts of Ministers of State—this all-powerful influence tending always to the maintenance of customary observances—should be firmly grasped by the mind.[24]

William Logan, who served in various capacities in Malabar, including magistrate and collector toward the end of the nineteenth century, faults "foreign" intervention for what in effect he deemed a loss of innocence in this unique region. He was a firm believer in the virtues of the Hindu Nair caste, which he deemed the backbone of Malabarian society.[25] He describes the extensive Nair household (*thara*) as constituting nothing short of "a small republic."[26] Those republics fanned out across the variegated landscape of Kerala and for millennia secured a happiness and relative prosperity not to be found in other lands; hence, according to Logan, it had no "history" until the foreigners began to arrive and upset the delicate balance.

In this land of mountains, hills, valleys, backwaters, and long coastline we find Lauren Benton's connected corridors, arcs, bands, and enclaves on one of "the edges of the Indian Ocean." These irregular geographical spaces and the fitful, uneven expansion of seaborne empires into them reveal the transformation of oceans and ultimately of territories from being "fluid" to "bounded legal space."[27] Logan was keenly aware that such a transformation in Malabar was only feasible when the intricate relations among land, economy, and politics were made intelligible, a knowledge project in which he found the EIC lacking. During the first two decades during which the EIC sought to consolidate power in Malabar, its geographical diversity and the related political "messiness" were sources of tremendous consternation, which in turn only drove the Company closer to the local rajas who seemed more pliant, thus insuring a fragmented order, structural instability, and recurring violence.

The first commissioners, representing the Bombay Presidency (Farmer, Page, and Dow), arrived in Malabar soon after the Treaty of Seringapatanam was finalized on March 18, 1792. Lord Cornwallis's handpicked commissioners from Bengal (Duncan and Boddam) arrived at the end of the year. Part of this joint commission's duty was to restore confidence in the Company, which had been lost in the previous decade. The rajas who had aligned with the EIC found it could not, or would not, protect them from Tipu's attacks in 1784. In 1790, recognition of this situation led to the following analysis of the postwar outcome. "In order to secure a willing obedience from the Malabar Chiefs, Government would be contented with their paying a very moderate Tribute, provided they would give the Company advantageous privileges."[28] The mode of government predicated on economy was by the late eighteenth century an established feature of seaborne empires, illustrated here in the summary of a letter from Lord Cornwallis to the Court regarding procedures for assimilating Malabar:

> It was of the utmost importance for the national character and for the interest of the Company that the British Government of the Countries on the Coast of Malabar should commence upon a good plan . . . it would be most prudent, before they should divide them finally into districts, to appoint Commissioners to make a temporary Settlement with all the Chiefs, for this season, and then proceed upon an active and earnest investigation of the amount of Revenue that those acquisitions were capable of paying, the extent of the different articles of Commerce, the nature of the tenures of the Rajas or other Chiefs, and the classes and numbers of the Inhabitants, in order that the Supreme Government might be enabled, from their Reports and the observations and suggestions of the Government of Bombay to propose a system for the future management of that Country, which might include Rules for the conduct of the Revenue and Commercial Departments, and above all, for a strict and impartial administration of Justice; and, as many of the Bengal Servants had great experience in conducting the internal business of extensive Indian provinces, it was the intention of Lord Cornwallis to depute two of those in whom he could place particular confidence.[29]

The attempt to copy the settlement in Bengal had disastrous consequences and led to recurring rebellions; that said, the selection of commissioners revealed an approach to government that engendered a gradual sharpening of the divide between private and public interests, with property and sovereignty serving as middle terms. Failure to appreciate or adeptly negotiate the divide seemed regularly to lose EIC employees their jobs, in Malabar and other provinces.[30] The "system for the future management" of their Malabar real estate, on the one hand, must secure revenue, and on the other, had to fight corruption—translated in loftier terms as ensuring "Justice."

In other words, Malabar was EIC-governed territory and not to be viewed as a personal fiefdom. An oath of office was administered to all the new recruits. The oaths were preceded by delivery of Abercromby's letter appointing William Farmer as the "Supravisor and Chief Magistrate of the countries henceforth to be denominated the Province of Malabar" and reiterating the Company's sovereignty and the responsibility its representatives now had.[31] With the letter, Farmer wrote in his diary, the "Government thus established was saluted by twenty-one guns from the field-pieces placed in front of the Government House."[32] The evolving economic logic of government, which may have had its origins in the special conditions of early modern seaborne empires, reshaped the terms of sovereignty globally. Yet in the management of populations in the Old World it met specific, nearly immovable limits. The Company's constitutional inability to translate market relations into political authority via "good" government (a feature of state formation back home), together with its strategic reliance on allies preventing annihilation of the enemy (a feature of state formation in the New World), produced conditions for continuous rebellion.[33]

Perhaps better than most, the Zamorin of Calicut recognized the impossible position that the EIC expected him to occupy, given the ancient terms of sovereignty that prevailed in Malabar in spite of the Mysorean interregnum. He was to convince the Nair rajas and the Mappilas, whom the EIC understood to be subordinates and subjects of the Zamorin, to accept the new dispensation. "This I tell them; but after all, you know they are not like the people of other countries, who live collected in cities where the hand of government can reach them and the tax gatherer has an easy task. *They live in woods and in hills, with every house separate, and that house defensible.*"[34] Benton's connection of anomalous geographical zones to modern political sovereignty's nonlinear progression cannot be better expressed.

Logan noted how the commissioners accepted the not completely accurate description the Zamorin gave regarding taxation as being beyond his jurisdiction and how that led to disastrous interventionist policies:

The Joint Commissioners in express terms withdrew from the great families
to whom they committed the revenue management of their ancient territories all authority except that of levying the land revenue, but the "authority"
and the land revenue collection had never before been so divorced from
each other, for in Mysorean times even the land revenue was collected direct from the cultivators by Mysorean officials. The result, of course, was
that the petty chieftains, accustomed to independence, shook their swords
or barred the doors of their defensible houses when the tax-gatherer came.[35]

He went on to explain how the glue that had held together the happy little
republics was dissolved by the Company's introduction of new relations of
protection and property. "Freed by the presence of British troops from the
restraints of having to consult the petty chieftains who had formerly been their
mainstays, Rajas naturally enough perhaps, sought their own aggrandizement
at the expense of their former subjects."[36]

In effect Logan laid the blame for rebellious conditions in Malabar squarely
at the feet of EIC policies, the new conception of sovereignty that underlay
those policies, and the resulting feudalization of social and political relations.
His historical insight about the changing nature of authority was quite sharp.
The intricate layers of the relationship between local rulers and the ruled were
gradually eroded as the conditions for patronage and protection were elimi-
nated or reduced ("withdrew") to insignificance by the rise of the colonial state.
Logan was preceded in this analysis by a military observer who had served in
Malabar and found the hybrid nature of the civil government of the EIC to
be seriously lacking, unlike the effective "military system" that he found to
be "original and self-derived." The tension between the two arms of colonial
service is palpable.[37]

In a nuanced intervention, Dilip Menon questions the teleological narratives of state formation for the period between the Mysorean invasions and the
British conquest of Malabar. In those narratives, the past merely forms a flat
landscape on which the given objects are plotted in various stages—emerging,
succeeding, failing—while the mystery of the "state" remains unexplained.
"The idea of the inevitability of the emergence of elaborate 'modern' state forms
does not allow the overdetermination of hindsight to be recognized."[38] Menon
coins the notion of "state experimentation" to capture the fluidity of historical
moments in which local power relations were being realigned with no clear
sense of larger and final outcomes.

State experimentation refers to Mappila efforts to capitalize politically on the opening created by Mysore's displacement of traditional authorities.[39] Menon argues convincingly that the militarization of Malabar in the wake of Mysore's expansion and the "peculiar circumstances of warfare" created a class of "political entrepreneurs" among Mappilas who started out as "military labor" and gradually expanded their bailiwick to include control of lands, trade routes, and revenue streams under the leadership of *moopans* (headmen; here, military recruiters).[40]

The EIC record of the scene in 1792 when its forces entered Malabar confirms Menon's description of the state of war that prevailed:

> The Coast of Malabar had been in a state of great distraction and confu-
> sion since the time that Tippoo's Troops and the Officers of his Government
> were driven out of it, the two great and inimical classes of the People, the
> Nairs and Mopillas, or Moplas, being almost at often war with each other;
> and great dissensions about Boundaries and revived old claims prevailing
> amongst the Nair Rajas themselves. But, as General Abercromby would
> immediately upon descending the Ghauts detach troops into the different
> districts Lord Cornwallis hoped that he should soon hear that tranquility
> had been restored, and the Company's authority completely established
> throughout these Countries.[41]

Cornwallis also wanted to know as quickly as possible what sort of military expenditure was required to hold the ports and the interior of the territory now added to the Company's portfolio. In particular, he was interested in reducing the size of the "Native" force, whose numbers had been increased during the Mysore wars. We can say with some certainty that this demobilization was the origin of at least some of the "roving bands" of armed men who appeared in later reports.[42]

From State of War to Lawful States: Reckoning with Fanaticism

With new players afoot, from warrior bands and rebel rajas to a company-state, unresolved issues of sovereignty formed the backdrop to Vaughan's 1817 re-port on Sayyid Alawi's role in the ongoing struggles in Malabar. At the heart of these issues were new claims to government that, while mostly rhetorical, also engendered one element that made it impossible for a full or final recon-ciliation with all parties: the law. As Benton and others have demonstrated in transimperial global locales being mapped for new forms of exploitation, the law was a critical and central site for the transformation of sovereignty that took place over a very long period, from the sixteenth to the nineteenth century.[43] The EIC initially inserted itself into prior relations of authority in India through innovative combinations of customary, Islamic, Hindu, and English legal traditions. The history of these innovations suggests their generalization and implementation were more often than not sporadic, uneven, and destabilizing.[44] In the second half of the nineteenth century, as historians of the British Empire have shown, there was a gradual move away from recognizing and working through "pluralities" of law toward a more centralized legal order. Magistrate Vaughan's attempts to arrest Sayyid Alawi mark the ambivalent beginnings of such a shift, when the later jurisdictional clarity was still unavailable to him and to the government in general.[45]

In large part and put simply, clarity of rule was forestalled as long as there was formidable resistance. Vaughan met with the kind of resistance that might be regarded as a precondition for any jurisdictional politics and for the existence of multiple sovereignties. In Malabar and other regions in South Asia, this took the form of confrontation between the EIC and another powerful transregional actor, the sayyids, with varying political outcomes between collaboration and prolonged conflict.

The relationship between Malayalis and Arab Muslims in Malabar extends back as far as the seventh century. This relationship, particularly the role of sayyids, is conspicuously absent from Menon's analysis of state experimentation. He takes issue with Stephen Dale's "overblown" *longue durée* analysis that ultimately reduces all political actions in Malabar to Islam and an oppositional, jihadi Muslim identity that began taking shape in 1498. However, in Menon's quest for contingency and synchrony something is also lost—the Alawi role in Indian Ocean world history generally and in Malabari politics specifically, a role with which the British were all too concerned.

The war footing on which many Mappilas remained in 1817 was apparent from the numbers that Vaughan cited as having taken part in the March attack, which he reported was carried out "by some hundreds of people . . . upon some Property formerly belonging to a noted Rebel of the name of Goorikul which was afterwards escheated to Government."[46] From the mid-eighteenth century on, at least three generations of Goorikuls (Kurikuls) sought to carve out an autonomous sphere of operations in Manjeri, not far from Mampuram and Tirurangadi.[47] Dale describes the family as "struggling to realize aspirations of local sovereignty."[48] By the end of the 1790s the revenue demands of the Company led Manjeri Kurikul to openly defy the latter's authority in the region. The EIC regarded his actions as rebellious warfare and dealt with him accordingly. Using a special police force composed exclusively of Hindus, called the Nair Corps and led by Captain Watson, the two major guerilla groups under Unni Mutta and Athan Kurikul's son, who had joined forces in 1799, were defeated in 1802 and Manjeri Kurikul killed. The Nair Corps was first established to undermine and counter the Mappilas' "police establishment" in the interior, which rose under Tipu and was in fact maintained by the EIC, until a policy shift of restoring upper-caste Hindus to the lands they arguably had fled during Tipu's invasion met with opposition.[49]

However, the draconian counterinsurgency measures prescribed by Lord Clive (son of the infamous "Clive of India"), when Malabar was transferred from Bombay's jurisdiction to Madras in 1800, affected a wider swath of Malabar's population. In 1801, "To Major Macleod and his assistants the Government committed all power, both civil and criminal, and the military were further authorized to punish, 'by summary process, crimes of every description.'"[50] The abuses to which the exercise of emergency rule led, not least in tax assessment and collection, resulted in a popular revolt; as Logan put it, "In the early part of 1803, the province rose *en masse*."[51] That Hindu rajas and their associates who saw their real power diminished under the new dispensation led the revolt was difficult for the Company and colonial officials who came later, such as Logan, to square with their vision of government as transacted on legal grounds and in complicity with landlords and nobles. This was especially true because the EIC justified its presence in Malabar as reversing the despotic Muslim rule of Tipu through the restitution of *janmi* rights to property; *janmi* here means Hindu upper castes, Nambudhri brahmins and Nairs, who were thought to have a birthright (*janmam*) to land.[52]

Looking back on the period, Logan argued that the Malabar Province was essentially founded on the commissioners' misrecognition of *janmam* as a right to land (a "European Idea") rather than a claim to authority over people on a land, which was repeated through its legal practices. He described this critical moment as one of willful ignorance; it was an original sin for which later administrators such as himself would have to pay.[53] The misrecognition as it was did not prevent early officials from noting that many Mappilas and far more of the lower castes possessed tenancy rights (*kanam*), which they correctly translated as de facto property rights.

This episode fits into a broader debate about property, which took place against the global backdrop of the commercialization of agriculture. Madras and London deliberated on whether to apply the Bengali *ryotwari* model—a bastardized view of precolonial land tenure presupposing ownership of all land by the sovereign—throughout India. For Malabar the question hinged on which relationship to land was closer to property ownership, janmam or kanam. By 1850, Lockean liberalism's conception of property as constituted through labor lost out to a conservative view of it as an ancient right of particular castes yet mediated now by the sovereign Company, thus effectively sealing the end of a dynamic mode of land appropriation that had developed since the seventeenth century.[54]

On the way to a resolution of the property debates was significant resistance on the ground. In Kerala, the popular mobilization of Pazhassi Raja, remembered as an anticolonial freedom struggle, had been crushed by 1805 after a massive military buildup. This left the Mappilas, at whose expense the administration of Malabar was established. For over a century their claims to land rights, when not ignored, were effectively dismissed by successive governments, which in turn faced recurring revolts of various forms, sizes, and intensities. Colonial officials tied Mappila opposition to British rule at least from 1817 on to religious motives and to the specific figures of Sayyid Alawi and his son Sayyid Fadl.

Rather than being dismissed outright as colonial, the "religious" explanations of rebellion require more serious consideration. In a global context that was characterized by jurisdictional flux, the transregional Islamic legal tradition of the Alawi sayyids could and did pose a formidable obstacle to a seamless advance of EIC claims on sovereignty. The formidability of this competing legal tradition was in fact more legible once open and violent rebellion was suppressed.

Colonial officials regularly used the language of fanaticism to describe and explain the violent incidents—often attacks on Hindu landlords—that took place in Malabar from 1817 to 1921.[55] However, treatment of what or whom they deemed the source of the violence was searching and more ambivalent, revealing yet another genealogy of "fanatic." In Vaughan's report on the 1817 attack, he initially held Sayyid Alawi responsible:

> The person who headed this is a mussulman Moplah of the name of Taramalle Coya Tangal an arab by Birth but who has been settled in this Province for upwards of 40 years and whose Reputation for Sanctity is so great that every Mopla Mussulman in malabar looks to him almost as a Prophet. Considering the conduct of this man as highly subversive of all subordination to the authority of Government and as tending to have the worst effect

upon the minds of the Natives I issued a summons for him to attend in Person to answer for his conduct and apprehensive from the former Violence of his conduct that the Peon who was sent with the summons might be maltreated or even murdered I backed it with a small Party of armed Colkars and a warrant for his apprehension in case of resistance.[56]

The summons to appear before Vaughan could not be delivered because Sayyid Alawi disappeared. The peon and his party did not find him in Mampuram or Tirurangadi. Once news of his resurfacing in Calicut was received, Vaughan issued a second summons, however, this time sending only the messenger without an armed force. He had learned from his sources that "violent resistance" by Sayyid Alawi was not a concern. Again he could not be found, and the summons could not be delivered.

Sayyid Alawi's avoidance of so much as an encounter with the new claimants to rule was very telling.[57] He could not have better expressed his refusal to recognize British authority over him if he had led an armed resistance, which it was quickly rumored he was in fact doing. These rumors attended him until his death and were inherited by his son as part of his patrimony and responsibility for the wider Muslim community and its actions. Vaughan's efforts to bring Sayyid Alawi before him were met by petitions from leading Mappilas pleading for a "pardon." He noted, "I did not conceive it proper to attend to their Petition as long as he persisted in refusing or rather omitting to attend my office."[58] This wavering between a reading of Sayyid Alawi's actions as refusal or as omission underlines a growing sense that he was no ordinary rebel. Indeed, the magistrate decided to forgo the use of military force to apprehend him precisely because of his "Reputation for Sanctity." Although in some respects such a reputation only mattered to Mappilas, who would in his estimation burn down the district for Sayyid Alawi, there was certainly a growing appreciation of it from the EIC's end as well.

Vaughan turned to the *qadi* of Calicut, seeking his mediation on behalf of the Company. He reflected on the exchange quite extensively, conveying several layers of sovereignty and jurisdictional politics:

I therefore sent for the Town Cazee a man of great respectability with whom I had a private conference and represented to him the consequence of the Tangul's ultimately refusing to obey my Summons, he seemed very sensible of the impropriety of the Tangul's conduct and said he would endeavor to persuade him to wait upon me, provided I would promise to treat him without offering any indignity to him, in fact that he was to attend me with

every Pomp and Ceremony to this I objected but said my office was open
to all Comers, but that if he did come thus attended I should consider it my
duty to represent to him the impropriety of his conduct after which I should
require Bail and that he might then appear in Person or by Vakeel which
ever he thought Proper. I soon found that so far from condescending to this
he would not even put his name to a Vakalatnamah.[59]

In this moment of encounter between two globally salient dispensations, one
hears the collision of law and symbols of sovereignty representing distinct traditions, even as echoes of centuries of Hindu-Muslim-Jewish-Christian exchange
facilitated by hybrid legal forms resound in the magistrate's vocabulary.[60] The
judge from an Islamic legal tradition appears here neither as collaborator nor as
rebel, the conventional categories for locating actors in the context of colonial
occupation. The qadi's very office in Calicut was a product of and reflected a
dense, ancient web of Hindu-Muslim relations, in which transregional and
transoceanic ties featured prominently. Thus, in 1817 the qadi could only view
the British and the EIC in terms of that prior history of exchange that could
accommodate multiple jurisdictional claims as long as they were recognized
as such. Vaughan's refusal to accord Sayyid Alawi the honors of a sovereign
entity foreshadowed the "militarization," that is, uniformity, in terms of rule
that would be realized in the form of a global empire-state.[61]

For his part, Sayyid Alawi issued fatwas condemning non-Muslim usur-
pations of law to serve the exclusive purposes of material gain at the expense
of Muslim life. His refusal to cooperate with the British remained consistent
with the Alawi Sufi tradition of steering clear of worldly powers that seek to
corrupt. The Alawi role as they saw it is the subject of the next chapter; here it
is worth highlighting that the changing terms of sovereignty in South India
and elsewhere were in part the outcome of negotiations between Company
states like the EIC and various "little kings."[62] Sayyid Alawi might be counted
in the latter category, but with some significant qualifications, which will be
elaborated later.

Vaughan was confounded by the persistence of Sayyid Alawi's refusal to
appear before him or even to sanction a proxy to appear in his stead. Asking
for guidance from Madras, he underscored the Tangul's (sayyid's) rejection of
his authority, saying he was so "adamant about not appearing that for a while
he was hiding in an Arab ship that was getting ready for a trip back to Arabia."
He left it to Madras to decide whether "coercive measures" were to be used and

intended to pretend he didn't know where the Tangul was hiding until orders came. He added: "Should it be deemed proper to resort to Compulsatory measures I cannot answer for the consequences, yet on the other hand the example thus set of an open attack on the Government property and a further contempt of its authority holds out an encouragement and example for others to adopt the same line of conduct."[63] Sensibly, the governor of Madras put the ball back in Vaughan's court, citing insufficient information and advising him to use "discretion in the exercise of those powers with which you are invested and for the right exercise of which you are responsible."[64]

By Vaughan's calculations the Tangul, Sayyid Alawi, was far too powerful to confront without the backing of Madras. He evidently did not want to risk a massive uprising just when their repeated occurrence seemed to be in the past. Incurring the cost of suppressing and policing a new popular movement, Vaughan knew, had the potential of harming his career prospects. Leaving the decision on how to proceed to his "discretion" was telling, because he replied immediately with a revised assessment of the situation: "On further inquiry I find that the Tangul is now far advanced in years, and in fact superannuated, that he has resided in Malabar during 50 years of his life and consequently during the most troublesome and rebellious times but it does not appear that he at any time took part against Government by countenancing or protecting those hostile to it."[65] He drives home the point by stressing the separation of spiritual and worldly concerns in the life led by the sayyid to the extent that he is depicted as literally projecting himself out of his mind:

> The Tangul is a man of little or no landed property, who evinces at all times a contempt of riches and subsists upon the donations of his disciples—his Chief concern being that of preserving unblemished the Character which he has obtained amongst all classes of Mussulmans for sanctity, not to say inspiration and these ideas are rather extravagant heightened at times by the appearance of Symptoms, which evidently bespeak a derangement of mind occasioned probably by intense thought and religious fanaticism.[66]

In Vaughan's April 10 letter to Madras, he did not use "fanatic" to describe the rebels. As late as 1817, "fanatic" retained its prior meaning: beginning in the mid-sixteenth century the word was used as an adjective in English to describe a person seemingly possessed by God or by a demon, or simply a person who seemed mad. The latter would, with the added sense of excess, become common usage by the mid-seventeenth century. It was derived from the Latin *fanaticus*, meaning "of a temple, inspired by a god," from *fanum* (temple); "profane" is derived from the same root, naming that which is outside the temple. So, if we take the original valence of "fanatic" as given in the *OED*, then it roughly represents the ecstatic states (*hal* in Arabic, *halillakum* in Malayalam) Sayyid Alawi and Fadl entered. Vaughan's use of "fanaticism" indexes a political universe that retrospective readings of political modernity consistently occlude.

Although his revaluation of Sayyid Alawi's role in rebellion against the newly constituted authority in Malabar may have been self-interested, Vaughan's conceptual tools for explaining the unlikeliness of the Tangul acting politically are instructive. He regarded Sayyid Alawi as a zealous devotee of a religion for which he had little respect; nonetheless, he possessed the intellectual resources to fathom Sayyid Alawi's "intense thought and religious fanaticism" as a domain of experience that intersected with individual and collective self-fashioning that was ultimately irreducible to politics or economy. In a few short decades after Vaughan's encounter with the idea of Sayyid Alawi, if not the person, colonial representations of religious life changed with the exigencies of rule, and anyone who was a Muslim rebel was branded a fanatic, gradually making the prior conception unintelligible. Perhaps not coincidentally, it was once the pluralities of law were less a feature of British rule in India that the fanatic and the rebel became indistinguishable.

The move toward greater uniformity in law and fixed identities—legal, religious, and political—was the story of the second half of the nineteenth century once the Company was no longer. It is almost impossible to say whether other choices could have been made when it came to engaging legalities and personalities that were other in the context of colonial rule, which came increasingly under pressure and exploded in 1857.[67] However, the prehistory of the Raj, or the history of the EIC, represented that moment when deciding on the exception was not so easy for a sovereignty that was layered and in a sense always deferred.

Vaughan feared that a genuine fanatic would rather become a martyr than be seized alive. He warned that he did not have the force at his disposal to manage the consequences of that eventuality:

> Under the impression of his own innocence and the total loss of Character which he conceives would result from his appearance in a public Court of Justice either in person or by Vakeel my information leads me to believe that on the first attempt to secure him, he would immediately put an end to himself in the event of its being found necessary to resort to compulsory measures, and what might be the Consequences of an infuriated and

fanatic mob, in a populous Town and Neighborhood containing not less than 20,000 Mussulmans being worked up to a pitch of frenzy in the idea of revenging one whom they would consider a Martyr it is impossible to say, but should, I conceive be previously guarded against by resorting to means more adequate than those which I at present command.[68]

In this projection of Sayyid Alawi's response to arrest and the subsequent reaction of his Muslim followers, Vaughan lays bare again the jurisdictional limits of the EIC's sovereignty over Malabar. The magistrate's political universe had to accommodate multiple constellations, of which a few are indicated or implicit in the above: imperial state, Company government, revenue demands, public Court of Justice, *vakeels* (legal proxies), a fanatic mob, and at least twenty thousand Muslims. These points are typically mapped as an oppositional system that inexorably produced anticolonial nationalism. This teleological thrust of most narratives of modern Indian history misses much about "India" and the world beyond prior to the mid- to late nineteenth century. Finally, if we regard fanaticism as a mode of glimpsing the unity of life and if the shores of the world beyond to which Sayyid Alawi journeyed were on no known maps, then in the later colonial conflation of rebel and fanatic we arrive at a different moment in the history of sovereignty in relation to life.

Imperium in Imperio: Recognizing Sayyid Sovereignty

In 1817, the terms of accommodation redolent in Vaughan's reports evince the sedimentation of a long history of polyvalent engagements.[69] That sediment formed a ground of mutual intelligibility in spite of the proliferating rhetoric of difference. The reconceptualization of sovereignty that hardened lines between the "conquerors" and the "natives" would still be a few decades in the making. The career and actions of the magistrate H. V. Conolly, who lost his life in the "conclusion" to the Sayyid Alawi and Fadl Ibn Alawi story in 1855, demonstrate the hardening of those lines.[70] Vaughan ultimately recommended that it was best to send a warning to Sayyid Alawi, to "reprimand him for the past and caution him for the future," and this is what was done. However, when another series of outbreaks of violence in the province seemed to follow a similar pattern, implicating Sayyid Alawi and his son as well this time, the question of arresting the revered figures surfaced again.

Thirty-two Mappila uprisings were recorded between 1836 and 1921, the year of the last, most widespread, and best-known rising labeled a full-scale rebellion; about half occurred between 1836 and Fadl's exile in 1852.[71] Hagiographic texts and some histories point to the sayyids' influential status, but the colonial officials went further to suggest that Sayyid Alawi and Fadl were proponents and/or instigators of the violence. Dale writes, "The Mambram Tannals were almost certainly responsible not only for the beginning of these more ritualized and increasingly serious attacks but also for the major fluctuations in the rate of outbreaks during the 1840s and 1850s."[72] The years Dale zoomed in on coincided with the death of Sayyid Alawi (1844), the departure of Sayyid Fadl for an extended stay in Mecca (1844–49), and his return and subsequent exile. Meanwhile, according to Ronald Miller, "The Pukkoya Tangal [Fadl] issued a fatwa that no one should rebel against the British, that the learned should discourage the uneducated from doing so, and that the government should be informed of such possible events in advance."[73] In any case, there is disagreement about the level of Alawi participation in what the British attempted to define as "Moplah Outrages," the majority of which were attacks on Hindu landlords or their agents. Dale notes that the legal definition of what constituted an outrageous outbreak was constantly in flux, even after the issuance (1854) and renewal (1859) of the Mappila Act, an emergency measure that allowed the state to decide what constituted an outrage, act more aggressively, and employ harsher punishments. The religious and suicidal character of the attacks, though, was central to the definition, signaling the hardening of lines mentioned above.[74]

Conolly, Malabar magistrate from 1840 to 1855 during the height of the Mappila "outrages," was key in shaping the colonial view of the Alawis and responsible for arranging Fadl's departure from India. The colonial view formed over time—at least a decade—and is as a result not always consistent. He writes, for example:

> The Tangul, as I said in a former letter in treating of similar cases, may not have been fully aware of all the horrors that were designed by those who came to visit him. He may have blessed their enterprise for "the good of the faith" without knowing to what atrocities he was giving his sanction: but even were this allowed, his moral responsibility would not be lessened. The man who knows what tragedies may ensue from his simple blessing, and the Tangul (allowing his former exculpations to be sincere) has had long experience of this, is bound to be thoroughly careful on whom his blessing descends. I am taking the most charitable view. It is hard to be fully persuaded that the young and ignorant fanatics from the north would or could have concealed their devilish intentions from a person like the Tangul, whom they too much venerated to deceive, or to think indeed capable of being

deceived. That the Tangul is in every respect a dangerous person—that *the Police is powerless against him*—and that he really enjoys an *imperium in imperio* is a matter of no doubt.[75] (emphasis added)

Written in the wake of an unusual and especially gory attack in a northern district at least eighty miles from Mampuram and Tirurangadi, Conolly nervously and tacitly recommended deportation, which was carried out within two months after the letter was received at Fort Saint George.

This was the last violent event that took place while the Alawis were present in Malabar. The appreciation of Fadl's role here as nothing less than representing an "imperium in imperio" and beyond police control is insightful, but Conolly did not push the point much further. Dale viewed this limited analysis as part of a broader failure of colonial officials to fully absorb the significance of the transregional Islamic-revival context and the role of Alawi sayyids as reformist missionaries within it.[76] However, his own haste to debunk some of the colonial rhetoric and to resituate Kerala as a "frontier" of a broader Islamic world history stops him short of providing a sustained analysis of the nature of the roles of sayyids in relation to the changing historical context of sovereignty. A question that emerges when the "outrages" are viewed through a global history lens and as coming at the end of the saddle period is whether they are the desperate last gasps of the "revolutionary" uprisings witnessed everywhere starting in the eighteenth century.[77]

In this regard, Conolly may have been closer to appreciating the entwined political, economic, and religious claims of different classes among the Mappilas, wherein reformists like Sayyid Fadl were reconceived by relatively poor recent converts as revolutionary leaders, and he in turn began to view himself in the same light. Folded into an evolving colonial discourse on fanaticism was the dialectical relationship between, on the one hand, the commoner now willing to die for his freedom and the holy man willing to sanctify such death, and on the other hand, the consolidation of imperial sovereignty. Conolly became a relatively keen observer of how fanatic power vested in sayyids worked to escape the grip of the company-state and in a sense the sayyids themselves, thus rendering it a serious threat to the emerging colonial body politic. Through his detailed reports and glosses on subordinates' reports, he essentially reshaped the colonial understanding of that power. Although the "consistency" of his explanations for the Mappila outbreaks was questioned at times by the government in Madras, which went so far as to contradict his assumptions about Sayyid Fadl's involvement, by 1852 Conolly's view of the linkages among fanaticism, violence, and the Alawis was accepted by all.[78]

Conolly was desperate to explain the source of a power that seemed to come from nowhere. He transformed the vague pattern Vaughan had begun to no-tice—of Mappilas visiting Mampuram to seek blessings from the sayyids before carrying out attacks—into a narrative of sayyid power. Since it appeared in bits and pieces as reportage, however, it was easy to read him as being inconsistent and confused, which he also may have been. Perhaps for the same reason of form, it took him several years to establish to his own satisfaction the need to remove the Alawis from Malabar. Conolly wrestled with intelligence he received from various quarters about the precise role of the sayyids of Tirurangadi-Mampuram:

> The Tiru[r]angady Tangul asserts that he holds out no encouragement to fanaticism or rebellion against Government, that crowds of people come to do him reverence, that he is obliged to receive and bless them, often in a mass, and that it is his misfortune if any evil designing people, who partake of this blessing, in the mass, should hold that it warrants them to commit any atrocity, which their perverted minds consider a service to God. All this is specious enough, and I will not say, that it is altogether untrue; but I can-not shut my eyes to the fact, that somehow or other, this Tangul's presence in Malabar has been *the* cause, or *a* cause of most, if not all, of the outbreaks that have taken place.[79]

The confused and flustered analysis above is apparent in the rest of the "con-nected narrative" of events Conolly offered to Madras regarding an attack in 1849 that culminated in a major standoff between sixty-four Mappilas and several heavily armed Company units. All but one of the Mappilas were killed.

His explanation for why Mappilas acted the way they did swung between materialist and idealist poles. The latter engendered dreams of paradise through martyrdom nurtured by the sayyids of Mampuram, whereas the former re-mained unresolved land-tenure issues that he acknowledged were exacerbated by the alignment of British law courts, revenue policies, and Hindu elites' re-vised claims to private property in land. The impasse created by the two poles operating in tandem, with ground zero being Mampuram-Tirurangadi, was irresolvable because an Islamic tradition of sovereignty had literally taken root and could not be extirpated through normal means.[80] With the death and burial of Sayyid Alawi in Mampuram in 1844 the game changed yet again. Conolly danced around the notion of sayyid sovereignty being a real possibility but could not acknowledge it except in terms of a fanaticism that was now reduced to or displaced onto the irrational acts of the illiterate poor.

In one description of the power of the sayyids, Conolly comes very close to tying the geographical specificity of their base to their political viability: "I have in former letters, shewn the Government, the exact position in which the Tangul's family stands to us, and that the only hold we have over the Tangul himself, as a poor and abstemious faqueer, is an appeal to his fear of being removed from his influential post at Tiruwangady, to some place more remote from, and inaccessible to, his bigoted *country* followers."[81] Tirurangadi being an out-of-the-way place partially explained the sayyids' influence, and in turn Conolly recommended the family's removal to another location, such as Cannanore, with its army barracks and where better surveillance was possible.[82] Echoing Vaughan, in 1849 Conolly made clear that seizing the sayyid was still a risky proposition requiring full commitment from Madras to manage the fallout. The fallout that Conolly feared was extrapolated from the suicide attacks that began in the 1830s, which pointed to there having developed among the Mappilas a level of commitment to an ideal, no matter how "false," that was embodied in the person of the sayyid and that posed a grave danger to the order the Company sought to impose in Malabar.

Conolly surmised that the fear of death vanished among Mappila assailants who visited the Mampuram gravesite of Sayyid Alawi and received the departed saint's blessings in addition to Fadl's. The power of death and desire for it became a centerpiece of colonial analyses of Muslim politics; but it did not appear in the register of "the political," since the act of denying the sovereign's right over life foreclosed the political horizon being drawn by the colonial state. After describing in a half-admiring tone the zeal with which the fanatics fought, forgetting their own physical bodies in pain, Conolly wrote: "A feeling which can so denaturalize men, and prompt them to terrible excesses, is one, which it must be the anxious desire of any civilized Government to eradicate; but the power of so doing is, I am sorry to say, anything but apparent. The idea, instead of being weakened, has been strengthened of late, by various circumstances; the most important of which is, the celebrity that has been attached to the history of former Malabar 'martyrs.'"[83] The "history of former Malabar 'martyrs'" was indeed orally transmitted through song and story, forging a strong sense of a local Mappila Muslim identity.[84] However, the sayyid as powerful "cause" and the fanatic "idea" as irrepressible were tropes of a colonial narrative that accompanied and encumbered Fadl throughout his life. That life, tied as it was through revelation, genealogy, and *baraka*[85] to living and dead bodies, to semidivine beings, to talismans, and to the divine, could not easily be brought into the sovereign jurisdiction delimited through the Company's land appropriations and its evolving legal form in the first half of the nineteenth century. Neither could that life be fully excluded. To that extent Sayyid Fadl and Sayyid Alawi before him were simultaneously *homo sacer* and not *homo sacer* to a tradition partially drawing on Roman law for its (re)conceptualizations of empire while confronting another formidable tradition—not just barbarians across the Rubicon.[86] There was certainly a desire among colonial officials to see the Alawis disappear, yet they could not allow them to become martyrs. From the perspective of most Mappilas, the sacredness of sayyids became indisputable, and their killing would have been considered a significant sacrifice.

Multiple forms of life and sovereignty remained a feature of the mid-nineteenth-century global moment of empire. Hence, negotiating jurisdictional boundaries and drawing inchoate lines between custom and law, private and public, religious and political was the norm. However, confirming the notion of sovereignty as grounded in the exception, the lines became clearer through repeated emergencies. Conolly's final points in the report entailed a recapitulation of his recommendation to the government in Madras four years earlier to hit hard individually and collectively: disarm the population, expropriate the holdings of insurgents' families, and fine the leader's district. He appealed to the directors not to reject his counterinsurgency proposal as they had done previously on the grounds of being "opposed to justice and policy"; he begged that at least the first recommendation, for a policy of disarmament, be accepted. This minimal bid for action follows directly upon making a strong case for the provision entailing collective punishment, which he acknowledged was "severe" but insisted was necessary given the state of "emergency."[87]

He defined the emergency as a situation of recurring terror unleashed by Muslims in the heart of Malabar making Hindus of all castes feel unsafe and creating a persistent climate of "animosity . . . between two opposite races, which increases in intensity by each fresh instance of outbreak."[88] At various points over the next century, all of these counterinsurgency techniques were tried, along with some partial land reforms and limited social development projects.[89]

Conclusion: Life in Death, Politics in State, and Transregional Ruptures

English East India Company officers charged with administering Malabar in the early years were attuned to how distinctions within and relations among the religious, political, and economic spheres played out on the ground over time and attempted to locate their position in relation to those histories, of which by the turn of the nineteenth century the EIC had been a growing part for two hundred years. During Conolly's tenure as Malabar magistrate, those histories became less and less significant, as the Company's position in a vast global imperial state formed part of the local, regional, and international calculations, establishing a "colonial" rule of exclusions and "inclusive exclusions." Much of the history of the British in India is told from this postconsolidation perspective.[90] Accordingly, the nature of colonial rule and resistance to it has undergone voluminous treatment from scholars across disciplines.

The relative centrality of the colonial archive for modern Indian history and the determining force of responses to colonialism (scripted in terms of that archive) for Indian and British futures have meant that the nature of non-state sovereignty and its historical transformation through operations of power quite different from those that attended the formation of the modern state is a relatively new arena of investigation.[91] For colonial administrators like Conolly, other forms of sovereignty were a real and present danger to which they gave much thought:

> It has been debated at times whether the Tangul is in full possession of his faculties. I have no doubt as to his real sanity and consequent accountableness, though I am aware that he is at times "besides himself," and in a sort of supernatural ecstasy, in consequence of long-continued fasting and prayer. This is one of the chief means by which he obtains the extraordinary hold he possesses over the feelings of the people. His face after one of these spiritual exercises, is said to show clearly (as did that of Moses) how intimate has been his communication with the Deity.[92]

Strangely, these were the last lines in the letter sent to Madras regarding the current situation in Malabar's continuing Mappila insurgency. It was an uncanny ending to an otherwise sober assessment of the sayyid's involvement in violence and of the force that would be necessary should the decision be made to remove him from the region.

That Fadl's power to compel subjects' affective (and as other accounts indicate, political, economic, and religious) submission entered the colonial record in terms of the supernatural evinces an ambivalent appreciation (fading even as uttered) of sayyid sovereignty as constituted in excess of the law, as a function of fanaticism in its original sense. The face became a site of revelation. Conolly's parenthetical citation connecting Fadl to the first exemplary shepherd suggests at least an implicit understanding of the ancient tradition of pastoral power as existing in relation to a people and constituting another form of government. In addition to security concerns, it may have been this recognition of Fadl as a sovereign in his own right that forced Conolly to show him, however begrudgingly, a certain level of respect in delicately handling the terms of his exile.

Whether deemed irrational, arbitrary, ultimately despotic, or utterly transformed in the encounter, law—Hindu and Islamic—was one of the comparative frameworks through which the humanity of secular law could be elaborated, defining proper and improper forms of life.[93] In the figure of the sayyid such comparison met with a further difference, in the form of baraka, *karamath*, genealogical authority, and sharia, braided to form a paradoxical order that could not be named in positive terms. It was not the same Islam the qadi represented, nor the Sufism of dervishes and fakirs, nor the sovereignty of sultans like Tipu. With only paradoxes to offer—immanent yet transcendent, singular yet multiple, living yet dead—the life of Sayyid Alawi and the life inherited by Sayyid Fadl reached beyond the sensible and governable world even as they offered a form of government.

By establishing a pastoral relationship of care for individuals and for the many at once, the sayyid's life became a political life characterized by government: conducting men to the good and protecting them on their way. The predicate of modern colonial rule, then, did not merely lie in the rejection of another's sovereignty linked to territory but also entailed the gradual derecognition of prior forms of political life that were not reducible to the emergent politics (police) of the governmentalized state. There were different outcomes for "the people" emerging in the interstices of and marking the distance between rejection and derecognition. Rejection and its accompanying repression were dialectically bound to produce a reversal in the form of anticolonial nationalism and a postcolonial order of nation-states with citizens of varying degrees of rights and protections. Derecognition saw an accumulation of knowledge as formulas that recoded the genetic makeup of a tradition such that its positive valence was masked, slowed down, to allow other trajectories from within and without to surpass it. However, signs of sayyid sovereignty and reaching for the unity of life remain across the Indian Ocean world and beyond.

The stakes of rewriting the history of transregional encounters between sovereignties are high. Though scripted in terms of emergency, the absence of normal rule in the first decade since the EIC conquest raises the question of the entirety of colonial rule being one long emergency. Pushing that logic further, if the postcolonial state inherited and reproduced many of the preexisting terms of rule, as some scholars have argued, then an exit from the state of emergency cannot be found in the embrace of modern sovereignty. Deconstructing life's relationship to sovereignty requires excavating its other histories.

2 "Where the Sun Rises to Where the Sun Sets"

Origins, Life, and the Faces of Sovereignty

THE CONFUSION ABOUT SAYYIDS in colonial records and in contemporary interpretations is not merely the result of a lack of evidence. The role of the Alawis is confusing. Or rather, it becomes confused as history is simultaneously read forward to and backward from the latter part of the nineteenth century—with the two historical perspectives colliding in a gray zone between the 1830s and 1850s. On the one hand, when read properly, that is forward, from the context of a global political economy growing more sophisticated since the seventeenth century, "religious" actors can be seen as remaining the norm through much of the nineteenth century, even as "secular" methods of government took robust new techno-political forms in seaborne empire-states, their settler offspring, and elsewhere, and as "scientific" cultures expanded. Magistrates like Vaughan straddled the religious and secular worlds as they had for centuries. On the other hand, when read backward from the "modern" late nineteenth century, the story becomes one of foreign secular agents meeting already surpassed "traditional" and religious despots, dervishes, and other deceivers with modernist indigenous reformers in between.[1] Confusion is political.

The scare quotes around religious, traditional, secular, scientific, and modern are intended to signal the making of those distinctions into a political problem over time and across space, challenging the premise of the secularization thesis and its assumptions about demystification and humanity's general, inevitable disenchantment. Nevertheless, on a global canvas a host of painters of different schools busily and self-consciously drew the lines of a modern world, filling in the regions of tradition and superstition in different colors. Take Egypt and the Ottoman Empire, both of which engaged in state practices understood in the nineteenth century to be departures from tradition. Until recently, those experiments were interpreted by historians in terms of outcomes—defeat, incorporation, bankruptcy, occupation, dissolution, and so on—that mattered for those who inherited the state.[2]

Such a reading is contingent on a peculiar decontextualization and elision of the interconnected global formation of state and society that had been taking place since the fifteenth century. The nineteenth century becomes reimagined in relation to the imperatives of the nation-state, such that "the modern Middle East" cannot *not* appear temporally out of sync and spatially truncated (long-standing exchanges with Europe, Africa, and Asia vanish), even in revisionist accounts focused on the state. In the past ten to fifteen years, there has been a move to retrace those transregional links, which was likely not accidental; as the bipolar post–World War II order collapsed, India's and China's (for example) "return" to the Indian Ocean world not only suddenly became more legible but was also marked by greater intensity. While there were certainly new kinds of state-level and corporate investments in the postcolonial period, to speak of a return requires first seeing Cold War formations such as "Middle East" and "South Asia" (as well as Southeast and East Asia) as discrete areas and as temporally constituting moments of rupture—separated by the history of modern sovereignty we are tracing here.

According to some historians, Malabar and South India more broadly were transformed from a dynamic, globally connected region that since at least 1498 had seen intense competition in trade, land appropriation, cultural practices, and the means of violence into an isolated backwater that by 1852, the year of Fadl's expulsion from India, was characterized by feudal relations in land and the alienation of labor from its social product. This is well-trodden territory, with perspectives ranging from those who would place all "blame" on, and hence all power in, the British to those who regard it as an outcome of overdetermined global forces that could not be reduced to intentions, good or bad. Ironically, it is nationalist and postcolonial scholars who tend to assign the most power to colonialism; even when refuting that power by pointing to alternatives, the colonial agenda sets the terms of debate.

Scholars such as David Washbrook have sharpened their analytical tools against the postcolonial "turn" and claims about an all-powerful colonialism. Curiously, while his recent work argues for a connected global history approach as better suited for retrieving the agency of Indians prior to the rise of bourgeois nationalism and in the face of momentous change that produced the latter's condition of possibility, the "pragmatic" decisions of the EIC are evacuated of power through an emphasis on the results not matching intentions. That is, during the "transition" from a commercial body to a colonial governing body the Company's policies for administering an Asian empire are assigned a quality of bricolage wherein individual decisions and consequences were just as much or even more up to Indians to impact through their local responses as the "will" of the British.[3]

The history of the Alawis in Malabar conforms to Washbrook's broad framework, but in the long run it is clear from the record that British intentions to sever Malabar's ties to Arab sayyids mattered more than Mappila efforts to bring back the family. That said, at the end of the day the power of sayyids did not operate along the same lines as the new power of states taking hold of life and consequently never posed the threat that early colonial officials projected. The voluminous records on figures like Sayyid Alawi and Sayyid Fadl express an anxiety of rule that marks the distance between old and new conceptions of sovereignty. Apparent in the classic example of anticolonial revolt that unfolded five years after Fadl's exile is the culmination of some of the processes sketched in the previous chapter: land tenure revisions, taxation, communal interferences, and expanding colonial legal jurisdictions.[4]

This chapter focuses on the role of the sayyids in relation both to the formation of a Mappila Muslim community and to a transoceanic Muslim public sphere. As Stephen Dale and, more recently, Sebastian Prange have detailed, Muslim merchants, sayyids, *ashraf*, and Sufis from the Arabian Gulf region have had real or imagined relationships with Malabar since the time of Muhammad. Those relations deepened and broadened over the centuries as the merchant communities established roots and became global actors centuries before the arrival of the Portuguese in 1498. In the previous chapter, it was knowledge in, of, and for empire that brought the sayyids and Mappilas into view. Here we rely on other sources.

Those sources require that the narrative ahead take a couple of sharp turns. First, we begin with the forging of a foundational Muslim connection to the land of Malabar as it was sought in the originary idea or mytheme of Cheruman Perumal, the founding father of *keralam*. Following this is quite a long treatment of a very important text that takes us more deeply into the thought worlds of Sayyid Fadl and Sayyid Alawi at a formative moment. The text's composition, dissemination, proscription, and later printing outside India overlap with the last years of Fadl's father's life (ca. 1836–44), his tenure in Mecca as a student (1844–49), his return and exile (1849–52), and his travels in Arabia, Egypt, and Turkey (1852–57). Despite the significance of this text, we remain in the realm of the fragment as far as perspectives on and into the life of these sayyids. Thus, rather than seek the ultimate truth of their lives, we direct our inquiry into life's possibilities in the face of sovereignty as it changed over time. This is the thread that ties together the chapter's fragments.

Mappila Muslims: Making the Fourth Vedam

A fascinating origin myth of Kerala that is a true testament to its deep Indian Ocean identity relates the foundation of a distinct Malayali polity with many and no borders to an act of both conversion and migration at once. The myth of Cheruman Perumal delineates a number of themes of Muslim life in Malabar that are repeated under different historical conditions well into the present while helping to better situate the changing role of sayyids.[5] It is related in a number of sources, including the well-mined sixteenth-century Arabic treatise *Tuhfat al-Mujahidin* of Zayn al-Din al-Malabari (al-Ma'bari), which is famous for its account of the Portuguese irruption into the Indian Ocean trading world, challenging the Islamic sphere of influence and endangering a Muslim way of life.[6] The *Tuhfat* circulated far and wide in the Arabic original and in translation, from Lisbon soon after it first appeared in India in the 1580s to Kuala Lumpur in 2006.[7] Various English versions of parts or the whole were published in the early nineteenth century and during India's freedom struggle in the 1930s–1940s. Soon after the British conquest of Malabar, the Scottish orientalist John Leyden translated excerpts of the *Tuhfat* without attribution, which appeared as part of a general collection of his translated Oriental manuscripts.[8] Leyden, who held various posts in the EIC's Indian administration from 1803 to 1811, in fact chose to translate the section relating to the origins of Muslims in Kerala. A complete translation was done by Lieutenant M. J. Rowlandson, the Persian interpreter to the army at Madras in 1833.[9]

The legend of Cheruman Perumal as the last of the benevolent Chera emperors is shared by all Malayali traditions, which claim him as Hindu, Jain, Buddhist, Christian, or Muslim.[10] It was deemed compelling even by normally skeptical British officials.[11] Before their time, beginning in the sixteenth century, it circulated via Portuguese, Dutch, and Danish sources.[12] In the Hindu tradition he was said to have divided the once unified lands into principalities and then vanished or ascended, to return some day. The account was reworked in the Mappila tradition to fit their uniqueness as a recent minority into a universal Islamic history and into a regionally specific Malayali history. According to Mappilas, he was likewise a Hindu sovereign who lived in the early seventh century and ruled over all of what is today the state of Kerala. On the night of a new moon, he had a vision of a full moon splitting in two. Although none of his astrologers could explain the event, he subsequently had a dream in which it was revealed to him that it was a miracle performed by the Prophet Muhammad.

Hearing about a group of Arab mystics (*faqirs*)[13] who had landed in Malabar on their way to visit Adam's footprint in Sri Lanka, the raja invited them to his palace, where they informed their host about their pilgrimage, Islam, and the life of Muhammad. Their corroboration of his dream instilled in him a deep desire to meet their prophet. After carefully dividing up his territory among various princes as governors, the king quietly left with the pilgrims on their return voyage to Arabia. There Cheruman Perumal was converted to Islam by Muhammad himself; he died on his way back to India.[14]

He was believed to be buried either between Mukalla and Shihr or somewhere in Dhofar on the southern Arabian coast. In that area he was known as the saint Abd al-Rahman al-Samiri (Samudri), and a British officer, Colonel Miles, who visited Dhofar in December 1884, reported that the tomb was still there in "Dareez," a half day's sail from Salalah. He found it standing a half mile in from the sea, though in a state of disrepair.[15] He reported that it was believed that rain fell in Dhofar as a result of the saint's blessing, and that out of fear that the rains would stop a small subscription was taken up in order to effect some mostly minor repairs. He interviewed an old qadi by the name of Sayyid Ahmad, who told him about the local tribes and the saint al-Samiri: "His tomb was now a ziarat or shrine, and visited by all sorts and conditions of men, and his name was included with the other Ameers, Anbias and Ulemas, and was prayed to whenever rain was required by the people of the district."[16]

Like a good historian formed within the Arabic historiographical tradition, al-Malabari discounted aspects of the popular account that he deemed unlikely and offered corrections, for example, that the Perumal lived in the ninth century rather than the seventh and that he could not have witnessed the miracle of the splitting moon at the exact time of the new moon over Mecca.[17] In the late nineteenth century, Logan explained the variance in interpretations as a split between "Malayali Arabs" who relied on Arabic manuscripts and the "indigenous Muhammadans (*Mappilas*)." The latter were keen to represent Islam's transmission to a Hindu sovereign as the Fourth Vedam.[18]

Coastal Malabar was a cosmopolitan hub of the medieval world; the Islamicate civilization that took shape there by the twelfth century included Arab, Persian, and North Indian Muslims along with growing numbers of Malayali Muslims. In the precolonial period, "mappila" signified a complex household economy and political relation more than the identitarian position implicit in Logan's definition, which the colonial administrator deployed in order to distinguish between indigenous and foreign at the apogee of imperial power.[19] By the sixteenth century, "mappila" could describe families such as al-Malabari's, in which a male Arab Muslim married a local Malayali woman, establishing a creole culture that is noticeable to this day in foods, rituals, physiognomy, and language. As the Chera dynasty came to an end in the twelfth century and before the arrival of the Portuguese in the last years of the fifteenth century, competition among Muslims from various regions for recognition by the rulers of the new fragmented polities may have grown.

Recognition brought with it protections and privileges such as land grants and the highly symbolic right to use roofing tiles on congregational mosques or private dwellings. The use of tiles was a marker of sovereignty that could only be possessed to the extent that it was bestowed. Technically, the leading rajas of the northern, central, and southern regions of Kerala possessed exclusive rights to tile and could both grant that right to others deemed worthy as well as revoke it. However, as a sovereign right it could only ever exist relationally and through acts of sharing. Temples, palaces, large houses, churches, congregational mosques, and so on were often tiled structures that were simultaneously the products of both material and symbolic negotiations over value, right, and duty.[20]

Accordingly, the myth's tying of the origins of Islam to the origins of a regionally differentiated Malayali polity authorized by a shared sovereign(ty) constituted the Mappilas as a translocal community that was Muslim-Arab-Malayali.[21] Engseng Ho's description of al-Malabari captures this complex reality: "Al-Malibari himself was from an eminent Malabar family of Muslim scholars who originated in Yemen, and his writing reflects the double perspective of being both insider and outsider, and of having both local and transregional concerns."[22]

Along with the deeply local sovereign, inscribed in the Mappila version of the Cheruman Perumal myth was the responsibility of the Arab Muslim for making possible and sustaining a Malayali religious life in Islam, at a practical political-theological level. According to the anonymous *Qissat Shakarwati Farmad* (The narrative of the universal sovereign), which gives a more elaborate account than the *Tuhfat*, a compact was established between the Perumal and a group of Hadhrami Muslims in order to realize the former's wish that Islam become the Fourth Vedam in all of his lands. While preparing to return he fell ill, and knowing that he would die he had his companions, Malik Ibn Dinar and his family (Habib Ibn Malik, Sharif Ibn Malik, and Malik Ibn Habib and his wife, Qamariyya), promise that they would carry out his mission.[23] When they wavered he wrote detailed letters to the Malayali princes about their responsibilities in their respective principalities and his wish that the reception and protection of the new religion be added to their remit. Upon his death, armed with these letters the party of Malik Ibn Dinar, which included the fifteen children of Malik Ibn Habib and Qamariyya, traveled to Malabar and began the process of disseminating Islam through the establishment of mosques in all of the major trading ports and training a cadre of ulama (scholars) who could serve as imams, qadis, and muftis.

No matter the particular historical conditions that gave rise to the Mappila Muslim version of the Cheruman Perumal myth, at its core are themes that repeat themselves through the centuries: miracle work, migration and pilgrimage, mysticism,[24] genealogy, responsibility, law, and divided sovereignty. These themes have formed and informed the politics and culture of Malayali society down to the present. The late nineteenth-century colonial usage of "Mappila" to label territorially bounded Malayalam-speaking Muslims elided the medieval distinctions, partly as a result of a conscious policy of restricting and regulating the flows of more mobile Muslims through British-controlled territories.[25] Those regulations and restrictions stretched across the Indian Ocean and (re) shaped relations among peoples just as Muslim merchants, scholars, and mystics did in earlier times, when the ocean was far more of a *mare liberum*.

The simultaneity (and possibility) of inhabiting different identity positions was especially characteristic of the Alawi and other diasporas around the Indian Ocean. That the colonial politics of fixing identities in place in communal, ethnic, or other terms had disastrous consequences globally is a well-worn truism. However, the constitution of sufi-sayyid as stranger and kin was mediated by a third possibility, which made this-worldly drawing of lines only ever partial in their sovereign claims. The sufi-sayyid as intimate friend indexed other potentialities of life. That potentiality can only ever be glimpsed in the interstices of the sovereignties—divine and modern—that Fadl negotiated during his lifetime.

Reconnecting the Muslim World: The
Alawi Way from Calicut to Cairo

Our access to Sayyid Alawi's and Sayyid Fadl's thoughts during the Indian period is provided by a text they are believed to have "authored" sometime in the 1830s or 1840s. It has been held in high regard by Mappilas until the present. The reason for focusing on this one text, beyond chronology and exigency, is that it represents a conceptual bridge between Fadl's religious-political life as heir to (an impossible) sayyid sovereignty and to his life of politics as a servant of the Ottoman sultan-caliph, which will be explored in the following chapters. Admittedly, this is an overly simplistic dichotomy and is only intended to serve a heuristic purpose. In this specific analysis of government and Islam, the two intercalated moments of divine sovereignty (sayyid and sultanic) index broad transoceanic transformations that form the backdrop for an inquiry into an irresolvable tension. That abiding tension in the entwinement of the political and the theological is brought to crisis again in Muslim empires in the mid-nineteenth century, with varying consequences for rule and for opposition to rule.

Uddat al-umara' wa-l-hukkam l-ihanat al-kufra wa abdat al-asnam (The preparedness of princes and governors for the affronts of infidels and idolaters) is a text made up of different parts, most assembled in Malabar and published as a whole in Cairo shortly after Fadl's exile.[26] The part of it said to have been composed by Sayyid Alawi—the fatwa collection titled *Al-Sayf al-battar* (The sharpest sword)—ostensibly circulated by way of mosques in Malabar before the British confiscated and destroyed all extant copies in 1851.[27] There is heated disagreement about the authorship of *Al-Sayf al-battar*, since the text itself only gives the name of Sayyid Abdallah bin Abd al-Bari al-Ahdal (d. 1271AH / 1854–55), of the famous family of scholars from Zabid in Yemen. The followers of Sayyid Alawi have argued that the Arabic verb *allafa*, which is used in this case, did not connote authorship at the time but still retained the classical meaning of joining or combining; thus, this esteemed contemporary, Sayyid al-Ahdal, was merely a relay for the answers to questions put to Sayyid Alawi.[28]

However, even if "authorship" were problematic, which it was in this context, a provincial outlook does not conform to the internal evidence, nor does it do justice to the vastness of the Islamic world the text instantiates.[29] Accordingly, it may indeed have been the reverse: that Sayyid Alawi and Sayyid Fadl, responding to conditions in Malabar, were nonetheless relays for a renowned scholar in the "center."[30] There is a chance that Fadl met al-Ahdal in Mecca in 1844, five years after the British occupation of Aden, when the legality of living under Christian rule and related questions assumed renewed significance. Whichever direction the "Q & A" went, its spatial and temporal dimensions reveal a quest for universality over and against the local and regional containers of specific historical conditions.

Regarded in this way, in which there is always only one Author of Law, the ulama appear as conduits for a transregional transmission of knowledge about legal-theological matters and world affairs, in which the ultimate horizon is the deterritorialized and ineffable hereafter.[31] In addition to the fatwas (which we will take to be religious opinions of Sayyid Alawi and others), the longer text of the *Uddat* contains introductory remarks by the Egyptian publishers, critiques of the religious establishment by Fadl, advice for true believers, "histories" of transoceanic Muslim communities, and commentary on the practice of good government. Formed against the backdrop of continual European incursions into India and the wider Indian Ocean world, where Alawis had been in circulation for just as long, the treatment in the *Uddat* of Christian invaders and Muslims' willing submission to their rule may seem predictable. However, given that not all ulama opposed the establishment of colonial rule in India and elsewhere, it remains to be explained why some did and how they differed from other oppositional stances, particularly the Wahhabi movement in Arabia that had picked up steam at the same time as Mappila encounters with the EIC across the ocean in Malabar.

I consulted a copy of the *Uddat* that was in the private collection of Abdurahman Mangad; he had made his copy from the one held at his mosque in Vazhayur, a sleepy inland village about twenty-five kilometers north of Mampuram. Lending weight to the claim that colonial officials had destroyed all the Malabar originals, this copy was of the manuscript printed in Cairo. When exactly the text circulated back into India in this form is unclear. At the bottom of every page is a prayer to the Ottomans, for their rightful guidance and victory. Specifically, the prayer is intended for the sultan of the time, who in a marginal note is given as Abdülmecid (r. 1839–61). At the end of the *Uddat*, a page of publication information indicates that the manuscript was printed at the Matba' al-hujra al-hamida in the Egypt of Said Pasha (r. 1854–63) and was edited by Shaykh 'Ali al-Mukhallalati in March 1857 (mid-Rajab 1273). Publication of the *Uddat* in Ottoman Egypt in the year of the Indian Mutiny and in the wake of the Crimean War is telling.

Fadl's itinerary after his exile from India would have put him in Egypt in 1857 on his way to Istanbul, his second trip. From his prior stint in Mecca

(1844–49), Fadl certainly knew that Sultan Abdülmecid had become deeply influenced by a growing movement for the revival of Islam led in particular by Sufi orders of the day. Butrus Abu-Manneh's revision of the dominant thesis, that the first equality edict issued during the Ottoman Tanzimat was a result of Western pressure and the product of the westernized Rashid Pasha's sole endeavor, entailed resituating the 1839 *hatt-i sherif* of Gulhane within the context of Abdülmecid's rededication to Islamic principles of justice.[32] Even though Abu-Manneh suggests that the direction of change had shifted quite decidedly toward the West from roughly 1850 onward, Fadl's publication of the *Uddat* in 1857 can be regarded as part of the earlier strands of thought that delved into the Islamic past and Islamic discursive tradition for answers to the social and political problems confronting Muslims globally.[33]

Abu-Manneh's characterization of the 1830s as a decade of ulama reasserting authority in the Ottoman Empire dovetails with the Mappila contention that the *Uddat*'s parts were produced in Malabar in response to the British consolidation of power there, which saw lines drawn between pro- and anticolonial ulama. At the same time, the EIC's seizure of Aden in 1839 also suggests that Yemen and al-Ahdal were the origins of the fatwa section, *Al-Sayf al-battar*.[34] Yet another, Hijazi, context for the text corresponds to Fadl's movements at the time: "The rebellions of 1855 and 1858 were caused in part by local rivalries for power, but a major factor involved was the detestation felt by the Muslim Hijazis for innovations desired by Christian Europe and the rising position of European protégés in commerce." William Ochsenwald's analysis maps almost perfectly onto the thesis of the *Uddat*.[35]

There was an overlap between the sources Abu-Manneh identifies for the Gulhane Rescript and the sources of the *Uddat*. Taking our cue from his reading strategy, any such similarity is unremarkable when we consider the circulation of ideas about kingship and justice in a post-Mongol Islamicate world; Muslim scholars had never ceased, in a sense, to contemplate the terms of inhabiting a post-Prophetic time.[36] The contemplation took place under very different historical circumstances and in very different locales, with the question of the *khilafa (caliphate)* occupying the center of debates at key moments. Fadl makes this explicit when, following al-Haddad, he distinguishes between the time of the Prophet and the time of history, which begins with the first successor, Caliph Umar. It seems that disagreements and conflicts about the succession were on parallel with debates about ulama deserving recognition as *mujaddids* (renewers) and drove a specifically Islamic history.[37]

The Ottoman sultans' fortuitous addition of Arab lands to their imperial holdings after 1516 brought with it the office of caliph.[38] The early sultans did nothing with this title, or so it was thought. Recent revisions of early modern Ottoman history show how it was precisely in entreaties from far-flung places such as Java and India and Ottoman responses to these that among Sunni Muslims the sultan-caliph came to be identified with Istanbul.[39] After the sixteenth- and seventeenth-century engagements, it is only in the second half of the nineteenth century that we see a meaningful return of the Ottoman sultan-caliph to a relationship with Muslims across the Indian Ocean. However, especially after the Mongol conquests, individual Sufis and Sufi orders, though competitors in many respects, played the most crucial role in stitching together a global Islamic ecumene.[40] A glimpse of Fadl's consciousness of that globality and capacity to plug into its network will be provided in the following chapter.

The Egyptian publishers noted in their introduction to the text, which acknowledges that Fadl had assembled it, that the *Uddat* is a "da'wa [calling] to follow God and his Messenger, a call to follow the Sunna and walk in the path" of Muhammad. They also noted that the text is "adorned" with a prayer for the "Ottoman state, which is the pride of states and the source of eternal happiness."[41] However, given the complex origins of the *Uddat*, the prayerful invocation of a universal Ottoman sovereignty appended to the bottom of the text, most likely at the time of publication in 1857, only belies a more nuanced treatment of the long history of grappling with religious and political entanglements in the quest to live a life that is good. Additionally, this marginal inscription and the publishers' egalitarian framing of the text signals a disjuncture between the Indian Ocean world of the Alawi *sada* (pl. of *sayyid*) and the Egyptian ulama. The latter had come to experience life as subjects of a centralized state and were adjusting to an ongoing imperial restructuring.

The term "subject" (*ra'iy*, pl. *ra'iyya*, or *abd*, pl. *abid*) is apt here, as the time of the "citizen" was yet to come. However, it does elide differences within and between groups bound together in various vertical and horizontal relations for which there was a proliferation of terms in Arabic, Persian, and Ottoman over the centuries. In the Ottoman context, for example, everyone in the empire was essentially the sultan's *abd* (servant, slave), his *ra'iyya* (subjects, charges), unless otherwise stipulated, by extraterritorial conventions, for example. In rank and administrative practice the stark divide between ruling classes (*askeri*) and the common folk (*ra'iyya*) was mediated by a host of other differences or oppositions. In a broader Islamicate context, ulama were responsible for the moral, legal, spiritual, and in some instances biological lives (soup kitchens, hospitals, and warrior Sufis come to mind) of the ra'iyya.

So in a sense, for ulama in the Ottoman Empire in the mid-nineteenth century, the Tanzimat and its corollary discourse of rights and citizenship threatened to make "subjects" of all, irrespective of learning and status. The Egyptian interlocutors noted: "Among the secrets of this book is that whoever reads it from beginning to end and understands its meaning will expand his mind and his religion. And whoever acts on what [he learns] therein becomes fit for sanctity/sovereignty (*al-wilaya*) and for the protection of his faith. Therefore, it is incumbent on each human being (*insan*) to strive with it and to take it as his personal companion."[42] Self-sovereignty as the marker of a "modern" Muslim identity was very much the stuff of the Egyptian *nahda* (renaissance or enlightenment). The long present slippage between the two registers of wilaya became amplified as the question of state and subject crescendoed through the second half of the nineteenth century, climaxing in the 1880s–1890s.[43]

At this point in the text, the Egyptians hand the reins over to the *qutb al-zaman wa ghawthuhu wa imamuhu ayn al-wujud lisan sirr wujud*, their Sayyid and Habib, Fadl bin al-Habib al-Imam al-Ghawth Alawi Ibn Muhammad bin Sahal Mawlay al-Duwayla. This extensive honorific bestowed by Egyptians on Fadl and his father is a testament to their significance in a large transregional area. It draws on very old Sufi designations for spiritually advanced mystics that had admittedly over the centuries lost some of their gravitas by, as Trimingham put it, being "vulgarized."[44] This string of "degrees" translates as "The Axis of the Age, Its Helper and Imam, the Eye of Existence, Tongue of the Mystery of Existence." "Habib" (friend and love) is a marker of someone known for having an intimate relation to the divine, which makes closeness to them desirable.

Fadl declares at the beginning that he is following staunchly the Alawi Way, and as such the *Uddat* is the work of multiple times and places. The guiding thread is the question of sovereignty for Muslims, the answers to which touch on moral, political, economic, and aesthetic dimensions of life. His conception of sovereignty was not the same as that which arose from the Egyptian and Shami nahda or through the practices of governmentality intimated by the publishers.[45] At times, the text reads as a story of loss and constant decline that only a radical reorganization like the Ottoman Tanzimat could reverse. However, taken as a whole, a metanarrative of renewal and salvation whose temporality is cyclical and eschatological comes into focus. Proper guidance and obedience are fundamental precepts. Hence, the text ascribes to individuals genuinely inspired by God and carrying the light of Muhammad a key role in the inauguration of such cycles and the maintenance of a virtuous order. Fadl was a vessel for the continuation of the work begun by his father, Sayyid Alawi, who was one of those renewers of the ages—an axis (*qutb*) along which change was again possible. Understanding Fadl's departures from the 1850s onward requires a sense of the prior generation's views presented in the fatwas of *Al-Sayf al-battar*, which follow from Fadl's introduction.

The fatwas reiterated the call for jihad, which one historian has suggested was an echo of the sixteenth-century call to arms made in the wake of the violent Portuguese intrusions into the Indian Ocean world. The difference from the nineteenth century was that the Portuguese did not extend their influence far beyond the coast, and even there, their authority was far from absolute. As we saw in the previous chapter, since the late eighteenth century the EIC's resources and imperial connections had enabled it to begin usurping the jurisdiction of prior authorities in ways that shaped a new legal-political sphere while relegating "Islam"— and other discursive traditions that would fit—into the separate sphere of religion.[46]

Did these historical specificities matter to Sayyid Alawi, and if so, how? The key to explaining Sayyid Alawi's opposition, its form and historicity (or not), is to locate the fatwas within a chain of transmission descending from the Prophet, which Alawis extended in space, accumulating their own tradition along the way. They did this in spite of the early European trading ventures that competed with Muslims and others, seeking to displace them through various means, including violence of a new order. In the nineteenth century, Muslim trading networks and even fundamental Islamic concepts, though still not extirpated, had to be modified to accommodate an emerging system of states and their accompanying capitalist economies *within* imperialism. The old Asian networks—through which European mercantile firms made themselves and both of which were in turn transformed—were by the last third of the nineteenth century subject to the new conditions of a global economy and growing interimperial competition.[47]

During most of Sayyid Alawi's lifetime, however, the situation remained uncertain, not yet primed for anticolonial nationalism or anti-imperialism per se. Accordingly, it may be apposite to label the position at which he had arrived by the 1830s as anticolonial without being nationalist, or more awkwardly, anti–modern sovereignty. This position marked the newfound vulnerability of Islam's universal mission as Muslims, like others, began to feel the impact of a globalized world on the cusp of being "Europeanized," wherein the terms of encounter and exchange were increasingly determined unidirectionally.

That said, Sayyid Alawi's call to jihad is also located in the *longue durée* of Islamic history, which comprises a continuous narrative of religious, imperial, and both commercial expansion and retraction, even though the particular call was made in a context where Muslims were in the minority and did not wield political power.[48] In the Indian Ocean world, the Alawis, absent an organizing imperial center, nonetheless represented a front or vector in Islam's outward expansion. Moreover, there is an additional dimension of jihad that makes those very historical contexts fade from view. As a calling from and to an elsewhere that exceeds the particulars of the age and of place, the "greater jihad" conditioned struggle and opposition (or "counter-conduct") in relation to forms of worldly power in general and at times to doctrinal orthodoxy.[49] Warrior Sufis aside, the effort to live a life that was good made the question of violence more than a juridical problem in Islamic history. Nonetheless, read on their own the fatwas also clearly call for a lesser jihad to counter Christian power.

Life of Jihad(s): Questions of History and of the End of History

The fatwa-seeker was a believer whose "heart drank the love of *al-din*" and the questions concerned "communities (*tawa'if*) of this noble nation (*umma*) neighboring idolatrous communities whose religions had advanced greatly in all freedom."[50] The first question was about Muslims moving to a place conquered by Christians or other non-Muslims and living under non-sharia rule while also benefiting and strengthening those lands with their productive activities, transporting goods to it and building its structures.[51] The answer was in three parts, centered on past judgments (*ahkam*, sing. *hukm*). The first part related the finding of Ibn Hajar (d. 974H/1566), who determined that if infidels seized lands that had been part of Dar al-Islam, its sovereignty legally remained Islamic even if it had formally fallen into a state of war (*dar harb*). His reasoning relied on the hadith that said, "Islam is exalted and there is no greater,"[52] and on the verse "The earth is God's and he bequeaths it to whom he wishes,"[53] in order to justify the judgment that "if the territory was Islamic then it was obligatory for the people of Islam to liberate it from the hands of the unbelievers" by all means necessary.[54]

The second part concerned Muslims who moved to lands conquered by *ahl al-dhimma* (protected people, typically Christians). "He is rebellious (*asin*) and godless (*fasiq*) and has committed one of the gravest of sins. He is a kafir whether he disavows unbelief and its rule or accepts it. Punishment of apostasy is suitable."[55] Only a Muslim of corrupt morals, defined as worldliness and indifference to tyrannical rule, would leave the ostensibly well-governed "Dar al-Islam free of unbelievers" and move to a conquered Islamic land dominated by non-Muslims. Quranic verses (Surat al-Anam 68 and Surat al-Nisa' 140) on sitting with "oppressors" who mock and insult God and becoming like them as a result formed the basis of a long argument supporting the principle of *hijra*, migration from or exit out of such an untenable anti-Islamic situation. There was a further practical implication of hijra that was strategic, that is, reconquest was made easier without Muslims as neighbors of the unbelievers.[56]

The third part treated the enrichment of the kafirs by way of Muslim merchants and artisans in their recently conquered Islamic lands who continued to trade with, finance the building and improvement of, or work in those regions. This economic cooperation was ruled a violation of sharia and God's compact with Muslims; thus, it was equivalent to aiding the enemy in a time of war, when all able-bodied Muslims—including the poor, young men, slaves, the indebted, and women of strength—had an obligation to combat aggression by kafirs.

The seven questions that followed further illuminate how the Alawis built on centuries of Muslim jurists' conceptions of a global condition of war and sovereign right in relation to migration, economic and cultural exchange, religious practice, and legal subjectivity.[57] The preceding discussion of the vectors of unbelief identified in the message of the last of the prophets sets the stage for a historical view of the world in which the worst—that is, the most threatening—of the infidels so far as Dar al-Islam was concerned were Europeans (*al-afranj*).[58] Accordingly, the second question was in regard to the status of Muslims in Dar al-Islam who happily claimed to be protected subjects of Christians. In view of the question-and-answer, the context for such a query could be either the medieval-modern Mediterranean or the early modern–modern Indian Ocean. The modern period of European imperialism is indicated by the questioner's example of Muslim-owned ships flying the banners of Christian kingdoms.[59] History was in one important sense irrelevant, because living in accordance with the law and in submission to God was the motor of change, the cause of Muslim success, but the jurists' answers were nevertheless nuanced.

Muslims were not summarily disavowed for their errant and dangerous thinking about the world or for being protégés of foreign rulers. As long as they had not begun "to uphold in their hearts blasphemy and its lords, they fell under the rule and judgment of Islam." As such, they required gentle admonishment, discipline, and instruction.[60] This was true for those ignorant of the rulings of Islam. Those "knowledgeable [ulama] of ahkam al-Islam" were to be given an opportunity to repent. If these Muslims refused to learn the error of their ways and if they continued to believe in the greatness of the unbelievers, then their thought was tantamount to blasphemy and they were to be treated as apostates. It is in this section that the most forceful claim for God's absolute sovereignty is made. "God is the sovereign guardian [al-Wali] of those who believe, he delivers them from darkness to the light. Those who disbelieve, their sovereigns [awliya'] are false gods; they lead them from the light to darkness . . . There is but the sovereignty of God or the sovereignty of false gods because there absolutely cannot be both."[61] Sovereignty, from this perspective, cannot be shared.

The European advances into the Islamic world since the Crusades formed the broader historical background for the compilation and recirculation of the fatwas. The more proximate context was circumscribed by the claims of the new imperialism as of the late eighteenth century. Christian claims of bringing justice, freedom, and security in trade and the practice of religion were heralded most dramatically by Napoleon upon his conquest of Egypt in 1798.[62] Similar statements had been issued earlier and informed administrative practices as the British expanded in India and offered protection to kingdoms and communities around the Indian Ocean.[63] However, it was the mid-nineteenth-century humanitarian claims of the European powers used to undermine the sovereignty of a Dar al-Islam centered on the Ottoman Empire that formed the most immediate context for the Uddat. The marginal note announcing that "the sultan of the time" was Abdülmecid made this clear.[64] The note was appended to the last lines of the answer to the third question, concerning the praising of non-Muslims as the bringers of justice and material advancements. In the answer, the diminution of the sultan's power, "God's shadow on Earth," was given as an undesirable and disastrous consequence of regarding the kuffar as capable of justice because of "their rule of [codified] law" (ahkamuhum al-qanuniyya).[65]

The other questions also presupposed a moral and legal dilemma confronting Muslims under the new dispensation spreading forcefully around the Indian Ocean rim. The fourth question raised the issue of the legality of blocking goods and violently preventing the movement of Muslim merchants into Christian-controlled lands. The example of the Prophet and others who traded with Syria and Iraq before their conquest was given as a reason for allowing unimpeded commerce with Christian or non-Muslim domains. When the trade was necessary, anyone obstructing it or molesting merchants was to receive the punishment for bandits and highwaymen. The situation was different in the case of Muslim lands conquered by Christians and still considered Islamic; then all means to liberate it were enjoined.[66]

The fifth question was about continued settlement of Muslims with property and family in lands conquered by non-Muslims. Settlement extending Dar al-Islam was legal as long as Islam or its mission was not compromised or harmed, otherwise emigration was recommended but not obligatory. Remaining in conquered territory was encouraged if the prospect of regaining political power would be aided thereby. The availability of sharia to pass judgment on right or wrong conduct was essential for Muslim life to persist in any context; the judgment of the infidel's law was no substitute. When individual and collective Muslim life was impossible through the practice of Islam or when reconquest was more likely through hijra, then the latter was obligatory.[67]

The sixth question raised another economy-versus-religion scenario: Is it better to move to a Muslim land that is certain to ruin one financially while preserving one's religion, or to move to the land of unbelievers where riches await but religion is ruined? As before, the primacy of living for the hereafter over seeking worldly gains determined the judgment: Din must always come before Dunya (world), if a good life here and after is sought. The seventh question asked whether one was more deserving of prayers if two funerals were being held, one for a Muslim subject of a Christian ruler and the other for a Muslim subject of a Muslim ruler.[68] The eighth and last question concerned the punishment for a Muslim choosing to be judged by Christian law rather than Islamic law.[69]

In each case the criteria for ruling on the righteousness or degree of sinfulness of an act hinged on the sovereignty of Dar al-Islam. Anyone who through his or her acts or failure to act compromised God's law, as relayed through the Prophet and his interlocutors, was to be judged severely. There was provision for less severe disciplinary measures in order to lead those who committed their sins out of ignorance or compulsion back onto the straight path. In sum, as Islam's jurisdictional hegemony was becoming diminished, even in territories and spaces traditionally considered to fall within Dar al-Islam, new fissures appeared among believers and between believers and unbelievers that ran along political fault lines whose nature was not yet fully apparent from the perspective of a tradition that viewed itself as final and complete.

Muslim Publics: The Transhistorical Sense of a Historical Text

The notion of a text that calls to jihad within the performance of a broader calling tethered to an original divine call was the framing offered in the first few pages of the *Uddat* for reading the fatwas and the remainder of the text, which sets it apart from and goes beyond the traditional "Mirror for Princes" literature.[70] This is done not only in terms of claims explicitly announcing the transcendent calling but also through the practice of citation authorizing the text, which moves readily from canonical figures like the fifteenth-century Egyptian polymath al-Suyuti and the seventeenth- to eighteenth-century Hadhrami saint al-Haddad to the eighteenth- to nineteenth-century al-Ahdals and Fadl's father Sayyid Alawi.[71] Ho has established that the writings of al-Suyuti and al-Haddad formed parts of a textual chain that by the seventeenth century already constituted a literary canon that was distinctly Alawi and represented its diasporic society while simultaneously anchoring it in relation to multiple times and spaces.

In Fadl's introduction, even as a list of centennial renewers (*mujaddidun*) is given according to historical time, he qualifies their mission as one directed from and for the sake of another time. He makes this move by locating a rupture in space-time that occurred when a prophecy was revealed. Or, as God's words pierced the normally impermeable boundary of heaven and earth, time was suspended. The time of revelation, when Muhammad ceased being merely human and became a prophet who was human, was an interruption of the flow of historical time; since Muhammad was the last of the prophets sent to the world, the truly historical age of humanity begins with God's silence. The engine of historical change was then transferred to the successors (*khulafa'*), and with their passing, the centennial renewers. Conflict and struggle over succession and recognition of new renewers constituted a specifically Islamic history, in terms of events and personalities as well as in terms of possessing a sense of urgency in the mission to call others to God.[72]

This inscription of historical time as pregnant with the intractable problem of succession to the Prophet allowed genealogy to be established as a possible though contested solution for the time after the last of the prophets. Fadl noted that there was disagreement about the renewer of nearly every century for the first thousand years of Islamic history since the hijra.[73] The end of the first millennium corresponded roughly to the end of the sixteenth century, when from the perspective of the Islamic frontiers the rising power of European maritime empires, whether regarded as a threat or an opportunity, was undeniable, even as Muslim land empires (Ottoman, Safavid, and Mughal) had witnessed a century of growth and prosperity. Indeed, in those Islamic empires novel justifications for dynastic succession were formulated that depended on various settlements with different stakeholders, to use a popular contemporary expression. Compliant ulama were central to the new dispensation. The entirety of the *Uddat* is to a large extent a critique of the ulama's submission to the absolute sovereignty of sultans, forsaking their own roles. Against that critical backdrop, sayyid sovereignty appears as a faintly audible principle with which to think a solution to the seemingly unresolvable problem of succession to the Prophet.

The genealogical question illuminates the religious and political dance moving Islamic history, a dance that periodically dissolved into a violent embrace. The differences and disagreements about the renewers marked the historicity of these times. For al-Suyuti, the determination of who was a renewer was based on whether or not the community of ulama who were imams accepted the renewal as complete; what was said and what was meant (*al-lafz wa-l-ma'na*) did not diverge. Fadl was trying to establish the point that whether the renewer was selected through agreement or not, if the *salaf* (pious ancestors) were not remembered and respected, the age went on, and no renewal was possible until God's will was realized. That will seems to have been one that privileged the Prophet and his family; there was a last prophet for a reason, after all—his bloodline is special in and for a Muslim life.[74]

The claim that is of significance here, derived from al-Suyuti, relates the political theology of Islam to a prophetic mission that extends back to and forward from Abraham. "When the revelation ceased with the death of the Messenger of God, the earth complained to its master that there would be no other prophet after to walk on it. And so God made within this umma those who would be like them, exemplars from among God's saints and those who seek to know Him. These are the heirs of the prophets and their successors and it has been shown that among them are those whose hearts are like the heart of Abraham."[75] This passage appears in the context of a harsh attack on ulama who are said to have allowed and even benefited from the negative transformation of their calling; they went from being moral guides to mere holders of sinecures in institutions (*majalis*) that now only purported to quest after knowledge and religion (*ilm wa din*). Going further, some ulama are indicted for being the reason for the moral failings of those under their care. "If the people see those responsible for knowledge and religion neglect and make light of undertaking God's command and his duties and not quicken to obedience it might compel them to neglect and to let lapse religious matters. Indeed it might hasten their fall, into destructive situations and terrible crimes."[76]

What is iterated in this mid-nineteenth-century text is a complex critique of an establishment Islam regarded as having lost sight of the totality (*ilm wa din*) that at least normatively and at times historically engendered a quest for the embodiment of perfection, self-knowledge. That quest was disseminated as a divine calling from the time of Abraham and included within its address the pastoral duties that bound subjects to a hierarchical complex of learning. Ho elegantly echoes this critique as it expands outward (or upward) to encompass failed rulers: "Tyrannies are islands surrounded by a wider sea of Sunni Shafi'i scholars; this sea ebbs and swells locally but ever dominates the horizon globally, possessed of multiple sources and resources."[77] In sum, projected on the horizon is a life that was decidedly extraordinary, reachable through the right guides. These were outsiders to the worldly operations of power, which in this reckoning is always a process of decline. In the middle of the nineteenth century, however, the very totality making life possible, which until then had been shared by the monotheistic traditions, was facing an unprecedented assault.[78]

The sharing was still legible in the fatwas, but the grounds of commonality and commensurability began to recede with colonial expansion and the return of Fadl (textually and geographically) to the Islamic world's center in the second half of the nineteenth century. In general, from the Islamic perspective, neither the flawed commitment of these traditions to the law and to prophets, and the violation of the prime monotheistic principle of *tawhid* (the Oneness of God) in the case of Christians, nor the historical enmity with Christendom could erase the shared ground among the distinct traditions. For that ground was formed from the (anti)historical relations among God, prophets, and humans, and only an act of God could erase it. The fatwas, following the typical question-and-answer format, reveal a repetition of tradition even as they register recognition of the dangers presented by the new historical era dawning on the Indian Ocean. "The Islamic perspective," if ever there was one, faced a radical transformation as those dangers were confronted.[79]

Islamic Sovereignty and the Government of Souls

The tear in the fabric of a shared totality is on display throughout this plural and performative text that announces itself as a call to jihad.[80] Already appearing in the Yemeni fatwas of al-Ahdal that circulated via Sayyid Alawi and Sayyid Fadl across the Indian Ocean in Malabar was a sense that the terms of the game, namely, boundary markers distinguishing Dar al-Islam and Dar al-Harb, were shifting in directions that were not entirely clear, yet were worrisome. In the remainder of the *Uddat*'s 168 pages, repetition of prophetic sayings and moments from early Islamic history pertaining to the differentiation and distinction of Muslims from Christians and Jews are arranged in a manner to suggest the sundering of the contract that had secured a relationship of protection that was grounded in the trust in good government brought forth by the universalizing Islamic empires. Whether this organization of the text was a response to the Ottoman equality edicts of 1839 and 1856, while not explicit, is likely.

However, even as the text in numerous places invokes the real and potential hypocrisy and treachery of the *ahl al-kitab* (People of the Book) through history, rising at times to the level of undoing the rule of just kings for personal gain, ultimately the blame is laid on Muslim rulers, ulama, and lay Muslims for losing sight of the principles of an Islamic universalism.[81] In the following meditation on the form of genuine sovereign power, it becomes clear how to read what otherwise can only be characterized as crude anti-Christian and anti-Jewish screeds.

> It is said that Din is the foundation and Sultan is the guardian: that which has no foundation will collapse and that which has no guardian will be lost. It is also said that al-Din and al-Mulk [sovereignty] are twins; therefore, if the sultan who becomes sovereign [*qa'im bi-l-mulk*] is just and good, the end [*akhira*][82] of his sovereignty in relation to religion is right and true. However, if the sultan only desires sovereignty and its mimicry [*taqlidihi*] and aspires to it in order to obtain for himself leadership, superiority over others, to command authority, to satiate his desire for a worldly life and its appetites, then the end of the sovereignty of religion, which he upholds, is neither right nor true. Rather, it is an image that does not agree with or fall within the purview of sovereignty which can be characterized as the defense of the interests of religion and the protection of the interests and security of Muslims in their persons and property, and that is through government in accordance to, and in agreement with, the condition and correctness of sovereignty and leadership—to which he is an obstacle.[83]

In a world of obstacles, where the perennial problem of sovereignty could be complicated by multiple and plural sources (Muslim, Christian, or Jew; worldliness, self-interest, or greed), the divine calling is only as good as the ears it falls on.[84] Evidently, the recurring possibility of deafness then becomes a moment of aporia in the political theology that ties religion to sovereignty. Thus, it was imperative that in the "family" those who possessed special insight, senses beyond the ordinary, were allowed and supported in their ministrations to Muslims and to a world in need of guidance.

The truth of the copresence of religion and sovereignty was manifested in and through the virtues of good government. From this perspective, the government of men remained deeply personal, in spite of the rationalization of the state occurring in the Ottoman and British Empires at the time of the *Uddat*'s publication. To the extent that the sultan was a mediating vessel and an earthly force that might or might not possess (be possessed by) al-Din and al-Mulk (sovereignty) simultaneously, the presencing of their truth was historically contingent on the capacity and motivations of individuals. At times in the text, the deficits that attended particular claims to embodiments of sovereignty seem to be attenuated by the appointment of capable ministers and governors better suited to the quest for a perfect order. Nonetheless, Fadl was aware that this practical fix did not resolve the problem of sovereignty, which after all was a problem because it marked the outer limit of human agency.

Although ultimately "the sultan is God's shadow on earth" and hence theoretically an embodiment of sovereignty, the text performs a high-stakes balancing act that alternates between discussions of the remit and responsibilities of sultans and their representatives, on the one hand, and the ulama, on the other.[85] The discourse on ministers, alluded to earlier, established their role as intermediaries between subjects and sultans. As one might expect, choosing them wisely could determine the rise and fall of kingdoms. More germane here, however, and usually overlooked in discussions of Islamic political theology, is the relationship of care that is emphasized along with the typical advantages gained by sultans who have ministers that transmit accurate information ("matters as they are") and provide just administration.[86] The principle of care is also expressed in an earlier section detailing a plan for achieving the ideal Islamic order through constant material (economic, technological, infrastructural, administrative, and military) renewal and reform of kingdoms (*tajdid al-mamalik*): "The kingdoms are like his [the sultan's] house, the subjects like his household, and each caregiver is responsible for his charge."[87]

Two hadiths are invoked to support the point that caring for subjects (here, care is defined as "placing subjects in a relation of friendly admonition") is God's will for His / the sultan's ministers. One hadith recounts the threat of banishment from paradise if a wali (governor) shirks his responsibility toward his subjects, while the other suggests that as long as he is good and good to them, it is the responsibility of his subjects to support him and to offer a prayer in his name.[88] A clause inserted earlier, according to which God is the final arbiter of good and bad ministers, leaves open the question of a sovereign's absolute power.[89] A political order based on sultans and ministers, who are responsible primarily for security and for guaranteeing conditions that encourage the welfare of society, incorporates the ulama as judges and moral guides. In the end, however, since the virtue of the individuals inhabiting these distinct roles through time would be variable, the entire order appears in the text as in a state of permanent crisis. Indeed, the times that were not would seem to have been quite the exception, since righteous sovereigns are said to be rare throughout history. "Only one who has perfected his knowledge, his reason, his (in)sight, and his patience can make for a good ruler, which is why that designation has only been given to very few, singular kings and sultans Islamic and Jahili. Imam al-Shafi'i said . . . the government of people (siyasat al-nas) is more taxing than the management of animals."[90]

One example of the balancing act that requires alternating between the theorization of sultanic sovereignty and the sovereignty of jurists, imams, and Sufi shaykhs may be found on a single page. Immediately after recommending the imam—whose heart is directed to God—for the mission of securing Muslims and their lands, the text offers the definitive Sunni view that even a tyrannical sultan (power) is better than the continuation of fitna (disorder, civil war). This statement is then qualified to indicate the (Sufi) checks on such tyrannical power, that is, in the embodiment of God's Way and dissemination of its knowledge to His people for their "uplift" through the persons of saints who can interpret the divine law, judge, and govern. In this formulation, the target of that government is human life, for it is over this domain that the tyrannical sultan is barred from having complete sovereignty, through the multiplication and diffusion across the social body of the responsibility for the care of the soul. There is a democratic element to such a government; toward the end of this section on sovereignty the hadith is invoked that says "Each of you is a shepherd and each of you is responsible for his flock."[91] This, however, is a limited flirtation with the power of the people, as it is made clear that such a relation exists within a hierarchy that assigns moral and material responsibility for the flock in an ascending order, from a cat (the very last point made is about the care of animals), slaves, children, and so on, upward to the sultan.

The bulk of the *Uddat*, which follows the excerpts from al-Haddad, is a compilation of hadiths and historical examples stressing the importance of maintaining a recognizable Muslim identity and rejecting mimicry of Jews, Christians, Zoroastrians, and polytheists.[92] Mimicry was destined to lead to doom for the umma, and only wise rulers exercising "divine legal politics" (*al-siyasa al-sharaiyya al-ilahiyya*) could ensure a universal Islamic order. This longest section has to have been a response by Fadl and his associates to the Ottoman Tanzimat edicts putatively enshrining the principle of equality before the law. The line that likely elicited the most consternation was from the later reform edict, the Islahat Firmani of 1856: "Every distinction or designation tending to make any class whatever of the subjects of my Empire inferior to another class, on account of their religion, language, or race, shall be for ever effaced from the Administrative Protocol."[93]

Thus, when sultans could be influenced by non-Muslims at the level of law and politics, there only remained the renewers of the age, such as those in the blessed Alawi line ("Sufi mystagogues" in al-Azmeh's rendering), to manage a constitutionally crisis-ridden order and ensure the reproduction of a universal Islamic sovereignty—over the entirety of the earth, from "where the sun rises to where the sun sets."[94] It is at this point that "pastoral power" is reintroduced for an era of new challenges, in a historical context different from both Sayyid Alawi's Dar al-Islam and that through which Foucault traces the emergence of modern governmentality. The difference, however, is one of degree or, in a sense, geographical coordinates. Before beginning his now well-known demonstration of how population became the central problematic of European state formation, displacing though not eliminating the question of territorial sovereignty, which allowed the development of a new "government of men," Foucault offers his non-Greco-Roman genealogy of governmentality, which has received less attention.[95] He traces to the ancient Near East the notion of government as being fundamentally a duty to a flock and to an individual in pursuit of the good. He argues that it was in the analogy with God as shepherd that a model for "pastoral power" was derived and distinguished from the Greeks, for whom gods were linked to cities as built spaces and not necessarily to their inhabitants in a constant relationship of care.

Understanding the reintroduction of pastoral power, or what we have termed sayyid sovereignty, in Fadl's specific historical context is pivotal in appreciating the temporality proper to an Islamic discursive tradition, one whose contours were reshaped in relation to a European/colonial history.[96] Given the particular historical mix of its contexts—Indian Ocean, Alawi diaspora, Hindu sovereigns, British Empire, Mappila resistance, mobile Arabian exile, and Tanzimat-era Ottomanism—the text carefully rematerializes pastoral power anew, alert to the politicization of life becoming the new raison d'être of sovereignty; this precise mix of histories together with the Islamic tradition to which Fadl was beholden ensured that life remained an elusive target. To that extent, the *Uddat* was located at an uneasy angle to at least two dominant traditions of political sovereignty: the Islamic, to which Fadl was ambivalently related as sufi-sayyid, and the imperial, with which he became increasingly entangled.

Conclusion

From Malabar to Mecca and from Mecca to Malabar, this was the Indian Ocean circuit that rewired for the fourth time in a millennium or more the overlapping identities of the Malayali polity of Keralam. In the story of Cheruman Perumal, a Hindu sovereign not only gives himself to Islam but is permanently returned to the soil of Arabia, where a shrine to him remains; in turn, Malabar receives the gift of the revelations given by God to the Prophet Muhammad. With that gift, as well as with the continuous flow of Arabs and Malayalis between Malabar and Arabia, multiple ways of conceiving Islamic sovereignty were inevitable—converging and diverging in the center, on the frontiers, and in movements in between.

The *Uddat al-umara'* represents a moment of convergence of several strands of the Islamic tradition of thinking about the good, struggle (greater jihad), and salvation, on the one hand, and difference, conflict (lesser jihad), and territorialization, on the other. However, because it is a text compiled by an "author" of a specific strand—Alawi sufi-sayyid—of the broader tradition, between these different faces of sovereignty we are able to glimpse something else that both troubles and inspires: the unity of life. This is not the same unity as in the totality of al-Din and al-Mulk given in the text. Rather, it is the remainder, the in-between, the unsaid, and the unseen. Rather than crystallizing, it recedes with every gesture toward the disorder of the world, with every solution for setting it right, with every invocation of otherworldly order.

The different levels of the *Uddat* may be teased out in relation to Foucault's outline of the dimensions of ancient pastoral power: (1) its field of application is not territorial but a "multiplicity on the move"; (2) "its only *raison d'être* is doing good, and in order to do good"; and (3) its effects are paradoxical, as an "individualizing power" that must simultaneously totalize.[97] As a performance of many voices and as a layered text, the *Uddat al-umara'* captures the sense of a collectivity in motion for whom space and time do not map onto a mere two-dimensional projection; the movement posited requires a third and possibly fourth axis to be represented properly. In this complex universe, with the good and self-knowledge as the function and end of being-as-becoming, the power of the sayyid is especially well suited to conduct and to govern men on paths that traverse earthly and otherworldly dimensions. But it is in the paradox of such power, individualizing and totalizing at once, that the potential for contradiction, conflict, and aporia arises, allowing a glimpse of there being more to life.

The text certainly belongs in the genealogy of Abraham and the good shepherd. Its markings of Ottoman imperial sovereignty supplemented by the authors' histories plotted in terms of an expanding British imperial sovereignty in the Indian Ocean world place limits on other readings of the sufi-sayyid life. However, the text also performs its own excess (multiplicity of voices, times, and struggles), reflecting centuries of a sufi-sayyid tradition that developed in diasporic movements around a specific oceanic space engaging heterogeneous life-forms with complex traditions. Thus, reading the *Uddat* in light of the Cheruman Perumal myth, which renders Islam the Fourth Vedam, unlocks its capaciousness as an Indian Ocean text and loosens its ties to the very sovereignty that is inscribed in its margins and aims to circumscribe its meaning.

The unity of life does not necessarily express the historical experience of a community or an individual, but it does signify a horizon of the greater jihad that in fact formed part of the teachings of the Alawi sufi-sayyids who made their homes in far-flung places around the Indian Ocean. A perspective on the call to jihad that views it in light of a broader calling to oppose tyranny, embrace the good, and know the self has tremendous implications for understanding Sayyid Alawi's thought and legacy as inherited and reworked by Fadl and by the Mappilas of Malabar in different contexts. Perhaps ironically, parsing the dimensions of the call to jihad as an appeal that pierces space-time as we know it will help to better situate Fadl, the Mappila community, and the universal umma in history, and not as being politically homogeneous or static. Moreover, and perhaps contradictorily, it will show that a glimpse of the unity of life that is presupposed in the call requires appreciating the temporality intrinsic to it, wherein historical time appears only in suspension.

By the middle of the nineteenth century, the (counter-)conduct of Sufi spirituality, which interfaced with Islamic conceptions of sovereignty in unpredictable ways through space and time, may have had no choice but to engage at some level with the claims and practices of modern imperial sovereignty wherever it was found. Sayyid Alawi's refusal to acknowledge the summons of the colonial magistrate could not be repeated by Sayyid Fadl, who voluntarily exited Malabar. Although confident in his ability to return, by heeding the call of a new type of sovereign he had opened the door to its claims on life.

3 "The Tear Will Widen"

Reordering Government Madras to Istanbul

INDIA, WHERE SAYYID FADL SPENT roughly the first quarter of his in some ways typical nineteenth-century life, provided a front-row seat to a world that was changing at an increasingly rapid rate. Historians have noted the intense competition for trade and political power in India in the eighteenth century, involving a very diverse set of players, which made it perhaps one of the most dramatically changed places in the world at the start of the nineteenth century. From European, Arab, and Indian merchants of various stripes to Mysorean rulers, Malabari pirates, and African soldiers, the forces of globalization unleashed by the seaborne empires in the sixteenth century raised the stakes or the scales of competition for resources and authority to new heights. In addition to the obvious technological advances that greatly accelerated the movement of people, things, and information, the increasingly sophisticated practices of managing empires stretching around the globe brought state formation to a new height, or as Philip J. Stern puts it in the conclusion to his revisionist study of the East India Company, which shows that it was much more than Adam Smith's dismissal of it as a "strange absurdity": "The history of modern state formation was a history of one form of corporation, the nation-state, triumphing over its rivals, both within and without its borders, from the East India Company to pirates, mercenaries, composite monarchies, municipal corporations, monasteries, even the church."[1]

The Madras Presidency managed the Company's southern block of holdings and assumed jurisdiction over Malabar in 1800. It evolved over two centuries from a minor commercial venture to the arm of a vast empire-state with responsibility for thirty to forty million souls by the twentieth century.[2] In the mid-nineteenth century, the EIC's twilight years, the uncertain, hazy, and experimental realities of state of early modern times were clarified even as new problems of political representation, rehearsed in the eighteenth century with some revolutionary consequences, remained largely unresolved in colony, metropole, and lands in between—and remained so for the entirety of the long nineteenth century. In the spaces where old forms and claims of sovereignty were unraveling, the political appeared differently—at least for a while—from the political that attended the disciplinary order of capitalist states that were busily "englobing": slowly but surely subjugating bodies and minds across registers of production and desire.[3]

The reach of the modern governmentalized state, though ultimately most extensive in northwest Europe and its settler offspring nations, would be felt in one way or another across the globe by the end of the long nineteenth century—even if only as the desideratum of representative elites. The liberal solution of expanding the franchise in the post–World War I period did not resolve fundamental problems of voice, interest, and values associated with political life. Rather, the nation-state and its institutions—whether liberal or not, whether explicitly political or not—enabled a gradual evacuation of meaning from "the political," which has now been reduced to the biological problems of life and their concomitant juridico-technological solutions.[4] Even as the biopolitical regimes of rich countries are far more powerful in this regard, the rise of an international technocracy, fueled by human rights and humanitarian discourses, has helped bridge some of the distance between life and politics that "collapsing" or "weak" states were never capable of.[5]

In this chapter, by following the trajectory of Fadl's exilic life from sufi-sayyid to amir (prince), the kernel of a modern form of sovereignty vested entirely in states is excavated from layers of ideological sedimentation. That kernel is the revised concept and practice of government. A vexing contradiction of modern history is the simultaneous expansion of rights discourses and politics, on the one hand, and of state power over individual lives, on the other. The great liberal and Marxist historiographical traditions have emphasized one or the other, with questions of agency being juxtaposed contradictorily to questions of determination. The resulting narratives cast political life as heroic or tragic depending on the weight placed on human struggle or structural effects. The Foucauldian moment in history writing seemed to find a happy middle in which power was at once subjecting and "subjectivating," negative and positive; in other words, one was formed by power and one possessed power—a subject *of* power in both prepositional senses.

Especially for historians, Foucault's intervention burst ideological bubbles and created historiographical dilemmas, as the question of emancipation was returned to the present—not relegated to the past, to an apolitically "dominated mass," or to non-Western societies. Just as "agency" and "structure" were theoretical (ideological) constructs pegged nevertheless to specific historical developments in European societies in the nineteenth and early twentieth centuries, Foucault's analytics of "power" were also intimately tied to European historical experience, now conceptualized in the nonideological terms of disciplinary apparatuses and biopolitical technologies. To the extent that even today a significant chunk of the world's population does not have the kind of state (or capital accumulation) necessary to secure its own territorial sovereignty, much less expand "capillary" forms of power over the social body, it should be clear that there are limitations to liberal, Marxist, and Foucauldian approaches to writing global history and making social theory when all roads lead back to Europe.

The main limitation has been the tendency to regard forms of life that defy the logics of sovereignty in the very same terms that made the latter historically intelligible, thereby rendering truisms such as the "politicization of life" seem absolute or inevitable.[6] It is especially in regard to Foucault's governmentalized state that the limitations become clear. As noted above, such states—though generalized around the world by the mid-twentieth century as units of international relations and law—showed significant divergence when it came to the capacity for disciplining subjects.[7] The glaring asymmetry of state-in-government[8] remains across the divide of what are now termed the Global South and Global North, the ostensibly more progressive ideo-geographical substitute for East and West.

Cutting an increasingly broad swath across these geographical and political-economic divides is the phenomenon variously labeled international terrorism, political Islam, global jihad, Muslim religious extremism, and so forth. Though excellent efforts have been made to demystify and contextualize this phenomenon, a historical perspective that takes within its purview the global formation of the relationships among modern sovereignty, state, and Islam is needed. Only in this way can we see that today's intersection of Islam with politics at a global level is neither new nor very old, and that is very much tied up with how the state is thought in relation to sovereignty and the particular kind of politics that this engenders. The question to consider is whether and how Islam has represented a refusal of the politicization of life, troubling sovereignty and making an Islamic state as such impossible.[9]

As the thirteenth Islamic century hurtled toward its close, figures such as Sayyid Fadl were compelled by global events to develop a new historical perspective on the interrelated conceptual complex of sovereignty, state, and Islam.[10] Government was the key concept around which the fundamental change in state (al-dawla) hinged and through which it was often perceived. The modern Arabic word for government, hukuma, is only used in Fadl's writings toward the end of his life. Conceptually, it was derived from the Islamic legal tradition. As we saw in the previous chapter, hukm (pl. ahkam), rule or judgment, was a crucial element in the elaboration of a universal juridical order in which all Muslims and their protected subjects were implicated as participants, with roles to play in the realization of a good life in the present and a blessed life in the hereafter.

In this chapter and in Chapter 6, we trace the route by which hukm becomes hukuma and inhabits the new dawla.[11] We have examined how the government of souls became pivotal to the redefinition of sovereignty in the saddle period, when its conceptual terrain was still shared by religious men, administrators, and merchants alike. A politics that briefly threatened to overthrow the old order was unleashed in both hemispheres of the globe.[12] The responses in the Islamic Indian Ocean world of the Alawis varied. In the previous chapter we saw the mid-century reiteration of prior calls to jihad that drew the horizons of Muslim life, a good life, in relation to a sovereignty that was at the same time of this world and the hereafter, reiterating a historically irresolvable ambivalence at the heart of Islamic political theology. Fadl's reterritorialization of Dar al-Islam in the figure of the Ottoman sultan-caliph in Istanbul at a time of Muslim loss, personal exile, and uncertain futures was enacted both through and under a deterritorialized cosmology in which the divine, angels, prophets, and dead saints formed a primary and indispensable alliance.[13] In the end, their role as defined was limited to offering good guidance; however, that theoretical limit and its dimensional boundaries were periodically crossed—a crossing that was constitutive of unity.[14]

The knowledge and visceral experience of a sufi-sayyid form of life placed Fadl in a curious position in relation to the concept and the new practices of government he both witnessed and was subject to, in Company India and again in the Ottoman Empire.[15] On the one hand, he was intimately familiar with a notion of government that was deeply individualized and quietly guided souls toward unity. It engendered a constant striving for perfection and self-knowledge, which was necessary for a good life in the present and after death, and for some, especially sayyids, the proper exercise of government of the self held the potential for a transdimensional power. Within this tradition, power could be at once pastoral and insubordinate (counter-conduct); its temporality defied human order, or as colonial officials put it in relation to the sayyid, "the ordinary powers of the Government are virtually in abeyance."[16] On the other hand, the human order that seemed ascendant in the second half of the nineteenth century posed challenges and opportunities for mobile sufi-sayyids like Fadl. In the next two sections we examine Fadl's evolving approach to the new imperial dispensation and government, from 1852 to 1879. In the third section, retracing some of the same steps, we witness how the imperial surveillance state developed as it attempted to follow and fix Fadl in an outlaw category.

The Middle Years: The Sayyid between
Two Modes of Existence

Three years after Conolly convinced Fadl to leave India, a group of Mappilas attacked the magistrate's Calicut home and assassinated him, partly in retaliation for what they believed to be the expulsion of their spiritual leader, "their almost deified high priest."[17] This act of violence against the state by his followers permanently branded Fadl as the "Moplah Outlaw." After vacillating for years, in 1852 Conolly had sought and was finally granted the writ by Fort St. George to charge Fadl with incitement and arrest him if he did not politely leave of his own accord. For his part, Fadl understood his exile as voluntary and temporary, but that wasn't to be the case. The British effectively imposed a permanent travel ban on him, on members of his family, and on his associates, prohibiting them from ever again entering British-administered or -protected territories. Moreover, he and those related to him were subjected to extensive surveillance, which continued even after Fadl's death, whether their movements were in India, Arabia, Egypt, the Sham, Iraq, or Anatolia (the subject of Chapter 5).

Upon his delicate apprehension and deportation from India back to his "home" country in March 1852, Fadl spent much of the remainder of the 1850s in a circuit between Arabian cities, Cairo, and Istanbul. In the 1860s he seemed to split his time between Mecca and al-Tai'f.[18] The British tried to keep close tabs on him during this period but noted his elusiveness; sometimes he disappeared into the Hadhramawt to evade surveillance. British agents outside of India, despite themselves, also acknowledged the respect he commanded and the authority he exercised. Intelligence from Cairo reported to Malabar in 1856 that "[Fadl] maintains even in Arabia a marked pre-eminence as a fanatical ostentatious Wahabee of considerable influence, refusing to recognize any dignitary, and, as my information runs, not taking notice even of a Pacha should he enter his house."[19] But even the "Wahabee-souled" ascetic who refused agents of worldly power might be forced to seek patronage, if only to house and feed his numerous dependents.[20]

Partly with this objective but mainly to secure diplomatic support for his return to India, Fadl made his way to Istanbul with all haste, possibly in late 1852. His voyage included a stop in Egypt, where he spent several months and was invited to stay permanently by the governor, Abbas Pasha, grandson of the great state builder Mehmed Ali. He declined this generous invitation and continued on to Istanbul. Successful in his mission, he began what he thought would be his return voyage to India, reaching Jedda in June 1853. When he arrived, however, and though he was carrying letters from Ottoman ministers and the British ambassador, Lord Stratford de Redcliffe, he was caught in the imperial surveillance net and found his onward journey to Malabar blocked. He attempted to circumvent the blockade by continuing to Yemen, hoping to find passage from Aden, but to no avail. He returned to Mecca in 1855, with the annual pension of a thousand dollars that he had been awarded by Sultan Abdülmecid. The pension and donations from Malabari pilgrims allowed him to maintain the sizeable retinue that had followed him into exile, a household numbering upward of sixty persons, including family members, advisers, servants, and slaves.[21] The visit to the sultan had also earned him recognition as an Arab notable; in that sense, he had come home.

His putative support of an Arab rebellion that broke out in November soon after his arrival in Mecca against Ottoman reform policies, particularly Istanbul's move to end the slave trade under British pressure, lost him his annual stipend. This blow may have precipitated his departure for Istanbul again.[22] He may also have been pressured to leave as a result of British insistence that he was a threat to their interests and their recommendation that he be removed from the Hijaz.[23] Once he was in Istanbul, his previous stature seems to have initially been difficult to regain.[24] A petition dating from September 1859, from the Sofular Sufi lodge in Istanbul, where he was staying, pleaded for a stipend

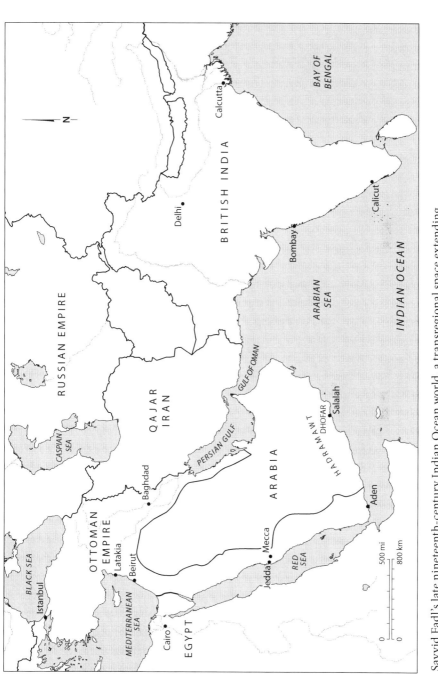

Sayyid Fadl's late nineteenth-century Indian Ocean world, a transregional space extending from Istanbul to Calicut and beyond.

for Fadl, who was described as belonging to a sharifian lineage but being utterly destitute.

> Sheikh Fazil, who is from the people of India and one of the Sherifs as well as one of the exalted successors of the great Kadiriyye Order, had emigrated to somewhere near Hejaz due to his devastating situation [*ahvali harabiyesinden*] in India that is known to all of us, and then came to Dersaadet [Istanbul] with the hope of obtaining a salary, and at the present he stays in our sacred lodge as a guest. He belongs to the eternal descendants of Shah [shaykh] Abdulkadir, and is one of those whose prayers are very much sought for. And his outward poverty is irrefutable. And because it is customary for the highest [people, officers] to take on the execution and application of required actions in these kinds of contemptible issues, I entreat you, the kindest person, to try and obtain a vizirial letter for the accommodation of the aforementioned Sheikh again somewhere convenient near the Illuminated Medina with a salary and rations, thereby making him happy.[25]

It is interesting that Fadl did not stay in one of the famous Indian lodges of Istanbul.[26] Also, the letter was addressed to the Sheikh of the Haram—the Prophet's tomb complex in Medina; this office, which typically involved administrative jurisdiction over the entire city, was held at the time by the Ottoman appointee Sheikh Mustafa.[27] The political fallout from his alleged involvement in the 1855 and 1858 rebellions may have restricted Fadl's access to the sultan and to those who wished to stay on the latter's good side.

At the same time, Fadl had established links with other networks as early as the 1840s during his student days, as suggested in the reference to him in the letter as a member and even a *khalifa* of the widespread and influential Qadiri Sufi order. Sayyid Alawi had been a member of the Qadiri order, so it is likely that Fadl was formally initiated before his study trip to the Hijaz. The cross-pollination of Sufi rituals and prayers intensified as technologies of print and steam accelerated the movement of texts, students, and shaykhs across lodge networks throughout the Islamic world. Sahar Bazzaz's study of the Moroccan sayyid Muhammad al-Kattani (1873–1909), for example, shows that there was mutual borrowing among the Kattaniyya, Tijaniyya, and Darqawiyya, especially as, she argues, tensions heightened between political and religious domains in the face of expanding European power in the Maghreb.[28]

Perhaps hoping that he would have better chances with Abdülmecid's successor, Fadl visited Istanbul again in 1871. He apparently impressed Sultan Abdulaziz with his advice for reforms in the Hijaz, which may have included a recommendation for the construction of a railway line from Medina to Damascus.[29] Between 1875 and 1879 he served as the amir of Dhofar. Finally, from 1879 until his death in 1900 he lived in Istanbul, as a special guest of Sultan Abdulhamid II. Despite having led a relatively itinerant life, and in spite of himself, he was a resident of Istanbul for many years.

During Fadl's first visits to the Ottoman capital, he raised the alarm about what he saw were dangerous developments in the Arabian Peninsula and beyond, while seeking improvement of his own status and welfare. During the third trip in 1871, he met with Sultan Abdulaziz and the great Tanzimat reformer Grand Vizier Ali Pasha just before his death.[30] The latter was apparently impressed with Fadl's knowledge of Arabian affairs and took to heart his advice for reforms in the Hijaz. Meanwhile, until the last years of his life, British officials in London, Istanbul, Cairo, Aden, Bombay, and Madras were exchanging letters about Fadl's attempts to return to India, his activities in Hadhramawt, the risk he posed to British interests along the Arabian coast, and his property claims in Malabar.[31]

A Changing Vision of Sovereignty, or, Fadl's Call to the Archives

In examining the terms of what for convenience we have called sayyid sovereignty, Fadl's involvement in the frontier region between Hadhramawt and Oman is of the utmost interest.[32] A delegation of tribal elders from Dhofar visited Fadl in Mecca in the mid-1870s to request his intercession in the bloody wars among tribes in the region, which had apparently brought life to a standstill. In exchange for using his sacred power, his baraka, to bring peace to the area, they promised to submit to his rule. Although he was successful in restoring order, his rule was short-lived (1876–79). It seems Fadl was not prepared to deal with an environmental catastrophe of global proportions wreaked by El Niño in those years. He was accused of overtaxation, expropriation of lands, and mismanagement of funds. With British backing and the about-face of the al-Kathiri tribe, which had initially submitted to Fadl, the Bu Sa'idi ruler Sayyid Turki was able to dislodge him from what Muscat considered a very sensitive region of Oman.[33] But rather than getting lost in the details of the absorbing stories of local, regional, and inter-"national" intrigues around this desolate spot in the world, we shall turn our attention to Sayyid Fadl's view of the governance of Muslims and his role therein.[34]

Even as Fadl represented himself formulaically as only an agent, a slave, of the sultan-caliph, between his departure from India and by the mid-1870s he seems to have reconfigured the special status his "noble" descent afforded him in a manner that approached notions of contract and commonwealth wherein sayyids assumed a representative and legislative political role in and through submission to the new terms of imperial sovereignty.[35] Sayyid Fadl supported the expansion of the Ottoman Empire beyond the coastal areas of the Arabian Peninsula, which it did, returning to the Yemeni highlands in 1871 after a long absence of over two centuries. To his political mind, shaped by his prior encounter with colonial rule in India, communal fragmentation and disunity were anathema. The Ottoman state represented the last hope for Islamic sovereignty. In the Arabian context during a period of expanding British influence, the tribes in their natural and permanent state of war became an issue of life and death for all Muslims. The tribes' own fear of death, Fadl argued, drove them into the arms of any superior power that could offer protection.

Although Fadl placed hope in the Ottomans reemerging from the Tanzimat as a powerful state, in the far south of the Arabian Peninsula their potential influence still seemed a distant reality. He made his way to Dhofar without prior approval from the Ottoman government, or so it seemed from official declarations. It was only after he had taken up the mantle of amir of Dhofar in 1875 that he contacted Istanbul:

> This time, on my arrival in the district called Zafar, one of the annexes of Hadhramaut, thanks to the fruits of the application of some effective admonitions, all the tribes have become tractable and obedient. The banner of victory representing the eternal State will be erected and distributed in the suitable places of the aforementioned district. Also, the coin of our sacred Sultan will be put in circulation in the market. In addition, for the execution of decrees, the council, constituted of Uluvvi [Alawi] seyyids and tribal chiefs, appointed me—this humble and simple emir, your well-wisher slave—to the task of issuing fetwas. *And the execution of the decrees was conducted as the way His Excellency, the Sultan of the sultans, had desired.* And the populace is now free of terror and fear, and they are totally obedient and in security.[36] (emphasis added)

Obedience, coins of sultans, and fatwas invoked a distinctly Islamic tradition of ordering the world, whereas the planting of flags was an acknowledgment that the Islamic tradition had encountered and must respond in the terms of modern sovereignty.

Fadl's prior experiences in Malabar conditioned his conception of sayyid power in terms of community survival, wherein the sovereignty vested in his noble personage, as a member of the *ahl al-bayt*, was the last resort. His time in exile exposed him to geopolitical scenarios of a different sort and on a very different scale, such that he came to view his role as sufi-sayyid, guide-sovereign, with a deep sense of past/tradition and with an anxious eye to the future and the claims of others. The physical and political situation of Hadhramawt, though always regarded as distant from Istanbul and other Ottoman centers, was repositioned, especially in the wake of Ottoman advances southward in the 1870s. Nonetheless, Fadl deemed for himself a special role in this the land of his ancestors, Arab and Indian. As we saw in the Cheruman lore, his Malayali Mappila side was also linked to Hadhramawt—Dhofar in particular—since ancient times.

The idea that the sayyid, possessing a sacred genealogy and possessed by baraka, is an arbiter of disputes and purveyor of justice has a long history that has often veered into myth.[37] Repeated within the narrative frame of the original migration of the Prophet to Yathrib, which becomes Medina, the City (as in *polis*), in this case Sayyid Fadl's presentation of his personal power in relation to the tribes inscribes traditional tropes of Islamic history while expressing quite modern political concerns centered on the state form. Immediately after his expulsion from Dhofar in 1879, he wrote a sober analysis of the strategic challenges facing the Ottomans in the wider region and the potential catastrophe awaiting all Muslims (specifically the loss of the holy cities, Mecca and Medina) unless these challenges were addressed in a timely and forceful manner.[38] This document of three pages, affixed with Fadl's seal and available in the original Arabic, is fascinating for the mix of styles employed: at times it reads like a policy paper produced by today's think tanks (complete with a concrete ten-point plan or "solution to the political problems"); at other times it reads like a revision of Islamic political philosophy.[39] Because of its rarity and richness, it merits careful and detailed analysis as a text and not just as a source that can be mined for details.[40]

The cover letter, addressed generically to the ministerial level, introduces the attached pages as bearing "beneficial information to revive your brilliant thoughts when necessary."[41] After that brief politesse, Fadl stresses the urgency

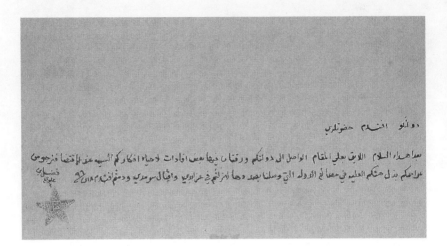

دولتلو الاسـلام حضرتلری

معاهدنا السلام الاین علی المقام الواصل الی دولتکم ورقنا ن فیها معن اوادات لاحیاء اذكارکم السبب عن الاقتضا فرحوص
مرا حكم بذل حنكم العليم في معا في الاوله الیح وصلنا بعد دها لمرنگم في حرامی و وانبال سرمدیه و دمن اننه م ۱۸۸۱ء

Sayyid Fadl's seal was devised while he was the amir of Dhofar (1876–79).
This particular seal was stamped on a cover letter addressing the Sublime
Porte and attached to the report discussed in the text. Thanks to the T. C.
Cumhurbaşkanlığı Devlet Arşivleri Başkanlığı for their kind permission
to reproduce the image.

and significance of what he has to say, emphasizing the need for consideration
at the highest levels of his assessment of the "interests of the state" (*masalih al-
dawla*).[42] He then begins the report on the next page with the none too subtle
"warning against a calamity" and moves immediately to consider the means
by which the British and others (though he does not name them, preferring
the construction "ba'd al-duwal al-ajnabiyya" [some foreign states]) had acquired control over the port of Aden. He argues, "If it had been by way of the
Sublime State or its ministers, then the matter would be simple. If you were
to say Aden was conquered through war, a war did not take place between
the Sublime State and the occupiers of Aden."[43] For Fadl, arguing that it was
"purchased" from tribal chiefs (*mashayikh*) raised a whole host of questions
about the historical, legal, and political relationships among state, territory,
and order. The answers to these questions could mean the difference between
the life and death of the umma.[44]

Hence the remainder of the first full page delineates potential points of
conflict in the Arabian Peninsula (*jazirat al-Arab*) and how to handle them. It
should be noted that the geographical bounds of Fadl's "jazirat al-Arab" are
more expansive than what is typically connoted by the English; here, "the

Arabian Peninsula" encompasses Arabia, Syria, Iraq, and Egypt—that is, the Mashriq. To better reflect both its geographical capaciousness and Fadl's Indian Ocean perspective on the Ottoman Empire, we shall render *jazirat al-Arab* as "the Arab subcontinent."

The flashpoints where foreign meddling was threatening to undermine Ottoman sovereignty, as it had already done with the British seizure of Aden, included an island in the Bab al-Mandab Straits (not named, but it is Mayyun, also known as Perim), the island of Socotra off the Hadhrami coast, and the island of Bahrain in the Gulf. In each case, he stresses the importance of establishing through the archives how foreign incursions were repelled. The example of Bahrain is most interesting for the number of intersecting geopolitical and historical vectors:

> And for the island of Bahrain, ask for the correspondence that took place between a foreign state and Shaykh Abdallah Faysal to learn the truth of its situation; he is one of the Arab shaykhs subject to [*al-tab'in*] the Sublime State. Demand from Mecca a search of its archives to see if there are any documents from the officials of Jazirat al-Bahrain that were sent to the commander [*al-ma'mur*] Muhammad Ali Pasha upon seizing power from [*inda istila'ihi ala*] Faysal in order [to know] if the Sahib of Maskat was paying *kharaj* [a tax] to Faysal. After Muhammad Ali Pasha's acquisition of power over the territories [*mamalik*] of Faysal, the Sahib of Maskat began paying the *kharaj* to Muhammad Ali Pasha. The documents of the correspondence on this matter are located in the Diwan of Misr al-Mahrusa, and it's necessary to search for them so that one of the foreigners doesn't establish the claim that he had a right to buy from Arab tribal shaykhs [*mashayikh al-Urban*] a slice of the Arab subcontinent, because the Arabs do not have that [right of disposition].[45]

In an imperial flourish that would make a historian proud in its emphasis on archival documentation, Fadl tied together Bahrain, the tribes of the Arab subcontinent, their chiefs, the highly successful Ottoman governor of Egypt—a state-builder in his own right—and the long independent Sultanate of Oman, through the right of conquest and payments of tribute. Right and facts on the ground during the time he was writing were discordant and alarmingly insufficient to support Ottoman or sayyid claims of sovereignty.

As a workaround, Fadl had earlier defined the terms of sovereignty in more specifically Islamic terms adapted for his time, making them at once spiritual/pastoral—a relation to population—and territorial. The sultan became the direct sovereign of some Arabs by conquering their lands, but he became the paramount sovereign for all Muslims by taking, in particular, the holy cities. Effectively, Fadl is arguing that more than the claimed title of caliph—which in his genealogical understanding of Islamic sovereignty could not have been unproblematic—the historical fact of making themselves the guardians of the Haramayn (Mecca and Medina) had entitled the Ottomans to the submission of Muslims everywhere. Moreover, unlike in the precolonial period of competing Islamic polities, in 1879 the fear of losing control of the Hijaz could easily be conflated with a fear of losing Islamic sovereignty more broadly. Following from the above, he continues:

> It is feared that if some succeed with such claims, then others will be made as well and the Arab subcontinent will become external to the domains [amlak] of the state [al-dawla] [and] internal to the domains of the shaykhs. This is what is desired by [foreign] states [al-duwal]: that they [Arabs] belong to areas neglected to the point of shame. Then what of that which is closer to them and more convenient for them? In this way they'll bring great evils to the Arab subcontinent. May God save it from their ruses and may He return their evil back at their own throats [fi nuhurihim].[46]

The terms of rule and sovereignty were in a sense all over the place in this text (which may explain the bullet-point format of the third page).

Nonetheless, these are not the confused mutterings of a sufi-sayyid stuck in a tradition of conceiving sovereignty exclusively in personal, embodied terms. The awkward use of the plural form of state (al-duwal) seems to be deployed to capture the emerging international order, wherein Ottoman sovereignty had become an easily violable (non)principle in the Great Game, whereas the singular form of state (al-dawla) denies the legal possibility of tribes' claims to sovereignty over territory because of prior conquests and a political-theological relationship—or hierarchical complex of care—that placed them as Arabs and Muslims under the protection of the Ottoman Empire and the sultan-caliph. What is clear, however, is that the cyclical sultanic order, with its relations among the settled and the nomadic connoted traditionally by al-dawla, had been superseded by the new political grammar that began circulating globally toward the end of the eighteenth century. At least this would have been the case for a well-traveled member of the ulama such as Fadl, who had become intimate with the modern imperial state in different corners of the Indian Ocean, and this state's trajectory did not fit neatly within a Khaldunian cyclical theory of history.[47] However, as

Ulrike Freitag shows in detail for Hadhramawt, in the intertwined and often conflictual relations among tribes, urban notables (including ulama), and sultans, al-dawla signified the one who subordinated contenders and acquired power for as long as he could hold it. This relation to sovereignty was changing yet true until as late as the end of World War I.[48]

Fadl proceeds to counsel the Ottoman ministers to be wary of foreign states' communications justifying their involvement in the region, because they were concealing their actual intentions, as the British did on the island of Mayyun with their claim of building a lighthouse.[49] In such a tense environment he recommends gathering intelligence about exact borders among the tribes. He maintains:

> It is necessary to send an expert [shakhs khabir] on the people of that [contested] region [jiha] and on their ways, someone acceptable to them and known among them for honesty and piety. He will find out from the shaykhs of those Arab tribes one by one to whom they owe allegiance. If they declare their allegiance to the Sublime State, then give them support; if they don't claim to follow anyone, make them understand the rules [al-qawa'id] that are going to protect their territories [amakin] from foreigners; if anyone claims the protection of foreigners [himayat al-ajanib], then he should declare the location of his borders in terms of the rules in force among the Arab tribes, not in terms of the rules of the state, because the Arab tribes still kill and pillage among themselves. As long as blood [feuds] and right [al-huquq] divide them, it's not possible to control them and to regularize security [ijra' al-aman] among them, except by someone with a big stick [shawka qawiyya, strong power]—which they themselves don't possess. Thus, they will submit even to the protection of foreigners. Some tribes [al-qabail] have segments that are the cause of corruption, that compel their protector to offer assistance to them when there's an attack on them from tribes or anyone who opposes them. That then leads to a conflict of protector states [al-duwal dhawat al-taba'iyya] with each other. This is a matter wherein the tear will widen, and afterward it will be difficult to patch. Careful attention to it is among the important matters [of state], and giving it thought may preserve sovereignty and the nation [al-mulk wa-l-umma].[50]

Much of Fadl's analysis of the geopolitical context of the Indian Ocean and Ottoman worlds was preparatory work to introduce his particular concern for Hadhramawt upon his loss of power in Dhofar. There, the distinctions among customary tribal laws, sharia, and imperial state laws collided and constituted a political field in which sovereignty was the pressing question for sayyids, tribes, and imperial states (Ottoman, British, and Omani). Before we move on, it is important to underscore the diasporic perspective of unity that is implicit here. His analysis of the politics of the Arab subcontinent was surely informed by developments in other regions to which both Islam and European states had spread. The "Indian Ocean world" that he knew and whose unity he feared was being torn asunder extended from Istanbul south and east. It was a world in which he had been operating, at this point, for four decades, observing as the "tear" widened.

Fadl describes Hadhramawt as "a vast province [*iqlim*] comprising approximately one million souls" and as being "the nation of sayyids [*watan al-sada*] of the Bani Alawi." Accordingly, there are in Hadhramawt cities and villages that enjoy justice. "Most of the merchants of Mecca, Medina, and Yemen are from there. Its largest ports are Shihr and Mukulla. Dhofar is the outer limit [*akhir hudud*] of Hadhramawt and the tribes [*qabail*] of its cities are part of the tribe [*min qabila*] of the Amir of Hadhramawt." An intriguing passage follows about interest politics and the devotion to future rewards in this world, that is, material profit. This was clearly intended to denounce the schemers who unseated him from power. The lack of *harakat* (short vowels) allows one to read the interests of the "rational kind" (*sanf aqil*) of men in terms of property (*al-milk*) or sovereignty (*al-mulk*), and on the basis of the context, a doubled economic and political sense is intended, while the very last line unsettles the entire quest for sovereignty in the world and opens the door to a universe unspeakable within the given terms of state, security, and territory:

> Know that there are [different] types of men of property/sovereignty. A rational kind expends his effort in securing the interests of property/sovereignty [*jalb al-masalih li-lmilk / li-lmulk*], even if he has to use force. So he looks to the one to whom victory belongs, and if it is his, he profits from it, [as he is] driven by interest [*tam'an fi al-maslaha*]. If it was not his, then he will substitute trickery for force in order that the advantage not be lost to him. If he is incapable of obtaining it, then he works hard [to ensure] that that interest does not lead to his loss even as it eludes him. Another rational type expends his effort in securing the interests of property/sovereignty without reaching the point of using force; indeed, when he sees difficulty with that interest, he relinquishes it. As for his mind's inability to solve political problems [*al-mashakil al-siyasiyya*], this is a part of, or a desire for, worldly ends [*al-aghrad al-dunyawiyya*]; this is another chapter.[51]

The next section, beginning on the third page, does not take up the question of worldly desires and its relation to politics as signaled; apparently, in a document for the eyes of imperial ministers the imperative of divine sovereignty could only ever be allusively conjured in short moral lessons. Rather, the following section, "A Statement of Some of Our Thoughts Summarized," outlines a sober, this-worldly plan to meet the challenges facing the Ottoman, Arab, and Islamic world in the face of "foreign" encroachments.

The first point states the right of conquest: "The prevailing fundamental principles [al-usul] among sovereigns [suggest that] if one king acquires sovereignty [istawala] over the capital [al-markaz] of another, all parts of the kingdom that were under the jurisdiction of the capital belong to the conqueror." The second point gives the names of the major capital cities of the Arab subcontinent: "Sana, Mecca, Baghdad, Damascus [al-Sham], Cairo [Misr], and others. After the Sublime State's acquisition of sovereignty [istila'] over all the [Arab] capitals they became its dependencies [sarat taba'n laha]."[52] In the third point he uses the term akhdh (take, conquer) to signify the historical events of the early sixteenth century versus the political-theological signification of "acquiring sovereignty" (istila'), which involves establishing symbolic and affective relations: "After the conquest [akhdh] of the capitals, the Sublime State gave the Arab shaykhs honors recognizing their ties to it."[53] The distinction between simple conquest and the complex process of acquiring and reproducing sovereignty over diverse geographies was essential to naturalizing the Ottoman Islamic order and de-naturalizing European claims in parts of the Arab subcontinent.

The remaining seven points all concern the current crisis of Ottoman and Islamic sovereignty brought on by the incursions (al-tadakhkhul) of "foreign states" into the Arab subcontinent through the establishment of independent ties (al-tashabbuthat) with Arab tribes and shaykhs by means of offers of protection.[54] Fadl notes first the obvious concern of any state with the movements of foreign states in territories it has claimed and the desire of that state to acquire intelligence about those movements. In the fifth point he states: "If it is learned that the object of the incursion was only to establish ties, then a warning is given against meddling harmful to sovereignty in accordance with the fundamental principles."[55] He moves on to indicate the importance of openly declaring the borders of a state's territories so that it becomes a mutually recognized fact, which can aid in obviating disputes. In his eighth point Fadl offers a more concrete discussion of the Ottoman situation: "If the Sublime State at this time looked at the intrusive movements [harakat al-tashabbuth] of foreigners into its territories, then the majority of the coast of the Arabian subcontinent is in the hands of foreigners, and from that results massive harm to Muslims of the Arabian subcontinent and to the most excellent places, the sacred Mecca and Medina, because they are in the same region."[56]

In the next point, he delves into recent history to demonstrate that when the political will is there, the Ottoman state is capable of not only defending its sovereignty but also extending its reach. He reminds Istanbul that France was forced to abandon some territory adjacent to the Bab al-Mandab it had claimed to have purchased from Arab shaykhs for a handful of *dirham*s because the Ottomans objected to it on legal grounds as violating the fundamental principles (*al-usul*) of sovereignty.[57] In another instance, he reminds the center that

> the Sublime State permitted the governor [*wali*] of Egypt to take [parts of] Africa that had belonged to it. He turned his attention there and organized its ports [all the way] to Ras Hafun,[58] despite the intensity [*quwwa*] of foreign involvement there, by giving salaries [*mahiyyat*] to some of its shaykhs and the like. He didn't pay attention to the relations that were in contradiction to the fundamental principles prevailing among states because they in essence were part of the Sublime State from a very long time ago.[59]

Fadl saves for the last point his own predicament as an Alawi sayyid in the context of global intrigues and tribal conflicts that he has sketched in the preceding two pages. He relates in vague terms how in the violent struggle between the Kathiri and Qu'ayti sultans over control of Hadhramawt's major port cities, al-Shihr and al-Mukalla, the Alawi sayyids were caught in the middle:

> Upon complaints from the Alawi sada about the shaykhs of the two [cities] during the reign of the late sultan Abdulmajid, Habib Pasha, the governor of Hijaz, and Sharif Muhammad b. Aun furnished two armed ships. They were ready to set sail when it began to storm. They made it to Shihr only with extreme hardship. Some troops were landed and entered the city. There was suffering among them and they couldn't stay at the port, so they returned. Afterward Habib Pasha sent honors and medals to the amir of Hadhramawt. Then during the reign of the late sultan Abdulaziz, the amir of Hadhramawt who was given honors and medals, entered and took al-Shihr, through battle, from the shaykh who was not in good standing with the Sublime State. He also wanted control of al-Mukalla. So the ruler of al-Mukalla sought the aid of a man from his tribe, named al-Qu'ayti, and he came and laid siege to al-Shihr from the direction of the sea. He was

able to remove it from [the control of] the amir of Hadhramawt because the amir of Hadhramawt doesn't have ships. The aforementioned al-Qu'ayti has been the governor of it until now. The Alawi sada complained a second time to the governor of Hijaz and to the amir of Mecca, Sharif Abdallah Pasha. They sent two officials [ma'murayn] to each of the port cities in a warship whose commander [qumandar] at the time was Ahmad Bey. They returned without any results, at which point the sayyids of Hadhramawt sent special envoys to the Sublime Porte during the reign of the late sultan Abdulaziz. The edict was issued to take the two port cities, and two warships were allocated specially for that. During that time it happened that the Asiri made a move on al-Hudayba, and the Sublime State ordered that Yemen be taken piece by piece. It is hoped that you will take as important within your purview and your administration the protection of the Arab subcontinent from the meddling and encroachments of foreigners. Trust in God to be your support and your protection from what may do you harm. Amin.[60]

With this plea and prayer, Fadl ends his report on contested sovereignty in the context of the Arab lands at the end of the 1870s.

Reproducing in Fadl's own words how the world appeared at a time of heightened imperial interstate competition is crucial to our argument. By the beginning of a heady decade of imperial expansions (the first salvos, in a sense, of what culminated in the Great War, that explosive global end of imperial hubris), he was seeing a world that was different from the one left by his father, Sayyid Alawi. In turn, as a sayyid from a venerable tradition, he sought in the report to make sense of that world in relation to the new international framework that was already operative in the Ottoman capital and elsewhere. Thus, the absence of what some might expect by way of detailed intelligence in fact only demonstrates that this document represented more of a policy recommendation and a political statement from the edge of empire by a caretaker of the Islamic patrimony than a technocrat's report.[61]

Previous accounts, based on British or Ottoman imperial sources alone, have depicted Fadl as driven mainly by self-interest or as a copy of one of those whom he himself described, motivated by calculations of worldly interests. As I've argued in the Introduction, such a view cannot fully account for the concerns that Fadl expresses in this document and that are evident in the risks he was willing to take, not to mention the overall conception of life in the tradition to which he belonged. The reductive view presupposes the absence of a sincere commitment to the welfare of Muslims, and there is no clear evidence to justify such a reading. In fact, if we assume that he was true to his word, then a far more generative reading of the globally changing conceptual landscape of sovereignty becomes possible, not to mention a more nuanced history of his life as irreducible to the emergent politics of state.

Surely it is undeniable from the above summary that Fadl had an imperialist perspective vis-à-vis what was domestic and foreign, particular and universal, local and global. The local was important to the extent that it played a supporting role in the universal mission of Islam on a global scale. The latter was impeded by the development of the international under the leadership of the Christian foreigners, not necessarily by the international itself. At this point political knowledge, will, and acumen were regarded as critical to the very preservation of Islamic sovereignty. The geography of Islamic domains and their legal boundaries were crucial to know and defend from the barbaric Arab tribes within and the barbaric foreign states without.

Tribes were cast as "still killing and raiding each other as is their constitution [da'b al-arban]," which, interestingly, makes them and their chiefs "our subjects," literally, "those in our care."[62] The "us" here consists of the Ottoman state and its agents, which had long ago (since the conquests of the sixteenth century) displaced the age of Arab kings (muluk), leaving the right of political decision-making—about administration, including the disposition of territory and delimitation of borders—absolutely and exclusively in the hands of the one true sovereign sultan-caliph.[63]

This story of sovereign power's materialization in the tribal areas of the Arab subcontinent is notably distinct from the classical liberal political fiction of contract as the journey out of the state of nature and its intrinsic dangers characterized by Hobbes as a war of "all against all." As Patricia Crone has observed, the freedom and equality supposedly intrinsic to tribal-type societies was not a celebrated "fact" in the tradition of Islamic political thought. Rather, the tribal as a mode of ethical and political life was necessarily rendered unintelligible through a rupture narrative that divided history into pre- and post-Islam.[64] Of course, the problem with this formulation is that the tribe continued to be a significant form of Muslim life for centuries—indeed, down to the present.[65] It is precisely around the persistence of tribal ways that Fadl's intervention into the question of sovereignty took shape.[66] He delineated historical, genealogical, legal, and political "sources" of Ottoman sovereignty over the entire Arab subcontinent. Aden itself and its surroundings, he argued, continued to show signs of Ottomanness in their buildings, defenses, and inhabitants.[67] Similarly, he noted how the region's tribes entered into agreement with the Ottomans, submitting as was tradition to the rulers of the Haramayn, and signs of recognition (edicts and honors) given to the chiefs could still be found in the imperial and other "archives" (*khazina*).

Thus, he generalized for the Arabs of the Mashriq as a whole—the Arab subcontinent—terms of sovereignty that were at once historical (hence, ostensibly mutable) and eternal or divine (fixed throughout time). Indeed, it was his keen sense of historical change taking place within an unchanging framework that arguably compelled him to enlist and insist on Ottoman sovereignty even as he made a move to bring sayyid rule to Dhofar, a mission to which he remained committed after his second exile and until his death in 1900. However, this imperialist agent was also a sufi-sayyid. While there was overlap between these positions (understood as subjectivities here), they were not reducible to one another. In the next chapter, we will inquire into the limits of this-worldly sovereignty and its pretensions. But first, in the following section, we will examine one of the pretensions undergirding a growing imperial surveillance state: the scientific identification of subjects.

Imperial Biopolitics and Modes of Existence

Previous chapters have shown that the British had trouble categorizing the Alawis for various reasons, perhaps mainly because across their empire they eventually encountered sayyids willing to collaborate with them in colonial and commercial projects, particularly after the failure of the 1857–58 Indian Rebellion. That indeed they were not a homogeneous group, especially when it came to ideas about the proper form of the political, is a point that has been neglected thus far in our discussion of "the sayyid"; we shall return to it in Chapter 6, treating it as a historical and theoretical problem of representation. Here, let us further investigate British efforts to neutralize Fadl, whom they chalked up as a radical and fanatic, in light of the expanding jurisdictional claims of empire to protect peoples and territories across the Indian Ocean world.

"I could not learn that he was in any way engaged in politics. It is however absolutely necessary, that a person of his character and influence should not be lost sight of," wrote Brigadier W. M. Coghlan in a letter to Madras reporting on the movements of Sayyid Fadl.[68] Coghlan was political resident and commandant at Aden around the time of the Mecca Revolts and the Indian Rebellion. Initially, as the mutiny spread and grew into a rebellion in the Indian subcontinent, the government of India had requested in December 1857 that Fadl be "closely watched" by agents in Arabia.[69] Madras seems to have feared that the ties he maintained with Malabar, "intriguing with his people," could become a transregional vector of transmission of rebellious sentiments. Of course, the fear of Fadl had predated the mutiny and rebellion and resulted in his expulsion from India in 1852. By 1858, such fears had reached the level of hysteria, and any potential route by which the rebellion in the North could spread was closely monitored, no matter how distant.

The emergency, which is what the Indian Rebellion was for the British Empire, as evinced by the exceptional and horrific kill orders and the dissolution of the East India Company, placed Company and imperial officials from Madras, Calcutta, and Bombay to Aden, Jedda, and Cairo on high alert. In that transregional context of imperial emergency, locating Fadl was given priority status; Brigadier Coghlan's and others' letters suggest a frantic search was on. The perception of Fadl as a fanatic rebel by nature with the power to rouse legions of Muslims from Arabia to India fueled a frenzy of correspondence. As intelligence reports repeatedly made clear even before the Rebellion, Fadl was offered information and financial support by Mappilas who regularly traveled to the holy cities. The Hajj of 1273 AH fell on the last days of July and first days of August 1857, after the start of the Rebellion, and the following one fell in the third week of July 1858, after the rebellion had been viciously put down.[70] Between those dates, a full account of the atrocities perpetrated by the British against Muslims certainly filled Fadl's ears.

Coghlan relayed the Indian history and current news of Fadl to one of his recently appointed colleagues, Captain Pullen, who was the commissioner at Jedda and commander of the H.M.S. *Cyclops*.[71] He reported from a reliable source "that of late the conduct of Seyed Fuzl the Moplah Tangul, has been of a character highly dangerous, and tending to foster the spirit of disaffection which is at present, unhappily so prevalent in India. You are aware that the Moplah race is notorious for the fanatical spirit with which they have on numberless occasions resisted our authority in Malabar, and over this sect, Seyed Fuzl's influence is unbounded. He affects the character of a martyred saint, and to such, Mahomedans of all classes are ever ready to render their sympathy and assistance."[72] The "highly dangerous" actions must refer to Fadl's alleged involvement in the June 1858 massacre at Jedda, after which he was said to have started making frequent visits to Mecca from his residence in Taif. Coghlan added that Fadl was now openly declaring hatred of the British and calling for all "true believers" to resist, to fight "to expel and destroy the Kaffirs." He noted the strategic threat to the British Empire of these calls being made in Mecca of all places, "where Mahomedans from every part of our Eastern possessions flock in great numbers, and whence they return to their homes, imbued with the baneful doctrines which they have there acquired, and ready and willing to propagate them still further."[73]

Coghlan thought the time had come to either seize Fadl or have the Ottomans deport him to somewhere remote. He expressed his preference for taking him into British custody, since "he would be confined for life in some fortress, remote from his native Country" and his "evil influence" would be neutralized. He concluded by reiterating the urgency of dealing with Fadl, citing the "cost" of Muslim fanaticism for "us." In reply, Pullen said he had finally cornered Namik Pasha, "Governor General of Hijaz," and got him to admit that he was aware of Fadl's activities and influence, after first denying that he knew who Fadl was. It was Pullen's suggestion that he would like Fadl delivered to him that forced the governor to tip his hand. Namik Pasha effectively refused, saying it would cause a massive uprising of Muslims and Arab tribes. Pullen was nonetheless happy, because Namik Pasha was "at any rate acknowledging that the Tangul possessed great influence."[74]

The reticent pasha proceeded to provide Fadl's itinerary since his exile from India, which essentially conformed to the one we reconstructed previously. He said that a person fitting the description had arrived in Mecca from Istanbul several years earlier and was living between Taif and Mecca. About two years into his stay, this person went to Suez and boarded a ship to Aden to try to get to India but was stopped. He went into Yemen, then back to Mecca. Pullen argued that Fadl was most certainly an instigator of the "melancholy events which transpired at this place [Jedda] on the 15th of June last," though he admitted tangentially that when he wrote his July report about the massacre he didn't know of Fadl. Pullen concluded that the Ottomans would not turn over Fadl, but the pasha had intimated that if it became possible at a later date to quietly hand Fadl over he would try to do so, and that he would attempt to get Fadl to soften the tone of his preaching. Pullen thought this was the best the British could expect and didn't want to push unless the government ordered him to do so, because he was "anxious" about the repercussions in that unstable moment.[75] The refuge Fadl sought in the Sofular Sufi lodge was likely to avoid being caught up in the post-massacre reckoning of imperial powers.

Going beyond the British sources, William Ochsenwald gives a detailed account of the Jedda massacre of June 15, 1858, and its aftermath.[76] Interestingly, a jurisdictional conflict over the nationality of a ship (the *Irani*) co-owned by an Ottoman and a British Indian subject provided the spark for the killings. Twenty-two Europeans and Christian protégés were killed.[77] The vice-consul, Stephen Page, was one of the victims. When Pullen felt that swift justice had not been meted out, he unleashed cannon fire on the town from the HMS *Cyclops*. Eventually, Namik Pasha, who had been in Mecca attending to Hajj preparations, took charge and de-escalated a situation that seemed ready to explode in full-scale war. After three rounds of Ottoman investigative council meetings, many of the rebels from the lower ranks of society were executed. Nonetheless, an international commission was formed in order to expose what the British believed was a local cover-up of the planned character of the massacre. The commission had Ottoman, British, and French representation. In the end, the leader of the Hadhramis in the Hijaz was also executed, on January 12, 1859, based on the recommendation of the commission.[78]

It seems the new British Raj in India and officials in London agreed with Pullen about not pursuing any further course of action, because Fadl was allowed to disappear again from their radar, that is, until his involvement in Dhofar in the second half of the 1870s. However, at that point, when the imperial bureaucracy sought information about Fadl's whereabouts, they were at a loss. The problem was that as the years passed—roughly two decades—his face was literally unfamiliar to the imperial agents who succeeded Page, Coghlan, and Pullen, making the task of keeping an eye on him difficult. The steps taken to identify and locate Fadl in the late 1870s might be regarded as reflecting scientific advances in statecraft or one of the many routes constitutive of modern sovereignty.

Efficiently identifying and regulating "the outlaw" became a preoccupation of states and a hallmark of sovereignty by the second half of the nineteenth century. Accordingly, manifold experiments were undertaken from angles that were both more and less scientific.[79] In the transregional space of empire, the difficulty of fixing the identity of a mobile and networked actor like Sayyid Fadl was compounded by the great diversity and porousness of jurisdictional and geographical boundaries that benefited the well-connected outlaw. At a very basic level, the border- and treaty-making practices promising protection and security, which underwent a boom after the mid-1870s, sought to close the holes in the net of imperial surveillance even as they were giving rise to an international order. The gaps were made visible, and filling them took on a sense of urgency for empire-states confronted by itinerant political figures such as Fadl and al-Afghani.

The new technologies of surveillance in some ways continued practices begun much earlier in combating pirates at sea and bandits on land. By the 1870s, however, a national form of the political subject accruing varying degrees of rights as citizens of territorialized bodies constituted publics within a global urban and imperial geography for whom the security of the state and the rewards of the market were intertwined and mediated by new secular imaginaries reproducing and reinforcing the claims of modern sovereignty. At the same time, the globalization of imperial, national, and urban forms constituted, confronted, and was contingent on the survival and even redemption of its rascals, marginals, frontiersmen, fanatics, and savages.[80]

The example I consider here is linked to Fadl's brief tenure as amir of Dhofar, a position that, as we suggested previously, he was asked to fill in the hope that he would bring peace to the area. It seems that the Jedda affair, whatever the level of his involvement in it, made him aware of the weakness of the Ottoman state in the post-Crimea international arena, wherein it seemed increasingly forced to compromise on the protection of Muslim lives.[81] His response to this constrained and diminished Ottoman sovereignty seems to have been to rededicate himself to the Alawi Way. He was devoted to a life of obscurity—that is, the life of *alim* (pl. *ulama*) and Sufi—when representatives of warring tribes from Dhofar reached him in Mecca sometime in early 1875. According to his own account, the tribes had sent him two documents with their request. The first was the Ottoman *firman* (appointment edict) held by the previous governor (*hakim*) Sayyid Muhammad Aqil; the second was a document swearing allegiance and an oath of loyalty (*waraqa al-mu'ahada wa-l-bai'a*) to Fadl by all of the tribes.[82] The meaning of the oath and the implications for Fadl of its being broken will be addressed in Chapter 6.

After receiving the entreaties and oaths, he set out for Dhofar to restore peace and rule as the prince. Fadl's movements in the direction of Dhofar in late 1875 activated the British surveillance net and put him back on their radar. A general call to be on the alert for his possible arrival in India was issued by Bombay after it received a description of him and news of his movements from Madras.[83] The latter had been informed by Aden in letters from the political resident J. W. Schneider dated September 6 and October 12, 1875. He included in each letter reports on the "movements of Syed Fazil the Mopla Outlaw."[84]

These letters and reports, whose quantity and quality increased, are evidence of an expanding web of imperial intelligence along the Indian Ocean coast.[85] In the September dispatch, Aden forwarded a letter from the consul at Jeddah of August 31, 1875, "reporting that Syud Fazil, the Moplah Outlaw left Mecca some days ago for Seet [*sic*] on the coast of Yemen, and that it has been ascertained he sailed for Maculla. I have written to the Nakeeb of that place to find out whether Syud Fazil has any intention to find his way to India."[86] Initially, the Dhofaris' invitation was unknown to the residents and consuls; so even as the intelligence grid was expanding, it remained rudimentary in its knowledge of peninsular politics.

Orders were issued from Bombay to British agents along the Indian Ocean coast "to prevent that individual finding his way into India" and recommending Fadl's arrest and detention as a "State Prisoner should he be found in the Bombay Presidency."[87] In order to make that order feasible, a request was sent out along the imperial net for the latest description of Fadl's appearance. Madras gathered from Malabar a "description roll" that was assembled by the most famous of its collectors, William Logan. Logan had previously sent to Madras and forwarded to Bombay a single description given by Fadl's nephew in November 1875.[88] Subsequently, several others who knew or claimed to know Fadl were interviewed and the information they provided was summarized and tabulated.

The resulting description roll is fascinating for its categorical precision, on the one hand, and its diverging content, on the other—rendering the instrument only minimally useful. Nonetheless, it was forwarded to imperial agents located in various strategic centers around the Indian Ocean. The columns were labeled Authority, Age, Height, Beard, Hair of Head, Teeth, Size, Colour, Appearance, Features, Face, Nose, General Remarks. There were seven rows, with the first being the account by the "authority," Fadl's nephew, Sayyid Abdulla Koya of Calicut. According to him, Fadl was about forty-nine years old, of ordinary height and weight, had a "round and bushy, more than black" beard and a receding hairline, "two fore-teeth lost; false ditto, removable at pleasure, substituted," was "bamboo brown, strong and not very fat or lean, marked with large smallpox scars," and had a "regular, neither too long nor round" face with a nose that was "long, and middle of bridge rather raised."[89]

In other descriptions, his age ranges from fifty to sixty years and his complexion "fair, and slightly reddish" to "somewhat fair" and "very fair." All except one noted there was something irregular about his teeth, and three of the seven mentioned smallpox scarring. Three remembered him being average height, two guessing five to five and a half feet, while the Mappila magistrate of Tirurangadi thought he was tall. As for "appearance," one suggested he was "fat and erect" and another "commanding." Some of the "general remarks" were interesting. The

Hindu *tahsildar* (tax officer) of Kurumbrunad said: "Nails not overgrown. Eyes black. Dress white with shirt and coat. Speaks Arabic and Malayalam." The Hindu magistrate of Quilandy said: "Voice soft. Speaks gently. Neither chews betel nor takes snuff." The Mappila magistrate of Chowghaut said: "Some hair on ear also. Forehead bears a callous spot from habitual worship. Feet and hands long. Eyes black." The Tirurangadi magistrate also noted his large black eyes.[90]

These descriptions reveal layers of connections between and among Mappilas, Hindus, colonial officials, and migrants moving between Malabar and Arabia.[91] When Fadl was expelled from India, he was less than thirty years old, so the accounts gathered in the description roll nearly a quarter century later were filtered through various sources and were not solely the memories of the agents listed. Thus the roll itself was a performance of multiple voices and movements projecting a physical image in words of a figure that was ultimately unrecognizable—which may have been very much the intention of the primary interlocutors.

Conclusion

In the years between what was his effective exile from India in 1852 and 1879, when he was forced to flee Dhofar, Sayyid Fadl lived a life of interconnected extremes: mobility and immobility, comfort and destitution, rebel and rebelled against, activist and reclusive mystic, powerful and powerless. Some of these opposing dualities were lived simultaneously, while others were sequential though potentially reversible. Living through these opposing aspects of sayyid sovereignty, he became a mature political actor with a deep ambivalence about the contours of the emerging sites and meanings of politics. By 1879, he could not be said to be ignorant of the modern state as the condition of possibility of all legitimate politics. Indeed, his report on the Arab subcontinent's vulnerabilities was a clear plea for more state.

He saw that state on two levels, both according with the modern terms of sovereignty. On the internal level, he deemed that it was only through an Ottoman imperial state capable of wielding the big stick that "the Arabs" and Muslims in general could expect to flourish. Similarly, on the external level, the erosion of Ottoman sovereignty, even as it was recognized formally by foreign states, meant the international order of empire-states dominated by Christians could only ever desire an end to a universal Dar al-Islam. It was on that emerging international level that his ambivalence toward the Ottomans grew as his efforts to return to Dhofar were thwarted in the 1880s and the empire seemed not only incapable of helping him but actively obstructed his efforts by holding him prisoner in Istanbul until his death in 1900. Thus, he turned his attention elsewhere. In part he appeared to throw himself at the mercy of the British and in part he seemed to turn more toward his Alawi Sufi tradition. The implications of both for his conception of sovereignty and his relationship to the unity of life will be discussed in Chapters 4 and 6.

4 "Time Is the Only Veil"

Sufism and the Politics of Recognition

WITHIN THE FIRST FEW YEARS of Fadl's ignoble ejection from Dhofar, as he found his movements restricted to the Ottoman capital, Tunisia and Egypt were being occupied by the "foreign states" he warned of in his 1879 memorandum. New protection treaties were signed, or old ones revised, with Arab shaykhs of the jazirat al-Arab, who in Fadl's mind were historically and legally bound to the sultan-caliph and geographically belonged to a transregional space between two subcontinents. In Istanbul, the recently enthroned Ottoman sultan Abdulhamid II had already lost patience with the Tanzimat reformers, abrogated the constitution in 1878, and was becoming increasingly authoritarian.

During the last two decades of Fadl's life in Istanbul, although he remained committed to the cause of securing Muslim sovereignty, he also appeared to become more committed to the Alawi Way, publishing more than twenty tracts about religious and spiritual matters along the lines according to which his sufi-sayyid brethren had come to understand them over the centuries. To say on the basis of his publication record that he was becoming more pious only begs the question of where the line was drawn between the religious and the political. In order to locate that line, or its movement, this chapter examines a sample of Fadl's "Sufi" writings in relation to his image in an Arab and Ottoman context of reform and revival.

Among Fadl's extant writings are texts that are conventionally categorized as Sufi mystical treatises. As a genre, they tend to be the academic province of religion scholars or anthropologists and are generally overlooked by historians.[1]

The focus of the former is generally on the distinctively spiritual and lived aspects of these types of texts, while the reason for the latter's neglect of them is similarly linked to the belief that they are spiritual and mystical in nature, with little to offer social or political history. Such an interpretation depends on a profoundly secular sensibility, which in turn presupposes an ethical and political subject whose limits and horizons were constituted through histories (of capital, colonialism, rights, psychology) that were contingent on ruptures with the past (of religion, tyranny, obedience, superstition).[2]

If no such subject is assumed, then the texts might be read for the cultural work they have performed in the world, constituting subjects and spaces of knowledge in relation to a power that was at once this-worldly and other-worldly. It would be a mistake to view these works as simply aspiring to assert the supremacy of Islam and the Alawis, in which case we might just read them as moralistic statements of narrowly interested parties. Even though this reading is not untenable and is even suggested by Fadl's career, it fails to appreciate not only the performative quality of the text but the outstanding fact that his was a complex life in which the politics of interest constituted only one dimension.

We might consider the section that follows an attempt to locate the missing "chapter" from Fadl's report on imperial sovereignty. Therein we saw that he advocated strong Ottoman government in the Arab subcontinent and indicated that he would at a later time explain the political shortcomings of the materially minded. Here, in short, Sayyid Fadl shows that a condition of political maturity is a life attuned to the soul, traveling simultaneously toward worldly and other-worldly ends within an order of divine sovereignty. In his mind, Islam as al-Din remained a total way of life that he was not prepared to reduce to private "religion" subordinate to the masalih al-dawla, or raison d'état, merely providing juridical support for a historically formed political-ethical system. In the second section, we consider how the passionate attachment to al-Din as total could be (mis)taken as a failure of character by others, fixing Fadl's identity within an expanding transnational Arabic public sphere.

Moment I: Tuning the Soul

The works I have been able to track down, which represent only a third of his production, form a rich corpus of writing whose neglect for so long by Middle East historians is surprising. The Mappila Muslim tradition in Malayalam shows, however, that Fadl has not been forgotten, renewing in nearly every generation a commitment to the preservation of his and his family's legacy. This is all the more puzzling since nearly two-thirds of his life was spent outside India.

Our argument about the unity of life in relation to the ends of sovereignty rests on catching glimpses of something that is and yet is not. Such a glimpse may be had by situating Fadl in relation to his future after death, which he may have anticipated on the basis of pasts that were also futures of other departed sayyids. Hence, before we turn to his Sufi writings, which engender these multiple temporalities, let us regard the future: twentieth-century Malayalam hagiographies (manaqib) of his father-friend Sayyid Alawi and of himself.

Hagiographic Waves of Time: Indian Ocean Frequency
Unlike the colonial accounts of Fadl's life, which viewed him through the lenses of fanaticism and insurrection, Malayalam hagiographies of the Alawis combine religious devotion, social reform, political activism, and miracle work under a single, unified rubric. In one text, Malayamma and Panangangara's *Mampuram Thangal*, such a unified account, aspiring to an account of unity, is proffered as a self-reflexive counternarrative to colonial, Indian Marxist, and Western readings of Mappila history; in it the biographies of the Mampuram *thangals* (sayyids) are scripted as nothing short of epochal and constitutional for Kerala Muslim history.[3] In each hagiography, the various dimensions of the saintly life combine to reflect the totality of Islam, though as we will see in Chapter 5, this has been and is contested. A certain "fanatic" approach to devotional practice is also encapsulated therein.

The hagiographic interest in both Sayyid Alawi and Fadl is not new, and as Anne Bang has shown, it extended far beyond the little corner of southwestern India. The subject of her book, Ahmad b. Sumayt, another Alawi from the East African coast, traveled to Istanbul in 1885 to study with Fadl.[4] During that time he worked with Fadl to compile a hagiographical account, *Manaqib Sayyid Alawi b. Muhammad b. Sahl*, published in a polyglot edition in Beirut in 1886 with a translation in Ottoman.[5] Through this account, she briefly discusses Sayyid Alawi's 1817 trouble with the collector James Vaughan, recounted in Chapter 1. In it, Sumayt, with what Bang rightly observes as Fadl's "input," relates the victory of spiritual authority over worldly power. Here no arms or direct confrontation are involved, rather a miraculous showing of God's protection and fiery punishment of usurpers: after a chance encounter between Sayyid Alawi and Vaughan on the road, "when the Christian came back to his house, he and his house burst into fire." Perhaps this divine intervention was what compelled the colonial magistrate to back off.[6]

Two easily procured Malayalam hagiographies are *Khuthubussamaan Sayyid Alavi Thangal, Sayyid Fasal Pookoya Thangal: Mampuram Charithram* and *Mampuram Makham Charithrakatha*. The first was written by Muhammed Mattath and published in 2008, the second by Ottamaliyakkal Muthukoya Thangal, its publication date unknown. Both were printed in the area (Tirurangadi) that conjured in Conolly's mind a fount—a veritable "hot-bed"—of nineteenth century fanaticism; I purchased them at one of the many small bookstands and souvenir shops surrounding the shrine complex of Sayyid Alawi. Between my first visit to Mampuram in 2008 and my visit in 2015, the complex had expanded substantially to include a new shopping arcade selling religious texts and paraphernalia. A new bridge from the main road on the other bank of the Kadalundi River was in mid-construction, and the Quran school, which was relatively new in 2008, having had its foundation stone laid in 2006, had been renovated and expanded by the time of my visit in August 2015. At the time, in order to access the shrine from Tirurangadi, cars and pedestrians had to rely on a very narrow, probably colonial-era bridge that could only accommodate one-way traffic.

Both texts are histories of the locality, that is, the shrine and its vicinity, and of the two Alawis. They constitute a moment in the reproduction of a distinct Malabari Muslim identity, which Menon rightly posits did not exist prior to the colonial period. Much of what is recorded in the hagiographies reflects the rich palimpsest of accumulated Mappila traditions, which was necessarily leavened with the stories of other traditions. Mattath's text is longer, beginning at the beginning with the myths of Kerala's birth. For example, Parasurama, the fifth avatar (other sources usually say the sixth) of Vishnu, threw an ax into the ocean southward, parting the waters and giving rise to the land that became Kerala. Here the sea plays a crucial role in the very geophysical formation of Kerala. In another version, as Adam was falling from paradise, he held on to a handful of its heavenly earth, and Kerala grew in the site where it was scattered—hence, "God's own country." After categorizing these stories as myths, Mattath takes the reader through a survey of Kerala's ancient history before arriving at the *kerala muslim charithram* (Kerala's Muslim history). This history features an account of Cheruman Perumal, who is called Banappalli Perumal; it is the version in which he met and was converted by the Prophet.[7]

The well-known story of the trade in spices and luxury goods between Arabia and Malabar, hundreds of years old by the seventh century CE, sets the scene for the less well-known story (at least in postcolonial South Asia) of the appearance in the South of the first Muslims in India as merchants and missionaries rather than conquerors. The genealogy of the migrants is traced to illustrate the "fact" that of the seventy-five major branches of the Prophet's line, at least twenty-five were represented in the long period of migrations from Arabia to Kerala, with the majority dating from the ninth century AH (fifteenth–sixteenth century CE).[8] Mattath attributes the appearance of Islam in Kerala's remote areas to those waves of *sada* (pl. of *sayyid*), some of whom settled there

"Mampuram Thangal Vamshaparampara." Genealogical table of Sayyid Alawi hung at the entrance to Mampuram Maqam. It traces his lineage back to the Prophet Muhammad via his grandson Husayn, son of Ali and Fatama al-Zahra'. Photo by author.

and served to spread Islam. The itinerary of the Alawi family, the hagiographic subjects, as they moved from the coast to the interior nearby, settling along the Kadalundi River, building mosques, disseminating knowledge of Islam, and attracting followers from near and far, fits well into the established template of Muslim missionary narratives.

In addition to the force of genealogy, the call of Islam, its form, and its means of delivery are shrewdly presented in both texts as key to attracting converts from among the largely Hindu population of northern Kerala. Here the call at times signifies the work of building the institutions and teaching the elements of Qu'ran and Sunna, which naturally included sermons on Islam's radical egalitarianism; but at other times it is clearly marked as a supernatural exercise of saintly power, echoing God's call to the Prophet. This power's condition of possibility is thus the specific Prophetic genealogy of the sayyid.

Fadl lived at a time of increased vigilance among Muslim scholars to avoid Wahhabi charges of *bid'a* (innovation), reflected in this case by statements he apparently made upon his return from the Hajj admonishing his followers to strictly observe Sunni worship rituals.[9] This was interpreted as enjoining Muslims to orthodoxy while not refusing the power of saints; hence, the hagiographers' textual inscription of miracle work proceeded cautiously.

Miraculous happenings took the form of a blessing that was later revealed; thus the results could always be attributed to God. There are numerous accounts of healing, protecting wayward mariners, and restoring lost or stolen property that often sound as if they are embedded in and repeat (with a difference) a long tradition of karamath narratives. In each case, the temporality of the miraculous event entails a past blessing in the form of a gift or a prescription for action, the value and logic of which only become intelligible to the initially puzzled and often skeptical recipient sometime in the future. For example, a traveler's supply of sugar provided by the sayyid is later shown to have healing properties, or his seemingly random instruction to burn a large stack of palm fronds becomes a beacon to a ship lost at sea.

While the hagiographies sought to trace a seamless line of sayyid power, connecting life and nonlife across oceans both literal and figurative, by the middle of the nineteenth century, when Fadl inherited his father's mantle, the threads had worn thin in the face of a global imperial consolidation and a new tradition of anticolonial resistance scripted in terms of modern sovereignty awaited its (re)invention. Fadl was not to be present for the birth of Indian nationalism; however, his deep exposure to modern political forms and movements in the Arab subcontinent and the Ottoman capital led to a kind of soul-searching in his twilight years.

The hagiographies attest to the historical and spiritual significance of Sayyid Fadl's life, while marking in part the future life he and numerous sayyids before him, including his father, consciously pursued in their engagements with the self, the other, and the world. Moreover, the Malayalam hagiographies underscore the need to explain the relative obscurity of Fadl both within the modern Arabic canon and within scholarship in English.[10] This explanation must step outside the penumbra of "Great Men," whose very constitution as such depended on excluding the likes of Fadl.[11] These choices in turn were made as the processes shaping modern sovereignty as a global dispensation aligned particular discursive and biopolitical apparatuses with the state. Illustrations of this point include, for example, the evolving relationship between Al-Azhar and the Egyptian state, between Wahhabis and the Saudi state, between Kemalism and the Turkish state, and between liberal secularism and the Indian state. In any case, we are left with the question of what was unintelligible about Fadl and his work in the time of the state: How did this problem of recognition materialize, and for whom? I will return to this question in the final section of this chapter.

The Veils of Time: The Unity of Life

Fadl's *Idah al-Asrar al-Alawiyya wa Minhaj al-Sada al-Alawiyya* (Visualizing the secrets of the Alawis and the pathway of the Alawi sayyids) is an excellent text to delineate the sufi-sayyid life of self-knowledge and to illustrate how such a life might also be a problem for modern sovereignty. First, it is worth noting its publication by the Egyptian al-Mu'ayyad Press, which was the vehicle that disseminated works by Abduh and his supporters.[12] It was published in 1898/99 (1316H), toward the very end of Fadl's life. The treatise is explicitly framed as a pedagogical instrument and addressed on the front cover to "those who desire to follow the path of *al-tasawwuf*" and wish to be instructed by a master if they don't have one (*shaykh man la shaykh lahu*). That using the terms "Sufi" and "Sufism" is apposite for describing the life and pathway of Fadl is indicated in the text. He provides a brief history and etymology of Sufism that seems compelled by a need to place it on par with other "systems" of his time. He locates its origins, which bear the names *al-sufiyya* and *al-mutasawwifa* in the second century AH (ca. eighth century CE). He explains its emergence in relation to an increasing worldliness within Islam, which caused some to aspire to find more meaning in their religious lives. Weighing in on the debates over the etymology of the word *sufi*—whether it was a loan word with no Arabic equivalent, which suggested it must have been a proper noun (name); whether it was derived from "purity" in Arabic, or from "quality," or from "wool"— he falls in with those who traced it to "wool."[13]

Bang suggests that like other similar instruments of the Alawiyya, the *Idah al-Asrar* was specifically written for the young Alawis who were adrift in the changing world of the late nineteenth century.[14] The publishers certainly intended it to have an even wider distribution, and the content also points in that direction. Nevertheless, in the context of Bang's study tracing the network of the East African Alawi saint Ibn Sumayt, such a reading is surely also correct. More on point, her analysis of the *Idah* supports our contention throughout that despite all his political entanglements, "Fadl Pasha had another side which does not emerge clearly in the records and reports of officialdom. He was also a scholar very definitely attached to the *tariqa* Alawiyya."[15]

I refer to "Fadl" as the author of the text even though long sections were copied from other sources. Since my objective here is not so much philological excavation as it is historically situating a specific kind of textual performance, the other voices will for the most part be left to serve the supporting roles for which they were scripted. In other words, the aim here is to glimpse the unity of life in this multipronged, specifically late nineteenth-century engagement with the Islamic tradition of conceiving individual responsibility to self/other/God in the face of novel, "ungrounded" claims to sovereignty and ethical imperatives. In such a historically specific engagement, authorship was an ambivalent performance, as it simultaneously presupposed a relation to sovereignty belonging to God and to the now displaced sultan—the state.

Fadl authorizes his text in the introduction through an initial invocation of the Prophet's family and its lineage, to which he belongs and which he describes as a "ship of rescue" and as "successful through the brightness of his light."[16] In the very next paragraph, he alerts the reader to his organization of the treatise as a distillation of an earlier elaboration of the best pathway to God, the *Minhaj al-Abidin* by the illustrious Imam Hujjat al-Islam Abi Hamid Muhammad bin Muhammad bin Muhammad al-Ghazali al-Tusi al-Nisaburi. He includes among other sources, or "excellent gems," that he planned to cite the *Muqaddima* of Ibn Khaldun.[17] Citing and even copying the luminaries of Sunni orthodoxy was de rigueur, but Fadl also critiqued them for their ambivalence when it came to the special role of the Prophet's descendants in the life of the umma. Accordingly, later in the text al-Ghazali is specifically named as having problematically promoted a populist conception of Sufism.[18] Thus, the text performs a balancing act between the juridico-theological and mystical-genealogical discourses of Islam, an act not entirely dissimilar from al-Ghazali's.

The "opening" section focuses on the general theory of spiritual enlightenment, or modalities of perfecting the soul on the path to God. Preceding the lessons is a prefatory statement of what will be presented in the work by way of four fundamental dispositions to be cultivated, which every "devotee must possess comprehensively." These are knowledge (al-ilm), conduct/acts (al-amal), faithfulness (al-ikhlas), and fear (al-khawf).[19] Copying from al-Ghazali's Minhaj, these dispositions are further divided and organized around seven challenges, or obstacles (aqaba: lit., steep road): knowledge, repentance, the Way, expositions, causes, trials (al-qawadih), and praise and thanks.[20]

Repentance is heavily emphasized throughout the text, creating a human-centered frame within which all else is elaborated. According to the text, the ulama historically categorized the modalities of repentance and its possibility according to four types of sin: one, god-like (arrogance, self-worship); two, devil-like (envy, hypocrisy, tempting others to do bad); three, animal-like (seeking satisfaction of the passions at all cost: fornication, sodomy, theft); and four, lion-like (seeking satisfaction of violent passions: insults, physical attacks, murder).[21] Hence, the desire for redemption was presupposed as a starting point for any prospective follower. Perhaps surprisingly, from our present vantage point, even those whose prior sins included sodomy and fornication are deemed redeemable. The taxonomies of sin and sovereignty are related in terms that place God, the Devil, and animals above and beneath human life, which possesses a government of souls exclusive to it.

One of the fundamental mistakes involved in striving for redemption and unity is that of confusing or conflating the zahir (external/manifest) and the batin (inner/hidden), which are two sides of the same thing though consequentially distinct. Devotees are cautioned against the false choice of investing exclusively in the zahir by pursuing ritual forms of worship and neglecting the batin, or investing exclusively in the batin by losing themselves in ascetic practices and hence neglecting the zahir. To the extent that exoteric and esoteric forms of knowledge and devotion are linked to this world (al-dunya) and the other (al-akhira), respectively, which are not disconnected opposites but are like the "sunrise and the sunset," then it is possible to regard them as working in tandem (*fa-bi-qadr al-ishtighal bi-ahadihima yahsalu al-a'rad an al-akhar*). The use of the gerund *al-ishti-ghal* (working) invites us to read the sentence in terms of Arabic gram-mar. It references one term governing another within a particular syntax through a relationship of differences and complementarities, suggesting the dependence of one term on another. Fadl's intervention here suggests that even prior to the binary linguistic logic of colonial modernity it was necessary to unveil the power of language, or a tendency within it, to associate individ-ual terms with seemingly discrete meanings and spheres of representation.[22]

Fadl supports the proposition that *al-dunya* and *al-akhira* are linked by drawing out the implications of this connection with a hadith: "One who loves his world harms his other [world] and one who loves his other [world] harms his world, so give preference to what remains over what comes to an end."[23] Thus the stakes are declared and the lines are drawn. Rather than celebrate complementarities and contingencies for their own sake, Fadl's argument in-tends to demonstrate that the secrets of the inner and hidden domains are more worthwhile both in this life and in the other. In short, the unity of life is entirely a question of knowing the self, which most crucially means also knowing life-as-other.[24]

To the extent that the soul is constantly exposed to an enemy within that is more dangerous than enemies without, it is knowledge of other-worldly ways that will aid most in the quest for redemption. Taming, controlling, or cultivating the animalistic instincts of the untrained and naked human soul requires methods different from those used to defeat other enemies. Compli-cating matters is the fact that the soul is simultaneously the object and "the means and the instrument, moreover it could not just be ignored since neglect also would result in its harm; therefore, one needs a path between two paths which can nurture and strengthen [the soul], so that in the end it may have the capacity to do good while weakening and containing it within a limit it does not exceed."[25] This in-between approach to the disciplining of the soul, which paradoxically seeks both to strengthen and to weaken it, to make it bounded and boundless at once, accords a special place to the heart. Humans mistake themselves for God or the Devil here. At the same time, the quest for the One, the ultimate Other, and the purpose of seeking redemption cannot but be located in the heart, since it is the receptacle of knowledge beyond that which is manifest.[26] The law and the sensible world it governs in a sense become props in this more central drama of life that seeks to simultaneously transcend the ordinary and the everyday and to bridge life and nonlife. Here, divine sovereignty is recognized, contemplated, and exercised on (and in some cases, through) individual souls.

In the everyday, life is subjected to the government or rule of hope (*hukm al-amal*), which entails a simple wish to live a long life. But the spiritually advanced believer has a different relationship to hope. On the one hand, she or he knows death might come at any time, and so regards life as God's will and doing God's will. On the other hand, the devotee has to remain focused on knowing/becoming life-as-other. Hence, the constant remembrance (*dhikr*) of God is key to escaping the banality of biological life.[27] It is also fundamental to the reproduction in this world of divine sovereignty.[28]

Fadl's Sufism might be characterized as a liminal quest for Being that is always becoming between this world and the other. Its historical modes of engaging with the world could claim to operationalize divine sovereignty, but they could just as well make it inoperative. The problem posed by the roughly translated mystical quest (*al-tasawwuf*) in relation to the legal orthodoxy is quickly addressed, lest any suspicion arise that Fadl is advocating a turn away from the law. Here, he introduces a distinction within sharia between lawfulness (*hukm al-jawaz*), which has the potential for being more lenient in terms of certain moral questions, and the cautiousness and stringency (*hukm al-ahwat*) associated with questions of piety (*wara'*). Deciding on the latter is essentially ruling on individual conscience and thus requires proceeding cautiously. His argument is embedded in a moral question about accepting rewards from sultans in "this age" (*zaman*), ostensibly a fundamentally corrupt one. He says that "ulama" are split on the issue: some (associated with the first rule) contend that if one is not sure the reward is *haram* (from a prohibited source), then one should take it; others (associated with the second rule) argue that if one is not sure the reward is *halal* (from a sanctioned source), then one should not take it. One might read this ethical dilemma as an allegory on tuning the soul in relation to divine sovereignty, to an omniscient yet distant God, because it is especially in the breach between the known and the unknown that the unity of life may be found. In a radical sense, it is only at the point of recognizing divine sovereignty as inoperative that the unity of life becomes legible to life.

Ultimately, Fadl's aim is to establish a distinction between sharia and Sufism at the level of the individual. The self-conscious moral actor is juxtaposed with and compared to the minimal subjects of the law: minimal in relation to a life predicated on becoming life-as-other, approaching the unity of life, which exceeds the law's field of application. The limits of the latter are determined by the law's main objectives, that is, securing social peace and reproducing political order. Arguably, this way of conceiving of the law reflects the exposure of Fadl to a post-Tanzimat Ottoman social and political order, wherein sharia had long been dislocated from its traditional ground and delimited in relation to modern systems and codes, in essence becoming "the Sharia" (Islamic law codes more than a dynamic field of legal praxis), with a similar development in British India and elsewhere.[29]

The distinction Fadl draws between juridical life (minimal) and life attuned to the soul (maximal) does not mean that in his mind sharia is necessarily an obstacle or opposed to a life of individual conscience and thus dispensable. Rather, the law, regarded in terms of regulating one's various relationships (to self, to others, to God) and from the perspective of transcendence, is one requirement for the preparation of an individual for the Day of Judgment. Indeed, he explains that in essence the law and morality are the same, and in fact, piety is of law.[30] However, when regarded from the perspective of the immanent potentiality of the unity of life, in which boundaries between the seen and unseen are not impermeable and judgment is not deferred until the final act, the law is merely a beginning. Therefore, the limits of the law are not simply being theorized as such; for even prior to the end times, it is precisely living in excess of the law but not outside its bounds or against it that is Fadl's pedagogical aim as a guide for individuals seeking the truth, questing after Unity.

The *Idah* is quite clear that submission to a kind of biopolitics engenders the grave risk of forgetting God. Putting all one's trust in sovereigns or economic actors in order to be fed, for example, places the soul on a dangerous path.[31] Genuine faith and reliance in the Absolute and only Sovereign for life—its care and protection—requires that one know fear. Living in total security and in the absence of fear is dangerous for the soul's future.[32] Thus, matters of security and population are manifestly of secondary importance and in some real sense must necessarily remain irresolvable in order for the remembrance of God to take precedence.

Within the changing order of government and economy confronting Fadl, wherein the ends of politics and religion were beginning to seem contradictory, it was perhaps clearer than ever before that submission to the law was only the beginning of the individual soul's quest. Going through the motions of worship or submission (fulfilling the five pillars of Islam) did not guarantee liberation, which in this case did not signify entry into paradise, since submission to the law could be a route to that ultimate end. Liberation lay in self-knowledge, which lay in becoming life-as-other, which lay in realizing the unity of life, which lay in this world and the other at once, which all lay with God and without. Tuning the soul for liberation required acting on oneself through specific techniques or exercises, which made one deserving while also developing the capacity to receive God's mercy. God must fill the subject with his mercy; this was just as true for the angels who had worshipped him constantly since creation and the Messenger of God himself. In other words, God must call the individual soul to Him, and that calling was not guaranteed through ritual or by fulfilling the minimum standard of worship alone.[33]

After making the case for seeking God through practices of the self, Fadl lays out a path that is not an easy one. Even (or especially) for advanced devotees, there is the risk of being misled by the promise of worldly rewards, unqualified shaykhs, and/or the *jinn* (spirits). The latter could be particularly mischievous with advanced aspirants, since they might begin to see into other worlds and believe that well-intentioned jinn were guiding them when in fact they were not.[34] This explication of the difficulties encountered in the quest then sets the stage for Fadl to introduce the Alawi path. Before beginning the discussion of the Alawis, he explicitly declares the superiority of the awliya' (saintly friends) in the management of the earth to the extent that its physical (oceans and lands, humans and animals) and noncorporeal beings all submit to them, while they only submit to God. Kings are beneath them.[35]

After laying out a set of almost impossible requirements for ordinary people to achieve self-knowledge and announcing the deputized sovereignty of saints, Fadl finally arrives at his particular order of Sufis, the Alawis: "They've trodden the path laid down by the prophets, companions, and those who followed of the righteous Salafis, these are the Banu Alawi bin Ubaydallah bin Ahmad al-Muhajir bin Isa bin Muhammad bin Ali al-Aridi bin Ja'far al-Sadiq bin Muhammad al-Baqir bin Zayn al-Abidin bin Sayyidna al-Husayn al-Sabt [grandson of the Prophet Muhammad]."[36] He explains that at first the name "Alawi" was not specific nor did it have the same meaning, as it referred generally to the children of Ali and his wives. Then, at some later point, it referred exclusively to the children of Hasan and Husayn, the sons of Ali and Fatima, daughter of the Prophet. The fame of this lineage spread until it was institutionalized as the Tariqa Alawiyya with the sons of Alawi b. Ubaydallah and became their moniker exclusively, while other names designated those whose genealogy could be traced to Hasan or Husayn.[37] He also reveals something of the process of establishing the genealogical truth of Alawi descent from the Prophet in an account of how their genealogy was verified when they settled in Hadhramawt (ca. tenth century CE). Essentially, the ulama of the area sent an investigator of their own (Abu al-Hasan Ali b. Muhammad b. Jadid) to Iraq and Mecca, who verified the Prophetic descent of the Alawis by means of witnesses in those places.[38]

The promotion of the Alawi Way includes a critique of unnamed orders that center their practices on something other (presumably ascetic rituals) than a path of learning, leading Fadl to describe them as lax. In fact, he adds, the major Alawi shaykhs forbid following anyone but an Alawi. Interestingly, he references a very pivotal moment in the structuration of the Alawi Way as both a sayyid and a "spiritual line," as Ho puts it, in order to underscore the fact that their own balanced and supreme approach to living a good life was developed over time, after initial missteps.

> The Way of the Al Ba Alawi sayyids is also the Madyaniyya Way, the Way of al-Shaykh Abi Madyan Shu'ayb al-Maghrabi, its Qutb, its verification (*tah-qiq*) inscribed by the singular al-Ghawth al-Shaykh al-Faqih al-Muqaddam Muhammad Ali Ba Alawi al-Husayni al-Hadhrami and it was passed from him from man to man. It was inherited from him by the elites, those of status and means. But in order to make it a pathway of verification, the senses, and secrets they leaned toward obscurantism, secret, and [more] secrets. *They did not put it down in writing* . . . And the first stage continued like that until the time of al-Aydarus and his brother al-Shaykh Ali; then the circle widened.[39] (emphasis added)

The reference to the thirteenth-century Moroccan saint Abu Madyan reveals an awareness of the historical and transregional formation of the Alawi Way, but more important, Fadl's tying of mysticism to scholarship evinces a deep understanding of his predecessors' Indian Ocean success. In the lines that follow the excerpt above, he argues that distance from the Hadhrami shrines combined with connections forged with strangers necessitated "writing, elucidation, and elaboration" (*al-ta'lif wa-l-idah wa-l-ta'rif*), which had flourished since the time of Abdallah al-Aydarus (d. 1461).[40] Thus, migration outward from Tarim across the Indian Ocean world, which began in the time of al-Aydarus's son Abu Bakr, "the Adeni" (d. 1513), provided a canvas for the expression of the balanced Alawi Way, with a specific emphasis on scholarship and its dissemination.

The text anticipates that reactions might range from support to raised eyebrows and open hostility to the idea of structuring a Sufi pathway around sayyid lineages. Preempting obvious criticism that their exclusivity was born of an economically self-interested decision, Fadl argues that the Alawi order is not in the business of granting *al-ijazat* (licenses, certificates), since "their path was based on the erasure of form [*mahw al-rusum*]."[41] In other words, the quest for self-knowledge could not be reduced to those signs of disciplinary progress granted and secured from an external human source, even if it was a saintly one.

Most Alawi sayyids, Fadl reports, have reached the level of *al-mashyakha*, that is, they have acquired the knowledge and skills required to be considered a master of a Sufi Way. They do not innovate improperly, and they follow the Prophet and his associates without compromise, modeling their comportment and dress on the sunna.[42] This celebration of Alawi shaykhs is preceded by a passage distinguishing their mission from the "popular mission" (*al-da'wa al-amma*) of al-Ghazali and "his supporters" to recruit from ordinary people (i.e., people with no spiritual commitments or uniqueness). Some Alawi ancestors described this approach to advocating Sufism as a self-interested gambit to attract followers with the promise of obtaining what is exclusive to *al-khassa* (elite by virtue of being committed to achieving excellence in life), but there is no evidence in their books whether this status was ever achieved.[43] In any case, it would have been impossible, since their Way does not include a regime of individualized care. Within the ideal praxis of discipline and care, the quality of the shaykh and the devotee are equally fundamental to their success.

Following tradition, Fadl describes the position and practice of the *mashayikh* as analogous to that of the science of medicine: "Each disciple appears to them [the shaykhs] according to his [unique] condition, personality, and time [*zamanihi*]. Because the position of mashyakha is like the science of medicine. One who is gifted [*mahir*] in it looks at each sick person in terms of the treatments and medicines appropriate to [that person], and the medicine may differ according to the illness. Thus, if the shaykh were [gifted] like this then he is truly the master [*al-murabbi*: pedagogue, cultivator, care provider]."[44] The relationship of master and disciple presumes a "science," or body of knowledge, to be transmitted, making it similar to any other pedagogical context. Sufism, however, simultaneously requires an ineffable connection to be made between two souls, demanding special insight on the part of the master into the particular condition of each disciple.[45]

Fadl invokes medicine not merely for the sake of analogy but rather to explicitly locate Sufi discipline as engendering techniques of caring for the life that concatenates body and soul. More precisely, the human being is targeted in Sufi discipline on the dual physical/metaphysical and interconnected levels of heart-spirit-soul-mind. Each of these levels or layers of the human has both material and immaterial properties. So the heart (*qalb*) can be both the bodily organ and the site of mystical knowledge; the spirit (*ruh*) can both be the liquid force, "a black blood," that runs through the body activating and energizing its parts, and convey the real meaning of the metaphysical heart, since they are of the same "texture"; the soul (*nafs*) can both be denoted by a collective noun that references negative emotions from anger to lust and indicate one of the meanings of heart and spirit, distinguishing humanity from other animals; the mind (*aql*) is both the seat of "knowledge about the truth of things" and "an instinct which knowledge follows by necessity."[46]

Interestingly, the perfection of the devotee has implications for the master as well. Fadl mentions that gazing at the *murid* (disciple) has been known to send many of the great shaykhs into a high spiritual state of perfect ecstasy (*al-jadhba al-kamila*).[47] The importance of time in the cultivation of a murid is also underscored, with a reference to Shaykh Abu Hasan al-Shadhili, who "used to say 'Time is the only veil' [*la hijab illa al-waqt*]."[48] This epigram is glossed in terms of the seeds of knowledge needing time to grow after their planting, being able to bloom, becoming unveiled, only after the passage of an unknown amount of time.

The temporality of perfection, or self-knowledge, is constitutive of Fadl's conception of life as becoming, an unfolding, and provides another inscription of sovereignty that not only exceeds the terms of this-worldly power but cancels it out at the moment of unity. The capacity for seeing other worlds and its relation to life and sovereignty are evident in his description of creation: "We can witness in the world creations that are all ordered and governed perfectly such that causes connect to effects, beings link to beings, and some presences transform into some other, and so on." His elaboration begins with the tangible, "interconnected" world layered in a rising trajectory from earth to water to air to fire, culminating in a layer of stars. The totality, the unity of life, however, was unintelligible to the senses; only movement (*al-haraka*) can be detected.[49]

Different forces govern the "worlds" of that unity. "The sensible world is affected by the movement of the planetary bodies. And in the formative world (*alam al-takwin*) there are influences from the movements of growth and [self-] realization (*al-numuw wa-l-idrak*)." The latter are spirit-related (*ruhani*) and come from yet another world, or realm of existence, namely, the world of angels. In Fadl's cosmology, this world must exist; otherwise, moving toward full presence would not be possible, because humans require the assistance of angels to approach the One who is the Truth of Being.[50] "The soul [*nafs*] requires preparation to detach from humanity and [material] possessions in order to be indeed among the race of angels [*jins al-mala'ika*] even for a moment or just a flash [*waqtan min al-awqat wa lamha min al-lamahat*]. And that is after the spiritual self [*dhatuha al-ruhaniyya*] is perfected . . . so that it may have connections to the horizon beyond it."[51] In that period of preparation, the soul seeks the aid of angels (ostensibly during ecstatic moments achieved through specific bodily techniques) to carry it closer to God.

Within this porous universe, the sovereignty of worldly kings is the least of sovereign powers. The horizon of a subject's quest to become closer to God is drawn on an ontologically different cosmic order from that constituted by the politics of kings and earthly interests; accordingly, the former may escape the latter's demands on it corporeally, spiritually, and epistemologically. The soul belongs to, or is possessed by, another formation of power, one awaiting realization but whose very possibility is disavowed by the rational principles underwriting modern sovereignty.[52] The possibility of overlapping sovereign powers arranged hierarchically within a universe of divine sovereignty, on the one hand, and the potentiality of realizing the unity of life, on the other hand, raises theoretical and practical "theologico-political" problems that remained aporetic in Fadl's life and work; it is not for historians to bypass them by identifying his actual historical personality.

As Fadl further elaborates the claims of Sufism and the Alawis in particular to a special status in the world of knowledge and as being a bridge between the worlds of humans and angels, the discussion reaches a sensitive and potentially dangerous place: the power of the supernatural ("being-in-other-space"). Rather than be circumspect, he chooses to start the section with an extremely unsavory example of saintly power in the eyes of late nineteenth-century Salafis and other modernizing reformers: the mad dervish (*bahlul*).[53] Dervishes, like madmen, were not legal persons, by virtue of their absent sanity; for that reason among others, he contends, there are jurists who reject the "wondrousness" (*al-aja'ib*) of their words and the fact that they channel being-in-other-space. His response to the *fuqaha'* (jurists) who argue that "saintliness [*al-wilaya*] could only be obtained through worship" is "That's wrong!"[54] It is God who decides upon whom he will bestow his grace, removing saintly powers from the domain of human calculations and deliberate acts. The dervish is not mad at all but a human soul sound in its being (*thabitat al-wujud*) to whom God has given a gift. Since what these dervishes (*bahalil*) possess is a gift that also possesses them, their condition cannot be considered the same as that of the mad, who are lost or dissolute. It would be more precise instead to regard their condition as one in which the rational mind, the site of legal capacity (*manat al-taklif*), is in a state of suspension. Indeed, Fadl seems to suggest that not having control and being open(ed) to receiving messages from other worlds constitutes the closest relationship to God.[55] Perhaps to know and to feel the interconnectedness of life and nonlife—the unity of life—is madness.

The dervish is only one of the human sites where the unity of life may manifest and appear paranormal. I use the term "paranormal" for its precision and proximity to the conceptual apparatus deployed by Fadl to discuss the actions of saintly figures who remain in possession of their faculties while being capable of *karamat*, that is, events piercing or interrupting the ordinary and everyday (*khariq al-ada*).[56] The word *karamat* (sing., *karama*) is typically translated as "miracles," and the concept is usually understood through a matrix of saintly attributes adhering to a person, living or dead.[57] Within Fadl's Sufi framework of divine sovereignty, it must also connote a sense of loaned powers that momentarily make present the unity of life. In order to remain true to the idea that paranormal work is God's gift rather than the product of a conscious personal decision, the definition of *karama* as a tear in the fabric of time, as a suspension of the ordinary self, secures the sense of being blessed. It is this blessing that powers the karamat, whether it is making the nonexistent exist and what exists nonexistent, making something hidden appear and hiding something apparent, answering a call and covering long distances in an instant, or being present in multiple places at once, to list but a few examples.[58]

Fadl makes clear the distinction in the notion of karama between common and "specialist" understandings in order to establish that not all paranormal events are divinely ordained. According to the common view of miracles, they are extraordinary acts performed by individuals possessing special powers, whereas the khassa regard karama as a "gifting by divine providence of good fortune and power in order to pierce/break the ordinariness/habits of their souls."[59] Apparently the reason that "perfect men" (*al-rijal al-kimal*) reject the common understanding is the tendency for it to be abused by charlatans and evildoers. The paranormal acts (*khawariq*) of such magicians could be confused with the gift of karama because the source (the Devil, bad jinn) is not known to common people, who evidently are easily impressed.[60]

Just when it seems to an untutored eye that he might lose himself in the world of paranormal acts, Fadl pulls in the reins, returning Sufism to its rightful place within Islam through a saying of the Alawi qutb Sayyid Abu Bakr b. Abdallah al-Aydarus, the Adeni, concerning the relationships among law, knowledge, and truth: "God has provided the one who wishes to serve him the possibility of knowing him through simultaneously [submitting] to the sharia bodily and to the Truth via the heart."[61] Knowledge "expressed through the body" (al-ilm al-mutajalli) was exoteric and needed to be shar'i. The knowledge revealed to the heart, the veiled and esoteric, is the knowledge of the Truth. The tongue, as the instrument for transmitting what is in the heart, becomes a bridge between the two, "so the Truth is connected to the sharia and sharia to the Truth."[62]

In the end, the claim Fadl stakes for Sufism is on life through the model of a perfect human being, life at the moment of becoming other, as exemplified by the Prophet in the state of being called to God (hal). A complex apparatus is required—the Alawis are masters of it and offer training in it—for seeking a similar perfection, bringing one closer to the divine sovereign, that is, an experience of life that has no beginning or end. This apparatus forms a "government of the soul" (siyasat al-nafs) and involves three interconnected yet irreducible techniques organized in an ascending level of difficulty: Islam, iman, and ihsan. Islam here means the basic pillars of worship expected of and governing all believers, constituting a body, individual and collective (qiyam al-badan bi-waza'if al-ahkam).[63] Iman, which is found among a smaller set of believers, is an excess (of worship), the means and end of Islamic practices of the self that cultivate a virtuous heart (qiyam al-qalb bi-waza'if al-Islam). Ihsan, found among an even smaller set of believers, is a practice of good actions directed toward obtaining a higher level of insight into signs of God (qiyam al-ruh bi-mushahidat al-alam).[64] The totality of the apparatus is predicated on repentance (al-tawba) and thus a desire for redemption.[65]

Idah al-Asrar closes with an afterword by Shaykh Mustafa Afifi, a teacher at the Masjid al-Haram, praising the book and its author. He refers to Fadl on the very last page by the title "Sahib al-Dawla wa-l-Siyada."[66] It is a telling honorific to accord to the author of a Sufi treatise on unlocking the secrets of the Alawi pathway with the putative objective of preparing followers to go beyond extant material forms, achieve self-knowledge, become life-as-other, and potentially connect to the unity of life, that is, life with/without sovereignty, for this honorific could be translated as "Possessor of State and Sovereignty" and signal a rather worldly life—indeed, perhaps Fadl's life as the ruler of Dhofar. If we return to the question of this life's intelligibility posed earlier and treated below, this discrepancy may in fact reflect our problem more than his.

Moment II: (Mis)Recognition, Subject, and State

The line between "us and them" in this case was not necessarily drawn geographically or historically. As many have now argued, the modern subject was a global one, formed at the same time at the intersection of a myriad of discourses.[67] Accordingly, the contemporary British official view of Fadl as an outlaw and fanatic and certain Arab views of him as a charlatan are two sides of the same coin. The autonomous religious and ethical domains of the Alawi sayyids were becoming increasingly untenable as a politics that sought to appropriate and domesticate the power therein for the ends of state, be they imperial, colonial, or national, encroached upon them.

Between Print Capitalism and the Politics of Pan-Islamism

Late nineteenth-century reformers more familiar to Middle East historians, such as the Druze "prince of eloquence" Shakib Arslan and the Egyptian journalist Ibrahim al-Muwaylihi, noted Fadl's presence in Istanbul at the time.[68] Ibrahim was the father of the soon-to-be-famous novelist Muhammad al-Muwaylihi, author of one of the canonical texts of a self-conscious Egyptian modernity, *Hadith Isa b. Hisham*, a sort of time-traveling allegory of national becoming.[69] Ibrahim and his son had been forced into exile after the sultan, bowing to British pressure, removed their patron, Khedive Ismail, from power in 1879, presaging the Urabi Revolt of 1881 and the British occupation of Egypt in 1882. While in Paris in the 1880s, they collaborated with the even better known modernizing Muslim reformers Jamal al-Din al-Afghani and Muhammad Abduh on the publication of their anti-imperialist and pan-Islamic magazine *Al-Urwa al-Wuthqa* ("support"; literally, "trusty handhold"). In 1885, Sultan Abdulhamid II invited Ibrahim to Istanbul, where he was bestowed with a rank and office in the Ministry of Education and where he remained for a decade.[70]

With this pan-Islamic background, it seems somewhat strange at first that when Fadl, whom Muwaylihi names as al-Shaykh Fadl Basha al-Malibari al-Makki, made an appearance, it was in Ibrahim's highly satirical account of the portion of his exile spent in Istanbul. The account was published in serialized form in the pro-British Egyptian newspaper *Al-Muqattam* between October 22, 1895, and February 8, 1896, and later published by the same press in book form under the title *Ma Hunalik* (What is there). In it, this bankrupt silk merchant who reinvented himself with the patronage of Khedive Ismail was highly critical of the sultan and his reliance for geopolitical advice on shaykhs like Fadl, whom Ibrahim regarded as uncultured charlatans. He called them *ammi* (common, vulgar, ignorant) to signify their lack of cosmopolitanism and learning, which ostensibly his tours of Europe, as a political exile, had fixed firmly in his mind as requiring modern schooling and knowledge. The other Arab shaykhs in this inner circle included Abu al-Huda al-Halabi, Ahmad As'ad al-Qaysarli al-Madani, and Muhammad Zafir al-Madani al-Maghrabi. Their expertise, or lack thereof, covered the various regions of the Arab world, as their names attest.

Al-Muwaylihi cast them as competitors for the sultan's ear and his patronage. He gives a brief account of each one's career in Istanbul, even if only to mock their roles, which he regarded as anachronistic.[71] He begins his biography of Fadl by noting that he was of the "famous" Alawi sayyids and hailed from "ahl Malibar."[72] That the Egyptian nationalist al-Muwaylihi, who was anything but sympathetic toward this breed of border-hopping ulama, could as late as the mid-1890s identify Fadl simultaneously as a Malabari and a Meccan suggests at the very least that even as fixed, national identities were becoming an object of political discourse, other possibilities remained alive in the Islamic world.[73]

Having identified Fadl as a region-hopping Alawi sayyid, al-Muwaylihi launches immediately into the Dhofar incident. He acknowledges that the people had chosen him (*ikhtarahu*) as their amir; yet the people soon rose up against him in revolt because of his despotic rule (*al-istibdad*). Perhaps the latter point served as a subtle critique of Sultan Abdulhamid's resort to repressive measures in the empire just as representative government seemed a real possibility. At the same time, he mentions the involvement of the British in expelling Fadl from Dhofar. Al-Muwaylihi's historical timeline of events is not entirely accurate. Fadl did not return during Abdulaziz's reign, "screeching" for the state to give him a military force to retake Dhofar. The satirist was less interested in accuracy than in making his point that Fadl was a loose cannon, untutored in modern ways and a fan of rigid hierarchy and autocracy.

Al-Muwaylihi adds that Fadl's ministerial (*wizara*) rank granted under Sultan Abdulhamid was due to the intercession of the sharif of Mecca at the time, Abd al-Mutallib. This allowed him to bring his children from Mecca to settle in Istanbul. In any case, the significance of Fadl as a player in imperial power politics and of concern to Istanbul and London (and Bombay) was clear to this contemporary Egyptian nationalist. He notes that while in Istanbul, Fadl continued to press his claim to "his Dhofar Kingdom" (*mamlakatihi al-Zufariyya*) with the British embassy and "continued to repeat the demand for military assistance from the State in order to regain his rule [*imarat*] over it."[74]

Al-Muwaylihi switches gears at this point to discuss Fadl's standing as a senior religious figure in what became by century's end the capital of the Islamic world. According to his account, owing to Fadl's advanced age and the prestige of his noble descent and reputation, other leading shaykhs (*al-masha-yikh*) would seek to kiss his hand. This show of respect soon ceased, however, as the shaykhs began to denounce each other. At one point, the sultan was convinced by one of the other shaykhs that Fadl had wronged him somehow and sent a police officer, Nazim Pasha, with Sayyid Ahmad As'ad to inform him what had vexed the sultan. Convinced that the shaykh who had spoken ill of him to the sultan was As'ad, Fadl grew angry, spat in his face, and was prepared to beat him when the messengers hastily took their leave. Apparently the matter ended there.

Whether true or not, the episode lay the groundwork for al-Muwaylihi's pronouncement that Fadl was "ignorant" despite the fact that he considered himself a writer and had "many books to his name which were mainly filled with stories of the miracles performed by his father and their ancestors." This is where the chasm that had formed between the *effendiyya* and the unreformed ulama—as Fadl was most likely regarded—appears most clearly. Next, Al-Muwaylihi announces that he is about to reveal something terribly strange and continues on to Fadl's claim that the *qutbiyya* (being the axis of the age) was a family legacy, inherited by the eldest of the line from the previous generation. Ostensibly it was for that reason that the enmity and rivalry between Fadl and al-Sayyid Abu al-Huda, one of the other Arab shaykhs competing for the sultan's favor, grew and intensified.

By revealing this conflictual link between two Sufi sayyids, al-Muwaylihi offered readers of this genre of writing additional grist for their mill, which in *effendi* cultural productions of the fin de siècle was set to grind up the *ancien régime* of truth and sift out an acceptable private Islam for the "compulsory" secular global order.[75] In the historical transformation of the relationships among religion, politics, and sovereignty, the secular state was installed as the norm through the closure of other options. Historians and anthropologists have shown that in the Middle East and South Asia, as everywhere, the broader culture of secularism (secularity) and its politics (of state) constituted a challenge to traditional ways of life, transforming them in some cases and obliterating them in others, while generating new hierarchies and divisions.[76]

If one doubts that Fadl had a global vision, the satirist al-Muwaylihi did not. Elaborating on the competition between the sayyids for the sultan's favor, he describes Fadl as promising the sultan the rule of India (*saltanat al-Hind*) and the Islamization of America.[77] He was said to have used the letters he received from India to justify his claim; meanwhile, Abu al-Huda attempted to neutralize his claims. The latter went as far as sending his associate al-Shaykh Kamal al-Din to India in order to promote the Ottoman cause and to undermine Fadl's exclusive claim to Indian contacts and expertise.[78]

Whether the political satire expressed Muwaylihi's true feelings about the sultan and his Arab advisers or if it constituted a ploy to return to British-occupied Egypt, which coincidentally he was successful in doing around the same time (he was preceded by his son), is not terribly relevant. The takeaway here for our purpose is how the particular form and content of print culture and its circulation signified the emergence of a new constituency with, for a lack of a better term, modernist views of Islam and its role in the world.[79] Put differently, Islam as al-Din (a total way of life) was reinvented as a "religion" suitable for a modern public sphere mediated by print capital.[80] Even as Sufi treatises traveled the waves of print, their impact was just as quickly drowned in the sea of reform-minded modernist texts, which were a better fit with the national projects that would expand or emerge in the new century. Without belaboring it, we may simply bookmark the point as belonging to the relatively well-worn Nahda, Arab and Islamic Awakening, thread of many narratives, a thread that stretched transregionally and "below the winds," as Michael Laffan and others have shown.[81]

The conventional historiography of the long nineteenth century understandably focuses on histories of empire and the nation-states that took shape within, or over and against, imperial terms of sovereignty; since then, the future-past of human political maturity around the globe has appeared as ordained in the robes of a secular order. The circulation of ideas about the world and how to belong in it as national families each with its own state was impossible for the Ottoman Empire to embrace if it were to survive, although Muslim authors such as Ibrahim al-Muwaylihi, and even more so his son, Muhammad, came to believe it inevitable. The major loss of European territories after the Russo-Turkish war of 1877–78 brought home in spades, especially to Sultan Abdulhamid, that some alternative form of positive identification had to be propagated if there was any hope of countering nationalist movements. By the 1890s, evidence of the propagation of a pan-Islamic ideology was abundant. The Ottoman Empire became the heart of that transnational Islamic world, another Mecca. The shaykhs, including Fadl, who were gathered from different corners of the Arab and Indian Ocean worlds were "kept" in Istanbul to serve the sultan-caliph's interests.[82]

Daily newspapers and weekly illustrated magazines, such as *Malumat*, edited by Mehmed Tahir Bey, gave the Ottoman reader virtual tours of the Islamic world and accounts of the various ways in which Istanbul reached out to its different corners.[83] This was one of the many periodicals that would have added to the American journalist and white-supremacist racist Lothrop Stoddard's fear that an exploding Islamic press was contributing massively to the formation of a new global Muslim identity that would be a danger to the West.[84] He cited the Hungarian orientalist Arminius Vámbéry to good effect, who in 1898 had warned of a "general war" and the "solidarity" of Muslim peoples in the face of overzealous imperialists:

> It may not be superfluous to draw the attention of our nineteenth century Crusaders to the importance of the Moslem press, whose ramifications extend all over Asia and Africa, and whose exhortations sink more profoundly than they do with us into the souls of their readers. In Turkey, India, Persia, Central Asia, Java, Egypt, and Algeria, native organs, daily and periodical, begin to exert a profound influence. Everything that Europe thinks, decides, and executes against Islam spreads through those countries with the rapidity of lightning. Caravans carry the news to the heart of China and to the equator, where the tidings are commented upon in very singular fashion . . . What the *Terdjuman* of Crimea says between the lines is repeated by the Constantinople *Ikdam*, and is commented on and exaggerated at Calcutta by *The Moslem Chronicle*.[85]

Fear-mongering aside, Vámbéry's depiction illustrates well the making of an interconnected, intertextual Muslim world conscious of itself. As Cemil Aydin has recently argued, the modern-day "Muslim World" was indeed the invention of Islamophobes as much as it was the strategic deployment of Ottoman and other pan-Islamists, all operating within an interimperial geopolitical framework.[86]

Stoddard continued the same line of analysis even after the conclusion of the "general war." His 1921 *New World of Islam* was translated into Arabic four years later as *Hadir al-Alam al-Islami* and underwent many subsequent printings, mainly because of the extensive critical commentary in it by Shakib Arslan.[87] The latter also made sure to include articles by two Alawi sayyids as part of his effort to recast the Muslim world in a different form.[88] The first was Sayyid Ismail Attas of Java, whose lecture on the history of the Dutch East Indies, delivered at the Young Men's Muslim Association in Cairo on January 6, 1929, was reproduced at the end of volume 1 of the second edition.[89] The second was a historian from Batavia, Sayyid Muhammad Ibn Abd al-Rahman bin Shihab al-Alawi al-Hadhrami, who offered "corrections and clarifications" of Arslan's account of Islam in East Africa. The piece was in fact a broader Indian Ocean history of the Alawis, some of whom he termed "futuwwa" for their leadership in advancing the mission of Islam.[90]

Stoddard regarded Sufi orders from around the mid-nineteenth century as one of the two main engines of a revivalist pan-Islamism, the other being the press, as mentioned above. A brief tour through the pages of *Malumat* offers a clear view of the stakes involved in the new world emerging toward the close of the nineteenth century.[91] The year marking Sultan Abdulhamid's twenty-fifth anniversary since ascending the throne and the year of Fadl's death is especially rich in images of imperial and Islamic reach and largesse. One issue published in November 1900 offers a several-page spread on the Imperial Jubilee celebrations in Ceylon. The photo illustrations are at once local and transregional, or pan-Islamic—representing the nature of the sultan-caliph. In one photo, Muslim men appear both in local dress and in fezzes and suits set against a backdrop of palm trees. Another photo shows locals gathering to inaugurate the Hamidian Commercial Office on the day of the Jubilee.[92]

Other examples of pan-Islamism displayed in *Malumat* include numerous photos of Islamic monuments in India; a medical expedition to Hyderabad;[93] a photo of the Omani governor of Dar al-Salaam, Sulayman b. Nasr Effendi;[94] and a school photo of the Hamidian madrasa in Colombo.[95] There were accounts and illustrations of other parts of the world as well. But even as world leaders, from King George of Britain and Empress Frederick of Germany to President McKinley, were featured on the cover, there were also clear attempts to fight back in the propaganda wars that cast the Ottomans as villains. On the cover in January 1901 was a sketch of white spectators in faraway Columbus, Texas, hurling stones for entertainment at black heads sticking through holes in a canvas sheet.[96] During the previous year, nearly every issue included reports, photos, and sketches of the Boer War in South Africa; there was one sketch of a black man being executed by a British firing squad for spying during the Siege of Mafeking.[97]

The claims and technological achievements of Western civilization were contrasted with its moral bankruptcy. Hierarchies of civilization were fully on display, showing a global patchwork of tribes and savages in relation to modernizing tendencies. An album of images from Samoa captures the divide between the progress the West promised to bring to every corner of the world and the native who continued to live in a state of nature yet subjugated to the state. The photos in the album are placed carefully: a Samoan dancer, a warrior, and a modern military squad plus scenes of a waterfall, cacao, and bananas are juxtaposed with photos of the port, the German consulate, and a European house.[98] The message is not meant to be nuanced: civilization is indeed a desirable end and new technologies are essential for its propagation at the fin de siècle, but unlike Islam and its Ottoman agents (numerous examples of Ottoman modernity are offered), the West is mainly in the game for its own advancement and world domination.[99] Colonialism brings the governmentalized state but in an emaciated and monstrous form devoid of a genuine ethics of care.

How did Fadl feature on this pan-Islamic and contested global canvas? According to one of the Malayalam hagiographies, *Malumat* and the major Turkish papers published an obituary of Fadl with his photo. While I was unable to locate the obituary despite carefully combing through every available issue, I did find a feature on the Mampuram Maqam from November 1900, a month after Fadl's death. The photo of Sayyid Alawi's shrine included with the article shows in front of it a crowd of people and three elephants.[100] That Fadl had a prominent place in the cultural and political life of the Ottoman Empire, had close personal ties to the sultan-caliph, and was recognized by the imperial Muslim capital in life and death was greatly consequential in the continuing recognition afforded him by Mappilas in Malabar, down to the present.[101]

Arslan appreciated better than most of the forward-thinking intellectuals of his generation the special position of sayyids like al-Afghani and Fadl who genuinely seemed to care about the fate of the global Muslim umma, in contrast to ulama who were self-interested, parochial, and unwilling to recognize the danger of stasis. Unlike the broad strokes of al-Muwaylihi's analysis, Shakib Arslan's was more attentive to the differences among the competing shaykhs in Istanbul. In an article on al-Afghani's career, Arslan discusses the trepidations of the latter about accepting an invitation to Istanbul in 1892 because of the sultan's established reputation as an autocrat and his own radical views on opposing tyranny.[102] Nevertheless, all went well initially, as Abdulhamid felt that al-Afghani could be of use to him in advancing a pan-Islamic agenda.[103]

In the next bit, a link is established between al-Afghani and Fadl by way of their common enemy, the notorious Sayyid Abu al-Huda, who was known for privately denouncing to the sultan anyone he considered a rival. As Arslan remembers it:

> A period passed during which Jamal al-Din enjoyed the favor of Amir al-Mu'minin. He didn't fear him and he didn't despair when the situation became chilly between himself and al-Sayyid Abu al-Huda al-Sayyadi. The situation stayed that way because of the stories maligning him to the sultan. Though it was a period to which [Afghani] attached little significance, al-Ustadh al-Sayyadi did not hesitate to direct his attacks against him to his master, rushing to charge Jamal al-Din with idolatry [al-kufr] and atheism [al-zandaqa], as was the habit of those with a certain rank, wanting to diminish another in front of the rulers. I had read a piece by Sayyid Abu al-Huda taking on three of his enemies: al-Sayyid Fadl al-Alawi al-Hadhrami Amir Zofar, al-Shaykh Zafir al-Madani al-Tarablusi, shaykh of the Shadhili tariqa, and al-Sayyid Jamal al-Din al-Afghani. All three were close to the sultan, and each was given a share of the insults found in this publication.[104]

Other connections between Afghani and Fadl of a more positive character surely existed. Arslan's recognition of Afghani as the archetypal political Muslim with a vision of a world free of foreign domination and an end to tyranny at home suggests at the very least that he would have found some political common ground with Fadl, whose outlook on the conditions of Muslim life developed through his own transregional peregrinations. That both Afghani and Fadl sought to leave, or more precisely escape, their imperial jailers in the last years of their lives testifies to their shared skepticism regarding the sultan-caliph's promise of pan-Islamic unity.[105] Indeed, al-Afghani nearly stated it outright in his letter to Abdulhamid:

> When I received the Caliphal edict ordering me to submit and expound my humble opinion concerning the possibilities of a unification of [the world of] Islam, I felt happiness as if the eight gates of Paradise had been opened to me, and I wrote down a summary of my humble opinion on this subject . . . Since not a word concerning this matter has been uttered until now, I have

unfortunately arrived at the conclusion that the project has been thrown into the corner of oblivion or that it has been burned by the fire of malice of partial and malicious persons, or its contents were misinterpreted by latter-day wise men so as to diverge from its sublime intention and it was consequently lodged among subversive literature.[106]

The shenanigans of "latter-day wise men" seemed to influence Sultan Abdulhamid significantly, while the likes of al-Afghani and Fadl formed another camp whose influence seemed to be on the wane and who sought other avenues for their work.[107]

The heightened propaganda appearing in various media from the last decade of the nineteenth century (and continuing into the interwar period, as noted earlier) was part of a great geopolitical struggle for survival, which was precisely how Fadl understood his time. Yet, judiciously, he did not put all his stock in the ability of the Ottoman Empire to secure the future of Muslims. In fact, it would seem that he was not convinced that this was within the capacity of worldly actors to deliver or to deny. This, more than some opportunistic politics on his part, may explain the complex position he occupied at the intersection of religion and politics at the close of the nineteenth century, when in contradistinction to "Eastern" nationalists' claims, he saw in the emerging international law and secular ethics an opening for spiritual life. We will take up this point in Chapter 6. For now, suffice it to say his view both accorded with and diverged from what Faisal Devji calls a "politics of responsibility" in his brilliant rereading of Gandhian nonviolence. Such a politics required a courageous embrace of death over life, hence opposing the governmental logic of state sovereignty and a future-oriented temporality.[108] While it would seem that Fadl took responsibility for his flock, it was not with the ultimate aim of protecting and reproducing life in this world but with a view to death and the hereafter, to another beginning.

Beyond potentially (mis)recognizing Fadl the physical person in the British imperial surveillance net, the (mis)recognition of his "essential" being as holy man, politician, ruler, charlatan, fanatic, or outlaw all say more about the process of state and subject formation and the attendant conceptualization of sovereignty than about this individual's historical life, and much less about his conception of life in relation to God the Sovereign. The recognition of Sayyid Fadl Ibn Alawi by modern political subjects such as Arslan and al-Muwaylihi or the modern Ottoman and British imperial states, through the intelligible categories that muscled forth in the second half of the nineteenth century, could only ever be a partial recognition, rendering a life that was a specter of itself.[109]

Conclusion

In the last quarter of the nineteenth century, Sultan Abdulhamid II attempted to reassert the power of the absolute sovereign in order, as one reading would have it, to save the Ottoman Empire from collapse. He blamed the failure to stem the tide of territorial losses and the empire's financial ruin on the Tanzimat's excessive devolution of power to bureaucrats and other stakeholders. In spite of Abdulhamid's successful efforts to concentrate power in his office as sultan-caliph with the suspension of the one-year-old constitution and to ratchet up pan-Islamist sentiments, the empire continued to suffer military defeats and territorial losses. In fact, Fadl arrived in Istanbul right on the heels of devastating losses in the Balkans, which were soon followed by foreign occupation of the two Arab provinces of Egypt and Tunis.

Fadl, as we have seen, had been an eyewitness to the expansion of Christian imperial power in India and the establishment of colonial rule, which brought with it new legal and political mechanisms. He was caught in the web spun by that colonial machinery, and his life might even be, and has been in Mappila histories, emplotted in terms of a long struggle to free himself of its powerful hold. From his voluntary or involuntary exile in Arabia, he was to witness the further expansion of British influence. In this context, and from his post as amir of Dhofar, he wrote reports advising the Sublime Porte on the need for a show of force in the region, only to face yet another humiliating ejection from his leadership role.

The life of this sayyid, or the *pookoya thangal* ("the younger"), straddled a moment of change of the tectonic variety, the kind of change that radically reconceives and reorders the fundamental terms by which the world is made sense of. On the one hand, while there is no denying that the nineteenth century was witness to the emergence of new habits of thought and new forms of order, this specific individual with the dispositions of a sufi-sayyid Way reflects the complexity, partialness, and incompleteness of that emergence. On the other hand, his life demonstrates—through its living, by its modes of knowing self/ other/God, in contemplating the potentiality of the unity of life—that an ancient tradition was not merely marginalized by the terms of modern sovereignty but was also opened up to questions of complexity, partialness, and incompleteness. The answers proffered by Fadl were layered, targeted, and sophisticated; nevertheless, for those enchanted by the modern, they could not but be regarded with disbelief if not disavowed entirely.

The calling that marked and authorized Fadl's trajectory as a sufi-sayyid, scholar, teacher, preacher, activist, and prince was of a different nature than the interpellative call of the law. As Agamben writes of the apostle Paul's calling, "The messianic vocation is a movement of immanence, or, if one prefers, a zone of absolute indiscernibility between immanence and transcendence, between this world and the future world."[110] Thus, my experimental translation of the Arabic word *al-akhira* as "life-as-other" rather than "the hereafter" (as it is usually rendered) is an attempt to mark the difference in Fadl's conception of his vocation, that to which he and others were called, from the law-bound mainstream Sunni tradition, while linking it to the broader unfolding of the unity of life. That is, Fadl's deployment of *al-akhira* located transcendence in the relationship to immanence, such that it did not delimit an exclusive, temporally deferred, unknowable future paradise, awaiting the end of history. Rather, al-akhira was constitutive of the temporality of souls: existing in the now and the not now, constantly striving to become one with the One, never arriving, but glimpsing in that return the unity of life.

The foregoing is neither the stuff of mystical nonsense nor of worldly re-nunciation. Fadl's life in exile and his claim on sovereign power demonstrate clearly that, in particular, the latter was not the case. If a cynical reading of his ambitions is bracketed, then the conceptual possibility of reinscribing divine sovereignty with simultaneously immanent and transcendent meanings is opened up—but only to be rendered inoperative in the process as life encounters the unity of life.

The techniques of government introduced by modern states and those theorized by Fadl in relation to the soul diverged in their ethics of care by how they approached the body. It is here that the political thinking of Fadl may be read productively through the "mystical" and recuperated from a reductive, modern biopolitics. The importance to the practice of politics of a mental and material universe that encompasses multiple dimensions and worlds and a plurality of life/nonlife forms becomes intelligible at the level of desiring bodies. At the end of the nineteenth century, the historical specificity of that desire for presence, for life-as-other, for Unity, was necessarily political; reproducing the distinction between naked, biological life and a life attuned to the soul marked the chiasmic divide between modern and divine sovereignty that enabled the birth of a new kind of state. Fadl's parsing of sharia in terms of juridical versus spiritual life, however, demonstrates that the question for him was one of complementary terms rather than of stark opposites demanding the exclusion of each other.

To the extent that the desire for presence materializes, the potentiality of the subject's formation is pinned to a horizon of otherness that is constitutional and deconstitutional at once. Theoretically, one could live in this world and not be of it. As the lines of flight between worlds become visible to the seeker, the discrete nature of form is defied and life is made anew in its interconnected plenitude. By the end of the nineteenth century, the multiplication of modes by which a state could decide life's meaning, worth, and trajectory had the effect of drawing the line between politics and religion ever sharper, making flights of freedom contingent on recognition by the state. In the next chapter, we shall follow this thread of recognition into the future, after Fadl's death, examining its implications for returns, both material and spiritual.

5   Uncertain Returns

Cyberspace, Genetics, and Genealogies

> If my identity is now determined by biological facts that in no way depend
> on my will and over which I have no control, then the construction of
> something like a political and ethical identity becomes problematic.
>
> Giorgio Agamben, *"For a Theory of Destituent Power"*

> Case and dispute going on in 2005 over the legal status of Mampuram
> properties while the family of Fadl, who are the rightful claimants to these,
> are alive and living in Latakia, Syria.
>
> *Madhribhumi, June 5, 2005*

IN THE SUMMER OF 2005, al-Sharif Muhammad Sahl al-Fadl of
Latakia, Syria, the great-great-grandson of Sayyid Fadl Ibn Alawi, visited
Malabar in the Indian state of Kerala. His visit marked a historic milestone:
it was the first time since Fadl's expulsion in 1852 that one of his descendants
successfully returned to the place of his birth.

The epigraph above, which references the legal dispute around the shrine,
is drawn from an exposé on the historical context of Sharif Muhammad's visit.
The six-page spread appeared in the widely circulating Malayalam magazine
Madhribhumi. The title of the article, "When the Mampuram Thangals Return,"
evokes or alludes to the themes of this chapter. First, the many levels of return:
circular movement, repetition, turning back, restoration, reward, and a final
denouement; they are all intended, as the article retraces prior attempts of
Sayyid Alawi's descendants to come home to Mampuram where he was buried
and their deportation by colonial authorities every time. Second, the continuity of sayyid sovereignty across the Indian Ocean world: *thangal* is a term of
reverence applied to descendants of the Prophet Muhammad and synonymous

with the Arabic word *sayyid*. Third, the significance of the Mampuram Maqam to Mappila Muslims: thangals and sayyids are not only revered, they are also believed by many to possess special powers, particularly when there is a shrine associated with them. In the previous chapters, we saw how various figures including sayyids viewed and sought to classify this power in the nineteenth century. In this chapter, we consider a "post-reform" Mappila view, a Wahhabi counterpoint, and the changing perspective of subsequent generations of sayyids.[1] In short, I argue that the dystopic present that Agamben problematizes in terms of life reduced to the biological may appear differently when regarded through the lens of return. The consequences for ethical and political identity are not as clearly mapped in history as in philosophy.

The hamlet of Mampuram is located approximately forty kilometers south of the port city of Kozhikode (Calicut) in the northern section of Kerala's historic Malabar coastline. An unexceptional and easily missed location even within Kerala, Mampuram is nonetheless, and perhaps strangely, not remote or insignificant by any stretch of the imagination. It is intensively and broadly linked to global circuits and networks of transnational labor and capital flows, innovations in communications technologies, and global political-theological debates and movements. More remarkable may be the claim that all of this connectivity was made possible by the death of one person on a January day in the year 1844.

The professional historian might note that the demise of this person, our Sufi shaykh Sayyid Alawi, did not by itself suddenly put Mampuram on the map. As we have seen, Mampuram had first achieved fame, or perhaps notoriety, while Sayyid Alawi was still alive, as British officials of the East India Company declared it the epicenter of "fanatical outrages" and illegal "outbreaks" occurring in neighboring areas within the Malabar District. The Company had annexed Malabar to the Bombay Presidency in 1792 with the defeat of Tipu Sultan's Mysorean forces. Meanwhile, a historian critical of Eurocentric framings of the past would note that Mampuram's founding and fame were determined by the agency of Sayyid Alawi and the Mappilas of Malabar, prior to and independent of British ambitions.

However, the continuity of Mampuram's significance was not a product of those histories, some of which we have charted in the previous chapters. Ironically, what kept Mampuram from fading into oblivion was the death and burial of this Arab migrant from the Hadhramawt in Yemen and the enshrinement of his life, a life possessing a Prophetic genealogy. And it would be the meaning ascribed to such a life that arouses certain passions today in actual territories and in deterritorialized space.

Appreciating the significance and multidimensional boundaries of such a life, as lived or aspired to, must begin with relatively bland maps of transregional and global geopolitics. Its specter, which is all that can appear on such maps, gives rise to praise, ridicule, concern, and even violent denunciations. Sometimes, however, it is by reading between the lines or against the grain of an explicit rejection of something that its true nature may be gleaned. So we begin with a contemporary Wahhabi denunciation of the Alawis and their

The shrine of Sayyid Alawi in Mampuram, Kerala, India. It was erected and renovated multiple times after his death in 1844. Photo by author.

kind in general, then return to Mampuram and a positive description of the sufi-sayyid life way, before considering historical efforts to restore Sayyid Alawi's heirs to their rightful place in Malabar.[2] The question of return raises the awkward further question of interest and if indeed the prospect of living life for other ends—glimpsing the unity of life—has any relevance to the politics of the shrine.

The latter is a big question and hence will be taken up only in the next chapter, Chapter 6. Here, the absent presence of a saintly friend's life as time passes might be regarded as animating the seemingly wild methodology of this chapter, which juxtaposes a postmodern archive on YouTube and social media with traditional hagiography and modern colonial archives. First, we look at how today's Wahhabism, particularly in its state-centered Saudi mode, views the world and the role of Sufism in it. Then we move to a Mappila, Sufi-aligned hagiographic view of the world and the Alawis in it. We conclude by considering the implications of colonial and postcolonial Mappila attempts to bring back the Alawi family along with their own efforts to return.

Purity, Life, and Islam's Cyberspace

Over the long nineteenth century, "Wahhabi" became shorthand for any expression of Islam that at least superficially appeared as a rejection of "modernity," usually meaning "Westernization." A synonym in this reductive discourse, found also among Muslims, is "Salafi." Much has already been written about the conceptual and political problems with both terms. From a historical perspective, it can safely be said that the eponymous founder of so-called Wahhabism, Muhammad Ibn Abd al-Wahhab, did not envision all the kinds of movements that would emerge under this umbrella.[3] What was at the heart of Abd al-Wahhab's message was purification; just like many before him and during his own time, he denounced accretions and innovations at the level of theology and sacred rituals. The meaning of the political alliance he forged with the House of Saud was and remains a major source of the conflicting interpretations of Wahhabism.

The Wahhabi opposition to Sufism is typically manifested in preaching against saints, shrines, and visitation to graves. As Engseng Ho has shown for Yemen and recent events have shown in Pakistan and elsewhere, the accompanying violent destruction of these holy sites is part and parcel of a larger political-theological discourse that intersects, though not always contradictorily, with neoliberal economic policies imposed by the US and international agencies.[4] The propaganda originates in large part from the staunchly pro-US Gulf countries and has found its way from traditional print and mass media to new media and now to social media. Meanwhile, the same evolution has required the Saudis to step up their game. The propaganda may have increased in recent years as the struggle to define orthodoxy leans in an anti-Saudi direction, the ebbs and flows of which are arguably tied to US policy in the Middle East and the Islamic world. At a recent conference of leading Sunni ulama convened in Chechnya, not only were Saudi scholars seemingly not invited, but an initial definition of Sunni Islam, or who could be called "ahl al-sunna wa-l-jama'a," excluded the Salafi Wahhabi tradition—the predominant legal and theological schools in Saudi Arabia—while recognizing Sufism. Not coincidentally, one of the organizers of the meeting was Habib Ali al-Jifri, an Alawi and preacher with a significant media presence.[5] A violent Twitter response originating mainly in Saudi Arabia followed, with over one hundred thousand tweets denouncing the conference.[6]

Scholars, journalists, and policy analysts of various political stripes have covered this mediated terrain for some time now.[7] Moreover, in the age of exploding social media, which seems to be in a state of constant flux, it becomes nearly impossible to make any meaningful observations about the media forms of this "smooth" cyberspace.[8] Hence, I provide only one brief example of how the Wahhabi material is developed and disseminated, with an eye to the content more than the form.[9] The focus is on Saudi Arabia rather than Malabar because it is the Indian Ocean and global epicenter in terms of discourse generation and funding.[10]

After witnessing the power of Khomeini's cassette recordings in fuelling the Iranian revolution in the 1970s, and before that the power of radio, cinema, and television in spreading Nasserism, Saudi Arabia invested heavily in media and communications. It is often noted that the real explosion came in the wake of the Gulf War (1991), when the Saudis entered the satellite television business. This use of petrodollars to influence media, first in the form of newspapers, then to gain a presence in the satellite market, and now to dominate the airwaves and cyberspace, suggests that the field of potential study would be vast and that our brief foray into it barely touches the tip of the iceberg.[11] Such studies might focus, as we do here, on the media personalities Saudi Arabia produces or manages.

On a call-in show on the satellite channel Wisal (Coming together), the topic for the day is DNA testing and how it can be used to verify the authenticity of claims to belong to the ahl al-bayt, those in the bloodline of Abraham and particularly those descended from the family of the Prophet Muhammad.[12] The expert, Shaykh Umar al-Zayd, says these claims are most numerous and least accurate among Sufis and Shi'a. According to his Facebook page, al-Zayd's highest qualification is an MA in comparative *fiqh*.[13] He runs a website, ijtehadat .com, with the aim of introducing the Muslim public (in Arabic and Persian) to the work of early twentieth-century reformers, Sunni and Shi'a, who were ostensibly silenced before they could reach a mass audience. To that end he features summaries of some of these "suppressed" works of "self-criticism" that elaborate how Shi'i rituals, beliefs, and practices, mainly, were errant. He also tweets about the website and about events of significance to Muslims on his "unofficial" Twitter page maintained by his followers.

The satellite channel on which al-Zayd makes frequent appearances describes him as a prominent Saudi analyst of Iranian affairs. He also appears on other channels, such as Safa and al-Majd.[14] He regularly hosts shows on Iran with clearly Sunni missionary objectives; the shows have titles such as "Shiite Revisions," "A Window on Iran," and "Iran from Inside." Unsurprisingly, he views Iran as a threat to Saudi Arabia and the entire Gulf. He claims it has sleeper agents (*umala' na'imun*) everywhere that are ready to be activated at any point to destabilize the region. This is especially true during the Hajj season:

> Iran's main purpose is to prove that Saudi Arabia is not capable of protecting pilgrims, which helps in the call for the internationalization of Islam's two holiest sites, Mecca and Medina. Iran has been wanting to [discredit the Kingdom] since the Islamic Revolution erupted in 1979, but they will never get what they want because Saudi Arabia is honored to serve and protect the two holy sites, and the entire Umma Islamiyya stands with her.[15]

Through his rhetorical attacks on Iran, al-Zayd styles himself as a defender of the Muslim umma and the Saudi monarchy's custodianship of its holiest sites. His mission to purify Islam of Sufi, Shi'i, and other accretions is motivated by perceived threats both to his Wahhabi views and to Saudi geopolitical interests.

In the special two-hour episode on DNA and prophetic genealogy, al-Zayd argues that genetic testing would demonstrate that 99 percent of the "black-turban-wearing Shi'i sayyids" are nothing but impostors.[16] He begins discussing the Ba Alawi without naming them. Minutes earlier, in response to a caller's query about the ahl al-bayt status of a family from Medina, he repeatedly begs to be excused from naming names. This largely disingenuous move in turn allows him to generalize about entire groups hailing from disparate geographical regions: North Africa, the Indian subcontinent, Iran, and Hadhramawt in Yemen.

Al-Zayd suggests that the Alawis are the biggest and most dangerous impostors. He says, of course without naming them: "There's a well-known Sufi clan in Hadhramawt descended from one man. It's a very large clan and has spread to Africa and Indonesia. They have missionaries now calling people to mysticism [*al-tasawwuf*] and they appear in the media. This clan possesses the non-Arab genetic marker "G." He refers to their missionary zeal and significant online presence to highlight the threat Sufis pose to good Sunnis. It could be argued that the Alawis, who are doctrinally Sunni, also represent an implicit threat to ulama like himself who are "shaykhs" by learning alone and not by claims to prophetic genealogies. In a battle for authority, this advantage has to be checked, literally. Therefore, he challenges the Alawis along with all other claimants to the title of sayyid to undergo DNA tests to prove their claims.

In short, al-Zayd's "scientific" argument runs along the following lines. J1C3D is the genetic marker, or haplogroup, for the indigenous inhabitants of the Arab subcontinent going back as far as five or six thousand years, including within its fold Abraham and Muhammad. Those possessing other genetic types therefore cannot be considered Arab, much less part of the Abrahamic bloodline. And this is the case for the vast majority who claim to be sada or ashraf (also descendants of the Prophet). In fact, he argues, in typical shock-jock fashion, that the Sufis of Hadhramawt do not even belong to the broad J1 haplogroup but instead to G. He reveals that Georgia, in the Caucasus region, has the highest percentage of G subjects, building to the scandalous conclusion that rather than being descended from the Prophet Muhammad, the Alawis are far more likely to be genetically related to the infamous Joseph Stalin! Earlier in the show he asserts that if we were to accept the genealogical claims of Sufi and Shi'i sayyids with G types, then "Eskimo tribes can also claim descent from the ahl al-bayt, as can tribes from the jungles of the Amazon."[17]

Shaykh al-Zayd's case for DNA testing may seem at first like a facile effort to bring identity politics of the one-drop variety, infamous from American history, to the Arab Muslim world. Moreover, his equation of DNA and identity seems to confirm the fears of the Italian political philosopher Giorgio Agamben in the epigraph earlier. Agamben continues: "What relationship can I establish with my fingerprints or my genetic code? The new identity is an identity without the person, as it were, in which the space of politics and ethics loses its sense and must be thought again from the ground up."[18] Does Wahhabi Islam conform to this feared end of biopoliticization, wherein life is reduced to the management of bare essentials?[19] Pascal Ménoret's account of Abd al-Wahhab's often misunderstood original aims paints a different picture. "Much as the French Revolution would locate the criterion of all legitimacy in an ideal and transcendent general will, so did Abd al-Wahhab's reform locate the criterion of good government beyond the particular will of this or that ruler, in the ideal and transcendent norm represented by God's law. In either case, the return to self is inseparable from the positing of an absolute *norm* or *gauge* or *criterion*."[20]

Similarly, the content of al-Zayd's tweeting, blogging, and video broadcasting paints a more complex picture than Agamben's terms would allow, and at stake is far more than a liberal vision of qualified political inclusion or a fascist discourse of racial purity.[21] In fact, following Ménoret, it might be argued that al-Zayd's call for DNA testing is pegged to "democratic" ends: the Sufi sayyid or anyone else claiming special prerogatives based on blood is enjoined to prove that claim. He expresses deep contempt for and opposition to the *quburiyyun*,[22] who profit from grave visitations; according to him, Sufi "sayyids" are for the most part impostors, who exploit the ignorance of ordinary people by claiming special powers to bless or heal for personal gain.[23]

As a loyal subject of the Saudi king, however, al-Zayd does not reject the legitimacy of worldly dynastic power. The proof, at least to some extent, is in the blood. In al-Zayd's conceptual universe, kings, ahl al-bayt, and sayyids are neither obsolete nor to be judged according to liberal democratic standards. Nonetheless, in spite of his own "official Wahhabi" intentions, to borrow Madawi al-Rasheed's distinction, taken as a whole and when related to Wahhabi thought more generally, his project of dismantling un-Islamic discourses of power appears to implicitly contain a (limited) critique of inherited power. To the extent that it is deployed as attacks on Sufis and Shi'a, it eludes the radar of Saudi authorities and is even rewarded.

As a student of fiqh (jurisprudence) who has also become a media personality, al-Zayd is an active participant in what may be termed the ongoing struggle to define Islam in the absence of prophecy, dating from 632 CE—the year of Muhammad's death.[24] Political scientist Thomas Hegghammer would categorize al-Zayd within a specifically Saudi pan-Islamist tendency with an intellectual pedigree that goes back to the late nineteenth century.[25] Al-Zayd, like many with his level of learning and especially like many who have found a media voice, knows exactly what Islam is: "Islam is quite concisely belief, worship, and the compendium (*manzuma*) of values, morals, and laws. 'That is Islam.'" In his version there is little room for debate, shockingly so, given the vagueness of his definition and the many questions it raises—for example, what exactly is law, and in what do belief and worship consist? Struggling to answer these questions since the ninth century CE, Sufis have given what may be seen as a value-added response to the standard premodern Sunni model of *madhahib* (legal streams, typically translated "schools of law") and *shahada* (profession of faith), followed by the other four or five pillars of Islam.[26] Rehearsing a modified version of the centuries-old rant about the dangerous basis of Sufism, al-Zayd tweets, "Esoteric thought [*al-fikr al-batini*] . . . was undertaken for the splintering of the fundamental truths of Islam in terms of belief, worship, ideals, values, morals, and laws."[27] He goes on in the same vein for several more tweets. The horizon of his ethical and political identity, as well as the basis of Islamic law, is the state, a vastly different reality from that of the premodern critics of Sufism.

However, even as al-Zayd struggles to delimit the boundaries of Islam in relation to modern sovereignty, the internet demonstrates its capacity for showcasing contrary views, if not exactly serious debate. Al-Zayd's DNA episode was posted on YouTube, where it was met with both approving and disapproving comments. One of the most colorful criticisms was posted by "Alghomari," who writes in Arabic: "God curse this tiresome cheat. His unscrupulous shaykhs on the Permanent Fatwa Committee don't believe the fact that the Americans landed on the moon because those transmitting the news are Kafirs. Meanwhile we find him absolutely trusting in the American [DNA-testing] companies, making them an authority on the genealogy of Muslims."[28] Ironically, and beyond the vitriol, there is and has been much room for agreement between Sufis like the Alawis of Hadhramawt and strains of Wahhabism, particularly concerning the necessary distance from or propinquity to political power.[29]

The tendency of conservatives such as al-Zayd to highlight the heretical dangers of mystical obscurantism for achieving Islamic universalism elides, perhaps purposely, Sufism's far more troubling consequences for religious orthodoxy and political power. As we turn now to the Alawi Way, we will see, as the first Muslims saw, that there is something strangely simpler at work within and not against the broader normative order that could nonetheless disturb, destabilize, and even displace its power: genuine piety and faith.

Submission, Freedom, and Life of Struggle

Saba Mahmood's research in another context, the women's mosque movement in contemporary Egypt, demonstrates the unintended consequences that result from pursuing ethical practices of the self.[30] These women, without joining any social or political movement, unsettled the power of the patriarchal order both in the home and in the secular Egyptian state through seemingly benign "private" efforts to become better Muslims. *Pace* liberal, Marxist, and post-structuralist feminism, Mahmood argues that, paradoxically, the force of submission, in this case to God's will, opens a space of freedom and agency. In her account of pious women's lives, such concepts are intelligible only insofar as the social relations in which they are always already embedded are historically and ethnographically grasped, which in turn renders the concepts theoretically more capacious. The unexamined liberal genealogy of freedom and agency constrains most analyses of life in Muslim contexts within a normative horizon that makes transcending the religious a necessary step toward emancipation. Colonial and liberal assumptions about the proper political subject pervade studies of Islamic movements, rendering them reactionary a priori. However, studies such as Mahmood's show that arguments within Islam are potentially more generative for thinking life and freedom than the exhausted domain of liberalism.[31]

The tradition to which Sayyid Fadl belonged, from which I contend sprang an ambivalent relation to sovereignty, was far from liberalism's heartland. Nonetheless, as with Mahmood's piety movement, freedom and agency are operative concepts. Yet as I argue below, they are somewhat beside the point. The unity of life glimpsed as a foil to the Wahhabi critique in the present also constituted a limit to its political theology, which, not unlike liberalism, cannot disentangle the sovereignties of umma and state. In the project to return Fadl's descendants to their rightful place is embedded a history of Muslim religious and political life different from the terms in which it is conventionally cast. Excavating that history requires borrowing instruments that are typically in the anthropologist's toolkit.[32]

The hagiographic literature in Malayalam that constitutes part of the broader shrine complex at Mampuram—the control of which was in dispute in the early twenty-first century—offers a particular version of that history. The links among the Mappilas, sayyids, and a transregional Islam as viewed through hagiographies have been discussed in Chapter 4. Here we take up the text alluded to in that chapter as evincing a self-conscious counternarrative to the colonial, Indian Marxist, and Western readings of Mappila history, a text published after the 2005 return of Sayyid Sahl.

Commissioned by the new custodians of the Mampuram shrine, Malayamma and Panangangara's *Mampuram Thangal: Jeevitham Aathmiiyatha Poraattam* (The Mampuram sayyid: A life of spiritual struggle) was intended as the official biography of Sayyid Alawi and a claim on history. The foreword to the book by Malayamma states that the history of Muslims in Kerala may be divided into pre- and post-Mampuram sayyids, such that their age represented a "determining stage in the evolving history of the Mappilas. It was with them that a Mappila-Malabar way of life ended and a new . . . one began." The rupture that is indicated here posits the quest for a new, universal mode of existence as the other side of a fragmented history. The biographies of the Mampuram thangals are inscribed as nothing short of epochal and constitutional for Kerala Muslim history. In this attempt to craft an official history for a specific location within the wider geography of Islam and Sufism, early Muslim history was the unmistakable template.[33]

The more popular hagiographic literature we considered previously was less engaged with the historical, serving mainly as a guide to the power that was locally enshrined at Mampuram. Perhaps because of its relation to the current politics of the shrine, Dar al-Huda's more substantial biography sought to make a decisive claim for the saintly life of the "Mampuram Thangal," for which history was an important vehicle. History could aid in the demonstration of the cosmopolitan, transregional mission of the Alawis while simultaneously showing the importance of the latter's (trans)localization through temporally and spatially particular saint shrines. In other words, Sayyid Alawi belonged to a long diasporic Sufi Way, of Arab Tarim, of Malayali Mampuram, of antecedents and descendants, of guides and followers. And upon his death and the recognition of his saintliness, he also belonged to other Indian Ocean shrine locations and of life-as-other (al-akhira).

What I am calling the "official biography" runs to 669 pages, with a 23-page appendix of photos of mosques, graves, texts, and sacred objects—items that had belonged to Sayyid Alawi such as his swords, walking stick, and clogs. In the title of the book, Sayyid Alawi's life is already framed as a jihad, or struggle of the soul. The contents, however, are mainly historical accounts that extended beyond his lifetime, specifically relating the itinerary of Sayyid Fadl in quite some detail.

The document authorizing the biography appears immediately after the acknowledgments: the letter from Sayyid Sahl sent from Syria and congratulating the authors on completing the biography. It is reproduced in the Arabic original, followed by a Malayalam translation. Sahl meditates briefly on the transitory nature of nations, states, and earthly life, noting that if anything at all remains, it is in the form of "fading pages and lingering memories." He regards history as a capricious mode of remembering, which at times may remain "silent" as "disasters" unfold and "the sources of truth overflow." In his view, the biography of Sayyid Alawi represents in that flow of time a sudden moment of awakening to and "discovery" of the truth of a past life as if for the first time.[34]

The volume is divided into three "books" titled "Life," "Spirit," and "Struggle." The life history, which opens with the "family tree," naturally begins with the Prophet and the Islamic connection to Malabar through the Cheruman Perumal account. Then the Hadhrami and Ba Alawi linkages to Malabar are established, with individual chapters dedicated to the eighteenth-century migrants Sayyid Shaykh Jifri and Sayyid Hasan Jifri, before Sayyid Alawi's story is told. At this point the story is mostly filled with the names and trajectories of his family members, especially Sayyid Fadl. Sayyid Alawi's miracles are listed after the genealogical accounts. They include predicting the demise of British rule in India and the rise of communism in Kerala.[35] The transition to reporting his last days battling sickness and his death on a Sunday night (7 Muharram 1260 / January 27–28, 1844) is very quick.

He was ninety-four and had spent seventy-seven of those years in Kerala. As news of his passing spread, throngs of people of all faiths and from many regions began arriving in Mampuram; the funeral prayers had to be recited several times because of the large number of mourners. In one lifetime, Sayyid Alawi had transformed the Muslim community, and "that [time of devotion to its elevation] implanted his life [*jeevitham*] in the hearts of the people."[36] The final chapter of "Life" gives an account of the composition and publication of several memorials to Sayyid Alawi that were meant to accompany *mawlid* celebrations, all dating from the late nineteenth century and after. The list and brief descriptions of more than ten texts is preceded by an unusual definition of the *mawlid* (celebrations of the Prophet's and saints' birthdays): "Mawlids are the story of a genealogical tradition told through the remains of a saint" [*Paarampariyaththinde katha parrayunna thirushayshshippukalaanallo mawildugal*]." A prophetic hadith is also invoked as authorizing the recognition and remembrance of those who achieved closeness to God.[37]

The first chapter of "Spirit" traces the historical linkage between the Ba Alawi and the Qadiriyya, which Sayyid Alawi helped to spread in Malabar. The following two chapters relate how his spiritual life and his work as a shaykh of the Qadiri order were interrelated, that teaching his many disciples through example was how he acquired his reputation for saintliness, a reputation that went far beyond Malabar and earned him the status of *khutbusamaan* (qutb al-zaman). The hagiographers emphasize that scholars have noted the special blessing a place receives through its qutb; hence, "in Sayyid Alawi Thangal's time Malayalis obtained blessings from this [qutb]."[38] The status of qutb indicates that he was at once a local and global figure. "The truth is, [though, that] embedded in the Malayali earth, Sayyid Alawi Thangal observed and directed the affairs of not only here but of the entire world."[39]

As might be expected following such claims, accounts of his miracle work follow, providing evidence of his omnipresence. In one case, Sayyid Alawi sent a letter with a messenger to a holy man living atop Adam's Peak in Ceylon. When the messenger arrived on the mountaintop, he found Sayyid Alawi there, and when he returned to Mampuram with the reply, he was there too; to lessen the messenger's shock, Sayyid Alawi told him, "I will be everywhere."[40] The chapter ends with an account of Sayyid Alawi's miraculous intervention leading to a regime change in Mecca while never leaving Mampuram. He knew instantaneously when the ruler of Mecca had killed a good man in the Masjid al-Haram (likely intended was the dispensation following the Wahhabi-Saudi conquest of 1803). Because the spilling of blood in the sanctuary space was forbidden by sharia, this blatant violation naturally "flew on the winds." When it reached Sayyid Alawi, he screamed in the midst of a lesson to bewildered students that the person who defied the law should be removed from his position immediately. Only much later did they grasp the significance of his puzzling outburst.[41]

Sayyid Alawi's ability to disseminate proper Islamic civilization (*samskaranam*) in Malabar was due both to his assimilation and to maintaining his cultural difference. He mastered Malayalam within months of his arrival, but he continued to wear the "long robes of Arab countries" whenever he left the house. He wore Arab dress on his tours of the surrounding regions, where he observed the different ways of life. Through this knowledge—intensely local and of the present, on the one hand, and broadly transregional and historical (and a discursive tradition), on the other—Sayyid Alawi was able to mete out a kind of mutually recognized and accepted justice in seemingly intractable disputes.[42] The apparatus of mutual recognition, which aided conversion to Islam, did not magically appear but was, as the hagiography suggests later in the text, patiently constructed.[43]

Aathmiya navoththaanam (spiritual revival), *navajaagaranam* (reawakening)—these were Sayyid Alawi's achievements when Muslims lacked political power. This spiritual and cultural movement was felt not only in the Muslim centers of Eranaad, Walluwanaad, and Ponnani but throughout Malabar, including its remote hinterlands.[44] His own missionary peregrinations and those of his many disciples and companions, as well as the building of mosques, are credited as the vehicles for the diffusion of this Islamic renaissance and the increase in the Mappila population. The traditional distinction is made between miracle work (*muajisath*), the province solely of prophets such as Moses, Jesus, and Muhammad, and the granting of blessings (*karamath*), a "God-given aid" passed on to people through saints.[45] Nonetheless, the saintly capacity for performing acts popularly conceived as miraculous certainly served the broader apparatus of Sayyid Alawi's power, a source from which Mappilas and others drew power for themselves to act or even simply to subsist in the world.

In this account, the authority of Sayyid Alawi was based on a host of intersecting factors that could be reduced to racial or ethnic givens and moral-cultural choices that leveraged his status as stranger in the local context. His power, however, as distinct from authority, seems to have emanated from his actions and connectedness: learning, spiritual self-discipline, and movement through multidimensional space-time. In any case, his power and authority were in the end only as strong or as weak as the willingness and capacity of local interlocutors to read the signs and symbols of the Alawi sayyids, which had circulated around the Indian Ocean world for three centuries by the time of Sayyid Alawi's death.

Mappilas in turn became translocal through their reading and practice of distinguishing authoritative and powerful Muslim scholars from others.[46] A question that haunts the process of Sayyid Alawi's becoming a saint, however, is the degree to which the challenge from a colonial authority, with another claim to sovereignty and exercising a new form of power, mattered in the process of sayyid-becoming-saint. This is a historically specific question and a concern that was novel to the sayyid tradition at the turn of the nineteenth century.

Competing with the official biographical and more popular hagiographical representations of the Alawis of Mampuram is the vast corpus of colonial records. From these it is eminently clear that the power of the sayyids, wherever it emanated from, was to be reckoned with in life and in death. The recent struggles over control of the shrine complex referenced in the epigraph had a colonial precedent—a negative one. The British did not stop at restricting the entry of Fadl's associates and descendants into Malabar; colonial authorities effectively shut down the shrine after his expulsion in 1852. Conolly wrote: "My policy ever since the Tangul left, has been to let Tiruvangadi, so far as it was a place of religious veneration and support, fall into obscurity and neglect. With this view, I have prevented the only one of the Tangul's connexions who remained behind when he went to Arabia from paying any visits to that place . . . The name and prestige of the Tangul will no doubt die out . . . if not kept in recollection by the exertion of his family and adherents."[47] The rise of pan-Islamism and Abdulhamid's appeals to Indian Muslims a few decades later may have convinced the colonial authorities to revise their policy, supporting the reform-minded in Malabar as moderate bulwarks against potential fanatics.[48] The shrine was in turn permitted to reopen and to be renovated, while Sayyid Alawi's descendants were banned from returning.

Returns

After failed attempts to return on their own in the nineteenth and early twentieth centuries, a movement to bring Fadl's heirs back to Mampuram began with Muhammad Abdurahman Sahib in 1933. Sahib was a nationalist activist and president of the Kerala Congress Committee. He convened a public meeting in the Calicut town hall on January 16. With thirty-three people present, the Mampuram Restoration Committee was formed, which issued an invitation to heirs of Fadl to return to India. Fadl's son Sayyid Ali accepted the invitation, traveling from Cairo via Colombo to Madras and reaching Kozhikode by train. He saw Collector Russell, who demanded that he leave Malabar, which he unwillingly agreed to do. Abdurahman Sahib arranged a house for him in the French territory of Mahé and went so far as attempting to procure French citizenship for Sayyid Ali. "After eight months of being away from his kith and kin, his homesickness [girhathurathwam] grew intolerable so he went back to Egypt, where he died." In the 1934 National Assembly and 1937 Provincial Assembly elections, the "Mampuram problem" was a heated topic of debate. Throughout his life, Sahib continued his efforts to bring back the rightful holders of the Mampuram properties.[49]

Although Fadl's heirs' attempts to come back on their own ended in failure, their stories illumine a changing understanding of return, which in turn maps onto a reordering of the world. The British began receiving petitions and visa applications from Fadl and his family as early as 1893 and continued to deal with their requests to be allowed to return to Dhofar and then to India until at least 1925. While *Madhribhumi* offers a decidedly postcolonial view, with the attendant sense of national injury and redress, the treatment of their return in British sources provides a view of the changing international and imperial context in the years leading up to World War I and after. Since several of the Alawi letters and petitions were included in these sources for comment and reply by the relevant offices, a window is also opened onto the diasporic experience within the changing geopolitical context. The folder containing all these files, though located in the "Political and Secret" series for the year 1912, propels one into the future, as the story of the family is taken up to the year 1925. Perhaps as the result of an initial misfiling of a petition received in 1912 from Sayyid Sahl, Fadl's eldest son, who had left India with him in 1852, this document seems to have been lost in the bureaucratic shuffle until it was addressed internally during what seems to have been a pruning of files and receipt of new petitions from other family members at the end of 1924:

> This paper appears to belong to your Dept. [Economic and Overseas] rather than to P. & J. [Political and Judicial] or Political, dealing as it does with the question of refusing visas for India to two Arabs who, it is feared, would "disturb the peace" in Malabar if allowed to go there. They had already received visas for India from the responsible authority at Port Said and at Baghdad. Would you be prepared to take the paper for the required action? If so, a copy of it might be sent to this Dept for attachment to the past records of the *outlaw*, Saiyid Fazil, and his family.[50] (emphasis added)

A list of telegrams and meetings pertaining to previous attempts to return and the decision to refuse entry reveals that members of Fadl's family had made efforts in that direction in 1893, 1905, 1907, 1912, and 1919.[51]

After their failure to secure a return to Dhofar in the 1880s by flying under the radar, Fadl and Sahl began in the 1890s to petition the British directly, going all the way up to the prime minister and the queen for assistance. Sahl went to Egypt in January 1895 to seek the intercession of Lord Cromer in the family's bid to regain Dhofar. He met there with Milhem Shakour Bey, who had the ear of officials at the British residency, serving under Kitchener as Arabic secretary of the sirdar (during preparations for the campaign to retake Sudan from the Mahdists). That in the closing years of the nineteenth century the Indo-Arab Muslim Sahl Pasha and the Lebanese-Egyptian Christian Milhem Shakour Bey (whose brother Mansour Shakour had been a Christian missionary in Egypt before his early death in 1873) should have a conversation in Cairo about Alawi family history, Malabar, and Dhofar in Ottoman but British-occupied Egypt was testament to the still-unsettled terms of sovereignty during the height of imperial hubris. Shakour seemed rather taken by Sahl and his family's narrative.[52] Cromer was advised by the Foreign Office on the recommendation of the India Office not to meet with Sahl, who was staying at the Koubbeh Palace as a guest of Khedive Abbas II.[53] He left Egypt in the summer, unsuccessful in his mission, and returned to Istanbul with the khedive's entourage.[54]

The anxieties of the Raj and the India Office regarding Fadl and his heirs' efforts to return to Dhofar heightened in March 1896 as the same tribe that had forced Fadl out in 1879 rebelled against the governor sent by Muscat and raised the Turkish flag, calling for Ottoman protection.[55] An earlier report indicates that the revolt was popular and that Fadl's emissary was there with his flag. The Omani sultan pleaded with the British to "warn the Kathiris that they will not be allowed to establish Said Fadhl at Dhofar as their ruler."[56] India wanted Istanbul warned that the "Moplah Outlaw will not be permitted to go there and that no intrigues on his part or foreign interference will be tolerated."[57] However, Ambassador Currie deemed it undiplomatic to convey this message when his sources indicated that Istanbul had no designs on Dhofar and that Sayyid Fadl seemed to be staying put.[58] A rift concerning Middle Eastern affairs that would widen between London and Bombay-Delhi might be perceived in this exchange of telegrams.[59] For our purposes, it is sufficient to note how the mere prospect of Sayyid Fadl the Moplah Outlaw's return continued to cause significant perturbation at the highest levels of imperial governments in London, Bombay, Istanbul, and Muscat.

The 1905 petition, also from Sayyid Sahl, was directly addressed to King Edward. The king in fact reviewed the "prayer" to allow the Alawis to "visit all British territory and particularly the Malabar District" and decided he could not "issue any commands" after the family's history was discussed in council, and the secretary of state for India recommended denying the request.[60] The 1912 petition was addressed to the secretary of state for India, and again London agreed with Madras and Delhi that "in the interests of the public peace none of the descendants of the Mappilla outlaw should be permitted to visit [M]alabar." If anything, Sahl was persistent, and he tried his luck again with the next British sovereign, King George, in March 1919.[61]

Sayyid Ali Hyder Bey, whom the Mampuram Restoration Committee invited to India in 1933, had made a previous attempt to return to Malabar in April of 1925. His mother accompanied him on that trip, but they were only able to get as far as Colombo. The government of Madras recommended to the government of Ceylon that he be instructed to reveal his intent and itinerary and to seek the permission of the former before proceeding to India. Sayyid Ali complied, informing the government that his destination was Malabar and his aim was to reclaim custodial rights over the Mampuram Maqam and its revenues, as well as his share of the properties belonging to his late father. He also asserted that Fadl's half-sister's grandson Sayyid Ahmad b. Hasan Jifri of Calicut had appropriated his share and was trying to keep him out of Malabar.[62] After consultation, the Malabar magistrate concluded that the return of Fadl's heirs would be a danger to "the public peace": "The Mambram Mosque is inseparably connected in the minds of the Mappillas with the previous history of the Mappilla outrages. A descendant of Sayid Fuzul would certainly be regarded with veneration by Mappillas of the rebellion area and his presence would stimulate fanatical tendencies. Further, as his avowed object is to challenge the established rights of others to property, faction would be added to fanaticism and the results might well be disastrous."[63] In the wake of the Mappila Rebellion of 1921, which according to some historians began as a protest against British attempts to repress the pan-Islamic Khilafat movement, Fadl's descendants stood no chance of gaining entry into Malabar. Meanwhile, Madras requested advice from Delhi on laws that could be used to detain Ali if he entered India without its consent. The sections of the Moplah Outrages Act of 1859, which had been passed to disarm the Muslim population and collectively punish acts of rebellion in Malabar, did not apply in this case. Madras queried whether it could use the Madras State Prisoners Regulation of 1819 if it became necessary to take action.

Nevertheless, an extensive report was compiled in order to demonstrate that the claims Ali was making were unfounded: that Fadl had disposed of all his property by 1880 at the latest. Moreover, to discount the exclusive claims of Fadl's sons to the Mampuram Maqam, a genealogy of the family was drawn up showing the current relations with the Jifris descended from Sayyid Alawi, whose tomb-mosque complex (which Ali termed a *dargah*) was in dispute. The conclusion was that Sayyid Ali was merely using his property claim as a pretext to return to Malabar, presumably with the unspecified objective of causing trouble. Another brother, Sayyid Muhammad, who was traveling on a French passport issued in Latakia, Syria, and with a visa for Baghdad issued by the British consul general in Beirut, had managed to reach Bombay on August 29, 1925, with an Indian visa obtained from the passport officer in Baghdad.

Unsurprisingly, the government of India sanctioned the use of the State Prisoners Regulation to take action against Fadl's family.[64] Madras and the government of India wanted London to put all members of this family on a blacklist of personae non gratae that was apparently updated regularly and distributed to passport and visa offices throughout the empire. In 1919, London had already decided that petitions from the Alawis for the right of return could be refused without consulting India, since it had made its position clear in previous years. This move reflected a larger process by which a distinct Middle

East policy was carved out in relation to new imperial and international realities on the ground after World War I.

The dismemberment of the Ottoman Empire and the formation of the League of Nations and the mandates system, in which Britain assumed a leading Middle Eastern role, realigned the significance of Gulf-India relations to reflect the London-Cairo-Jerusalem-Aden-Baghdad axis. Interestingly, even in this case of return denied, as per Indian request, the geographical location of Dhofar received comment, indicating that the view from London had begun to matter more in Middle Eastern affairs: "It may be noted that while the memorialist [Sayyid Sahl] speaks of Zaffar as being in Yemen, Sir R. Ritchie [an old India hand and undersecretary of state for India, who had written a minute on the Alawis' desire to return in 1905] refers to it as being under the control of Muscat. As a matter of fact, it seems to be in *Hadramaut* at the extreme limit of the sphere of influence of Muscat."[65] The interests of the Indian Raj in the Middle East as regarded from Bombay, Calcutta, and then Delhi were no longer prioritized in the same way by the imperial center, which from 1919 was to some extent legally obliged—and politically committed by being a driving force behind the new international order—to treat developments in Arabia as politically linked to its mandates in Palestine-Transjordan and Iraq.[66] The politics of the Great Game in the pre–World War I period had already necessitated a shift toward regarding relations with Arabs, particularly the "notables," from a more global perspective than India was capable of.

The Ottoman drift away from the British camp, which could be dated to the latter's occupation of Cyprus after the Russo-Turkish War (1877–78), and the subsequent intensification of competition for Arab support is one way to explain the British government's entertaining petitions from the Alawis at the highest levels. So when the author of a Political Department minute wrote in 1911, "And although *it appears necessary* to transmit the present application for their [Madras's] report, it is hardly to be expected that their view will have changed [since 1905]" (emphasis added), the need for an Indian opinion was being gauged in terms of the contemporary politics of alliances in the Arab subcontinent.[67]

These politics of alliances assumed a new territorial imperative in the aftermath of the war, which did not bode well for diasporic futures in the Indian Ocean world or the new post-Ottoman Middle East. The trajectory of Fadl's son Sahl's arguments in support of his right of return to India poignantly reveal how the fortunes of even a notable family of sayyids shifted and forced a revision of their sense of historical purpose and the purpose of history. With the forced abdication of Sultan Abdulhamid in 1909, Sahl decided it was time to move the family from Istanbul. Once settled in Latakia on the Syrian coast, he wrote a petition to the secretary of state for India in 1911 after consultations with the long-serving British vice-consul there, N. Vitale, who delivered it to the consul general in Beirut, H. A. Cumberbatch, who forwarded it on to the ambassador in Istanbul, Gerard A. Lowther, who relayed it to London.

Cumberbatch's cover letter added something peculiar based on Vitale's intelligence. Apparently, the "Muslims" in Latakia received Sahl warmly at first, because he was a sayyid; however, when they discovered he was not a genuine descendant of the Prophet's family, their attitude changed. No further details were given about this intriguing local politics of recognition and who the relevant parties were in authorizing originals and outing copies. Nevertheless, Vitale reported to Cumberbatch that the downward turn in levels of hospitality along with the smallness of the stipend from the Turkish government were Sahl's immediate reason for wanting to return to India.[68]

By the time of his move to Syria, Sahl seems to have developed a keen sense of the nascent international order. He used the context of the Great Powers' relations with their subject Muslim populations to advance his claim for compensation and restitution of his legal right of residency in India. Here he also dropped a clue as to the possible origin of the challenge to his status as sayyid. After reproducing the letter rejecting his 1904 petition to the king, which ended with a note of "sincere friendship," he wrote:

> I demand consequently your consideration of the matter as justice requires, and if the Indian Government will also approve I demand from the Great English Government to allow me a sum of money for my being banished, after a due enquiry into my standing, the revenue of my properties, my influence and prerogative and then to be treated on the same footing as my equals who have been treated by other Powers such as France has treated Ul-Sayd Abdul-Kader, Emir of Algeria when they exiled him from his country after a long war with the said Power. As for me, I have nothing with the exalted Government of England besides the calumnies and intrigues against me. I demand from the Great and just Power of England who rules over millions of Moslems to do justice to the family of their Prophet so as to oblige them.[69]

Competition among Sharifian families heightened as the Great Game intensified and local alliances were sought in the region by multiple major powers. Of the transregional migrants to Syria, the Algerian family of the world-famous resistance leader Abd al-Qadir al-Jaza'iri became relatively wealthy in exile, aided by French subsidies beginning in 1856, and played a significant role as intermediaries among local communities and between them and imperial powers.[70] Even after Abd al-Qadir's death in 1883, the al-Jaza'iris retained their status among the leading Damascene families; the grandson Amir Said, for example, headed a delegation that sought to mediate between rebels and French Mandate officials during the Great Syrian Revolt.[71] In the case of Fadl's descendants, the long period spent in Istanbul obviated the potential for developing a local Arab constituency, which in turn seems to have diminished their value in the network of notables regionally and alliances internationally.

Appreciation of that deficit perhaps made India seem a more promising home, since it was there that the family had had an independent, historically deep base. And given their brief yet significant political investment there in the 1870s, in later petitions Sahl proposed Dhofar as another, albeit less attractive, option in case the British were yet again to refuse the family entry into India. Distancing himself more explicitly from his father's anti-British stance and from transregional Islamic movements also seemed necessary after the rejection of the 1912 petition. In 1919, he tried once again to place the family on the radar of the king-emperor, but for good measure he also sent a letter under separate cover to the "Minister of Justice."[72]

In the letter to King George V, Sahl references the petition from 1904 to King Edward and how it was rejected because of the intervention of the Government of Madras, information that was relayed to him by the embassy in Istanbul.[73] He indicates that there was a perfect conspiracy involving Madras and Malabari "libellers" who bore "ill will" toward Fadl's heirs. The government's unchanging position was based on misinformation passed on by those who did not want to give up the benefits they accrued from "our name, good will and the income of our lands."[74] The first agent for the family who was responsible for managing their assets was Sayyid Hasan b. Ahmad Jufri, who, Sahl explains, was dismissed with the help of the British embassy in Constantinople and replaced with Sayyid Ahmad b. Abd al-Rahman Jufri.[75]

He proceeds to relate the history of the family since its expulsion from India in order to reveal the "oppression, unfairness and damages" they have had to endure as a result. He mentions a letter Queen Victoria had sent thanking Fadl for the care of her subjects in Dhofar, to which he replied from Constantinople and received another letter from her "most graciously ordering our welfare to be forwarded in all ways."[76] He links Victoria's interest in their welfare to Fadl's inability to return to Dhofar, insinuating that Sultan Abdulhamid was suspicious of their ties and "ordered that my father should not leave Constantinople."[77] He appeals to the sense of "right and justice" of the king to help him resolve his case. Then an unusually sharp distinction, elaborated further in the next petition, is drawn between him and his father: "Should the reasons for which my father was prohibited from returning to [Mal]abar have been *political*, I was then only ten years old and had nothing to do with them. But as the Madras Government did not inform my father of the reasons for which he was kept away, I claim my rights at the courts of justice to all damages, the income of my lands during sixty-five years' absence, as well as any value to which our name and good will may have been put in our absence" (emphasis added).[78] Sahl is at once acknowledging the local legacy of the Alawis in Malabar and disavowing it for its anti-imperialist implications as perceived by the colonial government. The latter required severing the "political" Fadl from other Alawis, who were more pliable and docile.

When Sahl received the same reply he had received in previous years, he wrote again to the king toward the end of 1919.[79] In this correspondence he essentially disavows his father as stubbornly anti-British and as a result foolish in his actions. In one fell swoop Sahl dismantles his family's history of principled rejection of British imperialism as simply the product of one man's obstinacy. Examples are given to demonstrate that Sahl would have made different choices.

He first relates how Fadl refused to accept a stipend of one thousand pounds a month from the British government. He intimates that it was offered in 1854 as just compensation through the high commissioner in Jeddah after he revealed that Fadl and his family would not be allowed to return to India. Then, after the Dhofar episode, Sahl claims his father had developed "intimate relations of friendship" with Lord Dufferin, the British ambassador in Istanbul. The latter was apparently prepared to allow the family to return to Dhofar as agents of the British and presented terms that Sahl deems "advantageous" but that Fadl, "who was then the favorite of Abdul Hamid," rejected:

> Being the eldest of my brothers, I venture, for myself and on behalf of my brothers, to ask to be granted either of the favours which our late father refused. During his life we had to give unquestioning obedience to our father's decisions, whether we liked it or not, but now that he is dead and that we are responsible for ourselves, we beg to accept the offer which our father then rejected. We do not know the grounds which actuated Great Britain

to prohibit us from going back to India. If this prohibition was meant for our late father (and it cannot be otherwise, because we were all young then), this prohibition should cease by the very fact that the man aimed at died.[80]

Sahl's disavowal of Fadl and embrace of the British, at least rhetorically, suggests that a desperation had set in after the war, surely due in part to the end of Ottoman stipends to the family.[81] Charting a future course for them in a post-Ottoman world thus entailed severing ties to that past and reconstructing their history as individual Alawis unbeholden to the ways of prior generations.

Feeling that he had accomplished that objective, Sahl makes three demands of the king:

1. To be compensated for the loss which we have sustained through our being expelled from India. (I leave this to the wisdom of H.M. The King.)

2. To go to India in order to remove the reasons (of which we are unaware) of our expulsion.

3. If it is not possible to go to India I should be glad to come to terms and go to Zaffar.

In return, he offers to pledge his "loyalty" to the British government in India, and in Dhofar to "strive for the progress of the country and for the enhancement of the prestige of the King."[82]

As noted briefly above, after Sahl's death his brothers continued unsuccessfully in the 1920s to try to break through the British surveillance net to reach and stay in India. According to *Madhribhumi*, in the 1930s Muslims in Kerala launched their own campaign to support the return of the Alawis. After the deportation of Sayyid Ali, the Mampuram Restoration Committee managed in 1936 to bring Fadl's great-grandsons Sainul Abidin and Sayyid Fasal as far as Madras.[83] The colonial officials there deported them on arrival. A pamphlet issued by the Kerala Muslim Association of Kozhikode in 1938 gave an account of their attempted return and reproduced the letter from the two addressing Malabar's Muslims.[84] In the letter, the brothers portray their family as wandering in distant lands (Zafar, Hijaz, Misr, Turkey, Syria, Iraq) for over half a century after their exile from India. They note that the Alawis had always advised the unity of Muslim society (*sanghadana*) irrespective of race and sect and preached the importance of doing good works. They emphasize the fact that they were never troublemakers but always counseled otherwise, and that if permitted to enter Malabar the British would be able to witness their support of the status quo.

In 1936, another letter was sent to the Kerala Muslim Association, signed jointly by Sainul Abidin, Fasal, and Muhammad Mahdi. In it they express their desire to return to Mampuram. They add, "We know that Sayyid Ahmad Aatakoya Thangal has through trickery [taken possession of our property and] is enjoying its fruits."[85] They mention that two family members had come to India in 1931: these were their sister and grandmother—the wife of Sahl Pasha. This means the authors of the letter and the sister mentioned were all Fadl's great-grandchildren through Sahl's son Ja'far Bey.[86] That trip too met with no success, and by 1931 the large family seems to have been suffering; the Great Depression must have shrunk their fortunes further. The letter continues in more dramatic language, which *Madhribhumi* paraphrases: "On a ship from Bombay to Karachi they actually run into Aatakoya Thangal. He tells them first they don't really have much in Malabar. Then he tries to blame others for their misfortune and paint himself as their advocate but they say that God will give him his due because they know all about his ill-gotten gains."[87] The article then turns to the reflections of al-Sharif Muhammad Sahl al-Fasal, the Alawi who visited Kerala in 2005 and great-grandson of the Sahl who had been so persistent in petitioning the British government for his family to be allowed to return to India.

In keeping with the long-established tradition of seeking recognition by locating and authorizing oneself in relation to kinsmen, Sahl provides information about his family tree. Sayyid Fadl left India with two male children, Sahl and Hasan, from his first marriage. Five more sons were born abroad after the second marriage: Muhammad al-Fatih, Sayyid Ali Bey, Muhammad Yusuf Bey, Ahmad Bey, and Muhammad Basha. The first two died without leaving any heirs. The others, including Sahl and Hasan, left heirs who are now living in Latakia. Four generations of Fadl's family numbering a hundred persons were said to be living under the same roof! In 2005, as the article went to press, Sainul Abidin (93) and Fasal (92) were still alive.

The historical details remembered by Sharif Muhammad were slightly at variance with the information his great-grandfather, Sahl, had given in his letters. For example, he credits Sahl's brother, Hasan Basha, with plotting the family's course out of Turkey and only after the caliphate fell.[88] Latakia was considered suitable in terms of climate and location. He does suggest that Sahl had departed Istanbul earlier by sea, bound for Jeddah, but that his boat broke down in a Lebanese port, where he ended up staying for three years before he was able to make his way to Latakia. Fadl's other son, Muhammad Yusuf Bey, also left Istanbul with his family and went to Latakia. He recounts Muhammad's attempt to return, prevented by the British, as recounted above. He adds that on his way back from India Muhammad received an invitation from "Hasan Onnaman Rajav"[89] to reside in Baghdad and to serve as the director of Islamic *awqaf* (charitable endowments). He accepted the post, and his line of the family was still in Baghdad in 2005.

Sharif Muhammad's grandfather, Ja'far (Sahl's son), chose to make Beirut his home in the post-Ottoman years. Nonetheless, he also attempted to return to Mampuram. He reached Madras and even met with the chief secretary. Before any decision was made, however, he fell ill and returned to Lebanon, where three months later he died. Subsequently Ja'far's family also joined the clan in Latakia.

Muhammad notes that his father (Fasal) and his uncle (Sainul Abidin), who were alive at the time of publication, still longed to see Mampuram. Since the failed 1930s efforts to bring the family back, no other attempts had been made, and the family had essentially been forgotten until the present. According to *Madhribhumi*, the parties who assumed the role of custodians of the shrine, under the title of Khan Bahadur, were British toadies who tried to bury the significance of the family.

Conclusion

Efforts to return by and efforts to make return possible for the Alawis might be narrated as failure in the face of a powerful new dispensation in the Indian Ocean world, the sovereignty of states. The positioning of Fadl's lineage might be read in terms of purely worldly interests, whether from the perspective of the family or the Mappilas, as suggested by the story's "end." In the postcolonial period following World War II, the family finally found a secure footing in Syria and Iraq, hence abandoning their efforts to return to India. Conversely, the independence of India evacuated the anticolonial imperative from the Mappila-led campaign to rectify the neglect of Sayyid Fadl, a "courageous leader of the freedom struggle," rendering it defunct.[90] And as the *Madhribhumi* report essentially reveals, the recent return efforts might be regarded in terms of a struggle over the custodial rights to the Mampuram Maqam, which simply made the family pawns to be maneuvered on a legal-moral battlefield involving different Mappila constituencies. The question to be decided in 2005 was whether the shrine complex should continue as a waqf-administered institution, become public property, or pass to the Chemmad educational trust, Dar al-Huda. These conclusions—of failure and of worldly interest as prime motivator—are all possible in light of the accounts offered above. Once the

Wahhabi discourse, emanating from Saudi Arabia but exceeding its official state representation and bounded territorial spaces, is also factored in, then sayyid sovereignty appears to be a long-lost cause. The genetic encoding and decoding of life's meaning may mean the final victory of a kind of sovereignty that began its march forward three to four centuries earlier.

In these human-centered accounts a key actor is absent or given only a bit part: the shrine itself. The Mampuram Maqam in fact was and remains a stage unto itself, on which theological disputes, economic interests, and the political ramifications of state sovereignty are played out under the watchful though buried eye of a departed and returned, singular and plural, life and nonlife. On this stage that beckons to its own audience, surely the human agents seeking its control or some authority to represent it are the bit players. The Mampuram Maqam, like similar shrines around the Indian Ocean world and beyond, focuses claims of and on the power that paradoxically belongs everywhere and nowhere at once, which in turn enables the further paradox of a relation to sovereignty that is also a release from it. The life, or unity of life, that appears at the center of those paradoxes is the subject of the next chapter. Suffice it to say here that the sovereignty of God did not give up the ghost or the ground, as the grand secularization thesis would have it, nor was it fully domesticated by a disciplined clergy subject to modern government—perhaps because the story was never and is not about sovereignty after all.

In the shrine, in the relations of devotees and supplicants who make entreaties to it, we are allowed to imagine a vortex of powerful energy that is neither divine nor human, a product of the conjoined efforts of many souls and many things unfolding as many and one across eons. It provides a glimpse of what we have termed the unity of life. The latter is not reducible to God or to the mystical life and mysticism associated with Sufism, though this is the specific route by which we have sought to obtain our glimpse. In this context, the danger of the unity of life lies not in doctrinal departures or a reconstitution of hierarchies beyond the legal-political order but precisely in a potentiality that promises a state no longer tethered to the law nor to master-disciple relations . . . nor possibly to sovereignty of any kind.

6 "This True and Merciful Way"

Sovereignty and Life's End(s)

Unzur kayfa faddalna ba'dahum ala ba'din wa l-al-akhira akbar darajatin w-akbar tafdilan (See how We have preferred some over others, but life-as-other is the greatest achievement and the most preferred.)
—*Quran, 17:21*

Fa innahu al-iksir li-lqalb al-jari? (It is an elixir for the tormented heart.)
—*Fadl Ibn Alawi*

ONE OF MY LAST VISITS to Sayyid Alawi's shrine in Mampuram began with a sumptuous lunch and a lecture at the Darul Huda Islamic University in August 2015.[1] According to its promotional literature, "Darul Huda was established in 1986 with a cherished dream of revival of [the] Islamic educational system in the country, where Islamic institutions were neither appealing to the soul nor to the world."[2] The global and universal ambitions of its revivalist mission were laid down by the founder, Dr. U. Bapputty Haji, in a self-conscious desire to reverse prior histories of empire and orientalism:

> Insha Allah, I aspire that, a bunch of highly talented scholars coming out of this institution; a group quintessentially grown up under and groomed by the strict directives of Islam; the sheer favour of Allah the Almighty would flow out of their veins; with sterling behavior, eloquence and writing ingenuity, they would capture the hearts of society. A day will come, when the meadows of this institution would be crowned with white skinned Europeans, dark-skinned Africans and blonde-haired Americans, who flock to this citadel of knowledge to imbibe its pleasures and sweetness.[3]

Dr. Haji set his religious sights high, though one may be forgiven if one hears the language of the global higher-education administrator in an Indian Muslim register. While there was no sighting of blond-haired Americans imbibing pleasures, the college did have the air of a thriving institution. Recognition of the problem of secularization and "academic dependency on the Western countries" forms the backdrop to Darul Huda's mission to "revive [the] Islamic way of understanding the world, not merely as a way of life, but also a way of knowledge."[4]

The students were mainly from Kerala, though there were some from North India and instructors who had trained there or in Malaysia and Egypt.[5] My talk was quite basic, covering the life and times of Sayyid Fadl. Nonetheless, it was necessary to switch between English, Arabic, and Malayalam in order to be intelligible. In the question-and-answer session that followed, I gained a better sense of the students' priorities and their anxieties about my presentation of Fadl's life and its relationship to power. I had tried to dislocate the Alawi story from local and national frames and to suggest what we might gain, in terms of our understanding of history and of life, as a result. Their questions, while indicating a certain amount of knowledge, also revealed a certain amount of forgetting, mainly expressed in silences.[6] Or more precisely, the historical Alawis were not especially the objects of memory or even interest beyond a vague understanding of their Arab origins and migration to India once upon a time. Moreover, in the context of reformist Islam in which the students' formation was taking place, the saintly quality of Sayyid Alawi and the continuation of his baraka also seemed to be deemphasized. The question of authorship of the *Al-Sayf al-battar* collection of fatwas (discussed in Chapter 2) was of far greater importance to them than a past that had been superseded or a Sufi saintly tradition that was under attack from elsewhere.

Or perhaps authorship was indeed connected to a present danger that I did not fully grasp at the time. The students' interest in *Al-Sayf al-battar* may have had something to do with its circulation through cyberspace as a "jihadist" text since its translation in 2009 as *The Slicing Sword: Against the One Who Forms Allegiances with the Disbelievers and Takes Them as Supporters Instead of Allah, His Messenger, and the Believers.*[7] The author's name is given as Eminent Scholar Abd Allah ibn Abd al-Bari al-Ahdal (d. 1271 AH) and the text is provided with a foreword by Anwar al-Awlaki. Awlaki was an imam and US citizen living in Yemen; he was killed by the US in 2011.[8]

The forgetting was of a past that was at once genealogical, historical, and global. The forgotten kinships and the forgotten history of Alawi entanglements with empire were not the result of some amnesia induced by modernization, nationalism, and the attendant religious reform impulses that seemed to overtake the worlds of Islam from the late nineteenth century onward.[9] A specific politics of the present linked to an economy of saints' shrines conditioned and perhaps even determined the students' knowledge or lack thereof. This politics of the present, while specific, was not exclusively local or without precedent, as recent studies of the Indian Ocean's sacred geography have shown.[10] It is simultaneously entangled in two *longue durée* processes of globalization and universalization that have played crucial roles in determining the economy (and map) of Muslim saints as well as other objects.[11] One of the processes is the mission of Islam, which at the time of researching and writing this book was going strong well over a millennium since its launch. The other is the secular state project, which, whenever and wherever its beginning, could hardly be avoided by anyone on the planet by the interwar period of the twentieth century.[12] The form and content of the knowledge that has accompanied these two massively important phenomena have changed over time whenever and wherever their powers waxed and waned. It is in order to track these changes and approach the truth of a power that evades total capture by either process that we have made forays into the present.

History's continuing tendency, conditioned in part by economic and political necessity, to play handmaiden to national(ist) projects relies heavily on foundational narratives that in turn rely on establishing a cordon sanitaire between putatively self-evident pasts and presents. Often the law and history share and mutually reinforce the foundations, which makes them fundamental discourses for the reproduction of modern sovereignty. We return in this final chapter to Sayyid Fadl's negotiation of divine and imperial sovereignty in the face of various dangers, while also continuing to try to gain a glimpse through him of the unity of life.

Sayyid or Sultan for "an India in the Arab Subcontinent"?

Let us begin at the peak of Fadl's "political career," when he was amir of Dhofar in the 1870s. Using the lens of the political-as-career to regard the role he assumed and the activities he pursued can from the outset prejudice an appreciation of these as anything but examples of worldly power grabs. Certainly, the wider geopolitical universe enfolding Fadl in its warp and weft involved dynamic relations among empires, regional powers, tribes, city-states, and mobile religious men that were already several decades old by the latter third of the nineteenth century and had transformed the political relations of the Indian Ocean world, including the Middle East. One could say that as the Tanzimat came to an end of sorts in 1876, with bankruptcy and a constitution, the modern political subject had already become a globally intelligible creature. It marked a future horizon, new ends of sovereignty that departed dramatically from the past and would touch every life on the planet. Nonetheless, the confrontation or negotiation between Islamic and secularized Christian traditions of conceptualizing sovereignty, which we have argued fundamentally shaped the meaning, direction, and outcome of global politics, was for many actors still unfinished business in the 1870s.

Sayyid Fadl's experience after the 1840s with the new kind of sovereignty emerging from within imperial projects would suggest that it was with a sense of unease at what the world was becoming that he set out from the Hijaz for the easternmost part of the Hadhramawt in 1876, heeding the call of tribes (the Ghara, the Kathiri, and others) from the area of Dhofar on the frontier of the Sultanate of Oman. These tribes or Muslims, depending on the type of relation sought with or within the group, did not reveal much about themselves—at least as far as the historical record shows. The call itself, however, spoke volumes, as it was made through ancient channels that reflected a complex dynamic of power irreducible to the purely political or religious or economic. This in turn made the labeling of these groups as tribes and/or Muslims contingent on the specific relationship that was being (re)established. It is as warring tribes that the story began, as Muslims that Fadl's intercession was intelligible and possible, and as unruly and rebellious tribes that it ended.

The confusion that Fadl experienced in the process of assuming responsibility for the lives and property of others only to have them revolt against his rule is revealed in a rare letter preserved in the India Office Records at the British Library in both the original and translation, written to Sultan Turki of Oman on 24 Muharram 1296 (January 17, 1879).[13] While some historians would take the request for military aid in the letter as the key to unlocking Fadl's true intentions, I am more interested in his professed surprise at the breaking of the oath originally taken by the rebellious parties.[14]

Seema Alavi interprets the episode in essentially the same way as British officials who were keeping tabs on the Arabian coast and reporting to London and Bombay.[15] The role of British agents in fomenting rebellion and dissension among tribes is barely considered, nor are Fadl's accusations to that effect. In a long chapter, Alavi analyzes Fadl's actions under the rubric of "career broker," under which she also represents several other Muslim figures who seemingly played imperial powers against each other for personal gain. Fadl is said to have "nurtured the political ambition of becoming the independent ruler of Dhofar" and "was in the end a typical transcultural and transimperial entrepreneur.[16] While these may be useful categories for making legible the mobile networks of Muslim activists and scholars at the twilight of empire as "global rather than simply pan-Islamist," much work remains to be done to flesh out how in fact figures such as Fadl viewed the world around them.[17] Alavi's often harsh interpretations of Fadl's motives are shaped by a nearly exclusive reliance on British records in English.[18] She writes, "Fadl played on Ottoman political ambitions in order to further his own ends in the region. He hoped to put Muscat and the Ottomans onto a collision course and then reap the benefits."[19] How Fadl conceived these "ends," political, personal, and religious, appears more nuanced when his writings in Arabic and Ottoman sources are also analyzed.[20]

In Fadl's letter to Sultan Turki, a key phrase was omitted in the English translation. Even though the latter claims only to be a "translated purport" of the original, that is, capturing the gist, it is for the most part a literal word-for-word translation; hence, if for no other reason than querying the practice of colonial translations from Arabic, the elision is worth considering.[21] When the translator reached Fadl's statement of the oath in religious terms, these terms were not rendered into English. Emphasizing the binding nature of the oath taken by the tribes, Fadl noted that the alliance with him was "bi ahd Allah al-matin wa urwat Allah al-wuthqa ala al-kitab bi-l-sam'a wa-l-ta'a." With these few words he expressed shock while simultaneously conveying a millennial tradition of conceptualizing power, so they are weighty words to gloss over as if "the oath" were always the same in every place and time.[22] Rather, the oath was an oath here because it was with "God the Steadfast and the unbreakable bond of God in the Book that [they will] hear and obey." An entire universe of revelation and knowledge, of reciprocity and trust, of promise and faith was contained in the language of the oath. Thus the oath's significance and the shock of its breaking can only be appreciated if the specificity of that language, its signature, is preserved and decoded.[23] Therein were terms of divine sovereignty facing their "modern" translation and transformation.

The subsequent request for military aid from the Sultanate neither invalidates the tradition of the oath nor establishes Sayyid Fadl as a typical opportunist driven only by interest and given over to the new dispensation. Surely,

Fadl was not unaware of the geopolitical backdrop of imperial rivalries and the implicit internal contradictions of empire exposed in the birthing process of the modern state. His location at the intersection of two modes of inhabiting and exercising power has been amply demonstrated in the preceding pages. How we read his engagement with this creeping secular governmentalization of life is made more difficult, not simpler, by the various reports he sent to Istanbul while becoming involved in Dhofar. Yet no simple narrative of interest can do justice to this engagement, nor can it illuminate the power at stake. At the end of one of his reports, in which he argues analogically that since all major Arab cities are Ottoman, then "all Arab lands should also be considered as lands of Devlet-i Aliye," he offers the following postscript, titled "Warning" (Ihtar): "If one considers some European maps, one can see that there are some horrible mistakes about the abovementioned places and to whom they belong. Especially the colors and marks showing these places are extremely misleading."[24] In a time of danger—as Fadl clearly perceived it—he adapted for his own ends the Tanzimat's objectives of state recentralization, which was in effect a fundamental reconfiguration of relations among population, territory, and security, not a return to some sixteenth-century golden age. It is those ends that are in question. Did they engender new conceptions of the Good and of Muslim society, or were they exclusively self-interested, or a position in between?

In another report from the same period, titled "The Statutes [ahkam] Executed in Dhofar in Consultation with the Ruling Parties [askerin]," he details the juridical form of his government. Here are the first five points:

1. We made a treaty [mutual swearing of an oath] with members of all the tribes on terms of their obedience to me—to this humble slave—and to the Ottoman State following the principles ordered by Allah and His Prophet.

2. The towns of Salalah and Mirbat were chosen as the centers of legal proceedings, and it was ordered that four people from every tribe should come to the council of government [hükümete] every day to discuss the affairs and the state of pacification of their respective regions and to exchange views.

3. Prior to the constitution of the government in Dhofar, the treatment of all the claims other than the claims resulting from the battles between the tribes were postponed for two years, and since with the prolongation of the time it would be easier for the government to settle them gradually,

at the end of the first two years the period could be prolonged for two more years.

4. If anyone violates the treaty, all the signatories of the treaty shall be in concord to take a contrary stand against that person. Hence his property will be squandered and his blood will be shed in vain.

5. A frontier [*hudut*] will be designated for each tribe separately, and each of the tribes will be responsible for whatever happens within their own frontiers.[25]

As with the previous document, the contents suggest that the Arabic original was written in Dhofar between 1876 and 1879. Fadl's approach to Dhofar's frontiers seems to subscribe to older conceptions of territory. Meanwhile, in this period empire-states were delimiting territorial holdings with greater precision, replacing the old, soft frontiers or borderland regions that were often the domain of multiple tribes with new, hard borders cutting through tribal regions.[26]

Fadl's contribution to this imperial mission and to its archive suggests that the formation of a Dhofari society nested within the wider Hadhrami-Yemeni world, as well as within the yet even wider Arab, Ottoman Indian Ocean, and Islamic worlds, was the object of his governmental ministrations in the region. As we have seen, however, a perspective based on the British archive could result in a very different view: granting government to Company and colonial officials and enclosing Fadl in a domain of exclusively religious and/or individual private interest. Yet clearly the concerns over security and territory in this case are being mediated by a new conception of population pointing explicitly to a keen desire to bring government to the ungoverned and in turn mapping the Islamic world in global terms:

10. The preservation of some customary rules—compatible with sharia and the siyaset ["kanun," or secular laws of the Ottoman State]—that were in use among the tribes for the protection of their properties and lives before the constitution of the government became a political necessity. Since the tribes do not have known residences, in places where the execution of punishment presents difficulties for the government, the execution of aforementioned customary laws is allowed in order to facilitate arrest and imprisonment [*zajr*].[27]

Point 10 delineates a shared sovereignty, neither fully Ottoman nor Islamic nor tribal, which is avowed precisely in order to make government possible at a time of "political necessity." Its contours shifted with the shifting boundaries of imperial maps and the nature of the population, in this case (semi-)nomadic and (semi-)urban denizens of port towns at a great remove from imperial centers. The use of "political law" in order to reconcile competing claims of authority in favor of empire was documented for the same period as a practice used in the consolidation of British rule in India, in which geographic "anomalies" could be reflected in the terms of sovereignty.[28] Also, as recent studies of different *tanzimi* and *nahdawi* contexts have demonstrated, in the nineteenth century the ends of politics and religion became the reconfigured minor legal-theological concept of public good, or *al-maslaha al-amma*.[29]

This is made manifestly clear in what is likely an addendum to the legal-political (*ahkam*) document above, which begins, "The land of Dhofar district is matchless of all the coasts of Arabia and that of Arab Africa," and details the geographical advantages, natural resources, and productive capacities of the region. On the one hand, the purpose of both documents is quite narrow: to secure Ottoman imperial commitment to holding and maintaining the territory; on the other hand, these documents more broadly illustrate a process of learning to think the political anew under conditions of global colonial modernity. These conditions posited subject and state in relations extending beyond taxation and protection and continually expanding to include life in all its forms. Indeed, Fadl's reports might just as well be read as a contemporaneous effort to represent the change so that he might intervene in it.

The value of Dhofar is represented in terms of its utility as measured mainly in geographical and economic terms. Its Indian Ocean location and natural bounty are presented as raw materials waiting to be processed and plugged into circuits of global trade, communication, and politics; meanwhile, the presence of a foundational sayyid gravesite in Dhofar roots the place in Islamic time and the itinerant Fadl in that place. Obviously, Fadl aimed to make the imperial center take notice of him and the emirate that was his. Less obvious is how the specific content and form of the appeal can reveal a global process by which biological, religious, and economic life changed—and became inescapably political. This process of politicization entwined with the law (or the law's making) was not, however, exclusively a matter of rights and/or property but that of a concatenation of the government of man and things, living and dead.[30] Tracking the politicization of life along these lines is not only salient for appreciating the multivalent formation of the global and the possibility of a global history but can also reveal gaps, fissures, and fault lines that constituted openings for constant reinvention and renewal.

The following passage from the report is rich in detail, floating between an Arab-Muslim tradition of geographical writing and a modern secular discourse of political economy, worth quoting at length:

> The valleys and mountains are covered with all kinds of trees and plants yielding myrrh, gum, and rubber. Were they to be extracted they would fill up ships. The myrrh that is used in every corner [of the world] comes from Dhofar. The majority of cattle consist of cows. The oil is delicious here. In certain months, one can find plenty of sardines in the sea. Sometimes these fish are so abundant that they throw them on the beaches. And people collect them to use in their fields as fertilizer and use their oil in the construction of boats. And they dry some of them and use it in barley to feed their cattle in winter. In this district there are not only numerous flowing water sources but also there are wells. The waters of wells are so close to the surface of the earth that it is possible to perform an ablution from them. And these waters are generally fresh. The waters of wells do not seem to diminish by consumption. One of the water sources was ameliorated and enlarged, and named "Hamidiye." The population is Sunni and belongs to the school of Shafii. There are coconut trees all along its coasts. All kinds of trees growing in India, Arabia, and Anatolia also grow here. Some valleys are covered in lemon trees; in one valley there are trees of tamarind, another is full of grape vines, and in one of the other valleys there are henna trees. *None of these valleys belong to anyone. Currently, being legally appointed Emir of Dhofar, all of them are my own property/domain.* [*Butun kitanin arazisi elyevm tevliyet-i sheriyye ile Zafar emiri bulundugumdan kendi mulkumdur.*] Lemon trees yield fruit continuously in summer and winter. The soil of Dhofar is suitable for cultivating coffee; and by the reason of the fertility of the land, had we grown coffee here the product would be much better and tastier than the coffee of Yemen. The weather is really good for health. One of the wonders of this district is that the tops of the mountains within the boundaries of the rainy area are dry and their skirts are wet and green. So much so that some animals can graze in rainy places during the days and stay the night in dry places. Also, there is a valley in Dhofar where it never rains but there are huge and flowing sources [of water], and it is covered with date palms. There are many mines in Dhofar, such that there is coal for steamers, iron, glass, and so on and so forth. *Dhofar district resembles an India in the Arab subcontinent and is considered a natural wonder because the*

rainy season lasts uniquely three months. Unlike other parts of the Arab sub-continent, in Dhofar there are trees yielding myrrh and rubber. The tomb of Esseyidesherif Muhammad Aliyyul Ulvi [Alawi], the forefather of all the Ulvi sherifs living on earth today, is in Dhofar.[31] This district is in equal distance from Basra, Yemen, the coasts of Africa, and India by sea. There is a port for the steamers to harbor. Today, with the existence of steamers and the telegram, and considering the fertility of the soil, this place could be built up and made prosperous in a very short time, because it's situated on the coast and has many advantages.[32] (emphasis added)

In this view of territory, approximating an imperial gaze, the natural wonder that is Dhofar has long existed in a primitive state of exploitation and accumulation, one that has not required sophisticated legal or political forms of order. Even tribal wars were fairly simple affairs normally resolved with little to no mediation from legal-spiritual authorities (sayyids). But something had changed in Arabia to despoil the state of nature and innocence in which tribes and villagers had lived for so long—the other side of the intensifying connectivity of the Indian Ocean celebrated above. Fadl was keenly conscious of the change from the time of his arrival in the early 1850s from India. After a period of dormancy, when he seemed to recede into a life of study and meditation, he was reactivated, so to speak, by the call of the Dhofaris. Perhaps no other reference above evokes the experience of epochal change in the nineteenth century as that to coal and the power it released into the world.[33]

Going in the other direction and riding the waves of steam power was Henry Maine, who arrived in India in 1862. Maine made an analogous observation about tribes, territory, security, and sovereignty that unwittingly supported Fadl's apprehensions about British encroachments in the Indian Ocean world having fundamentally altered older terms of sovereignty:

But the motives of the Government of India in effecting an arrangement of the affairs of Kathi'awar are above suspicion, and the course which it is proposed that we should take has its justification, not only in the indefinite obligations contracted by us in the capacity of Paramount Power, but in the fact . . . that *our government of India has, in a sense, been the cause of this anarchy in Kathi'awar.* One of the many difficulties attending the application of international law in India arises from the circumstance that the whole system of the law of nations was framed by its authors subject to the contingency of occasional war. The British Government has prevented the Kathi'awar States from going to war among themselves, and hence has arrested the operation of a natural process by which the endless sub-division of the chiefships occasioned by the law of succession would have been corrected or counteracted.[34] (emphasis added)

While most likely Fadl had never heard of Maine, the liberal imperialism of European powers and the power over planetary life that its forms of government sought animated Fadl's thought and shaped his political consciousness from the time he encountered the EIC—the target of Maine's criticism.[35] Accordingly, he felt it crucial to declare Ottoman sovereignty over Arab tribes as being of paramount importance.

While the terms Fadl used were decidedly not liberal, he likewise seems to have felt a compulsion to "fit" the Ottomans into the new international and interimperial global order through a hybrid discourse on sovereignty. As for the Ottoman state (from which Fadl was learning much and concerning which he had his doubts), Maine's arguments about law, divisible sovereignty, and the politics of recognition among states would certainly have been familiar, espe-cially with the establishment of the Office of Legal Counsel, one of the world's first such governmental bodies, which was to be wielded as an instrument of foreign policy after the British occupation of Egypt.[36] More broadly, the existential value of international law in interstate engagements and conflicts was made manifestly clear to the Ottomans as they were rescued from the clutches of the Russian Empire and formally inducted into the European family of nations with the Treaty of Paris (1856) that ended the Crimean War.[37] All of this tells us both something and nothing about the terms available to Fadl for processing the changes in sovereignty that he began to perceive in Malabar as early as the late 1830s.

For example, his concern with infiltrators, discussed above, was reiterated in these reports:

While I was in Istanbul, the people of Masqat, one in the guise of a judge [*hakim*] together with an officer and some others with evil intentions landed at some villages by the sea because the route took longer by land. But the people of Dhofar did not accept them and banished them from their villages. Then they wrote to me [saying] that this type of event occurred repeatedly. Consequently, those places fell into ruins as the tribes began to fight with each other. *But, these sorts of things happen only because of the provocation and incitement of the foreigners.* As a matter of fact, in Dhofar the flag of the Sublime State is drawn everywhere and its population subject to the Sublime State. Accordingly, [the inhabitants] explained to those people that their emir, your well-wisher slave, was [away] the guest of His Excellency the Sultan in the capital of the Exalted Sultanate.[38] (emphasis added)

"Foreign" incitements of tribal groups to violate the territorial sovereignty of the Ottomans and Muslims inevitably resulted in violence and chaos, which ultimately threatened the very future of Islam. Fadl made his own importance in negotiating that dangerous world patently clear, such that one may indeed read his documents in terms of self-interest and self-promotion. However, it was precisely in the distinction between Ottomans and Muslims that the problem of sovereignty was most acute for Fadl; taking this into account suggests a less reductive reading of his life.

Despite his in some ways typical treatment of sovereignty as deriving from good government, Fadl was torn between riding the wave of reform in the Indian Ocean world accompanying the sea change in sovereignty and leading a life free of the new, subjugating powers. As an Alawi Sufi and son of a sayyid whose trajectory "ended" in the best of all possible ways, namely, enshrined and made a saint, conceptualizing the relationship between life and sovereignty was no simple matter at any level: theological, political, mystical, or economic. The two-dimensional cartographic and ethnographic imaginaries invoked in one moment of political-economic activity in the context of interimperial rivalries did not exhaust the spatial and temporal universe to which Fadl, sayyid sovereignty, and the quest for the unity of life belonged.

Fadl's reports evince a time of searching for a language and style to represent sayyid sovereignty in a world where empire-states had expanded their capacity for government with ends that were avowedly material. That material reality was, from mid-century, increasingly legible across the Middle East and South Asia, in the built environment, in technologies of transport and communications, and perhaps most important, in the refashioned modern self. Whether in the person of tanzimi bureaucrats, trouser-wearing nahda scholar-journalists, or emancipated religious minorities, the modern subject was a life-form governed under new conditions of sovereignty and reproduced in relation to new, individualizing norms.[39] The legal and political dimensions of that sovereignty had started to impress themselves on the Alawis in their Indian Ocean encounters with the growing British Empire since the late eighteenth century (and possibly even earlier in encounters with the Portuguese, Dutch, and French Empires).[40] Thus, Fadl's compulsion to engage shifting terms of sovereignty was in a sense historically given. Indeed, the last letters we have from Fadl brilliantly illustrate the ambivalence of this engagement.

After being forced out of Dhofar in 1879, Fadl made repeated pleas to the sultan and the British to grant him clearance to return, all of which fell on deaf ears.[41] After he made his way back to Istanbul, it seems he was able to acquire the arms necessary to try to retake his lost amirate and sent one of his sons to do so. In 1886, the British seized a shipment at Aden "from a filibustering party of Arabs under Seyyid Muhammad bin Fadhl" who were said to be headed to Dhofar. The fact that Fadl's plan for Dhofar had the support of the sultan is indicated by the formal request made by the Porte for the return of the confiscated weapons in 1888–89. The request was denied with the claim that the arms had been destroyed. The matter seemed to fall silent, at least for the next few years.

Fadl made his last effort shortly before his death, as the political situation in North Africa, East Africa, and southern Arabia seemed to converge around Italian, French, and British suspicions of each other, which as even a casual observer could see threatened to explode in open conflict. For a while at least, these countries' shared fear of the region-hopping pan-Islamic threat fueled from Istanbul may have mitigated their mutual animosity.[42] Reading the situation astutely, Fadl initially set himself apart from these pan-Islamist movements, representing himself as a friend of the British Empire. But in a letter dated August 2, 1896, Fadl addressed the British ambassador to Istanbul, Philip Currie, in a more aggressive tone than he had used in his previous entreaties, revealing his deep frustration at what had essentially become a decade and a half's detention, which he blamed on Currie's superiors.[43] First he acknowledged receipt of Currie's letter delivering the British prime minister's decision to refuse Fadl or any of his envoys permission to enter Dhofar.[44] Currie's letter was in response to one Fadl had written in May of the same year indicating that he was planning to send an emissary to Dhofar to set the administration straight, after the representative of Sayyid Faisal b. Turki, sultan of Muscat, had bungled its affairs so much as to incite a revolt among the people.[45] In the letter from August, disappointed by the latest round of refusals, Fadl seems to deny or at least qualify his prior efforts: "I have never asked either for permission to proceed myself to Dhofar, nor for the official recognition of my envoy. For I am under no obligation to ask of any state permission to go to Dhofar. There are Governments which recognize the official character of my state and functionaries. I have at Dhofar a representative and officials who carry on the Government."[46] The translation at this point is very poor, but in any case, the letter denounces efforts by Muscat to hoist its flag over Dhofar and suggests that Fadl could not allow this to happen, being one who has "always tried to preserve intact and uninjured the rights of my principality."[47] He then softens his tone to note, "Even if the recognition or non-recognition of my envoy by England be considered as a political question, yet to admit [him] will be a proof of her friendship to me and will increase my friendship to her." He continues: "Thank God, I am known in many countries, and thousands of Mussulmans rejoice at my joy and grieve at my sorrow." After this rhetorically strategic claim on a sensitive and highly responsive constituency, he ends the letter by asking the ambassador to convey to Lord Salisbury, the prime minister, his "ancient and sincere friendship towards England," which "still exists and is even greater than ever. Signed Fadl bin Alawi, Amir of Dhofar."[48]

Alavi, Bang, and Buzpinar characterize Fadl as entrepreneurial, opportunistic, and an ambitious adventurer, respectively. And surely from a cursory reading of the British and Ottoman imperial archives, one is left with this feeling. In the May 1896 letter to Currie, Fadl enclosed the instructions he was planning to give to his emissary. These include a description of the "national flag of Dhofar" as "green with a pentagonal center" and orders that Dhofar would be in "complete friendship and unity" with the British government, which in turn should be "prepared to protect the rights and independence of the Principality."[49] In the letter and the instructions, Fadl essentially pledges loyalty to the British Empire, which he describes as always having protected Muslims and the caliphate from "hostile Powers." He announces that sixteen years of living in Istanbul have taught him that the Eastern policy of the British "will ensure completely the interests of Islam."[50] Here, Fadl can be slotted into one of those ethical-political categories, such as Alavi's "career broker," to which historians sometimes seem to assign negative moral value all too easily, effectively foreclosing the story of a complex life.

Fadl's petition to the sultan in 1897, a year after the failed attempt to convince the British of his friendly intentions, reinforces this view. As these are the last of his penned words as far as I know, I shall quote at length from the letter:

> Upon my most humble request for the permission of my departure to Medina, it had been commanded that I should continue my sojourn here waiting for the resolution of some issues and that I should bring my family from Hejaz. Yet I can no longer support the cold weather here, and even if I brought my family from Hejaz they would naturally fall ill like those that are with me here. Because of these reasons, I have repeatedly written petitions

requesting from the Shelter of the Caliphate to permit my departure. However, considering the fact that I haven't attained to the praiseworthy happiness of receiving the exalted royal order, it has become absolutely evident that His Excellency wished and demanded the prolongation of my stay here. And therefore I have had to sacrifice my comfort for the sake of obeying the orders of the Sovereign [*shahriar*]. However, the English, the enemy of the State and the people, and especially the enemy of your slave, try to prevent me from going there, because they've been casting covetous eyes upon the district of Zafar that is unique in the world with its moderate weather, power of vegetative growth, fertility of its soil, geographical importance and impenetrability of its location and many more advantageous aspects. And since they are unable to prevent me from going to Zafar openly and through legal and political means and because they know that your slave never takes them seriously, they try to reach their goal by spending freely and distributing many gifts [*bezli mal*] [in the region] to instigate rebellion. They have greedy aspirations for the coasts of the Arab Subcontinent and especially for the district of Zafar, since, like all the European states that have acquired colonies on the African coast they have found the weather there to be too hot. I do really hope that your majesty whose political genius keeps fascinating and bewildering all the political scholars of the world could protect that beautiful and important district that is full of thousands of Muslims and noble descendants of the Prophet [the Seyyids] . . . I am ready and waiting for the imperial order and *firman* of His Excellency, the Shelter of the Caliphate. In all circumstances, to command belongs unto him, the benefactor.

Your well-wisher slave, Fazil bin Ulvi Bey.[51]

He sent this appeal to the sultan on October 22, 1897, and died almost exactly three years from then at the age of seventy-five. Perhaps he was telling the truth about the effects that the wicked Istanbul cold was having on his health. In any case, it is clear that the temperate climate and fertile soil of Dhofar were not the only reasons he wished to return there. So the question remains, If it was not nature, opportunism, or a sheer will to power, then why Dhofar? Do we simply take him at his word, for example, when he wrote in the May 1896 letter to the British ambassador, "My object is to protect and insure the well-being of the [Muslim] elements"?[52] Interestingly, and despite the cynics among them, the British *did* seem to take him at his word, which was precisely the trouble for Sayyid Fadl, the Moplah Outlaw.

Life's Other Ends

Perhaps the final proof of Fadl's profound engagement with worldly power was the grand state funeral he was accorded after his death on October 26, 1900. Layers and layers of the imperial order, from palace attendants and Armenian merchants to top judges and high State Council members, were represented—the presence of the Ottoman ambassador to the United States confirms his global reach. His body was taken from his house in the Machka neighborhood of the Nishantashi quarter, and in a procession accompanied by police, gendarmes, imperial guards, city officials, and Shadhili Sufis, Fadl made his final trip. After funeral prayers held in the monumental Aya Sofia mosque, he was transferred to Mahmud II's cemetery—his final resting place decided by order of the sultan so as to be alongside Tanzimat luminaries.[53] It would seem the ambivalence of a lifetime's relation to sovereignty was finally interred.[54]

Even as spaces of autonomy and the concomitant potential for independent action shrank throughout the nineteenth century—explaining in part the different trajectories of father and son—the specific temporal and spatial dimensions of the Alawiyya exceeded the time(s) of the historical and gifted to Fadl another, unfaded "map" of life that promised to show the way to a relationship with a non- and even antihistorical, that is, transcendent, divine sovereignty. That life and its ways were marked by genealogical and mystical texts, spiritual exercises, disciplineships, and gravesites, which we have argued amount paradoxically to both less than and more than sovereignty: the unity of life. As he read this map of a multidimensional universe toward the end of his earthly time, modern political sovereignty and sayyid sovereignty could not but be mediated by the question of life in relation to the paramount sovereignty of God.

One of the maps that Fadl revisited and reconfigured for the time was titled *This True and Merciful Way* (*Hadhihi al-tariqa al-hanifa al-samha'*),[55] which was a guide to the Alawiyya, its long chain of sayyids and saints, its wise teachings, the performance of dhikr, and the fundamental truthfulness of the Way. Interestingly, the second printing in 1900 was done under government auspices, as a short note on the cover in Turkish indicates: "This was published with the authorization, number 181, of the Ministry of Education, at the printing house of the Crimean Abdullah Efendi, which is situated on Kiztashi Street (Istanbul)."[56] Hence, looking to this map of the Alawi Way—bearing its literal stamp (no. 181) of government approval—for unambiguous answers about Fadl's final years would be a mistake. The other Ottoman "intrusions" into the Arabic *risala* (treatise), which seem positioned to domesticate the text, make

Tomb of Sayyid Fadl. The first part of the inscription reads:

PRAISE TO THE EVERLASTING CREATOR.
This is the shrine of an Exemplar of the Prophet's Family,
Descendant of The Ascetic Virgin Fatamah Al Zahra [daughter of the
    Prophet]. Committed Scholar [al-'alim al-'amil].
Perfect Friend [of God], Eminent Sayyid, and Notable Prince.
Ruler of Dhofar, Our Lord [mawlana] Fadl Pasha al-Alawi al-Husainy.
May God have mercy on his soul and may we benefit from him.

Many thanks to Akif Ercihan Yerlioğlu and Aslihan Gurbuzel for taking this
beautiful photo and to Walid Asfour for helping to decipher some of the words
in the inscription.

reading *This True and Merciful Way* as some pure Sufi meditation problematic. Nonetheless, the marginal markings signify a moment of aporia that Fadl must have experienced in his last years and point to the unsettled and unsettling relationship of life to sovereignty. The marginalia are Ottoman translations of the Arabic, only appearing at strategic points in the text and mirroring strategic points in the world, that is, when the relevance of the Alawis to Hadhramawt is being elaborated.

This True and Merciful Way begins with the teaching of al-Arif Billah Abd al-Rahman bin Abd Allah bal-Faqih Ba Alawi. A fundamental pillar of the Alawiyya is explicated here in the very first line: "The time of the social yields no benefit in the absence of kinship" (*la tufid tul al-mujalasa ma' adam al-mujanasa*). Engseng Ho has extensively mapped the genealogical imagination and practices of the Alawis over the *longue durée*, so the intricacies of its development as a "society of the absent" in a diasporic context need not be rehearsed here. For the purposes of establishing the life that Fadl was heir to, beholden to, and challenged to forsake, we need only note the juxtaposition of sociality and intimacy, of which kinship is the primary and operative modality. Under the larger rubric of Islamic society and Islamic conceptions of sovereignty, the weight of the genealogical was felt strongly even as it was regularly contested—hence the need to reiterate it at the fin de siècle in the face of new challenges, specifically the governmentalization of the state discussed in previous chapters.

In this regard, the time or duration of the social formation was assumed to have a history and politics that often diverged from the Way, which presupposed a series of relations made possible and extended to humans by the grace of God, with sayyids and mystics playing leading roles. Overt critique of the former (orthodox dispensation, if you will) was always a problem; thus, Sufi orders that stressed intimacy with God, in some cases by way of an expansion of traditional kinship and prophetic lineages, always walked the line between acceptance and rejection. In the case of the Alawiyya, the kinship that truly mattered was that linked to the Prophet Muhammad. The nature of Alawi kinship was at once historical, when regarded from the perspective of the timeline of the social, and universal, when considered as an exemplary practice on a path to oneness with God and the suspension of time. All other relations of souls to bodies and people to each other remained chaotic and ephemeral, returning to dust, when deficient in the remembrance of God. Without the unifying power of God, souls remained but "conscripts" (*junud mujannada*) and bodies a bundle of contradictory passions (*al-ajsamu amzijatun mutadadatun*).[57] Within this cosmology, prophets and their descendants mattered: they helped facilitate a glimpse of the unity of life.

In reaffirming the universality of God's truth, sovereignty in its various worldly guises could not but become a problem. The historical "problem space" for which Fadl offers his map, however, was very different from the time of al-Faqih.[58] The standard solution grounded in genealogy was surely rehearsed extensively. Each person's birth and existence on earth is analogized to the familiar blank slate of human essence or nature (*kullu mawludin yuwladu ala al-fitra*) and the language that always preceded it, which was recursively inscribed upon it. The person born unmarked is conditioned into a tradition: "Judaized, Magiized, or Christianized" by fathers and mothers. Then, in the familiar monotheistic move, divine government, by definition impossible and inoperative on earth, is deputed to caretakers: "The shepherd of a flock [*abu al-ra'iyya*] is its sultan."[59] The genealogical ties binding person to person were indispensable to any community existing at any time. But without the knowledge and wisdom of God, which is self-knowledge, an empty existence—the soul a mere conscript to the will of bodily desires—remains.

The four marks distinguishing righteous people are then given: (1) fearing none other than God; (2) expelling the love of the world from their hearts; (3) acting in the world; and (4) "preserving the order for which prophets and messengers sacrificed their souls and bodies, when making legible the way [*al-shari'a*] out of compassion [*al-shafaqa*] for the umma and in observance of the [principle] of action without reward." From the four marks are distilled the four properties that will enable a select few to earn their just reward: reason (*al-aql*), knowledge (*al-ilm*), action (*al-amal*), and determination (*al-himma*).[60]

After closing this section with a prayer for those exemplars who travel in God's path, the uniqueness of the family of the Prophet Muhammad among men is elaborated. Through genealogical right and virtue the tariqa of the descendants of the Prophet that formed over time deserve a special status and have primacy, being a "fount" for other tariqas.[61] Following an elaboration of the Alawiyya's distinctiveness as a tariqa, major figures, and the appropriate *zikr*s (remembrance rituals for the saints), a history is given of the migrants and migrations that resulted in the establishment of Hadhramawt as home base. It is at this point that the Ottoman intrusion, or translation, begins. The narration is standard, with some attempts to bring the history up to date.[62]

The overlay of a Turkish voice upon the Hadhrami and Indian Ocean history of the Alawis should not be surprising, given the previous chapters charting Fadl's life as it intersected with the imperial geopolitics of the British, the Ottomans, and the Omanis. The wooing and co-optation of sada to an Ottoman imperial project in the Arab subcontinent forms part of Fadl's personal history. During the high point of Hamidian pan-Islamism, the intrusion of Ottoman into a Sufi tract would not have been unusual. The challenge, however, lies in retrieving, from the perspective of one inhabiting the Alawi tradition, the significance of this juxtaposition of politics and religion (or superimposition of politics over religion) at a point where the two had only in one lifetime become legible as distinct spheres.

There is no way to establish definitively a crisis of conscience or its absence when it comes to the historical life of Fadl, a life thoroughly enmeshed in questions of sovereignty in diverse settings spanning half a century and a vast geography, from Mampuram to Istanbul. Nonetheless, the unity of life, sought or not, flashes across the pages of *This True and Merciful Way*. Even as its historical and genealogical terms suggest a submission to the legal and normative shar'i order of Islam, its Sufi terms of intimacy among people and between people and God reveal the insufficiency of the latter as well as a quest to exceed, if not its bounds, its boundedness. Therein was presupposed a simultaneously historical and transcendent temporality, forming the Alawi sayyids' horizon of secular and religious experience for centuries and informing their actions in the world. Moreover, in their contemplations of God and their exercises of the soul, a state of immanence could be said to dissolve all other states. Thus, even as a biological life was necessarily lived out on this earth abiding by its human terms (secular and religious), the Way promised access to life and life-as-other, existing as unity.

In the second half of the nineteenth century, when Fadl was active in the world, the known horizons were called into question as the experience of time was reconditioned by technologies that shrank distances and accelerated the growth of "state" and "society," of dense new constellations of relations between sovereign and subject, among subjects, and even or especially between human subjects and nonhuman objects. We saw above how Fadl's attentiveness to the products of the earth and steamship trade in the government of Dhofar was framed just as much by a prevailing tanzimi logic entrammelled in global capitalist and imperialist networks as by the universal call of Islam. The accompanying intellectual projects of demystification and the experience of disenchantment—in short, the Nahda—posed a challenge to traditions such as the Alawiyya, especially when viewed from the growing urban conglomerations. Historians have more recently downgraded the significance of the challenge, yet examinations of life-worlds that fell out of the secularizing purview remain few or have a periodization that still presupposes the teleology of secularization.[63]

In this regard, Fadl's life offers a deeply historical view of the transformation in sovereignty and its cultural forms even as it opens a window onto another, ahistorical or possibly antihistorical, dimension we are calling the unity of life, which in itself renders all sovereignty inoperative. In the glimpses of that unity, death played an integral part, as did the rituals that surrounded it—subjects that defy and are in turn usually overlooked by modern historians. Yet struggling with closeness to God, from whom all else flowed, was a crucial aspect of being Alawi that Fadl would have been unable to ignore, especially as his biological life neared its end. What he may have made of it, and the unity of life it reflected, must be queried even if the answer necessarily remains speculative.[64]

That Fadl possessed a deep knowledge of the Alawi diaspora's significance in the Indian Ocean world and that he had an intimate and detailed understanding of the operations of life after death does not require speculation. From the example of his father, who was buried in Mampuram before his own expulsion from India, he gained an appreciation of how life lived in the pursuit of intimacy with God was a life of potentiality and never of simple beginnings and endings. The evidence for that is reports of his regular briefings by Mappilas on how the shrine built to Sayyid Alawi functioned and remained a matter of concern for the British colonial authorities in Malabar.

In a political-geographical sense, the Mampuram Maqam anchored the Alawis deeply in one more location and one more society forming a loose system of port towns and hinterlands strung around the Indian Ocean and reflecting a history of outward expansion dating back centuries. In a mystico-theological sense, the maqam tethered the generations of Alawis past, present, and to come to prophets, disciples, and supplicants in this world and to spirits, angels, and ultimately God in worlds between and beyond. The shrine thus entombed a historical person's corpse and was the physical repository of an interconnected transoceanic sacred geography that bespoke variable politics and economies across time and space. Paradoxically, the tomb-shrine also illuminates life in its mysterious unity. Marking and marked by an ethics of openness and an entreaty to remember, the shrine is a piercing of time and space, storing and releasing the force of generations of bodily and textual performances. We cannot say simply that these are fantasies of a religious type or ahistorical speculations of a scholarly type gone rogue, unless we wish to reproduce the secularist demystification narrative attending the transformation of sovereignty in the nineteenth century as the only possible history of that moment. More compelling than ideological and historiographical critiques is that the power of the shrine and the enshrined persisting into the future was both a fact known to Sayyid Fadl and an end that was, if not sought, at least contemplated by him. At the very least, such a fact of life, refusing the linearity in vogue at the fin de siècle, inserts a spiritual parenthesis in the biography of Fadl, a pause, that in the face of the shrine's enduring power, over and against the sultan's cemetery, we are also signaled to take.

Conclusion

"If I were just to open the gates and sit out front wearing a green shawl, I'd make crores."[65] This was Sayyid Ahmad Jifri's reply to one of my student guides from Darul Huda who had accompanied me to Mampuram and who had posed a question this distant relative of Sayyid Fadl deemed impertinent. We were being offered a tour of the Jifri house, which, he told us, had originally been built by Sayyid Alawi to accommodate the taller Hadhramis.[66] When we were shown the bed that purportedly belonged to Sayyid Alawi, the student guide innocently (or not, as the case may be) asked how someone so tall could have fit in such a small bed. This elicited a lecture peppered with colorful language about the fraught relationship between Sayyid Jifri and the Darul Huda administrators.

Then, as if he were transported back to the present from an imaginary plane on which he had delivered his rehearsed speech to all who had ostensibly wronged the Alawi sayyids past and present, Sayyid Jifri switched gears again and adopted a kinder tone, apologizing to the students who were, he conceded, innocent of institutional politics. He turned to narrating the history of the Alawis in Malabar from the seventeenth century to the present before taking us on a tour of the beautiful house, which had been renovated using a mix of traditional Hindu and modern architectural styles. He mentioned other items that had belonged to Sayyid Alawi that were still in his possession, including articles of clothing, walking sticks, and a sword. When I paused and possibly stared longingly at the display case housing the sword and other objects, he said he dared not touch it lest he fall dead immediately—such was its power.

The historical and genealogical account, the tour of rooms and objects, and the outburst are interlinked in a perception of the diminished role of the Alawis as historical actors, for some of the reasons outlined in previous chapters. This perception, while accurate in a sense, does not fully reflect the vectors of sayyid power, which do not rely exclusively on or reside in human/nonhuman intermediaries. The power that endures has in the end very little to do with individuals inhabiting discrete space-time envelopes. Nor is it best indexed by the long-running disputes over Sayyid Alawi's shrine (which have been going on since his death and burial in 1844), or by Sayyid Jifri's reference to the articles that had belonged to him. Of course, some sayyids in some places remained influential and in some cases even powerful personalities; and rituals and talismans do critical work in staging the dramas of saints.[67] Yet the life of power we have been investigating is not reducible to such tangible or easily recordable tropes despite their proliferation around the Indian Ocean world.

Buried in discussions of religions and saints, or debates about religion and politics, is often a secret of the life sought in a "religious" way: that in seeking it there was power—not in reaching it or in definitively giving it content or in rationalizing methods for the seeker, but in the seeking itself. Seeking implies a particular kind of motion; moreover, behind the act of going to the shrine, praying, or extending one's hand to touch it is a powerful mover that is unseen, begetting mystery. The mystery in turn is marked by a long history of efforts to define, order, and fix its meaning. However, the quest constitutes a relation to the unity of life and to divine sovereignty, rather than simply reaffirming and reproducing an exclusive, prior identity determined by communities and institutions. Because the power resides in the movement of life, in its unfolding, and not in some telos, it cannot be seized and commanded by sovereigns. In this way, we may see the plurality that is a recorded fact of the shrine—that is, its condensation of multiple temporalities, spaces, and agents—as distinct from both interest and the politics of property and as a reflection of life and nonlife connecting and producing moments of unity that are at once highly particular and universal.

In this shrine-centered account of the life of power as connected life constituted in the seeking, by both Muslims and non-Muslims, conventional historical markers of time are inadequate. From the ancient foundational figures of Abraham, Jesus, and Muhammad to the medieval monastic and mystical experiments on the self through Luther, Calvin, and Zevi to Sayyid Alawi and the pious women of Cairo, history neither stands still nor does it matter as much as we historians are fond of declaiming. The world that does not remember particular sayyids or know their histories nevertheless acknowledges and refracts their power in numerous ways, and that world is in fact far bigger and more interconnected than the terms of sovereignty make legible.

In the Islamic tradition, what is missed or covered over by the new dispensation working under the sign of modernity is precisely the relationship between life and power to which modernity or the secular modern state laid claim and which it territorialized. That a relationship between life and power could exist apart from sovereignty and its many political forms was in essence the Sufi experiment with/on the soul, an experiment that never ended. That all life grew in relation and died in isolation was a powerful discovery, even if in the time of the everyday it was self-evident. The dimensions of that truth were explored in manifold discourses within the two great globalizing traditions of Islam and secularism, hence making it a discovery with the potential for power. It is perhaps with this discovery and the development of technologies to tap the power of connected life that, while avoiding the limelight that comes with more spectacular statements of faith, Sufism, as a mystical tendency within Islam, has been viewed with concern in some quarters down to the present; the Alawiyya is merely one, albeit highly specific, example of this tendency.

Examining the history of Sayyid Fadl has shown us that this appreciation of connected life, wherein power resides in seeking (God), did not manifest itself as a renunciation of the world. To the contrary, his biography according to some historians points to the pursuit of a particularly instrumental politics during much of his life. Nonetheless, we are left with his attachment to a tradition and the need to explain it, especially given such texts as *This True and Merciful Way*. To invoke tropes of insincerity or of functionalism to explain this attachment will not solve the problem: under the conditions of the late nineteenth century, it made just as much sense to abandon tradition and seek a new path.

At the shrine of Fadl's father, Sayyid Alawi, in Mampuram, all those who are receptive to the powers of the unseen—Hindu or Muslim, religious or secular—may feel his presence and seek his blessing. There are no laws or sovereign commands compelling such an openness to being blessed or touched in some way by the absent presence marked by the shrine. Rather, the spiritual force of the maqam may be said to emanate a power capable of being possessed by (or possessing) any who approach it: the power, for example, to save a life from some physical or spiritual ailment, or the power to improve someone's material situation. It is a power *of* life rather than a power *over* life. Despite all his closeness to princely and sultanic rule, from Dhofar to Istanbul, Sayyid Fadl, the son, was never able to achieve the same kind of power that Sayyid Alawi, the father, seemed to possess both in life and even more so in death.

Some historians might accept Fadl's realization of this truth, and his feeling the need to find an "elixir for the tormented heart," as an adequate explanation of his turn to the Alawi Way in a more dedicated manner after his expulsion from Dhofar. Other historians might find his being charged with working his Sufi networks for the ends of empire as part of the Hamidian pan-Islamist project a more compelling explanation. In either case, he had to confront the tensions apparent by 1900 between Ottoman imperial ambitions and the Ottoman geopolitical location in an emerging international order.

This chapter has shown that not taking the leap into the future from Sayyid Fadl's time would lead, ironically, to an incomplete or impoverished history of his individual, historical life. As my translation of verse 21 of *Surat al-Isra'* (The night journey) in the epigraph at the beginning of this chapter indicates, his biography is bound up with life-as-other—a Quranic temporality that disrupts the human times of the now, the before, and the after.[68] Some aspects of the leap are speculative, while others are observed and observable facts of a life. Thus, this last chapter on the life of Sayyid Fadl has engaged questions of history and genealogy, property and politics, memory and mission, as they were negotiated in a continuous past, with the aim of arriving at a meaning of life both in and not in relation to sovereignty.

Reading Fadl's reports from Dhofar against his later Sufi writings such as *This True and Merciful Way* reveals how the ends of life were fraught with perilous contradictions as well as comforting reassurances. The reports signified, even heralded, that the Great Game was poised to change the global calculus again. Against this backdrop the future of Muslim lives appeared uncertain at best. There was a need to unbind them from the terms of state sovereignty and bind them again to divine sovereignty through the ministrations of sufi-sayyids. Such rebinding, as viewed by Fadl through the lens of Alawi tradition, had the potential in turn to generate a glimpse of the unity of life that momentarily or even permanently dissolves all relation to sovereignty. This unverifiable, immanent, paradoxical unity of life was neither of this world or the next, yet its power and desirability must have seemed all the more real to a Fadl who stared down the last days of his corporeal existence while peering into the future already present in the Mampuram Maqam and the many other Alawi maqams sown around the Indian Ocean world.

Conclusion

Sovereignty and Life's Mysterious Unity

IT IS PERHAPS FITTING, since discovering my mappila connection, that my last act in tracing the life of Sayyid Fadl was to cross the Indian Ocean and make the pilgrimage from Malabar to Dhofar, in search of Cheruman Perumal. And what a revelatory experience it was. I arrived in Muscat, capital of the Sultanate of Oman, in late November 2017. On a crisp early morning, I walked from my hotel to the Sultan Qaboos Grand Mosque, a distance of three or four kilometers. An impressive complex by any standard, the mosque, completed in 2001 and built entirely of Indian sandstone, sits on over one hundred beautifully landscaped acres.[1] It is flanked by five minarets and can accommodate twenty thousand worshippers. When it opened, the main prayer hall boasted the world's largest hand-woven Iranian carpet and its largest and most intricate Italian crystal chandelier.

At least, this is what my online research reveals. Unfortunately, I was unable to see the impressive features inside the mosque because I had arrived before official visiting hours had started, as I was soon to be notified. First, however, seeing a group of Omani elites in crisp white robes and distinctive colorful turbans entering in ones and twos after being greeted by a young imam or mosque official dressed similarly, I asked if I might also enter.[2] He seemed to signal that I was indeed welcome. After crossing under the first archway and before reaching the second, however, I learned his gesture was meant more as a dismissal than a welcome. Several even younger mosque attendants in brown robes and with ceremonial daggers at their side gathered around me and demanded in none too friendly a manner to know why I was there. Not satisfied with my answer or my appearance but amused by my Egyptian accent, the leader of the band declared that I could not enter at that time. From their brusqueness it was clear that they found it rather presumptuous of me to think I could visit outside normal hours and felt no need to explain why there were in fact people entering. The question of whether I was Muslim or not never arose.

By now, those well-versed in the prosody of Orientalism will be hearing alarm bells and chiding me: "Of course it was presumptuous, plus utterly arrogant and aggressive; you are not a local!" But that is to miss the point—a point that was lost on me as well, I confess, until my experience in a very different corner of Oman. I flew the next day to Salalah to locate the Cheruman Perumal burial site.

Initially, I expected I would have to rely on the clues left behind by Colonel Miles in order to locate the shrine. However, a quick search on Google Maps revealed its exact location, with attached images and comments regarding its modest stature, left mostly by (disappointed?) Muslim visitors from Malabar. Salalah in the Dhofar Governorate is lush and green from the seasonal monsoon rains; the shrine is set among groves of papaya, coconut, and banana. Having arrived from Kerala, I found the scene strangely similar, but then Sayyid Fadl had already prepared me for the geographical likeness of "India in the Arab subcontinent." The shrine can only be reached by an unmarked dirt path, which despite Google's help was not easy to locate, since there were many similar paths off the main coastal road, and no one working in the shops in the area seemed to know if there was a maqam nearby. Eventually, someone who was in fact from the area pointed me to a path that meets the road at the westernmost edge of Al-Baleed Archaeological Park.

I approached the shrine on foot early in the morning, as I did with the mosque. There was no one else on the path. The shrine is set far enough away from the main road that the sound of traffic disappears, and only the rustle of coconut fronds touched by the gentle breeze and an occasional bird cry were audible. I discovered the shrine entirely unattended (by living beings) and its two main chambers unlocked. Inside appeared to be at least two graves, but the signs to both chambers only indicated the presence of Cheruman Perumal under his different Arabic monikers (Taj al-Din Abu Bakr and Abd al-Rahman al-Samiri).[3] On closer inspection, one of the signs revealed a reclaiming by Mappila Malayalis of their founding father. Provided at the bottom was the

Sultan Qaboos Grand Mosque, Muscat, Oman.

Cheruman Perumal shrine, Salalah, Oman. Photos by author.

contact information (email, Facebook, mobile) for an E. V. Saidalavi (no less) of Kuttippuram, a town thirty-five kilometers south of Mampuram. There was no one present to clarify or explain, or none I could hear.

My experience of this relatively impoverished shrine space was not profound in any spiritual way that religious folk would recognize, yet it was a profound experience of the spirit nonetheless, diverging markedly from the encounter at the Sultan Qaboos Grand Mosque, named for the ruler of a prosperous nation-state built as a vanity project and for the glory of God, perhaps in equal measure.[4] Rather than towering minarets or grand domes, the shrine was marked by the simplest of architecture that did not hide the fact of its bricolage. Instead of being surrounded by geometrically arranged and meticulously maintained gardens, the shrine was nested within a patchwork of independently owned farmlands that, while beautiful, were being cultivated for their products.

Most important, the shrine was open. It was open for me to wander through undisturbed. It was open for the gentleman from Kuttippuram to put his mark on it and invite the world to communicate with him. It was open for many other visitors, some of whom would post photos of themselves "with" the shrine on Google Maps. The openness of the shrine was constitutive of its spirit and constituted a tradition of living with difference, of conceiving life as difference, which took shape over centuries of engagements and encounters around the Indian Ocean world. Surely its very existence today is a sign of the transregional connections (Dhofari, Hadhrami, Zanzibari, Malabari, etc.) that ensured that patrons and bricoleurs would eventually be found to patch up the roof, as Miles had written in 1884; the derelict state of affairs in his report had indeed been improved upon, but the shrine was still far from grand.[5] This lack of grandeur—indeed, its poverty—was an embarrassment to some visitors, yet for many religious traditions it was the key to unlocking self-knowledge and the unity of life.

As I finished writing the previous chapter, I allowed myself to start reading Arundhati Roy's much-anticipated second novel, which was twenty years in the making after her dazzling debut in *The God of Small Things*. I did so sitting on another verandah in Kerala. To my surprise she offered an account of the famous seventeenth-century Persian poet and Sufi, Muhammad Sa'id Sarmad Kashani, who came to India for trade and stayed for love of a Hindu boy named Abhai Chand. Sarmad lived in the streets of Delhi, a naked fakir, and was executed in 1660 by the Mughal emperor Aurangzeb for apostasy. Originally an Armenian Jew who converted to Islam and possibly to Hinduism, he clearly lived his life very differently than Sayyid Fadl. Nevertheless, the following words from Roy's *The Ministry of Utmost Happiness* almost seemed to be written as a personalized gift for the completion of my own long journey with Sayyid Fadl:

> To suppose from this that those who went to pay their respects to Hazrat Sarmad Shaheed without knowing his story did so in ignorance, with little regard for facts and history, would be a mistake. Because inside the dargah, Sarmad's insubordinate spirit, intense, palpable and truer than any accumulation of historical facts could be, appeared to those who sought his blessings. It celebrated (but never preached) the virtue of spirituality over sacrament, simplicity over opulence and stubborn, ecstatic love even when faced with the prospect of annihilation. Sarmad's spirit permitted those who came to him to take his story and turn it into whatever they needed it to be.[6]

This is what I learned from, and perhaps what I have done with, the plural life of the Arab-Mappila-Outlaw Sayyid-Pookoya-Thangal Fadl Ibn Alawi.

This book has not been an argument, however, in favor of shrine and Sufism over and against mosque and Sunni orthodoxy, in general. No significant analytical acumen or deep historical knowledge is needed to appreciate the relationship between sovereignty and congregational mosque architecture, for example; likewise, one can easily distinguish well-funded shrine complexes from lesser shrines and be correct in suspecting that major organizations with "worldly" interests are involved.[7] I recounted my particular, contrasting experiences of a specific mosque and a specific shrine to illustrate that these sacred spaces—both belonging to the same religious tradition and both capable of inspiring spiritual moments for those seeking them—manifested their power differently. That difference was contingent on a series of encounters and exchanges, claims and counterclaims, appropriations and exploitations, all of which involved a multitude of human and nonhuman actors, seen and unseen, over times historical and times immeasurable.

In Sayyid Fadl's story, we have witnessed a major ambivalence reflected in the title of this book, *For God or Empire*. While, as far as I could tell from the sources, this is clearly one way to frame his historical experience, there is in each term, "God" and "Empire," a series of other ambivalences. That the two terms need not be contradictory is so nearly self-evident that I have not belabored the point. That God might be found along different paths but never reached, no matter the path, and that empire might be served and opposed in different ways made up the stuff of Fadl's life. To some extent, his life has only ambivalences to offer, and perhaps in this way it was truly singular given the particular time and place he occupied, always and everywhere in between. However, exploring the dimensions of that liminality has, I hope, been generative for thinking the writing of a global Indian Ocean history in terms of sovereignty and the many approaches to life.

Sovereignty has typically not been studied through extra-European encounters, at least not until the political question of decolonization forced the issue historically and legally. More recently, whenever a global approach has been taken, the law of Europeans that came to define the modern international order on a global scale—no insignificant subject to be sure—almost always frames the terms of exchange and interaction that are explored. At a certain level, the fact that we are living in and still struggling to perfect that order plays no small part in shaping the post–Cold War outpouring of scholarship on sovereignty.[8]

Or, according to Martti Koskenniemi, "sovereignty persists as an instrument of analysis and polemics. The excess of sovereignty, we may now assume, results from the way in which the latter always infects the former. There is no analysis of sovereignty that remains unaffected by the polemical intentions of its author." Koskenniemi argues that these analyses/polemics are conditioned by a Eurocentric refusal to come to terms with the identity of those against whom protection is necessary, a geographical and theoretical blindness to how asymmetric military and economic power works to create an unnamed other.[9] Analysis that cuts through such blindness might start with appreciating the studies showing that Christian forms of subjugation were imported into modern terms of government, forming a biopolitical regime in which fantasies of sovereignty were naturalized.[10] From this perspective, then, any embedding of "Islamic" sovereignty in a modern state had necessarily to import aspects of the West's secularized political theology.[11]

A significant polemic in the form of analysis to which many scholars of sovereignty turn is The "Nomos" of the Earth, written by the German jurist Carl Schmitt during World War II. Schmitt begins his analysis of the emergence of an international order on a global scale from the foundational principle of Landnahme (land appropriation), that is, radical title, or a primary claim, that was historical and logical as well as the basis of all further law.[12] This leads him to distinguishing between pouvoir constitué and pouvoir constituant, the latter being the preferred starting point in the positive law tradition, as it enables the fact of state to appear self-evident. Through this distinction, he recovers the genealogy of land appropriation and territoriality projected across seas as literally constituting the ground of international law and a genuine world order. He ties this historically to the unique and self-consciously global moment of the discovery of the New World, which accounted for the first stage of formulating a distinctively "European" international law and interstate system as a secular solution to a religious problem.

Then toward the end of the nineteenth century, the liberal legal minds of Europe made the fatal mistake of diluting the concrete spatial and civilizational basis of the prior interstate order by succumbing to the lure of conceptualizing the rest of the world in universalistic terms, on the basis of putatively equivalent units: nation-states. The push toward such a reconceptualization had already begun in the eighteenth century, Schmitt argues, as the New World struck back and European global lines dividing the world were redrawn such that a US-dominated Western Hemisphere grew in importance.

His critique essentially builds to the unmasking of the uncivilized and destructive global order that followed the rise of the US, in accordance with an economic (more than political) logic. The earlier lines dividing the world helped to "bracket war"—that is, limit it to military relations between states—but the new global lines developed by the US worked "to upset the spatial order of the European world and to introduce a new concept of war into world history."[13] Under the Monroe Doctrine, a new "procedure" of intervention emerged that could be invisible to public law because it occurred through treaty regimes (between incommensurable political communities) and economic penetration. "Territorial sovereignty was transformed into an empty space for socio-economic processes . . . The space of economic power determined the sphere of international law."[14]

Schmitt's account—or "formula" in Lauren Benton's view—of the historical and legal relationships among space, politics, and sovereignty that shaped the twentieth-century world order has been roundly critiqued from various corners as factually inaccurate and theoretically deficient.[15] The romanticized view of a European spatial and civilizational unity opposed to an opaque, largely uncivilized "rest of the earth" might be read as symptomatic: a refusal of the perceived othering of Germany enshrined in the Treaty of Versailles and a mourning of the lost juridical opportunity for peace.[16] However, as Susan Pedersen has recently shown, it was not an American ascendance or internationalism but precisely a sense of European civilizational commonality that reinvigorated international law's justifications of colonial oppression and unregulated war against "savages," as displayed continuously from the 1890s through the interwar League of Nations period.[17]

Schmitt's world of imperial sovereignty undergirding a rationally ordered European international order may never have existed exactly as he theorized;

nonetheless, his *longue durée* global approach exposes the liberal and positivist conceits necessary for imagining a world order based on equivalent nation-states and governed by a universal international law.[18] From that perspective, Benton, Pedersen, and others might be read as adding historical texture to the critique without taking a civilizational, or for that matter moral-political, "side" but losing some of the critical edge. Hence, Benton's distinction between her historical narrative and Schmitt's binary formula of a Europe-centered order and an extra-European space brought into it by empire fails to recognize a certain shared ground. She is surely right that her study of sovereignty reveals that "[a] broad array of legal routines extended law transregionally, and European sojourners and settlers enthusiastically embraced law as a framework for accumulating knowledge about the extra-European world, defining membership in distant political communities, positioning themselves for patronage and authority, and interacting with indigenous peoples and polities."[19] During Benton's *longue durée* (1400–1900), the target, namely, sovereignty, was mobile and polymorphous, with a multitude of agents positioned in relation to and constituting it through their engagements with each other, with space, and with legal ideas. However, the critical perspective that enables her inquiry—that the state did not precede but was constituted through empire, with law and geography serving as central discourses in its formation—is essentially the same starting point as Schmitt's, and so her assessment of the theoretical value of *Nomos* may be slightly harsh. Indeed, the only, albeit significant, difference would seem to be in her historical narrative, which presents a view of the richly layered sovereignty that empires were out of necessity forced to accept and even at times promote in a world made of "repeating fragments."

That world or world-making, captured richly by Benton and starkly by Schmitt, however fragmentary or binary, was unmistakably shaped by European empires of law. This is a historical truth that informs nearly all legal, political, social, economic, cultural, and historical theories treating the modern transformation of life on a planetary level. This truth of *our* global history is indeed significantly more nuanced now that two or three generations of scholars have included in its realm a myriad of new agents—human and nonhuman—from sailors, slaves, traffickers, pirates, convicts, native princes, women, and preachers to prize courts, barracks Islam, merchant letters, *waraqas* (deeds), and graves.[20] Trying to see beyond that truth may be nothing but a fool's errand, but it's what we have tried to do.

For God or Empire accepts Benton's historical narrative of a diffuse yet coherent imperial sovereignty, layered and negotiated, and Schmitt's critique of the invisible juridical horizon in the universalization of the nation-state form. The account given here, however, of the Alawi encounter with the East India Company in Malabar, Fadl's entanglements with the British, Omanis, and Ottomans, and our forays into the present has sought to establish that life's relation to sovereignty was more elusive than a focus on subjective agency, structural determination, or even a nuanced mix of the two would allow. Pushing the historical and theoretical envelope to a more global and critical level has surely enhanced our understanding of human life's relation to modern sovereignty; however, appreciating the returns of and on a historical life lived in view of a death not signifying finality but potentiality has required both traversing the terrain of modern sovereignty and bracketing its reach while reaching for another conception of life.

In this book, we have seen that Sayyid Alawi and Sayyid Fadl of the Sufi Alawi Way self-consciously continued a specific tradition of growing and improving Dar al-Islam, first on the Indian frontier and then, in the case of Fadl, back in the homeland, which was also a frontier for Ottoman, Omani, and British imperial ambitions. From a certain perspective, their universal mission—the *da'wa*, or calling, which their lineage and diasporic history inflected in particular ways—was easily narrated in terms of an ancient rivalry between Christendom and Islamdom, updated to take account of the global scope of imperial rivalries and their juridico-political spinoffs in the form of revolutions, constitutionalism, and nation-states, on the one side, and reaction, religious retrenchment, and limited reform, on the other. Taking our cue from the complexity of living a life in any age, we have tried to tell a less simple story of life and what it might mean when the boundaries between past/present/future, between spatial dimensions, and between (non)humans/things/ideas were porous if not entirely nonexistent. This "life" in one sense encompasses everything, every atom and every subatomic particle; this is the sense encouraged and cultivated in the Sufi texts, wherein life is unity.

Sayyid Fadl's was certainly a life entangled with modern sovereignty, but it was also indicative, through glimpses offered in his writings, of the unity of life, our adaptation of the Sufi concept of wahdat al-wujud. The distinction and dialectic between divine sovereignty and forms of political sovereignty was always present in Islamic history; it merely came to a head in the age of (modern) empire in unprecedented ways. Fadl may have been playing a game that was already centuries old, even as toward the end of his life he began to realize that it was no longer the same game. Even if this is true, however, and much of the historical evidence points in that direction, the state of play must be carefully considered.

Rationalist assumptions of the interplay among time, structure, and agency can only ever produce "thin" histories of a figure like Fadl, because the very fabric of such a life, woven with materials organic and inorganic, contained layers that were not easily described even by the wearer. As I have argued, his life was not always and entirely his own—it was also a life of his predecessors and successors, of graves and texts, of followers and detractors, of one place and many. A strictly historical view would reach its limit at the psychologization of a disordered life-form or consciousness, revealing in the process the terms of its own modern disciplinary formation while mostly missing the target. The contours of the unity of life, of life unfolding in the singular and the plural, escape history, for they are but faint flashes felt and found while beside oneself in a state of *hal* (entered when being called to God) or by millions in the gathering and reaching for blessings, for a touch of care, compassion, or joy. This life was and is Fadl's as much as it was and is not.

Sayyid Alawi and Sayyid Fadl aspired to follow the way to self-knowledge, to perfection, to God, as their ancestors taught them in practice, texts, and rituals; perhaps the father did so more successfully than the son. In both cases, it is through their aspirations and dissimilar quests that life directed at becoming life-as-other has become legible to us as more than the sum of its legal-political, moral, economic, and technological parts, more than the experiences of any individual or group. The unity of life of which we sought a glimpse, however, is not the same as God's immanence or the presence of invisible life-forms as mystics have conceived it; therefore, it can not be reduced either to Sufi pathways or to the belief of "commoners" in some generic mystico-magical force. If precision is demanded, it may be said that the unity of life we have been gesturing toward exists only insofar as a diasporic Sufi pathway intersected with a plurality of (non)life-forms spread across multiple times and spaces, with this researcher and his research absorbed in its folds. Knowledge of it is only had in historical contexts, even as it has no need of history.

The repeated historical encounters of a coherent Alawi tradition that was at once discursive ("properly" Islamic) and mystico-governmental with others and their traditions across the Indian Ocean world led to various outcomes. The skeptical rationalist (secularist or not) may focus on "real" claims to political-economic power as being the most significant. I have devoted serious attention to these, but I have also chosen to highlight other possibilities, not because I am not a skeptical rationalist but because the evidence of a unity of life beyond, or in a conflicted relation to, sovereignty was so compelling even as I accumulated evidence to the contrary.

Ultimately, it was the ethnographic moment at the Mampuram Maqam, more than the hagiographies or Sufi texts, that demanded an explanation that the strictures of historical narration or purely social scientific analyses alone could not provide. Admittedly there was a carnivalesque aspect to the shrine complex, which invited economic explanations of why these enterprises survive. But other dimensions, harder to explain, of this and other maqams around the world involve a strong sense on the part of supplicants that some presence—which I consider a small but significant part of the unity of life—cares for them. As one Nair-caste Hindu male informant in his thirties stated—after leaving a donation—"there is something there." That something that so many feel at similar shrines around the world may be one of the avatars of the power to transform life, which I have tried to glimpse through a mix of history, theory, and ethnography as a unity—not so much to materialize that something which is not material but to take seriously the sense of others (that consciously or unconsciously pierces the veil) and to make it my own. This book has tried to show how individual historical lives that were "technically" bound to the Islamic tradition of that something specific to the Mampuram Maqam and Malabar, as well as to the wider Indian Ocean world, also carried that sense with them and with varying degrees of dedication sought for it to inhabit them and to inhabit it themselves.

They understood this habitation in terms of the revelatory model enshrined in foundational "places"—the Quran and the Sunna of the Prophet—interpreted over generations by the likes of the Alawis to accord with a particular need of many Muslims: for intimacy with God. The specifically Sufi Muslim relationship to God, cultivated through particular modalities and techniques of the self, developed by orders such as the Alawiyya and disseminated to Muslims through text and teaching, were distinct from the sense of "something there" experienced at the maqam by visitors of various stripes. Hence, when Loch, in the epigraph introducing this book, spoke of the false pretensions of the likes of Fadl and "the simple minds" of the East open to such "impressions," he was both overestimating the power of sayyids and underestimating the people's capacity to differentiate meaningful sources of power.

Between the disciplined quest for God and the senses of supplicants at shrines we might glimpse the unity of life—not tied to sovereignty and yet always located at sites of sovereignty. This is not so much a paradox as it is an instantiation of sovereignty's historical repetition (empires, caliphates, states, sayyids, etc.) as always already different and recursively differing from the original. The mystery of sovereignty thus operates through its very inoperativity, which is perhaps the scandalous revelation offered by glimpses of the unity of life (as opposed to revelations that reaffirm sovereignty-as-mystery). Whether grounded in the divine or (un)grounded in secular principles, the unseen in both moments of sovereignty has been said to have captured the hearts and minds of souls through much of human history. That unseen something has been mediated by prophets, priests, shamans, and ministers of varied traditions, yet its experience and the mediation tied to the reproduction of sovereignty cannot be conflated or regarded as a simple case of control or false consciousness. Accordingly, unity of life names the power that is of sovereignty but not in sovereignty.[21]

Despite all that the skeptical rationalists—likely the vast majority inhabiting academe—have assumed about the movement of history, that desire or need, as the case may be, to be close to a power that touches life at a level beyond the corporeal and intellectual, whether it be ascribed to a god or some other unseen force, has neither disappeared nor diminished in the world and may even continue to grow. This is legible when the geography of faith or landscapes of enchantment are viewed globally and not provincially—that is, from the contexts in which social and political theory still mainly arises. Once this faith and the unity of life it connects to is removed from exclusively rationalist deliberations and one-dimensional space—both of which have also become part of modernized "religion"—then we might begin to appreciate Sayyid Fadl's journey in life, as well as to life, as anything but simple.[22]

For it was a deeply connected life, albeit not in the ways historians might understand it or not only in those ways; Fadl as a sufi-sayyid, whether he liked it or not (one suspects that at times he did not) was tied to a life that was other, both here and after here. This was a relationship deriving from inherited responsibilities, for "real" lives, both human and nonhuman, including many that were in peril, and for bridging the latter to life-as-other. These responsibilities were a heavy burden that many like Fadl could not bear or bore half-heartedly. Fadl's attempts to meet the requirements of an Alawi sayyid navigating a changing world of imperial sovereignty and an unchanging multiverse of divine sovereignty were fraught.[23] And this is the story this book has tried to tell.

Finally, in order to release that story from the grip of sovereignty's mediations we looked to/for the unity of life. A leap of faith was necessary for me and for those who sought similar glimpses: an experience of solidarity—if that is what it is—that is impossible to represent. Traces of that leap are what we have tracked through histories of diasporic movement, colonization, identity formation, mystical flights, rebellion, reforms, reaction, and returns. Thus, through a long, multidimensional play of sovereignty and life, an obscure site in Dhofar shrouded in centuries-old Indian Ocean myth and legend was tied to another obscure site in Malabar vested with stories of Mappila Muslim community formation that was in turn tied to a grave in an imperial cemetery in Istanbul. And as my final act of tracing this relationship within a global Indian Ocean history has revealed, the play continues.

Notes

The following abbreviations are used in the notes:

AHR   American Historical Review

BOA   Başbakanlık Osmanlı Arşivi (Prime Ministerial Ottoman Archive)

BL   The British Library

CMO   *Correspondence on Moplah Outrages*, 2 vols.

CSSAAME *Comparative Studies of South Asia, Africa, and the Middle East*

CSSH   *Comparative Studies in Society and History*

IJMES   *International Journal of Middle East Studies*

IOR   India Office Records

TNA   The National Archives of the UK

Preface

1. Wilson Chacko Jacob, *Working Out Egypt: Effendi Masculinity and Subject Forma-tion in Colonial Modernity, 1870–1940* (Durham, NC: Duke University Press, 2011). For an opposing view, that the fitiwwa had few links to the medieval tradition of al-futuwwa but was rather a socially embedded actor and product of the modern state's assertions of sovereignty, see Nefertiti Takla, "Murder in Alexandria: The Gender, Sexual and Class Politics of Criminality in Egypt, 1914–1921" (PhD diss., UCLA, 2016), 85–86.

2. Engseng Ho, "Empire through Diasporic Eyes: A View from the Other Boat," *CSSH* 46, no. 2 (2004): 210–46, 212. Ho argues that distinguishing between imperialism

and colonialism is necessary for explaining the "new mode of domination" represented by US empire, when old modes of resistance shaped by anticolonial nationalists and the modes of knowledge associated with them are insufficient to grasp the global, plural, and open-ended powers at work in the present.

3. I was repeatedly "asked" after the incident, "Surely you stored everything on a cloud!"

4. "Al-Baltajiyya Changes the Shape of Politics in Egypt," Al-Jazeera Online (3 February 2011), http://www.aljazeera.net/news/pages/346ac5be-c8f8-4ee6-9b81-fc 908c31ac8c. See also Paul Amar, "Turning the Gendered Politics of the Security State Inside Out? Charging the Police with Sexual Harassment in Egypt," *International Feminist Journal of Politics* 13, no. 3 (2011): 299–328; and Wilson Jacob, "Revolutionary Mankind: Egypt and the Time of al-Futuwwa," *Cairo Papers in Social Sciences* 33, no. 1 (2014): 32–52.

5. In "Rethinking the 'Middle East' after the Oceanic Turn," *CSSAAME* 34, no. 3 (2014): 556–64, Nile Green argues that "the Middle East" needs a "conceptual pluralization" and offers three "arenas" that would "disaggregate and enlarge" it: Mediterranean, Inner Asian, and Indian Ocean.

6. Echoing Kantorowicz, Salvatore writes, "In contrast to this development, the Ottoman counterpart to the second, abstract, political body of the king or body-politic in Europe remained like a penumbra and was not able to materialize a vivid aura." Essentially, a society that was able to fit within the confines of a worldly state was never hived off from the transcivilizational Islamic dialectic of *din* and *dawla*, unlike the trajectory of *regio* and *religio* in Christian Europe. Armando Salvatore, "Repositioning 'Islamdom': The Culture-Power Syndrome within a Transcivilizational Ecumene," *European Journal of Social Theory* 13, no. 1 (2010): 99–115, 112, doi: 10.1177/1368431009355756. Salvatore elaborates his arguments further in *The Sociology of Islam: Knowledge, Power, and Civility* (Malden, MA: Wiley-Blackwell, 2016). One of the few works by a historian frequently cited in studies of sovereignty by philosophers, political scientists, anthropologists, sociologists, and others is Ernst Kantorowicz, *The King's Two Bodies: A Study in Mediaeval Political Theology* (Princeton, NJ: Princeton University Press, 1957).

7. Unfortunately, I discovered Bhrigupati Singh's exciting recent ethnography of Rajasthan, *Poverty and the Quest for Life: Spiritual and Material Striving in Rural India* (Chicago: University of Chicago Press, 2015), too late for serious engagement; however, we seem to share similar concerns about and approaches to conceiving life and power. I thank Andrew Ivaska for the reference.

Introduction

Epigraph: Francis Loch Pol Resident Aden to John Jardine Sec'y to Govt, Bombay, November 20, 1877, in TNA FO 78-3615.

1. Although *tariqa* when applied to institutionalized Sufism is conventionally translated as "order," following Engseng Ho I opt for the more literal "Way," to preserve the sense of movement over fixity important to Sufi history and to spiritual exercises. Ho, *Graves of Tarim: Genealogy and Mobility across the Indian Ocean* (Berkeley: University of California Press, 2006), 28.

2. I started making trips to India to research the Indian history of the Alawis starting in 2007.

3. The origins of the Syrian Christian community and its churches in South India are hazy. It has held for centuries that the arrival of St. Thomas, first on the eastern coast, then in Kerala, around the year 53 CE planted the roots of Christianity in India. If a nineteenth-century Anglican missionary can make a good argument for its plausibility, then "hard" evidence can't be everything. W. J. Richards, *The Indian Christians of St. Thomas Otherwise Called the Syrian Christians of Malabar: A Sketch of Their History, and an Account of Their Present Condition, as Well as a Discussion of the Legend of St. Thomas* (London: Bemrose and Sons, 1908), 65–94.

4. Or in a moment of rightward political drift, that history may be deployed quite ironically. In the first visit of an Indian prime minister to Israel, in July 2017, Narendra Modi of the Bharatiya Janata Party (BJP) gifted Prime Minister Binyamin Netanyahu with a replica of ninth-century copper plates from central Kerala belonging to the Syrian Christian Church. They document a land grant to the church and the existence of trading associations that had West Asian members, including Jews, Zoroastrians, Christians, and Muslims. That the nation-state and its international order had wiped out a prior Indian Ocean world is of course only part of the irony in this case.

5. TNA FO78-3615 and FO78-4790 (Public Record Office [PRO] at the time). I stumbled on these fascinating sources, which in their scope traversed the Indian Ocean world and beyond, purely by chance and boredom in 2005. Tired of reading police reports on Egyptian Boy Scouts, I wandered the open stacks and thumbed randomly through catalogues when the entry for "Moplah Outlaw" jumped out at me

6. Nile Green, "The Waves of Heterotopia: Toward a Vernacular Intellectual History of the Indian Ocean," *AHR* 123, no. 3 (June 2018): 846–74. For how far the study of the Indian Ocean has come, one could start with the review of the field in India offered by one of its leading historians, Ashin Das Gupta, "India's Quest for the Indian Ocean: The Collection at the National Library," *Proceedings of the Indian History Congress* 49 (1988): 420–24; the role of the vernacular was deemed virtually unworthy for writing maritime history. Other helpful reviews include Markus P. M. Vink, "Indian Ocean Studies and the 'New Thalassology,'" *Journal of Global History* 2 (2007): 41–62; Isabel Hofmeyr, "The Complicating Sea: The Indian Ocean as Method," *CSSAME* 32, no. 3 (2012): 84–90; and Jeremy Prestholdt, "Locating the Indian Ocean: Notes on the Postcolonial Reconstitution of Space," *Journal of Eastern African Studies* 9, no. 3 (2015): 440–67, http://dx.doi.org/10.1080/17531055.2015.1091639.

7. For recent iterations of this point, see Jane Burbank and Frederick Cooper, *Empires in World History: Power and the Politics of Difference* (Princeton, NJ: Princeton University Press, 2011); John Darwin, *After Tamerlane: The Global History of Empire since 1405* (New York: Bloomsbury Press, 2008); and Christopher A. Bayly, *The Birth of the Modern World, 1780–1914: Global Connections and Comparisons* (Malden, MA: Wiley-Blackwell, 2004).

8. Philip J. Stern, *The Company-State: Corporate Sovereignty and the Early Modern Foundations of the British Empire in India* (New York: Oxford University Press, 2011);

Ritu Birla, *Stages of Capital: Law, Culture and Market Governance in Colonial India* (Durham, NC: Duke University Press, 2009); Christopher Bayly, *Rulers, Townsmen and Bazaars: North Indian Society in the Age of British Expansion 1770–1870* (Cambridge: Cambridge University Press, 1983). See also the classic by Ranajit Guha, *A Rule of Property for Bengal: An Essay on the Idea of Permanent Settlement* (1963; Durham, NC: Duke University Press, 1996). Manu Goswami makes a strong case for seeing the post-1857 dispensation as markedly different for shaping a global "colonial state space" in her *Producing India: From Colonial Economy to National Space* (Chicago: University of Chicago Press, 2004).

9. Sugata Bose, *A Hundred Horizons: The Indian Ocean in the Age of Global Empire* (Cambridge, MA: Harvard University Press, 2006), 39.

10. "The name of the Tangul [*sayyid* in Malayalam], according to the passport furnished by the magistrate of Malabar, dated March 10, 1852, is Syed Fazil, son of Syed Alibi Bin Saib [*sic*]." T. Pycroft, Secretary to Government of Fort St. George to Capt. S. B. Haines, Political Agent at Aden, September 10, 1853. *Correspondence on Moplah Outrages in Malabar for the Years 1853–59*, vol. 2 [henceforth *CMO*] (Madras: United Scottish Press, 1863). The most well known of ancient Muslim travelers, Ibn Battuta, carried such letters with him on his voyages from Morocco to China and back. As James Leduc astutely commented on an earlier draft, European empires and companies had begun introducing passes to travel and to trade centuries prior. Yet Sayyid Alawi's travels in the eighteenth century suggest that the borders they created were highly permeable.

11. By the mid-nineteenth century, the word *dhow* in English usage denoted a class of "native" ships of various names and builds—"bagalas, bedans, jalboots, kotias, ganjas, jahazi, sambuks, mtepes, and more"—that were regarded by the British as categorically different from Western ships. Erik Gilbert, "The Dhow as Cultural Icon: Heritage and Regional Identity in the Western Indian Ocean," *International Journal of Heritage Studies* 17, no. 1 (2011): 62–80, 65–66. See also, for earlier periods, George F. Hourani, *Arab Seafaring in the Indian Ocean in Ancient and Early Medieval Times*, rev. and expanded by John Carswell (1951; Princeton, NJ: Princeton University Press, 1995).

12. For a more detailed account of how conquests and nomadic movements affected trade routes and constituted a unified Indian Ocean world of sea and land, see the now-classic K. N. Chaudhuri, *Trade and Civilisation in the Indian Ocean: An Economic History from the Rise of Islam to 1750* (New York: Cambridge University Press, 1985). For general works, see Auguste Toussaint, *History of the Indian Ocean* (Chicago: University of Chicago Press, 1966); Michael Pearson, *The Indian Ocean* (New York: Routledge, 2003); and Edward Alpers, *The Indian Ocean in World History* (New York: Oxford University Press, 2014).

13. Ho, *Graves of Tarim*, 100. See also Nancy Um, *The Merchant Houses of Mocha: Trade and Architecture in an Indian Ocean Port* (Seattle: University of Washington Press, 2009); Roxani Eleni Margariti, *Aden and the Indian Ocean Trade: 150 Years in the Life of a Medieval Arabian Port* (Chapel Hill: University of North Carolina Press, 2007); Nelly Hanna, *Making Big Money in 1600: The Life and Times of Isma'il Abu Taqiyya, Egyptian*

Merchant (Syracuse, NY: Syracuse University Press, 1998); and Janet Abu Lughod, *Before European Hegemony: The World-System, AD 1250–1350* (New York: Oxford University Press, 1989). And, of course, revolutionizing the study of medieval commerce was the "India Book"; see S. D. Goitein and Mordechai Friedman, *India Traders of the Middle Ages: Documents from the Cairo Geniza* (Leiden: E. J. Brill, 2008). On Calicut and Malabar's history of defending its maritime trading autonomy, see K. K. N. Kurup, ed., *India's Naval Traditions: The Role of Kunhali Marakkars* (New Delhi: Northern Book Centre, 1997), and Kurup, *The Ali Rajas of Cannanore* (Trivandrum: College Book House, 1975).

14. The classic early revision of the old Orientalist decline thesis is Marshall Hodgson's magisterial three-volume work *The Venture of Islam*, vol. 1: *The Classical Age of Islam*, vol. 2: *The Expansion of Islam in the Middle Periods*, and vol. 3: *The Gunpowder Empires and Modern Times* (Chicago: University of Chicago Press, 1974–1977). See also A. Azfar Moin, *The Millennial Sovereign: Sacred Kingship and Sainthood in Islam* (New York: Columbia University Press, 2012); Rifaʿat Ali Abou-El-Haj, *Formation of the Modern State: The Ottoman Empire, Sixteenth to Eighteenth Centuries* (Syracuse, NY: Syracuse University Press, 2005); Rula J. Abisaab, *Converting Persia: Religion and Power in the Safavid Empire* (New York: I. B. Tauris, 2004); and Kathryn Babayan, *Mystics, Monarchs and Messiahs: Cultural Landscapes of Early Modern Iran* (Cambridge, MA: Harvard University Press, 2003); Richard M. Eaton, *Sufis of Bijapur 1300–1700: Social Roles of Sufis in Medieval India* (Princeton, NJ: Princeton University Press, 1978).

15. Aside from sharp dismissals of other views, in "The Economic Crisis of the Seventeenth Century after Fifty Years" Jan de Vries gives a rather thorough overview of the problem in his contribution to "The Crisis of the Seventeenth Century: Interdisciplinary Perspectives," special issue, *Journal of Interdisciplinary History* 40, no. 2 (Autumn 2009): 151–94.

16. Similar (trans)formations existed elsewhere. As Peter Brown's classic study *The Cult of the Saints: Its Rise and Function in Latin Christianity* (1981; Chicago: University of Chicago Press, 2015) demonstrates, dead human beings transformed into intercessors between heaven and earth formed a key vector in the rise of Christianity in the ancient Mediterranean world. He also indicates in the preface to the 2015 edition that his travels in Iran and the scholarly inspiration of anthropologists of the Islamic world were crucial to the framing of the book. See Ernest Gellner, *Saints of the Atlas* (Chicago: University of Chicago Press, 1969); and Michael Gilsenan, *Saint and Sufi in Modern Egypt: An Essay in the Sociology of Religion* (Oxford: Clarendon Press, 1973).

17. This is an oversimplification of a vast literature from within Sufism and Shiʿism that treats the complexity of wilaya from multiple perspectives, though the shared paradox—a life of and not of sovereignty—is the one we grapple with here. For an introduction, see J. Spencer Trimingham, *The Sufi Orders in Islam* (New York: Oxford University Press, 1998), 133–65. Vincent Cornell nicely draws out the distinctions in the Islamic history of saints' tombs in *Realm of the Saint: Power and Authority in Moroccan Sufism* (Austin: University of Texas Press, 1998).

18. Ahmad Ilyas, *Sovereignty: Islamic and Modern* (Karachi: Allies Books, 1965), 1. In a humorous yet serious concluding moment in the text, he responds to his colleague

Harold Laski, who suggested out of frustration that "the whole concept of sovereignty [be] surrendered," saying: "It would remain of immense value to Political Science if it is placed where it ought always to remain—that is, in Allah (as in Islam) and all the competing and conflicting views of sovereignty will vanish away by themselves" (483). The quote from Laski's *A Grammar of Politics* (London: George Allen and Unwin, 1925) continues: "That, in fact, with which we are dealing is power; and what is important in the nature of power is the end it seeks to serve and the way in which it serves that end. These are both questions of evidence which are related to, but independent of, the rights that are born of legal structure" (45).

19. For an introduction to Ibn Arabi's thought, see William C. Chittick, *Ibn Arabi: Heir to the Prophets* (London: Oneworld, 2005), and *Imaginal Worlds: Ibn al-Arabi and the Problem of Religious Diversity* (Albany: SUNY Press, 1994).

20. The relevant verse from the Quran is 38:44.

21. I thank Zozan Pehlivan for linking the fortunes of Fadl to the global environmental catastrophe that unfolded during the period when he was attempting to establish a government in Dhofar. See Mike Davis, *Late Victorian Holocausts: El Niño Famines and the Making of the Third World* (New York: Verso, 2001); I also thank her for the reference. There is an account of the drought's impact in Loch, Political Resident Aden to Gonne, Sec'y to Govt Bombay Pol Dept, November 22, 1878, FO 78-3615.

22. Kantorowicz, *King's Two Bodies*; Aziz al-Azmeh, *Muslim Kingship: Power and the Sacred in Muslim, Christian, and Pagan Polities* (New York: I. B. Tauris, 1997).

23. Carl Schmitt, *Political Theology: Four Chapters on the Concept of Sovereignty*, trans. George Schwab (Chicago: University of Chicago Press, 2006).

24. Andrew F. March, "Genealogies of Sovereignty in Islamic Political Theology," in "Political Theology," special issue, *Social Research* 80, no. 1 (Spring 2013): 293–320. Available at: https://ssrn.com/abstract=2166953. In an otherwise admirable attempt to theorize Islamic conceptions of sovereignty—the classic Orientalist leap from medieval to modern aside—it was precisely the elision of the sufi-sayyid trend in Islam and of nineteenth-century imperial sovereignty that makes this critical work of "political-theology" less critical. The global imbrications of modern sovereignty's genealogy must be mapped if Orientalist categorizations are to be truly displaced.

25. Green, "Waves of Heterotopia," 846–53.

26. Bose, *A Hundred Horizons*, 10–14, 20–21. "Interregional arena" signifies the diverse geographies intersecting around the Indian Ocean, opening up the latter to the actual historical, hence changing connections that extended well beyond its waters and littorals.

27. Green, "Waves of Heterotopia," 848.

28. In Western scholarship, significant treatment of Sayyid Fadl's life in English begins with Dale's (re)discovery of these Alawis while doing research on the Mappilas of Malabar over a long stretch of time and in relation to European incursions into the region; as such, most of his account ties their life histories to a trajectory of violent local resistance. Stephen Frederic Dale, *Islamic Society on the South Asian Frontier: The Mappilas of Malabar, 1498–1922* (New York: Oxford University Press, 1980). For similar though

narrower treatments that were primarily interested in tracing the roots of modern peasant protest, see Conrad Wood, "Historical Background of the Moplah Rebellion Outbreaks, 1836–1919," *Social Scientist* 25 (August 1974): 5–33, and *Moplah Rebellion and Its Genesis* (New Delhi: People's Publishing House, 1987); Roland E. Miller, *Mappila Muslims of Kerala: A Study in Islamic Trends* (Hyderabad: Orient Longman, 1976; rev. ed. 1992); and K. N. Pannikar, *Against Lord and State: Religion and Peasant Uprisings in Malabar, 1836–1921* (New Delhi: Oxford University Press, 1989). On Fadl's Arabian adventure, see Ş. Tufan Buzpinar, "Abdulhamid II and Sayyid Fadl Pasha of Hadhramaut: An Arab Dignitary's Ambitions, 1876–1900," *Journal of Ottoman Studies* 13 (1993): 227–39. One of the earliest mentions in modern scholarship of Fadl's pan-Islamic orientation is B. G. Martin, "Notes on Some Members of the Learned Classes of Zanzibar and East Africa in the Nineteenth Century," *African Historical Studies* 4, no. 3 (1971): 525–45, 542. More recent treatments using an Indian Ocean framework include Anne Bang, *Sufis and Scholars of the Sea: Family Networks in East Africa, 1860–1925* (New York: Routledge, 2003); Ulrike Freitag, *Indian Ocean Migrants and State Formation in Hadhramaut: Reforming the Homeland* (Leiden: Brill, 2003); and Ho, "Empire through Diasporic Eyes." Fadl did earn a brief entry in the Arabic biographical dictionary of Abd al-Rahman al-Mashhur, *Shams al-zahira al-dahiyya al-munira fi nasab wa-silsila ahl al-bayt al-nabawi*, 1st ed. (Hyderabad, 1911); 2nd ed., ed. Muhammad Diya Shihab, 2 vols. (Jeddah: Alam al-Maʿrifa, 1984); a family tree of Fadl's descendants is also provided in vol. 1, pp. 308–9. Other references to him in Arabic sources will be cited below.

29. Fiction often inspires and leads the way in inquiries into historical and more broadly humanistic limits; this project had many inspirations, but a major one when I first began to think of it as a "book" was J. M. Coetzee's *Elizabeth Costello* (New York: Vintage, 2003).

30. Huri Islamoğlu and Çağlar Keyder, "Agenda for Ottoman History," *Review* 1, no. 1 (Summer 1977): 31–55.

31. This revisionist literature is too extensive by now to cite here in full for all three Muslim empires. There are citations to notable works in places throughout the book. A key intervention in recasting the old world history is Sanjay Subrahmanyam, "Connected Histories: Notes towards a Reconfiguration of Early Modern Eurasia," in "The Eurasian Context of the Early Modern History of Mainland South East Asia, 1400–1800," special issue, *Modern Asian Studies* 31, no. 3 (July 1997): 735–62. See also his two-volume work *Explorations in Connected History: Mughals and Franks* and *Explorations in Connected History: From the Tagus to the Ganges* (Delhi: Oxford University Press, 2005).

32. On Istanbul's imperial reinvention, see Mostafa Minawi, *The Ottoman Scramble for Africa: Empire and Diplomacy in the Sahara and the Hijaz* (Stanford, CA: Stanford University Press, 2016). On Mehmed Ali's changing vision of an Egypt ruled from Cairo, see Khaled Fahmy, *All the Pasha's Men: Mehmed Ali, His Army and the Making of Modern Egypt* (New York: Cambridge University Press, 1997). On how Bombay's geopolitical and techno-economic positioning enabled the fashioning of a distinct Islamic formation, see Nile Green, *Bombay Islam: The Religious Economy of the West Indian Ocean, 1840–1915* (New York: Cambridge University Press, 2011).

33. Antoinette Burton and Tony Ballantyne, eds. *World Histories from Below: Disruption and Dissent, 1750 to the Present* (New York: Bloomsbury, 2016); Michael Pearson, ed., *Trade, Circulation, and Flow in the Indian Ocean World* (New York: Palgrave Macmillan, 2015); Jürgen Osterhammel, *The Transformation of the World: A Global History of the Nineteenth Century*, trans. Patrick Camiller (Princeton, NJ: Princeton University Press, 2014); Abdul Sheriff and Engseng Ho, eds., *The Indian Ocean: Oceanic Connections and the Creation of New Societies* (London: Hurst, 2014); Jane Burbank and Frederick Cooper, *Empires in World History: Power and the Politics of Difference* (Princeton, NJ: Princeton 2011); Christopher Bayly, *The Birth of the Modern World, 1780–1914* (Malden, MA: Wiley-Blackwell, 2004); Prasannan Parthasarathi, *The Transition to a Colonial Economy* (New York: Cambridge University Press, 2001); Kenneth Pomeranz, *The Great Divergence: China, Europe, and the Making of the Modern World Economy* (Princeton, NJ: Princeton University Press, 2000); and Bin Wong, *China Transformed: Historical Change and the Limits of European Experience* (Ithaca, NY: Cornell University Press, 2000).

34. Sanjay Subrahmanyam asks global historians—the "presentists"—seeking to give an account of globalization: "In sum, what of world historians of the past who happen to be somewhat more ancient (and less derivative from a single Anglo-European locale) than the usual tired list of William McNeill, Lewis Mumford, Arnold Toynbee, Oswald Spengler, or H. G. Wells?" Subrahmanyam, "On World Historians in the Sixteenth Century," *Representations* 91, no. 1 (Summer 2005): 26–57, 30. For examples of the latter-day innovators he finds problematic, see J. R. McNeill and William McNeill, *The Human Web: A Bird's-Eye View of World History* (New York: W. W. Norton, 2003); and Bruce Mazlish, *The New Global History* (New York: Routledge, 2006). A trailblazer by any standard, Marshall Hodgson began the project of rethinking world history in non-"ethnocentric," "interregional" terms in lectures given in the early 1950s, as he notes in "The Interrelations of Societies in History," *CSSH* 5, no. 2 (1963): 227–50; see also the collection of his essays edited by Edmund Burke III, *Rethinking World History: Essays on Europe, Islam and World History* (New York: Cambridge University Press, 1993).

35. Seema Alavi makes a similar point in *Muslim Cosmopolitanism in the Age of Empire* (Cambridge, MA: Harvard University Press, 2015), Kindle edition. Reinhart Koselleck's *Begriffsgeschichte* is instructive in thinking about the historiography of the nineteenth century in terms of a transformation in the experience of time, "an inversion in the horizon of expectations," which conditioned a particular approach to historical time. Koselleck, *Futures Past: On the Semantics of Historical Time*, trans. Keith Tribe (New York: Columbia University Press, 2004), 12, and *The Practice of Conceptual History: Timing History, Spacing Concepts*, trans. Todd Presner, Kerstin Behnke, and Jobst Welge (Stanford, CA: Stanford University Press, 2002).

36. See Timothy Mitchell, ed., *Questions of Modernity* (Minneapolis: University of Minnesota Press, 2000); and Dipesh Chakrabarty, *Provincializing Europe: Postcolonial Thought and Historical Difference* (Princeton, NJ: Princeton University Press, 2000). The collaborative formation of an asymmetric global order has historical value in deconstructing stark East/West binaries but often seems to come with an odd placement of

emphasis; see, e.g., Christopher Bayly, *Empire and Information: Intelligence Gathering and Social Communication in India, 1780–1870* (New York: Cambridge University Press, 1996); and Thomas Metcalf, *Imperial Connections: India in the Indian Ocean Arena, 1860–1920* (Berkeley: University of California Press, 2007).

37. On a method to disrupt that hold of empire on bodies and the imagination, see Antoinette Burton, *The Trouble with Empire: Challenges to Modern British Imperialism* (New York: Oxford University Press, 2015).

38. For evidence that this nineteenth-century way of seeing the world is alive and well, see Robert Kaplan's explanation of realism in the twenty-first century and his invitation to all of us to think like Victorians, "The Revenge of Geography," *Foreign Policy*, no. 172 (May/June 2009): 96–105, 98 and 105.

39. For an impressive examination of this emerging order that stitches (back) together the "Middle East" and "South Asia," see M. C. Low, "The Mechanics of Mecca: The Technopolitics of the Late Ottoman Hijaz and the Colonial Hajj" (PhD diss., Columbia University, 2015). See also Low, "The Indian Ocean and Other Middle Easts," *CSSAAME* 34, no. 3 (2014): 549–55.

40. Andrew Sartori, "Global Intellectual History and the History of Political Economy," in *Global Intellectual History*, ed. Samuel Moyn and Andrew Sartori (New York: Columbia University Press, 2013), 110–33; quotation from 113. The literature on ideologies of empire is quite large; see, among others, Anthony Pagden, *Lords of All the World: Ideologies of Empire in Spain, Britain, and France c. 1500–1800* (New Haven, CT: Yale University Press, 1995); David Armitage, *The Ideological Origins of the British Empire* (New York: Cambridge University Press, 2000); Duncan Bell, *The Idea of Greater Britain: Empire and the Future of World Order, 1860–1900* (Princeton, NJ: Princeton University Press, 2007); and Robert Travers, *Ideology and Empire in Eighteenth-Century India: The British in Bengal* (New York: Cambridge University Press, 2007).

41. For a critique of the impossibility of reassembling the fragmented world through the figure of the consumer, see Gayatri Spivak, *A Critique of Postcolonial Reason: Toward a History of the Vanishing Present* (Cambridge, MA: Harvard University Press, 1999).

42. This historical world system was not quite the same as the famously elaborated world system of Immanuel Wallerstein, *The Modern World System: Capitalist Agriculture and the Origins of the European World Economy in the Sixteenth Century* (New York: Academic Press, 1974). Other, more nuanced views of that world history now abound; see, e.g., Christopher Bayly and Sanjay Subrahmanyam, "Portfolio Capitalists and the Political Economy of Early Modern India," *Indian Economic and Social History Review* 25, no. 4 (1988): 401–24; Stephen Dale, *Indian Merchants and Eurasian Trade, 1600–1750* (New York: Cambridge University Press, 1994); Rajat Kanta Ray, "Asian Capital in the Age of European Domination: The Rise of the Bazaar, 1800–1914," *Modern Asian Studies* 29, no. 3 (July 1995): 449–554; Claude Markovits, *The Global World of Indian Merchants, 1750–1947: Traders of Sind from Bukhara to Panama* (New York: Cambridge University Press, 2000); Sebouh Aslanian, *From the Indian Ocean to the Mediterranean: The Global Trade Networks of Armenian Merchants from New Julfa* (Berkeley: University of California Press, 2011); and Pedro Machado, *Ocean of*

Trade: South Asian Merchants, Africa and the Indian Ocean, c.1750–1850 (New York: Cambridge University Press, 2014).

43. Mark Mazower, *Hitler's Empire: How the Nazis Ruled Europe* (New York: Penguin Press, 2008). See also Jürgen Zimmerer, "The First Genocide of the Twentieth Century: The German War of Destruction in Southwest Africa (1904–1908) and the Global History of Genocide," in *Lessons and Legacies: Generation to Generation*, vol. 8, ed. Doris L. Bergen (Evanston, IL: Northwestern University Press, 2008), 34–64. Figures such as Robert Kaplan ("Center Stage for the Twenty-First Century: Power Plays in the Indian Ocean," *Foreign Affairs* 88, no. 2 [March–April 2009]: 16–29) analyze the global future as if that history did not exist.

44. There was another sense of difference—*exister c'est différer*—articulated by Gabriel Tarde at the end of the nineteenth century, which saw in human and nonhuman organisms the same tendencies to associate and differentiate. Tarde considered the rush toward identity (as the contemporary starting point for asserting difference) as a problematic trajectory in the new social science driven by explanatory laws and theories. Bruno Latour observes that perhaps it's not surprising that Tarde's science of society, privileging the small and the singular, was buried. Latour, *What Is the Style of Matters of Concern? Two Lectures in Empirical Philosophy* (Amsterdam: Royal Van Gorcum, 2008), 16.

45. For a homologous argument about capitalism's global formation in the breach of licit and illicit exchange, see Johan Mathew, *Margins of the Market: Trafficking and Capitalism across the Arabian Sea* (Berkeley: University of California Press, 2016).

46. A future world governed by soulless states was one Fadl came to fear by the end of his life. On an antistatist trajectory that went into the twentieth century, see Karuna Mantena, "On Gandhi's Critique of the State: Sources, Contexts, Conjunctures," *Modern Intellectual History* 9, no. 3 (2012): 535–63.

47. The literature on sovereignty is too extensive to cite here, but references to relevant works will be given throughout.

48. When "sovereignty" appears with no adjective, I mean to indicate the family resemblance or shared genealogies of historical forms of divine and modern sovereignty wherein worldly submission/subjugation of souls is presumed.

49. For a refreshing departure from this conventional view that aligns with our argument about the unity of life, see Paulina Ochoa Espejo, "Does Political Theology Entail Decisionism?," *Philosophy and Social Criticism* 38, no. 7 (2012): 725–43, doi: 10.1177/0191453712447780. On returning to metaphysics in political theory today, see Espejo, "On Political Theology and the Possibility of Superseding It," *Critical Review of International Social and Political Philosophy* 13, no. 4 (2010): 475–94, doi: 10.1080/09692290.2010.517967.

50. S. M. Mohamed Koya, *Mappilas of Malabar: Studies in Social and Cultural History* (Calicut: Sandhya, 1983).

51. See, e.g., Lauren Benton, *A Search for Sovereignty: Law and Geography in European Empires, 1400–1900* (New York: Cambridge University Press, 2010).

52. "His long stay in the Ottoman capital and the intimate knowledge acquired of

the Empire's affairs have [left] him completely disillusioned." Enc. in Confid. Currie to Earl of Kimberly, Foreign Secretary, October 12, 1894. TNA FO 78/4790.

53. Ibid.

54. "Il est convaincu que la protection de l'Angleterre seule pourrait sauver l'existence politique et religieuse des Arabes et Turcs." Ibid.

55. Michel Foucault, *The History of Sexuality*, vol. 1: *An Introduction*, trans. Richard Hurley (New York: Vintage, 1990).

56. This is "necessarily an incomplete tale," in a slightly different sense than intended by John-Paul Ghobrial, "The Secret Life of Elias of Babylon and the Uses of Global Microhistory," *Past and Present* 222 (February 2014): 51–93, 55. Fadl's life story cannot be told in full, nor is it exactly over.

57. M. Taussig, "History as Sorcery," *Representations* 7 (Summer 1984): 87–109.

58. Ottamaliyakkal Muthokoya-Thangal, *Mampuram Thangal (Makham) Charithram*, 2nd ed. (Tirurangadi, Kerala: Nur al-Islam Press, n.d.); K. K. Muhammad Abdul Karim, *Hasratt Mampuram Sayyid Alavi Thangal* (Tirurangadi, Kerala: Amir al-Islam Power Press, 1975); Muhammed Mattath, *Khuthubussaman Mampuram Sayyid Alavi Thangal Fasal Pukkoya Thangal, Mampuram Charithram* (Tirurangadi, Kerala: Nur al-Islam Press, 2008); Moyin Hudawi Malayamma and Mahmood Panangangara, *Mampuram Thangal: Jeevitham Aathmiiyatha Poraattam* [The Mampuram sayyid: A life of spiritual struggle] (Tirurangadi, Kerala: Asas Book Cell, Darul Huda Islamic Academy, 2009). Written from within the discipline of history, K. K. Mohammed Abdul Sathar, the son of K. K. Muhammad Abdul Karim and inheritor of his private archive, was far more sensitive to the hagiographic tradition than Western scholars in his dissertation, "History of Ba-Alawis in Kerala" (Calicut University, 1999); see also his *Mappila Leader In Exile: A Political Biography of Syed Fazl Tangal* (Calicut: Other Books, 2012). When I first set out on this project, I interviewed Dr. M. Gangadharan, who had a great interest in the anticolonial role played by the Mappilas in shaping the history of his district; he was very helpful in steering me in the right direction. He has published two books: *Mappila Padanangal* in Malayalam (Calicut: Vachanam Books, 2004) and *The Malabar Rebellion* (Kottayam: D. C. Books, 2008).

Chapter 1

Epigraph from BL IOR/R/20/E/198, Item 1.

1. See also Freitag, *Indian Ocean Migrants*, 79–81.

2. On the development of a British imperial information order marked by a relationship between state intelligence and local networks of knowledge production and dissemination, see Bayly, *Empire and Information*. On the role of the culture broker or go-between in contexts around the globe, see Simon Schaffer, Lissa Roberts, Kapil Raj, James Delbourgo, eds., *The Brokered World: Go-Betweens and Global Intelligence, 1770–1820* (Sagamore Beach, MA: Science History Publications, 2009).

3. On similar historical formations through the lives and shrines of saints in the Deccan, see Nile Green, "Stories of Saints and Sultans: Re-Membering History at the Sufi Shrines of Aurangabad," *Modern Asian Studies* 38, no. 2 (May 2004): 419–46.

Green's concluding line is relevant here, "Whatever the epistemic breaks experienced by other historical traditions, the continued topographic presence of the shrines of the Sufi saints and the saints' continued miraculous intervention in the lives of their communities has in turn helped to ensure the continuity of history itself" (446).

4. Linda Colley, *The Ordeal of Elizabeth Marsh: A Woman in World History* (New York: Pantheon, 2007). There are many such works now, including an Oxford University Press series titled "The World in a Life"; see, e.g., Omar H. Ali, *Malik Ambar: Power and Slavery across the Indian Ocean* (New York: Oxford University Press, 2016).

5. I am aware of the modernist assumptions of this statement. By "biography," I mean a genre of modern history writing that consciously departs from prior forms of life- or self-narratives. This departure can also be located in traditions of *tarajim/ tarikh* in Arabic and *charitram* in Malayalam. See Dwight F. Reynolds, ed., *Interpreting the Self: Autobiography in the Arabic Literary Tradition* (Berkeley: University of California Press, 2001); and V. N. Rao, David Shulman, and Sanjay Subrahmanyam, *Textures of Time: Writing History in South India, 1600–1800* (New Delhi: Permanent Black, 2001). A work that has become controversial in part for its assertions of radical alterity over time and space but is nonetheless erudite and useful for thinking about multiple modes of writing life is Sheldon Pollock, *The Language of the Gods in the World of Men: Sanskrit, Culture, and Power in Premodern India* (Berkeley: University of California Press, 2006); see also Ronit Ricci, *Islam Translated: Literature, Conversion, and the Arabic Cosmopolis of South and Southeast Asia* (Chicago: University of Chicago Press, 2011).

6. Daniel Headrick, *The Tools of Empire: Technology and European Imperialism in the Nineteenth Century* (New York: Oxford University Press, 1981).

7. Ashin Das Gupta, *Malabar in Asian Trade, 1740–1800* (New York: Cambridge University Press, 1967). See also K. V. Krishan Ayyar, *The Zamorins of Calicut: From the Earliest Times Down to AD 1806* (Calicut: Norman Printing Bureau, 1938). For a broader view of contemporaneous travelers' lives reconstructed from recently discovered letters, see Gagan D. S. Sood, *India and the Islamic Heartlands: An Eighteenth-Century World of Circulation and Exchange* (Cambridge: Cambridge University Press, 2016).

8. Hasan al-Jifri may have been in Malabar from as early as 1699. Appendix 3, "Examination of Syed Mahomed Tangul, son of Syed Hussan Tangul," in Conolly to Montgomery, October 12, 1849, *CMO* (Madras: Graves, Cookson, 1863), 1:56–57. Colonial officials' investigations into cases of Mappila rebellion reveal parts of the Alawi genealogy, making clear to Malabar magistrates like Conolly the breadth and depth of their influence.

9. Early European colonialism was not dissimilar, though the intimate alliances do seem to have been fraught with more tensions; see Durba Ghosh, *Sex and the Family in Colonial India: The Making of Empire* (New York: Cambridge University Press, 2006).

10. In his *Oriental Memoirs* (London: White, Cochrane, 1813), 1:322–24, James Forbes made drawings of and recounted the appearance of Calicut in the 1770s as a city whose past greatness as a trade "emporium" had literally been buried under the sea for over a century.

11. In *Graves of Tarim*, 55–58, Ho contrasts the emptiness of frontier imagery in the American discourse of Manifest Destiny to its fullness in the Alawi vision of pushing back the frontier by civilizing the Bedouin with correct religious instruction and "revivifying 'dead' land" with irrigation and better land management. Fadl's reproduction of this view in the context of Dhofar will be discussed in Chapter 3.

12. Michel Foucault, *The Birth of Biopolitics*, trans. Graham Burchell (New York: Palgrave Macmillan, 2008), 31–33. Looking at a later period, in *Stages of Capital*, Ritu Birla has argued that it was precisely in the context of colonial sovereignty that government remained pegged to market.

13. *A Collection of Treaties, Engagements and Other Papers of Importance Relating to British Affairs in Malabar*, ed. William Logan, 2nd ed. (Madras: Madras Civil Service, 1891; repr., Madras: Superintendent Government Press, 1951), 178–80.

14. Clive, Stuart, Petrie, and Fallofield to Spencer, September 5, 1801, in ibid., 345–46.

15. William Logan, *Malabar Manual* (1887; New Delhi: Asian Educational Services, 1989), 1:533.

16. Dale gives 1801 as the year of the first official recording of the Alawis' involvement in anti-Company activities. It's difficult to say with certainty, however, that the ambiguous mention of a "priest" in this account refers to Sayyid Alawi. Dale, *Islamic Society on the South Asian Frontier*, 116 and n71.

17. Vaughan to Secretary to Government, Judicial Department Madras, April 10, 1817, BL IOR/P/323/33.

18. For an overview, see Anand Yang, ed., *Crime and Criminality in British India* (Tucson: University of Arizona Press, 1985).

19. There are many accounts of the conflicts that explain them in stark communal terms (Hindu/Muslim), though there is sufficient countervailing evidence to suggest that what was always at stake from the Mysorean period on was the question of sovereignty, which could take on communal flavor but did not necessarily have to. This is evident from the EIC's own record; see, e.g., April 5, 1792, BL IOR/H/606.

20. Logan, *Malabar Manual*, 1:449.

21. For how Tipu fits, or fit himself, into the new global history as an enlightened monarch, see Sebastian Conrad, "Enlightenment in Global History: A Historiographical Critique," *AHR* (October 2012): 999–1027, 1013. Conrad draws on Kate Brittlebank, *Tipu Sultan's Search for Legitimacy: Islam and Kingship in a Hindu Domain* (Delhi: Oxford University Press, 1997), ch. 5. Brittlebank's emphasis, however, is on the local appropriations that enabled Tipu's success.

22. David Armitage, *The Declaration of Independence: A Global History* (Cambridge, MA: Harvard University Press, 2008).

23. The postcolonial Indian state, the heir to absolute sovereignty, is regularly mocked in Malayalam popular culture (in cinema, television, and now social media) from the perspective of this local, individualized conception of power.

24. Logan, *Malabar Manual*, 1:vi. The "Parliament" reference was from a report compiled by the EIC's representative in Calicut about unrest there: "These Nayars being heads of the Calicut people, resemble the parliament, and do not obey the king's dictates

in all things, but chastise his ministers when they do unwarrantable acts." Tellicherry Factory Diary, May 28, 1746 (cited in ibid., 89).

25. Anecdotal evidence suggests that the Nairs are still held in high esteem by other communities in Kerala precisely for their fairness and openness just as much as they may be vilified by other castes.

26. Logan, *Malabar Manual*, 1:88.

27. Signaling her revisionist move, Benton notes, "In my sea yarn, the oceans have a quality of lumpiness about them, pirates strain not to break the law, and international norms take shape not at Westphalia but at the edges of the Indian Ocean." Benton, "Legal Spaces of Empire: Piracy and the Origins of Ocean Regionalism," *CSSH* (2005): 700–724; quote from 701–2.

28. August 15, 1790, BL IOR/H/606.

29. April 5, 1792, BL IOR/H/606.

30. Corruption among its employees was viewed as seeking personal profit as opposed to legitimate Company profit and was fought assiduously, as the records make clear. The line between legitimate government/trade and illegitimate self-aggrandizement established the further distinction between legitimate (EIC) and illegitimate (Oriental despotism) forms of state. On the role of violence in drawing and maintaining the line, see Benjamin Madley, "Reexamining the American Genocide Debate: Meaning, Historiography, and New Methods," *AHR* 120, no. 1 (February 2015): 98–139.

31. For samples of the oaths Farmer swore for each of the offices (Revenue, "Phouzdarry," and "Sadar Adalat") he assumed in 1793, see Logan, *Malabar Manual*, 1:487–89.

32. Ibid., 1:487.

33. David Washbrook, *The Emergence of Provincial Politics: The Madras Presidency 1870–1920* (New York: Cambridge University Press, 1976). Lisa Ford and others have shown that alliances and diplomacy were also features of an earlier competitive imperial jurisdictional politics and "legal ferment" in the New World, and annihilation more a condition of settler state building. Ford, *Settler Sovereignty: Jurisdiction and Indigenous People in America and Australia, 1788–1836* (Cambridge, MA: Harvard University Press, 2010).

34. Logan, *Malabar Manual*, 1:506; emphasis in the original translation. Dale refers to the Zamorin's "imperfect control" in a competitive political field, with a new entrant making revenue claims the former could not fulfill. Dale, *Islamic Society*, 100.

35. Logan, *Malabar Manual*, 1:507.

36. Ibid., 1:508. Though he did not intend his analysis to be generalized, Logan's insight goes a long way toward explaining some of the intractable and often intense violence found in the colonial and postcolonial world. Faisal Devji, *The Impossible Indian: Gandhi and the Temptation of Violence* (Cambridge, MA: Harvard University Press, 2012); Mahmood Mamdani, *Citizen and Subject: Contemporary Africa and the Legacy of Colonialism* (Princeton, NJ: Princeton University Press, 1996); Dilip Menon, *Caste, Nationalism, and Communism in South India: Malabar, 1900–1948* (New York: Cambridge University Press, 1994); Nicholas B. Dirks, *The Hollow Crown: Ethnohistory of an Indian Kingdom* (New York: Cambridge University Press, 1987). See also Ruchi

Chaturvedi, "'Somehow It Happened': Violence, Culpability, and the Hindu Nationalist Community," *Cultural Anthropology* 26, no. 3 (2011): 340–62.

37. Lieutenant William Heude, *Journey Overland from India to England in 1817 Containing Notices of Arabia Felix, Arabia Deserta, Persia, Mesopotamia, The Garden of Eden, Babylon, Bagdad, Koordistan, Armenia, Asia Minor* (London: Longman, Hurst, Rees, Orme, and Brown, 1819), 6–7. Heude began his military career in India when he was fifteen (1804) and received furlough from his station at Cannanore thirteen years later, which is when he started his long trip home.

38. Dilip Menon, "Houses by the Sea: State-Formation Experiments in Malabar, 1760–1800," in *Economic and Political Weekly* 34/29 (July 17–23, 1999): 1995–2003; quote from 1995.

39. In Menon's account, "mappila" is in lower-case, though it is unclear why, since he does not provide a definition and leaves Hindu and Muslim as proper nouns. One possibility is that it indexes the lack of a fixed Muslim identity in Malabar at the time and a porous boundary between and among communities; whereby movement into mappila (an outsider position?) or nair (Hindu designation for landed non-Brahmanical caste) could be effected through one's actions in the political and economic fields.

40. Ibid., 2000–2001.

41. April 1792, BL IOR/H/6065.

42. On the EIC as a military-patronage as opposed to fiscal-military state, see Mesrob Vartavarian, "An Open Military Economy: The British Conquest of South India Reconsidered, 1780–1799," *Journal of the Economic and Social History of the Orient* 57 (2014): 486–510.

43. Benton, *Search for Sovereignty*, and *Law and Colonial Cultures: Legal Regimes in World History, 1400–1900* (New York: Cambridge University Press, 2002); Ford, *Settler Sovereignty*; for a broader theoretical critique, see Peter Fitzpatrick, *Modernism and the Grounds of Law* (New York: Cambridge University Press, 2001).

44. The dissolution of the EIC and the ascension of Queen Victoria as the ruler of India in 1858 came with the promise not to interfere in and to protect the traditions of its various communities. Thereby, the Company and its excesses were reassimilated to a narrative of the progressive unfolding of a liberal imperialism, while its hybrid formation was purified. See Faisal Devji, "The Mutiny to Come," *New Literary History* 40 (2009): 411–30.

45. P. G. McHugh, "'A Pretty Gov[ernment]!': The 'Confederation of United Tribes' and Britain's Quest for Imperial Order in the New Zealand Islands during the 1830s," in *Legal Pluralism and Empires, 1500–1850*, ed. Lauren Benton and Richard J. Ross (New York: NYU Press, 2013), 233–58, 234. In the same volume, see also Paul D. Halliday's insightful essay "Laws' Histories: Pluralisms, Pluralities, Diversity," 261–78.

46. Vaughan to Madras, April 10, 1817, BL IOR/P/323/33.

47. Nonetheless, members of this Mappila family served in various revenue-collecting and policing capacities under Hyder, Tipu, and the EIC. Contrary to reductive confessional explanations for conflicts in the period, it was Tipu Sultan who moved against the Kurikuls in support of the Manjeri Raja when Athan Moyen Kurikul, a revenue official for Mysore, overreached in a 1784 attack on the raja's home and the

local temple. Athan and his son Manjeri Kurikul were captured and imprisoned. The son escaped and managed to reassert control over his family lands in part through service to the EIC after Mysore's defeat. Dale, *Islamic Society*, 87–88.

48. Ibid., 88.

49. See Conrad Wood, *The Moplah Rebellion and Its Genesis* (New Delhi: People's Publishing House, 1987), "The First Moplah Rebellion against British Rule in Malabar," *Modern Asian Studies* 10, no. 4 (1976): 543–56, and "Historical Background of the Moplah Rebellion: Outbreaks, 1836–1919," *Social Scientist* 3, no. 1 (August 1974): 5–33.

50. Logan, *Malabar Manual*, 1:534.

51. Ibid., 1:536.

52. Dale, *Islamic Society*, 105.

53. Logan, *Malabar Manual*, 1:491, 495–96, 506–8.

54. David Washbrook, "Sovereignty, Property, Land and Labour in Colonial South India," in *Constituting Modernity: Private Property in the East and West*, ed. Huri Islam-oğlu (New York: I. B. Tauris, 2004), 69–99. The law was crucial in fixing property relations and vice versa. Many studies have now shown that the importance of the legal profession as it matured out of more fluid engagements with natural law was connected to growing empires of the late eighteenth and nineteenth centuries. Land and tax cases in particular constituted quite a boon to lawyers as significant actors and as an interest group in the modern bureaucratic state. Bayly, *Birth of the Modern World, 1780–1914*, 144–45.

55. On the colonial career of the figure of the fanatic from Sayyid Ahmed's revolt in Northwest India in the 1820s to Sudan, northern Nigeria, and Somaliland later, see Benjamin D. Hopkins, "Islam and Resistance in the British Empire," in *Islam and the European Empires*, ed. David Motadel (New York: Oxford University Press, 2014), 150–69.

56. Vaughan to Secretary to Government, April 10, 1817, IOR/p/323/33. "Taramalle Coya Tangal" is a basic transliteration of the Malayalam phrase meaning "the noble sayyid from Tarim," that is, Sayyid Alawi.

57. In taking this stance, he was following a Ba Alawi custom based on an ancient conviction that pious Muslims risked moral pollution by interacting with rulers and political agents. Sathar, "History of Ba-Alawis in Kerala," 57.

58. Vaughan to Secretary to Government, April 10, 1817, IOR/p/323/33.

59. Ibid.

60. *Vakeel*, a Persianized Arabic word still used in Kerala, is a legal proxy or advocate. *Vakalatnamah* is essentially a document assigning power of attorney. See Bishara, *A Sea of Debt*.

61. It was precisely the layers and circles of sovereignty that confused Lieutenant Heud and made him appreciate the "unity" of military service. He noted that the fault did not lie with individuals but with "the establishment in general." He also did not seem to appreciate the constant resort to military force for tax-gathering purposes. Heud, *A Voyage*, 5–6.

62. Dirks, *Hollow Crown*. David Washbrook's critical survey of recent histories of South India's colonial past takes issue with studies that read back from a late nineteenth-century perspective, when British power was paramount, to earlier periods, when

British ascendancy was not yet a sure thing, making "hollow" crowns an inaccurate metaphor for the transitioning political landscape of the eighteenth and much of the nineteenth centuries, obscuring the precise ways in which paramountcy was achieved, if it ever was. One of Washbrook's many excellent insights is that ancient conceptions of sovereignty in both India and Britain were changed through their complex entanglement with one another, specifically as a mercantilist economic and governmental logic became the logic of state by the middle of the nineteenth century. "South India 1770–1840: The Colonial Transition," *Modern Asian Studies* 38, no. 3 (July 2004): 479–516; see esp. 512–13. His reading, however, of Dirks as overstating a structural argument about colonialism's power to "hollow" out prior authorities is not entirely fair; in fact, his own interest in explaining the specific ways the EIC affected the course of South Indian history obscures indigenous agency by an exclusive reliance on British sources.

63. Vaughan to Secretary to Government, 10 April 1817, IOR/p/323/33.

64. David Hill, Secretary to Government to Vaughan, 28 April 1817, IOR/p/323/33.

65. Vaughan to Madras, 29 April 1817, IOR/p/323/33.

66. Ibid.

67. Devji, "The Mutiny to Come."

68. Vaughan to Madras, 29 April 1817, IOR/p/323/33.

69. Another vivid example of the multidirectional engagement is a 1738 treaty signed by the Muslims of Peringatur with the French East India Company based nearby in Mahé for protection against the Nair landlords of the surrounding region. "The signatories agreed to have the French patrol the bazar [*sic*], to mediate in disputes concerning the 'manners and customs of the country,' and, probably most important, to defend the Muslims if any of the 'Lords' of the country caused trouble in the bazar, their shops, or at the mosque. To defray French expenses the inhabitants agreed to tax their houses and shops two rupees each." Dale, *Islamic Society*, 70–71.

70. While a particular historical chapter may have ended, in this case Sayyid Alawi's lineage in Malabar (though collateral descendants remain), there will be no conclusion to the story of the sayyids as long as the shrine at Mampuram stands, prayers are offered, and blessings sought through their mediation.

71. Dale, *Islamic Society*, 120; Sathar, "History of Ba-Alawis in Kerala," 103. Ronald Miller, in *Mappila Muslims of Kerala*, puts the number at fifty-one, which as Dale's explanatory footnote (251n1) suggests probably included "suspected incidents."

72. Dale, *Islamic Society*, 126–27.

73. Miller, *Mappila Muslims of Kerala*, 114. I could not find the source that he used to verify this claim.

74. For a view of the legal futures of "outrage," see E. Kolsky, "The Colonial Rule of Law and the Legal Regime of Exception: Frontier "Fanaticism" and State Violence in British India," *AHR* 120, no. 4 (2015): 1218–46, https://doi.org/10.1093/ahr/120.4.1218; the Mappila Act is discussed on 1229.

75. Conolly to Pycroft, January 29, 1852, in *CMO*, 1:240–41.

76. Dale, *Islamic Society*, 160–61.

77. R. Travers, "Imperial Repercussions: South Asia and the World, c. 1760–1840," in

The Age of Revolutions in Global Context, c. 1760–1840, ed. David Armitage and Sanjay Subrahmanyam (New York: Palgrave Macmillan, 2010), 144–66; V. Aksan, "Locating the Ottomans in Napoleon's World," in *Napoleon's Empire: European Politics in Global Perspective,* ed. Ute Planert (New York: Palgrave Macmillan, 2016), 277–90. Recontextualizing the outrages this way offers a prehistory to Talal Asad's reading of suicide terrorism as belonging to liberalism rather than Islam. Asad, *On Suicide Bombing* (New York: Columbia University Press, 2007), 92.

78. Minute by the Honorable President Henry Pottinger, December 16, 185[1], on Letter from the Magistrate of Malabar, No. 1,014, dated November 29, [1851], in *CMO,* 1:231.

79. Conolly to Montgomery, Secretary to Government, Judicial Department, October 12, 1849, in *CMO,* 1:33. *Tangul* or *thangal* is the Malayalam equivalent of *sayyid* and refers here to Sayyid Fadl.

80. Ibid., 1:35. Conolly's characterization of Mampuram and its sayyids as the epicenter of the Malabar outrages is repeated in Dale's analysis.

81. Ibid., 1:34.

82. Tirurangadi is a market town across the river from Mampuram. Since the eighteenth century at least its significant Muslim population had posed a challenge to the status quo.

83. Ibid., 1:35–36.

84. F. Fawcett, "A Popular Mopla Song," *Indian Antiquary* 28 (March 1899): 64–71, and "War Songs of the Mappilas of Malabar," *Indian Antiquary* 30 (November/December 1901): 499–508, 528–37.

85. Rendered roughly as "sacred charisma" when inhabiting a human subject, *baraka* broadly denotes a blessing from God that can be passed on via saints, shrines, relics, and so on.

86. By the last third of the nineteenth century it was precisely the history and laws of the Romans that united a Europe of big and small states as a civilization aspiring to the government of the world. Martti Koskenniemi, *The Gentle Civilizer of Nations: The Rise and Fall of International Law, 1870–1960* (New York: Cambridge University Press, 2001), 100–116. See also Antony Anghie, *Imperialism, Sovereignty and the Making of International Law* (New York: Cambridge University Press, 2005); and Karuna Mantena, *Alibis of Empire: Henry Maine and the Ends of Liberal Imperialism* (Princeton, NJ: Princeton University Press, 2010).

87. For a welcome focus on the brutal and everyday violence of colonial rule rather than its economic and bureaucratic or cultural spheres, see E. Kolsky, *Colonial Justice in British India: White Violence and the Rule of Law* (New York: Cambridge University Press, 2010). Kolsky writes: "Although the archive is replete with incidents of Britons murdering, maiming, and assaulting Indians—*and getting away with it*—white violence remains one of the empire's most closely guarded secrets" (2). See also Kim A. Wagner, "'Calculated to Strike Terror': The Amritsar Massacre and the Spectacle of Colonial Violence," *Past and Present* 233, no. 1 (2016): 185–225.

88. *CMO,* 1:37. Conolly first made the recommendation to revert to the policy of disarming the population in 1841; after the settlement, the possession of arms had

been made a punishable offense, but it seems the policy was rescinded in 1816 (Section 49, Regulation XI). Conolly argued in 1841 that Malabar was exceptional in southern India and perhaps in all of India for its population of fanatics "notorious for turbulence and lawlessness." Ibid., 1:38.

89. For an account of the history of Muslim rebelliousness that starts with the first attack on British interests, in 1756, prior to the annexation of Malabar, see R. H. Hitchcock, *A History of the Malabar Rebellion, 1921* (Madras: Government Press, 1925); repr. with introduction by Robert L. Hardgrave Jr. as *Peasant Revolt in Malabar* (New Delhi: Usha, 1983). Though he relied heavily on the trope of fanaticism, even giving it a periodization (that roughly coincides with the arrival of Sayyid Alawi), he did admit that land tenure issues and a desire for lives "worth living" were sometimes the actual causes of rebellion. Indeed, he pointed to the reform and development projects pursued after the 1896 "outbreak" as responsible for Malabar's longest period of peace. But the efforts (building roads and bridges, more schools, and "a higher standard of religious education," thus creating job prospects beyond Malabar) quickly slowed, mainly owing to "prohibitive cost." Ibid., 175–76.

90. For the kinds of epistemologies and the new objects of colonialism that are often inscribed as the history of power in India, see, among others, Ranajit Guha, *Elementary Aspects of Peasant Insurgency in Colonial India* (New York: Oxford University Press, 1983); Bernard Cohn, "The Command of Language and the Language of Command," *Subaltern Studies* 4 (1985): 276–329, and *Colonialism and Its Forms of Knowledge: The British in India* (Princeton, NJ: Princeton University Press, 1996); Ronald Inden, *Imagining India* (Cambridge, MA: Blackwell, 1990); Dirks, *Hollow Crown*; Lata Mani, *Contentious Traditions: The Debate on Sati in Colonial India* (Berkeley: University of California Press, 1998); and Peter van der Veer, *Imperial Encounters: Religion and Modernity in India and Britain* (Baltimore: Johns Hopkins University Press, 2001).

91. See the collection edited by Thomas Blom Hansen and Finn Stepputat, *Sovereign Bodies: Citizens, Migrants, and States in the Postcolonial World* (Princeton, NJ: Princeton University Press, 2005), especially Hansen's chapter on the power of local big men, "Sovereigns beyond the State" (169–91). Drawing on Tocqueville and Charles Tilly, Engseng Ho references the "leveling" of asymmetrical and multiple jurisdictions through the destruction of local sources of sovereignty as the definitive characteristic of the state form, which was replicated everywhere but whose territorialization of power in the nation was always incomplete. Ho, *Graves of Tarim*, 294–95.

92. Conolly to Pycroft, January 29, 1852, in *CMO*, 1:241.

93. Samera Esmeir, "The Work of Law in the Age of Empire: Production of Humanity in Colonial Egypt" (PhD diss., New York University, 2005), and *Juridical Humanity: A Colonial History* (Stanford, CA: Stanford University Press, 2012); Nasser Hussain, *The Jurisprudence of Emergency: Colonialism and the Rule of Law* (Ann Arbor: University of Michigan Press, 2003); Radhika Singha, *A Despotism of Law: Crime and Justice in Early Colonial India* (Delhi: Oxford University Press, 1998).

Chapter 2

1. The relative significance of the question of enduring religiosity versus the source of secular culture is reflected in Simon Goldhill's five-year (2012–17) research program engaging a team of postdoctoral fellows investigating "Bible and Antiquity in Nineteenth-Century Culture" at Cambridge University's Center for Research in the Arts, Social Sciences, and Humanities. See Gareth Atkins, ed. *Making and Remaking Saints in Nineteenth-Century Britain* (Manchester, UK: Manchester University Press, 2016).

2. Those reform efforts then tend to be regarded as derivative, or in a revisionist register, "defensive developmentalism," always a reaction. For the latter, see James L. Gelvin, *The Modern Middle East: A History* (New York: Oxford University Press, 2015).

3. Washbrook, "South India 1770–1840."

4. See Faisal Devji's *The Impossible Indian* for an analysis of the rebellion as realigning Hindu-Muslim relations along moral and political lines, superseding the ancient bonds of friendship and enmity through acts of sacrifice for the sake of unity.

5. Based on archaeological evidence dating the period of Chera rule from only the ninth until the twelfth century and pointing to the fact that "Cheruman Perumal" was more likely a title than a name, Sebastian Prange argues that the Muslim origin myth emerged and circulated as their benefactors vanished and at a time when the Muslim community had expanded and diversified across the region, possibly feeling pressure to justify its indigeneity, rights, and privileges to the Hindu majority as well as to each other. Prange, "Monsoon Islam: Trade and Faith on the Medieval Malabar Coast" (lecture delivered at the Indian Ocean World Center, McGill University, Montreal, April 28, 2016). Also see Prange, *Monsoon Islam: Trade and Faith on the Medieval Malabar Coast* (New York: Cambridge University Press, 2018). I was only able to consult the book after my manuscript entered production, but I would say that Prange's analysis should be considered authoritative.

6. I worked with multiple versions of the text and references to it in Arabic, English, and Malayalam. Citations will be given as required. The full title is *Tuhfat al-Mujahidin fi-b'ad akhbar al-Burtughaliyyin* (Gift of the mujahidin in some reports on the Portuguese).

7. The history of the *Tuhfat*'s reproduction in different times and places is in itself worthy of a book-length study. See Engseng Ho's brief introduction to his translation of an excerpt from the *Tuhfat*, "Custom and Conversion in Malabar: Zayn al-Din al-Malibari's *Gift of the Mujahidin: Some Accounts of the Portuguese*," in *Islam in South Asia in Practice*, ed. Barbara D. Metcalf (Princeton, NJ: Princeton University Press, 2009), 403–8. He suggests that one of the virtues of this early modern Muslim text is to reveal how multiple perspectives on self and other could be maintained at once; the excerpt, a rare ethnographic moment in the *Tuhfat*, illustrates how the elaboration of exclusivist laws was paradoxically the condition of possibility for cross-cultural interactions.

8. "History of the Mapillas from the Arabic," in *Miscellaneous Notes and Translations of Oriental Literature by Dr. Leyden c. 1805*, BL Add MS 26578, ff. 4–28.

9. M. J. Rowlandson, *Tohfut-ul-Mujahideen: An Historical Work in the Arabic Language* (London: The Oriental Translations Fund of Great Britain and Ireland, 1833). See

also S. Muhammad Husayn Nainar, *Tuhfat al-Mujahidin: An Historical Work in the Arabic Language* (Madras: University of Madras, 1942).

10. Andre Wink, *Al-Hind: The Making of the Indo-Islamic World*, vol. 1: *Early Medieval India and the Expansion of Islam 7th–11th Centuries* (Boston: Brill, 2002), 77.

11. Colonel S. B. Miles, *The Countries and Tribes of the Persian Gulf*, 2 vols. (London: Harrison and Sons, 1919), 2:501, 552–53. Miles, who had several imperial postings including resident at Aden and political agent and consul at Muscat, was one of the many officials in the Gulf who kept track of Sayyid Fadl's movements in the 1870s.

12. In Barbosa's version, Cheruman Perumal converted to Islam before dividing up the land and leaving for Mecca, dying en route. Duarte Barbosa, *A Description of the Coasts of East Africa and Malabar in the Beginning of the Sixteenth Century*, trans. Henry E. J. Stanley (London: Hakluyt Society, 1866), 102–3. A short mention of the Perumal is made in the translator's preface to a peculiar Danish missionary text (in "High-Dutch") that is made up of answers to questions put to the "heathens" by their "wise men," *An Account of the Religion, Manners, and Learning of the People of Malabar in Several Letters Written by Some of the Most Learned Men of That Country to the Danish Missionaries*, trans. J. Tho. Phillips (London: W. Mears, 1717), i–ii. Here he was said to have died upon his return, and since he had no heirs, his ministers divided the land into five sections. In an early eighteenth-century Dutch account, he apparently divided the land before going to the Ganges "in fulfilment of a vow, or, as the Moors say, to visit Mahomet in Arabia for the purpose of embracing his religion." Jacobus Canter Visscher, *Letters from Malabar*, trans. Major Heber Drury (Madras: Gantz Brothers, 1862), 49–50.

13. No commentary mentions how the use of the Arabic term *faqir* or the Persian synonym *darvish* (dervish) might be useful in dating the myth of Cheruman Perumal as a Muslim story. From what is known of the history of Sufism, it would seem that the myth could only have been generated around the twelfth or thirteenth century, aligning with Prange's dating.

14. That the myth is still relevant today, even in far-flung exotic locales such as North Carolina, is evinced in online blogs and amateur history sites. The blogger going by the name Maddy who is an electrical engineer in North Carolina maintains the blog *Historic Alleys: Historic Musings from a Malabar Perspective*, on which he posted a well-researched piece titled "The Perumal and the Pickle," querying whether the latter had given a heavenly Kerala variation on ginger pickle, *injipuli*, to the Prophet: http://historicalleys.blogspot.ca/2008/12/perumal-and-pickle.html. He has revisited the myth recently, armed with more research: http://historicalleys.blogspot.ca/2015/03/cheraman-perumal-and-myths.html. See also http://blog.calicutheritage.com/2008/11/tale-of-two-conversions.html. Prime Minister Modi's recent reference to the Perumal's conversion to Islam provoked a response: see http://varnam.org/?s=cheraman.

15. Miles, *Countries and Tribes of the Persian Gulf*, 552–53. A preliminary archaeological survey from 2010 of the shrine landscape of Dhofar reveals its continued existence just outside the bounds of Salalah's al-Baleed archaeological site—the derelict medieval port where Miles would have made landfall. Lynne S. Newton, *Death and*

Burial in Arabia and Beyond: Multidisciplinary Perspectives, Society for Arabian Studies Monographs No. 10 (Oxford: Archaeopress, 2010), 335 fig. 8.

16. Miles, *Countries and Tribes of the Persian Gulf*. My own visit, a pilgrimage of sorts, will be narrated in the Conclusion.

17. It is likely that the correction was also of the account that had prevailed until Malabari's writing in the sixteenth century contained in the undated medieval text *Qissat Shakarwati Farmad* (The narrative of the universal sovereign). The figure of a *chakrawarti*, or universal sovereign, is derived from ancient Sanskrit and was common in Malabar and elsewhere in India to refer to the idea of a most supreme or paramount world(ly) ruler. The Cheruman Perumal portion of the Arabic manuscript copy held at the British Library appears in Y. Friedmann,"*Qissat Shakarwati Farmad*: A Tradition Concerning the Introduction of Islam to Malabar," *Israel Oriental Studies* 5 (1975): 233–58. Friedmann believes that al-Malabari's account clearly borrowed but in a "haphazard" manner from the more thorough and earlier *Qissat*.

18. From this perspective the first Vedam was Hindu, the second Jewish, and the third Christian. Logan, *Malabar Manual*, 1:191.

19. In precolonial Malabar's history, *pardesi*, translated loosely from Malayalam as "foreigner," did not evoke the sharp distinctions that attended the category in late colonial times.

20. Dale, *Islamic Society*, 12; Prange, "Monsoon Islam." Prange notes how the early mosque architecture borrowed heavily from the Malabar temple style rather than repeating the pan-Islamic domed/minaret standard, which, however, became the norm in modern times. Although he does not make the connection, the form of sovereignty also changed along with the architecture.

21. In her recent *Islamic Sufi Networks*, Bang argues that in the study of the Indian Ocean world, "translocality" has been a useful lens with which to view networks forged by mobile Muslim scholars and saints in exchange with local communities that in turn became part of a larger Islamic geography of centers and peripheries. See also the introduction by Ulrike Freitag and Achim von Oppen, eds., *Translocality: The Study of Globalising Processes from a Southern Perspective* (Boston: Brill, 2010), 1–21.

22. Ho, "Custom and Conversion," 404.

23. It is debated whether these Muslims included his original traveling companions or were new friends he made in Arabia. In either case, the names are usually agreed upon.

24. For lack of a better term, I use "mysticism" to label variegated practices and personalities of the mystic, who as a figure occupies the threshold of a paradoxical unity of life that is and is not of the law, history, or politics. In the *Qissat Shakarwati Farmad* the Sufis were given as "derawish" and "fuqara,'" who were led by Shaykh Zuhayr al-Din b. al-Shaykh Zaki al-Din al-Madani.

25. "Mappila," according to some scholars, is a compound word from Tamil meaning great (*maha*) child (*pilla*), which was applied to merchant guests on the southeastern Coromandel Coast. On the Malabar Coast, in Malayalam, the word was also applied to esteemed guests who stayed and married local women; and it means "husband" in contemporary usage. In either case, new kinship relations established through marriage

and reproduction are signaled, which made the Mappila simultaneously Arab and Malayali, child and husband, guest and host.

26. I will discuss the version of the manuscript that I consulted later in this section. Interestingly, a recent Kuwaiti initiative has published this text as part two in a new series of Fadl's works edited by Anwar ibn Abd Allah Salim Ba'umar: Fadl ibn Alawi Mawla al-Duwaylah Ba'alawi, *Majmu' thalath rasa'il ilmiyah* (al-Kuwayt: Dar al-Diya' lil-Nashr wa-al-Tawzi', 2018).

27. The full title is *Al-Sayf al-battar ala man yuwali al-kuffar wa yakhudhhum min dun Allah wa rasulihi wa al-mu'minin ansar* (The sharpest sword against the one who aids the unbelievers and takes them as supporters instead of God, his Prophet, and the Believers).

28. Malayamma and Panangangara, *Mampuram Thangal*, 278. Another member of the al-Ahdal clan, Sayyid Abd al-Rahman al-Ahdal, migrated to Kerala during Sayyid Alawi's time. He married a woman from the prominent Makhdum family of Ponnani and had a child with her, named Abd al-Qadir al-Ahdal. Abd al-Rahman returned to Hadhramawt by himself and died in Mocha in 1298 (1881). Ibid., 161.

29. On the changing conception of authorship and authority as forging part of a new "machinery of truth" in the nineteenth century, see Timothy Mitchell, *Colonising Egypt* (New York: Cambridge University Press, 1989), 128–60.

30. The fatwas end with a reference to the fatwas of another, better-known Ahdal, Abd al-Rahman bin Sulayman al-Ahdal.

31. This "religious" dimension has been reduced to geopolitics again in the present as the text entered the "9/11" networks of interrelated discourses of terror and jihad. It has been deemed significant enough to be archived online: https://archive .org/details/sayfAlBattar. The translation and routes of dissemination of *Al-Sayf al-battar* in the twenty-first century are part of a new story taking shape, in which the future of sovereignty is uncertain; the plot lines and where they will end are anybody's best guess.

32. Abu-Manneh, "The Islamic Roots of the Gulhane Rescript," *Die Welt des Islams* 34 (1994): 173–203.

33. On the ways in which the very same approach could be deployed to shore up new terms of modern sovereignty, see Adam Mestyan, *Arab Patriotism: The Ideology and Culture of Power in Late Ottoman Egypt* (Princeton, NJ: Princeton University Press, 2017), 21–49, 125–63.

34. The Wahhabi-inspired response to the Christian European threat to Dar al-Islam was perhaps most extensive in the context of the waning Mughal Empire. Seema Alavi maps the change in the Urdu belt somewhat starkly as a "shift . . . from a Persianate inclusivity to an Arabicist exclusivity." Alavi, *Muslim Cosmopolitanism*, 35.

35. William Ochsenwald, *Religion, Society, and the State in Arabia* (Columbus: Ohio State University Press, 1984), 137–38. The lines drawn—local actors versus central state(s)—in 1855 revolved around recent Ottoman edicts banning the slave trade. A transregional figure such as Fadl likely allied with the local camp in the "dual sharifi-al-Ottoman power structure" in opposing innovation demanded by Christians.

36. This moment is a prehistory to the Egyptian Muhammad Abduh (1849–1905) and especially his Syrian student Rashid Rida (1865–1935), whose reformist views on Islam, which included limiting sayyid claims to authority, traveled across the seas to India and on to the East Indies, being adapted and reworked. The reception of this "modernist Islam," as it is termed by some, has been studied by a number of scholars. See, e.g., Ho, *Graves of Tarim*, 173–84, 271–85; Natalie Mobini-Kesheh, *The Hadrami Awakening: Community and Identity in the Netherlands East Indies, 1900–1942* (Ithaca, NY: Cornell University Press, 1999); Michael Laffan, *Islamic Nationhood and Colonial Indonesia: The Umma below the Winds* (London: Routledge, 2003); R. Michael Feener, *Muslim Legal Thought in Modern Indonesia* (New York: Cambridge University Press, 2007); Amal Ghazal, *Islamic Reform and Arab Nationalism: Expanding the Crescent from the Mediterranean to the Indian Ocean, 1880s–1930s* (New York: Routledge, 2010); Amira K. Bennison, "Muslim Internationalism between Empire and Nation-State," in *Religious Internationals in the Modern World: Globalization and Faith Communities since 1750*, ed. Abigail Green and Vincent Viaene (New York: Palgrave Macmillan, 2012), 163–85; Jose Abraham, *Islamic Reform and Colonial Discourse on Modernity in India: Socio-Political and Religious Thought of Vakkom Moulavi* (New York: Palgrave Macmillan, 2014); Anne K. Bang, *Islamic Sufi Networks in the Western Indian Ocean: Ripples of Reform* (Boston: Brill, 2014); and Scott S. Reese, "Shaykh Abdullahi al-Qutbi and the Pious Believer's Dilemma: Local Moral Guidance in an Age of Global Islamic Reform," *Journal of Eastern African Studies* 9, no. 3 (2015): 488–504.

37. Fadl borrows liberally from Abdallah bin Alawi bin Muhammad al-Haddad, who died in 1720 and is one of the greatest of Tarim's saints. His writings were widely referenced in forging the Alawi Way across the Indian Ocean. Ho, *Graves of Tarim*, 207, 211.

38. As the story generally goes, a descendant of a member of the Abbasid family who had survived the Mongol devastation of Baghdad in 1258 by escaping to Mamluk Egypt passed on the cloak of caliphal investiture to Sultan Selim after the Ottoman conquest of the holy cities.

39. For a riveting and far-reaching revisionist account, see Giancarlo Casale, *The Ottoman Age of Exploration* (New York: Oxford University Press, 2010).

40. Nile Green, *Sufism: A Global History* (Malden, MA: Wiley-Blackwell, 2012).

41. Shaykh ʿAli al-Mukhallalati, editor's introduction to Fadl, *Uddat al-umara*' (Cairo: Matbaʿ al-ḥujra al-hamida 1857 [mid-Rajab 1273]).

42. Ibid., 2.

43. See Mitchell, *Colonising Egypt*; and Jacob, *Working Out Egypt*. It is unsurprising given the earlier and deeply entrenched British presence that similar questions about the Muslim individual were first posed in South Asia. Seema Alavi notes in chapter 1 of *Muslim Cosmopolitanism* that the early nineteenth-century Urdu reinterpretation of the Arabic tradition focused on individual Muslim sovereignty in a Protestant manner.

44. Trimingham, *Sufi Orders in Islam*, 163. See also Annemarie Schimmel, *Mystical Dimensions of Islam* (Chapel Hill: University of North Carolina Press, 1973).

45. The classic remains relevant here: Albert Hourani, *Arabic Thought in the Liberal Age, 1798–1939* (New York: Cambridge University Press, 1983).

46. Talal Asad, *Genealogies of Religion: Discipline and Reasons of Power in Christianity and Islam* (Baltimore: Johns Hopkins University Press, 1993), and *Formations of the Secular: Christianity, Islam, Modernity* (Stanford, CA: Stanford University Press, 2003). See also Peter van der Veer, *Imperial Encounters*; Nandini Chatterjee, *The Making of Indian Secularism: Empire, Law and Christianity, 1830–1960* (New York: Palgrave Macmillan, 2011); and J. Barton Scott, *Spiritual Despots: Modern Hinduism and the Genealogies of Self-Rule* (Chicago: University of Chicago Press, 2016). A defining study such as Durkheim's *The Elementary Forms of Religious Life* (1912) was partly a product of the author's genius and partly a product of prior colonial engagements with religion.

47. Ray, "Asian Capital." Chris Bayly and Sanjay Subrahmanyam, in their groundbreaking article "Portfolio Capitalists and the Political Economy of Early Modern India," argue that the EIC had its start as a major player in South Asia once they became portfolio capitalists, a particular genre of the Indian merchant class serving as intermediaries between sovereigns and agrarian producers. Subrahmanyam further elaborates that medieval and early modern forms of trade and politics were much more complex than allowed in the received wisdom of a monolithic "Islamic world economy" overtaken by an equally monolithic European mercantilism in his "Of Imarat and Tijarat: Asian Merchants and State Power in the Western Indian Ocean, 1400 to 1750," *CSSH* 37, no. 4 (1995): 750–80. See also Prasannan Parthasarathi, *Why Europe Grew Rich and Asia Did Not: Global Economic Divergence, 1600–1850* (Cambridge: Cambridge University Press, 2011); and the excellent pieces in Giorgio Riello and Prasannan Parthasarathi, eds., *The Spinning World: A Global History of Cotton Textiles, 1200–1850* (New York: Oxford University Press, 2009).

48. The minority status of Muslims did not always mean the absence of power. In Malabar, the rulers of Cannanore were Muslim since the sixteenth century. Similarly in Southeast Asia, before conversion by the majority to Islam in certain parts, it was precisely the stranger status of individual Muslims that helped them establish polities. Jeyamalar Kathirithamby-Wells, "'Strangers' and 'Stranger-Kings': The Sayyid in Eighteenth-Century Maritime Southeast Asia," *Journal of Southeast Asian Studies* 40, no. 3 (October 2009): 567–91.

49. Michel Foucault, *Security, Territory, Population: Lectures at the Collège de France, 1976–1977*, trans. G. Burchell (New York: Picador, 2009); see chs. 8–9. Counter-conduct is usually understood in terms of puritanical refusals within Islam, establishing stark splits between, for example, Wahhabism and Sufism or between traditional Sufi mysticism and a politicized neo-Sufism. An excellent article that demonstrates the analytical payoffs of rejecting the stark binary is Darryl Li, "Taking the Place of Martyrs: Afghans and Arabs under the Banner of Islam," *Arab Studies Journal* 20, no. 1 (Spring 2012): 12–39. See also Ho, *Graves of Tarim*, 314–20, 324–28.

50. Fadl, *Uddat al-umara'*, 25. This framing suggests that the direction of the question-and-answer was from Malabar to Yemen.

51. For a historical overview of this problem, see Alan Verskin, *Oppressed in the Land? Fatwās on Muslims Living under Non-Muslim Rule from the Middle Ages to the Present* (Princeton, NJ: Markus Wiener, 2013).

52. *Al-Islam yalu wa la yala alayhi* may also be translated as "Islam dominates and is not dominated."

53. Quran, Surat al-Araf, 128. Interestingly, the context for the verse is Moses relaying to the children of Israel the need for patience after the pharaoh's rejection of God's prophecy. The preceding verses move from creation, Adam and Eve, through Noah (Nuh) and others to whom God spoke, ultimately without success as far as faith and submission to law were concerned.

54. Fadl, *Uddat al-umara'*, 25.

55. Ibid.

56. The difficulty of conducting jihad under these circumstances led the Prophet to declare, "I am innocent of [not responsible for] every Muslim living in the midst of polytheists." Ibid., 26.

57. On Shi'i fatwas from the same time dealing with the more famous case of Ayodhya in the face of Sunni calls for jihad, see Juan Cole, *Sacred Space and Holy War: The Politics, Culture and History of Shi'ite Islam* (New York: I. B. Tauris, 2002), 161–72.

58. Ibid., 28. The Dar al-Islam in this case seems to be at once a spiritual domain, where there was submission to the Word and its finality as represented by the Quran and hadiths, and a territorial domain of shifting boundaries. The questions and answers of the fatwas assume a situation in which Christians have seized worldly power, affecting spiritual and material realms.

59. The flags were called *rayat*. Although *raya* is an old Arabic word found in hadiths and defined as "flag" in the magisterial *Lisan al-Arab* of thirteenth-century lexicographer Ibn Manzur, its appearance in this context makes the parallel with the Iberian use of the word uncanny. In the Indian Ocean world of the Alawis, the flags could have been read as a symbolic representation of the papal-approved *raya* of the Spanish and Portuguese treaties of the fifteenth century. Those "first global lines" divided the world into spheres of Christian mission and colonial expansion and were discussed by Carl Schmitt as marking the beginning of an international order centered on Europe in *The Nomos of the Earth in the International Law of the Jus Publicum Europaeum*, trans. G. L. Ulmen (New York: Telos Press, 2003), 86–92. *Raya*, like the English *ray*, is derived from the Latin *radius*.

60. The text suggests that some Muslims out of ignorance and narrowness of vision see the expansion of Christian fortunes in the world as a kind of divine providence (or their fortunes in the next world) and regard them as the most appropriate preservers and caretakers of this world. Fadl, *Uddat al-umara'*, 29.

61. Ibid., 30.

61. Napoleon's proclamation to Egyptians that he was freeing them from the tyranny of Mamluk rule so that they could practice their religion and become better Muslims was famously deconstructed to reveal its poor use of Arabic and mocked by Abd al-Rahman al-Jabarti in his chronicles of the French occupation. This text formed part

of the canon that those publishing the *Uddat* most likely read. See Juan Cole, *Napoleon's Egypt: Invading the Middle East* (New York: Palgrave Macmillan, 2007).

63. In a later section of the *Uddat*, Fadl transmits the Alawi lessons from Java's Islamic history and encounters with Dutch colonialism. This includes a mention of how the towns fell to Dutch rule through a combination of the use of terror (*al-irhab*) and trickery. The latter involved using local propagandists to spread the word throughout the country that the Dutch "loved the religion of Islam" and were mighty enough to protect Muslims. Fadl, *Uddat al-umara'*, 54–55.

64. Ibid., 33.

65. Ibid., 31–32. The Cairo edition of *Al-Sayf al-battar*, which was interpolated into Fadl's *Uddat*, has a marginal note naming the sultan of the time, but others seemingly did not, as indicated by the al-Tibyan translation discussed in Chapter 6 of this book. This reinforces the point that the fatwas of al-Ahdal belonged both to him and to those who would use them in their own contexts: Malabar, Yemen, Arabia, Egypt, UK, etc.

66. Ibid., 33–34.

67. Ibid., 34–36.

68. The dead subject of a Muslim ruler was more deserving of prayer unless the other was compelled or unable to emigrate. Ibid., 37.

69. The ruling was apostasy and its punishment, if the Muslim's intent was guided by hate. Accordingly, the judgment was mitigated if expediency were the cause, and an appropriate punishment for what was still a sin was prescribed. Ibid., 37–39. This judgment was underscored by the insertion of an account from the fatwas of the more famous al-Ahdal, Sayyid Abd al-Rahman b. Sulayman, regarding errant Muslim tribes of the Hijaz who innovated customary legal practices that went against the sharia and were judged to be in danger of committing apostasy.

70. For some of its themes over time, see the following recent survey, Mehrzad Boroujerdi, ed., *Mirror for the Muslim Prince: Islam and the Theory of Statecraft* (Syracuse, NY: Syracuse University Press, 2013). For a tentative comparison, see Linda Darling, "Mirrors for Princes in Europe and the Middle East: A Case of Historiographical Incommensurability," in *East Meets West in the Middle Ages and Early Modern Times: Transcultural Experiences in the Premodern World*, ed. Albrecht Classen (Berlin: De Gruyter, 2013), 223–42.

71. Ho, *Graves of Tarim*, 123, 207, 211, and the entirety of the excellent chapter on "Hybrid Texts."

72. The urgency was not suddenly discovered but built up, especially in the Indian Ocean world, where the Alawis had operated since at least the sixteenth century. Ho provides an account of the "Islamic Indian Ocean" conception of a multidimensional space-time in his reading of Abd al-Qadir al-Aydarus's millennial text *The Travelling Light Unveiled*, a biographical compendium completed in Gujarat in 1603. He notes in particular the inclusiveness implied by a Prophetic genealogy in this text, wherein it is not simply "a scarce commodity subject to contestation" as it seems to become in a later period; "[r]ather, it is merely the front of a rising tide that lifts all boats." Sayyid Alawi belonged squarely in the earlier world, and Fadl straddled the two. Ho, *Graves of Tarim*, 125.

73. Apparently only the first (Umayyad caliph Umar bin Abd al-Aziz al-Qurashi), second (Imam Muhammad bin Idris al-Shafi'i al-Muttalabi), and fifth (Imam Hujjat al-Islam Abu Hamid al-Ghazali) were undisputed.

74. Fadl, *Uddat al-umara'*, 7.

75. Ibid. Among these exemplars with "the heart of Abraham," who formed a widely recognized lineage of mystics, was al-Junayd b. Muhammad, "sayyid of the *ta'ifa* of his age"; that is, in the third century AH / ninth century, he was a progenitor of Sufism *avant la lettre*. Others in the chain include Abi Hamza al-Baghdadi, Yahya b. Mu'az al-Razi (tenth century) "of the first preachers" (*mutaqaddimin*), al-Imam al-Ghazali (eleventh century), al-Shaykh Muhyi al-Din Abd al-Qadir al-Gilani (twelfth century), al-Shaykh Safi al-Din Ahmad b. Alwan, and al-Shaykh al-Suhrawardi (twelfth century), "master of recent Sufis" (*al-awarif*). Ibid., 9.

76. Ibid., 4.

77. Ho, *Graves of Tarim*, 121.

78. The intensity of the truth of Oneness in divine sovereignty and its ineluctable potential for dilution in the many ways of being and organizing humans was always a problem and was partially resolved by viewing that truth as only ever possible in individual experience, which was bound to be contested. Fred Donner, *Muhammad and the Believers at the Origins of Islam* (Cambridge, MA: Harvard University Press, 2012).

79. For a spirited and compelling demonstration of "the Islamic," see Shahab Ahmed, *What Is Islam? The Importance of Being Islamic* (Princeton, NJ: Princeton University Press, 2016).

80. Fadl, *Uddat al-umara'*, 23, 52.

81. The source that Fadl excerpted in order to deliver this message is *Al-Dawa al-tamma wa al-tadhkirat al-amma* (Dar al-Hawi, 1421/2000), penned by the well-known scholar and poet Abdallah b. Alawi al-Haddad (d. 1720). Many of his texts were among the first disseminated in print form throughout the Indian Ocean world. His devotional text, *Ratib al-Haddad*, is used in moments of *dhikr* as an aid to "remembering" God to this day in East Africa, South India, and Southeast Asia. Bang, *Islamic Sufi Networks*, 143–62; Ho, *Graves of Tarim*, 211, 327.

82. The version of *Al-Dawa al-tamma* that I consulted has "fraternity" (*ukhuwwa*) instead of "end" here, which would seem to follow better after "twins." The brotherhood of sovereignty and religion is also more in keeping with the family and household metaphors found elsewhere in the text. Al-Haddad, *Ratib al-Haddad*, 135.

83. Fadl, *Uddat al-umara'*, 83.

84. In his treatment of the concept of Muslim kingship, Aziz al-Azmeh made a similar point, perhaps more evocatively: "All Muslim discourse on political association is premised on a pessimistic anthropology." This sentence introduces the chapter titled "The Absolutist Imperative." Al-Azmeh, *Muslim Kingship*, 115. See also Saiyid Athar Abbas Rizvi, *A History of Sufism in India* (1983; New Delhi: Munshiram Manoharlal, 2009), 2:348–89.

85. Fadl, *Uddat al-umara'*, 89. The complete quote is "The sultan is God's shadow on earth and the oppressed (*mazlumun*) seek refuge in him."

86. Ibid., 85, 87.

87. Ibid., 48. In a short yet suggestive piece that resonates here, Wilferd Madelung's "detective work" uncovers the reason why the philosophically minded Nasir al-Din Tusi wrote a Sufi treatise on ethics (1235 CE) near the end of his life: "In the catastrophic and chaotic conditions during and after the Mongol conquest, he, more than anyone else, was in a position to protect its members' lives, property, and interests, a position he used fully." He also notes the post-Mongol ascendance of Sufi orders as the relevant context. Madelung, "Nasir al-Din Tusi's Ethics: Between Philosophy, Shi'ism and Sufism," Institute of Ismaili Studies excerpt of Richard G. Hovannisian, ed. *Ethics in Islam* (Malibu, CA: Undena Publications, 2011); downloaded from http://iis.ac.uk/research/academic-articles/nasir-al-din-tusi-s-ethics-between-philosophy-shi-ism-and-sufism, quote from p. 11/14 in PDF.

88. Fadl, *Uddat al-umara'*, 87.

89. This problem of sovereignty had been identified when Islamic political thought first began to coalesce as such in the Abbasid period. Azmeh analyzes the approach to the problem in terms of practical versus formal theology of power. Al-Azmeh, *Muslim Kingship*, 66.

90. Fadl, *Uddat al-umara'*, 84.

91. Ibid., 90. The possessive pronoun in this case might be read as ultimately referring back to the ultimate guardian of all.

92. Ibid., 91–165.

93. http://www.anayasa.gen.tr/reform.htm.

94. Fadl, *Uddat al-umara'*, 165.

95. Foucault, *Security, Territory, Population*, ch. 6.

96. In *Genealogies of Religion*, Asad famously examines the time of religious traditions as having historical (variable) and cosmological (stable) dimensions that are rescripted in specific ways to reflect modern concerns.

97. Foucault, *Security, Territory, Population*, 125–26, 128–29. The paradox is elaborated somewhat more complexly than I've schematized here, for it has two related dimensions. In the first, the shepherd has the responsibility for keeping watch over each and every sheep at once, "omnes et singulatim," giving rise to technical problems of surveillance. In the second, there is the problem of potentially sacrificing himself for one errant sheep, a necessary wager that could cost him the entire flock: "the sacrifice of one for all, and the sacrifice of all for one."

Chapter 3

1. Stern, *Company-State*, 213.

2. David Washbrook approvingly cites Lord Curzon, who said government in India was "a mighty and magnificent machine for doing absolutely nothing." Revising the notion of an all-powerful, monolithic colonial government, his work nonetheless reveals how by the beginning of the twentieth century this form of government—in its actions and inactions—carved out a space within which new kinds of politics grew. Washbrook, *Emergence of Provincial Politics*, 41.

3. Gilles Deleuze and Félix Guattari, *Anti-Oedipus: Capitalism and Schizophrenia*, trans. R. Hurley, H. Lane, and B. Massumi (Minneapolis: University of Minnesota Press, 1983), 238.

4. Giorgio Agamben, *Homo Sacer: Sovereign Power and Bare Life*, trans. Daniel Heller-Roazen (Stanford, CA: Stanford University Press, 1998), and *State of Exception*, trans. Kevin Attell (Chicago: University of Chicago Press, 2005).

5. See Didier Fassin, *Humanitarian Reason: A Moral History of the Present* (Berkeley: University of California Press, 2012); and Samuel Moyn, *Human Rights and the Uses of History* (New York: Verso, 2017).

6. Judith Butler critiques the apocalyptic philosophy of those like Agamben by showing the narrowness of their conception of the political in *Notes toward a Performative Theory of Assembly* (Cambridge, MA: Harvard University Press, 2015), ch. 2.

7. Partha Chatterjee, *The Politics of the Governed: Reflections on Popular Politics in Most of the World* (New York: Columbia University Press, 2004).

8. I use this admittedly clumsy formulation in order to distinguish it from "state capacity" as used in the social science literature during the return of the state to the study of politics in the 1980s. For an overview, see Peter B. Evans, Dietrich Rueschemeyer, and Theda Skocpol, eds., *Bringing the State Back In* (New York: Cambridge University Press, 1985); and Michael Mann, "The Autonomous Power of the State: Its Origins, Mechanisms and Results," *European Journal of Sociology* 25, no. 2 (1984): 185–213. For a brilliant deconstruction, see Timothy Mitchell, "The Limits of the State: Beyond Statist Approaches and Their Critics," *American Political Science Review*, 85, no. 1 (March 1991): 77–96.

9. The very Christian genealogy of government that Foucault traces to the heart of modern sovereignty has been shown to be the source of many "distinctly Islamic" practices—for example, suicide bombings. Asad, *On Suicide Bombing*; Faisal Devji, *The Terrorist in Search of Humanity: Militant Islam and Global Politics* (London: Hurst, 2008); Wael Hallaq, *The Impossible State: Islam, Politics, and Modernity's Moral Predicament* (New York: Columbia University Press, 2013).

10. On the perspective of comparable personalities over time, see, among others, Abdallah Hammoudi, "Sainteté, pouvoir et société: Tamgrout aux XVIIe et XVIIIe siècles," *Annales: Économies, Sociétés, Civilisations* 35, nos. 3–4 (1980): 615–41; Knut S. Vikør, *Sufi and Scholar on the Desert Edge: Muhammad b. Ali al-Sanusi and His Brotherhood* (Evanston, IL: Northwestern University Press, 1995), and *Between God and the Sultan: A History of Islamic Law* (New York: Oxford University Press, 2006); Ayesha Jalal, *Partisans of Allah: Jihad in South Asia* (Cambridge, MA: Harvard University Press, 2008); and Scott S. Reese, *Renewers of the Age: Holy Men and Social Discourse in Colonial Benaadir* (Leiden: Brill, 2008).

11. In *Working Out Egypt*, I drew a conceptual link between "physical culture" (*al-riyada al-badaniyya*) and the older "spiritual cultivation" (*riyadat al-nafs*).

12. On eighteenth-century efforts to reconceptualize the political in the Ottoman center, see Ali Yaycioğlu, *Partners of the Empire: The Crisis of the Ottoman Order in the Age of Revolutions* (Stanford, CA: Stanford University Press, 2016).

13. Echoes of Michael Taussig, *The Magic of the State* (New York: Routledge, 1997), are intended.

14. For another view of loss, which looks at moments of rupture in the global history of the "caliphate," see the learned study by Mona Hassan, *Longing for the Lost Caliphate: A Transregional History* (Princeton, NJ: Princeton University Press, 2016).

15. For many ulama, and Sufis especially, the sovereignty of nation-states posed a direct challenge by the turn of the twentieth century. Gilsenan, *Saint and Sufi in Modern Egypt*; Frederick De Jong, "Opposition to Sufism in Twentieth-Century Egypt (1900–1970): A Preliminary Survey," in *Islamic Mysticism Contested*, ed. F. De Jong and Bernd Radtke (Leiden: Brill, 1999), 310–23. Valerie J. Hoffman, *Sufism, Mystics, and Saints in Modern Egypt* (Charleston: University of South Carolina Press, 1995), shows that challenges by states can be met to some extent. See also Mark J. Sedgwick, *Saints and Sons: The Making and Remaking of the Rashidi Ahmadi Sufi Order, 1799–2000* (Leiden: Brill, 2005); and J. S. Schielke, *Perils of Joy: Contesting Mulid Festivals in Contemporary Egypt* (Syracuse, NY: Syracuse University Press, 2012).

16. Strange to Montgomery, February 21, 1852, in *CMO*, 1:352.

17. Robinson to Pycroft, November 18, 1856, in *CMO*, 2:388.

18. Mecca was perhaps always a transnational hub, which in the age of steam and through the annual hajj pilgrimage became a vibrant meeting point for Muslims from all over the globe. See, e.g., C. Snouck Hurgronje, *Mekka in the Latter Part of the Nineteenth Century: Daily Life, Customs and Learning* (Leiden: E. J. Brill, 1931); Eric Tagliacozzo, *The Longest Journey: Southeast Asians and the Pilgrimage to Mecca* (New York: Oxford University Press, 2013); and Nile Green, "The *Hajj* as Its Own Undoing: Infrastructure and Integration on the Muslim Journey to Mecca," *Past & Present* 226, no. 1 (2015): 193–226.

19. Robinson to Pycroft, November 18, 1856, in *CMO*, 2:388.

20. Ibid., 387.

21. Page to Playfair, October 31, 1856, in *CMO*, 2:390–91. On the importance of the "household," see Jane Hathaway, *The Politics of Households in Ottoman Egypt: The Rise of the Qazdağlıs* (New York: Cambridge University Press, 1997). For the Alawi and Hadrami context, see Michael Gilsenan, "Topics and Queries for a History of Arab Families and Inheritance in Southeast Asia: Some Preliminary Thoughts," in *Southeast Asia and the Middle East: Islam, Movement, and the* Longue Durée, ed. Eric Tagliacozzo (Singapore: NUS Press, 2009), 199–234, and "Translating Colonial Fortunes: Dilemmas of Inheritance in Muslim and English Laws across a Nineteenth-Century Diaspora," *CSSAAME* 31, no. 2 (2011): 355–71; and Kazuhiro Arai, "Arabs Who Traversed the Indian Ocean: The History of the al-Attas Family in Hadramawt and Southeast Asia, c. 1600–c. 1960" (PhD diss., University of Michigan, 2004).

22. British sources closer to the scene, while intimating his support for the rebellion, which began with ulama and sharifian leadership, state: "This man was one of the chiefs (although not appearing to take a prominent part) . . . He endeavoured to retire, and appears to be absorbed only in his religious duties. This feint I am informed did not however succeed so fully as he anticipated, as His Excellency Kiamih [Kamil] Pasha previous to his departure gave orders the pension should not be continued." Stephen

Page, Her Majesty's Acting Vice Consul and Honorable Company's Agent at Juddah to R. L. Playfair, Assistant to Political Agent, Aden, October 31, 1856, in *CMO*, 2:391.

23. Robinson to Pycroft, November 18, 1856, in *CMO*, 2:388; and Edmonstone to Pycroft, December 5, 1856, in *CMO*, 2:389. See also Janet Ewald and William G. Clarence-Smith, "The Economic Role of the Hadhrami Diaspora in the Red Sea and Gulf of Aden, 1820s to 1930s," in *Hadhrami Traders, Scholars and Statesmen in the Indian Ocean*, ed. Ulrike Freitag and William Clarence-Smith (Boston: Brill, 1997), 280–96, 291; see also Stephen Dale, "The Hadhrami Diaspora in South-Western India: The Role of the Sayyids of the Malabar Coast," also in *Hadhrami Traders, Scholars and Statesmen in the Indian Ocean*, 175–84, 179.

24. Robinson, who was acting magistrate of Malabar after Conolly's assassination, was in Istanbul in 1855. He reported that Fadl was "well known and considered a remarkable person there." Robinson to Pycroft, November 18, 1856, in *CMO*, 2:387.

25. BOA, Auikt. uui. 1276 S. 6 / September 4, 1859. Dosya no. 363. Vesika no. 77. I owe a debt of gratitude to Zeynep Turkyilmaz for locating Ottoman files on Fadl and to Zehra Gulbahar for translating the documents that were in Ottoman Turkish.

26. Rishad Choudhury, "The Hajj and the Hindi: The Ascent of the Indian Sufi Lodge in the Ottoman Empire," *Modern Asian Studies* 50, no. 6 (2016): 1888–1931. What Choudhury calls the "Indo-Ottoman Sufi assemblage" had many centers. Of the two important *tekke*s (lodges) in Istanbul that were known as "Hindular," one goes back to the very founding of the city as the Ottoman capital by Sultan Mehmed II. For other movement along Sufi networks, see Thierry V. Zarcone, *Sufi Pilgrims from India and Central Asia in Jerusalem* (Kyoto: Kyoto University Center for Islamic Area Studies, 2009); and Lale Can, "Connecting People: A Central Asian Sufi Network in Turn-of-the-Century Istanbul," *Modern Asian Studies* 46, no. 2 (2012): 373–401.

27. For a list of the names of all the sheikhs who held this office from 1839 to 1908, see Ochsenwald, *Religion, Society, and the State in Arabia*, 51.

28. Bazzaz, *Forgotten Saints: History, Power, and Politics in the Making of Modern Morocco* (Cambridge, MA: Harvard University Press, 2010). On Sayyid Alawi's Qadiri affiliation, see Moyin Hudawi Malayamma and Mahmood Panangangara, *Mampuram Thangal*, 114–18.

29. Bang cites an unpublished paper by Sultan Ghalib al-Quayti in which he states definitively that the Hijaz railway idea was Fadl's, based on his knowledge of its benefit to the British in India. Bang, *Sufis and Scholars*, 85.

30. Another petition presented by Fadl himself to the Ministry of Interior dates from 1871. BOA, Hariciye Nezareti, Tercume Odasi. HR. TO. 25/5/1871. Dosya No. 454. Gomlek Sira No. 64. Orijinal Kayit No. 143. Arzuhal 51.

31. See, e.g., TNA FO 78-3615 and FO 78-4790.

32. Ho uses a similar rubric, "sayyid sovereign rule," to distinguish the mobile and territorially fluid form of sovereignty developed in and through the Hadhrami diaspora from the state-centered version that was in ascendance in and through empire in the nineteenth century. Ho, *Graves of Tarim*, 210.

33. The political history is much messier than this account reveals, but for our purposes it will suffice. See Buzpinar, "Abdulhamid II and Sayyid Fadl Pasha of Hadramawt."

34. For some of the details, see Freitag, *Indian Ocean Migrants*, 79–88, 194–95.

35. Evaluating whether it was a commitment to pan-Islamism that determined Fadl's actions in the latter part of his life, Bang concludes, "Fadl's alleged pan-Islamism was most manifest in the political realm; claiming political power on behalf of the Ottoman Government, etc." She describes the complex political and religious affiliations of Fadl more sensitively than others but ultimately concludes he was "opportunistic." Bang, *Sufis and Scholars*, 88. On the Ottoman center's changing relations to religion and religious movements, see Kemal H. Karpat, *The Politicization of Islam: Reconstructing Identity, State, Faith, and Community in the Late Ottoman State* (New York: Oxford University Press, 2001). See also Brian Silverstein, "Sufism and Governmentality in the Late Ottoman Empire," *CSSAAME* 29, no. 2 (2009): 171–85.

36. BOA, Hariciye Nezareti, Tercume Odasi. HR. TO. 24/11/1875. Dosya No. 460. Gomlek Sira No. 29. Orijinal Kayit No. 320. Arzuhal 18. The highlighted line suggests that he was possibly acting with the knowledge of the sultan, who in that period of geopolitical troubles on nearly every front needed plausible deniability.

37. The distinction is an effect of modern power's truth games, which merits further interrogation than is possible here. For this reason, or what he termed ethnocentrism, Marshall Sahlins eschewed myth for "charter traditions" to describe similar founding narratives. Sahlins, "The Stranger-King or, Elementary Forms of the Politics of Life," *Indonesia and the Malay World* 36, no. 105 (2008): 177–94, 178. For a treatment of aspects of sayyid authority along these lines, see Kathirithamby-Wells, "'Strangers' and 'Stranger-Kings.'" See also the classic study by R. B. Serjeant, *The Sayyids of Hadramawt* (London: SOAS, 1957).

38. BOA, Yildiz Esas Evraki. 8 Ramadan 1296 / September 5, 1879. Dosya No. 35. Gomlek Sira No. 10. Varak Adedi 3/3. E. Tas. Nu.18-93/553-182.

39. Caesar E. Farah had discovered the same value in the document, and though he did not offer more than a line or two of analysis, he did translate it in full except the cover page. Farah, *The Sultan's Yemen: Nineteenth-Century Challenges to Ottoman Rule* (New York: I. B. Tauris, 2002), 133 and Annex E, 282–86. I consulted the original for this section; the translations are my own.

40. For a recent reading of Ottoman archival documents as text with the end being an evocative history of the Red Sea, see Alexis Wick, *The Red Sea: In Search of Lost Space* (Berkeley: University of California Press, 2016).

41. BOA, Yildiz Esas Evraki. 8 Ramadan 1296 / September 5, 1879. Dosya No. 35, 1/3.

42. This formulation of state interest signals a departure in Fadl's thought that will be taken up in greater detail in Chapter 6.

43. BOA, Yildiz Esas Evraki. 8 Ramadan 1296 / September 5, 1879. Dosya No. 35, 2/3.

44. On how prior forms of colonial knowledge (and even older networks of Indian actors) formed the basis of a new imperial geography such that "Aden and the Aden Protectorate constituted one of the westernmost parts of India," see John Willis, "Making Yemen Indian: Rewriting the Boundaries of Imperial Arabia," *IJMES* 41 (2009): 23–38.

See also Metcalf, *Imperial Connections*; James Onley, *The Arabian Frontier of the British Raj: Merchants, Rulers, and the British in the Nineteenth-Century Gulf* (Oxford: Oxford University Press, 2007); and R. J. Gavin, *Aden under British Rule, 1839–1967* (London: Hurst, 1975). On the Ottoman expansion in Yemen, see Thomas Kuehn, *Empire, Islam, and Politics of Difference, Ottoman Rule in Yemen, 1849–1919* (Leiden: Brill, 2011).

45. BOA, Yildiz Esas Evraki. 8 Ramadan 1296 / September 5, 1879. Dosya No. 35, 2/3. The othering of the Arab tribes and their leaders evident here was perhaps Farah's cue to translate *mashayikh al-Urban* as "Arabian chieftains."

46. Ibid.

47. On the renaissance of Ibn Khaldun studies and the dangers of assimilating the fourteenth-century genius into modern Eurocentric categories of time and theory, see chapter 2 of Mohammad Salama, *Islam, Orientalism, and Intellectual History: Modernity and the Politics of Exclusion since Ibn Khaldun* (New York: I. B. Tauris, 2011). For an example of this form of "exclusion" that depends on an idealized trajectory of the West to Enlightenment, see Hayden White, "Ibn Khaldun in World Philosophy of History: Review Article," *Comparative Studies in Society and History* 2, no. 1 (October 1959), 110–25.

48. Freitag, *Indian Ocean Migrants*, 137–85. See also James Onley and Sulayman Khalaf, "Shaikhly Authority in the Pre-Oil Gulf: An Historical-Anthropological Study," *History and Anthropology* 17, no. 3 (September 2006): 189–208.

49. He again does not name the British as the invading party, but the island was seized by the latter in 1857 and was held until 1967, the year of British withdrawal from Yemen.

50. BOA, Yildiz Esas Evraki. 8 Ramadan 1296 / September 5, 1879. Dosya No. 35, 2/3.

51. Ibid.

52. In points 1 and 2 it makes sense to use "acquire sovereignty" to translate *istawala* because the broader argument about establishing a relationship of care suggests it over the simpler "conquered." After the original Islamic conquests (which were also termed differently, as *futuhat* [openings]), what followed among Muslims was a jockeying for worldly power among dynasts, and the Ottomans were but one of the contenders; however, that would be difficult to state outright and not really the point for a sufi-sayyid trying to elaborate terms of sovereignty that were Islamic under the new global conditions of what in *Working Out Egypt* I have called "colonial modernity."

53. BOA, Yildiz Esas Evraki. 8 Ramadan 1296 / September 5, 1879. Dosya No. 35, 3/3.

54. The word *al-tashabbuth* (-*at*) is used frequently, perhaps because it has the efficiency of connoting simultaneously the establishment of connections/relations/ties and taking over.

55. Ibid.

56. Ibid.

57. It is not clear which territory is meant here, but given the example that follows it was likely on the East African coast.

58. Ras Hafun, or Xaafuun, is the bit of Somalia that sticks out into the Indian

Ocean and is the easternmost point of continental Africa, a very short distance from the island of Socotra.

59. Ibid.

60. Ibid.

61. That the center was primed to receive these kinds of missives is evinced in movements to consolidate state authority in frontier domains such as Jordan in the second half of the nineteenth century. Eugene Rogan, *Frontiers of the State in the Late Ottoman Empire: Transjordan, 1850–1921* (New York: Cambridge University Press, 2002).

62. On the Ottoman center's (re)conceptualization of sovereignty in a changing relation to subjects in a changing global context, see, among others, Selim Deringil, *The Well-Protected Domains: Ideology and the Legitimation of Power in the Ottoman Empire, 1876–1909* (New York: I. B. Tauris, 1999); Einar Wigen, "Ottoman Concepts of Empire," *Contributions to the History of Concepts* 8, no. 1 (Summer 2013): 44–66, doi: 10.3167/choc.2013. 080103; and Will Smiley, "The Burdens of Subjecthood: The Ottoman State, Russian Fugitives, and Interimperial Law, 1774–1869," *IJMES* 46 (2014): 73–93, doi: 10.1017/S0020743813001293.

63. Although he does not state it explicitly in this document, Fadl does say elsewhere that the power of the Omanis was illegitimate, considering its British backing, and had to be checked. But even the right of the Ottoman sultan as the "true" sovereign becomes questionable when read against his other writings, notably his Sufi treatises, in which he explicitly—albeit buried in the text—locates descendants of the ahl al-bayt, the awliya', well above political rulers in matters of governing souls (*siyasat al-nafs*) and in terms of the capacity to govern others. See Fadl, *Idah al-Asrar al-Alawiyya wa Manahij al-Sada al-Alawiyya* (Cairo: Matba'at al-Adab wa al-Mu'ayyad, 1316 [1898/99]), 75–76.

64. Patricia Crone, *God's Rule—Government and Islam: Six Centuries of Medieval Islamic Political Thought* (New York: Columbia University Press, 2004).

65. The classic example of the endurance of tribe as a real political and cultural force that provoked long reflection centuries after the rise of Islam yet centuries before Fadl and Crone is Ibn Khaldun's magnum opus, the multivolume *Kitab al-Ibar*, particularly in the theorization of forms of *asabiyya* in the introductory volume, *Al-Muqaddima*.

66. On the Ottoman state's view of tribes in the general vicinity, which was quite similar to Fadl's, see Thomas Kuehn, "Shaping and Reshaping Colonial Ottomanism: Contesting Boundaries of Difference and Integration in Ottoman Yemen, 1872–1919," *CSSAAME* 27, no. 2 (2007): 315–31. The prevailing Ottoman discourse on tribes as "savages" problematizes the origins of Fadl's own view. See also Selim Deringil, "'They Live in a State of Nomadism and Savagery': The Late Ottoman Empire and the Post-Colonial Debate," *CSSH* 45, no. 2 (2003): 311–42. For another quite compelling view that shows how the Ottoman experience of "empire" can thicken the concept, see Marc Aymes, "Many a Standard at a Time: The Ottomans' Leverage with Imperial Studies," in "Concepts of Empire and Imperialism," special issue, *Contributions to the History of Concepts* 8, no. 1 (Summer 2013): 26–43, doi: 10.3167/choc.2013.080102.

67. He names the al-Abdali and al-Fadli as tribes descended from *abna' al-atrak* who had been sent to Yemen in the first military campaigns.

68. Brigadier W. M. Coghlan to T. Pycroft, Chief Secretary to Govt. Madras, October 25, 1858, IOR/L/PS/6/463, Coll 36/16.

69. Stephen Page, Her Majesty's Acting Vice Consul and Honorable Company's Acting Agent at Jedda, to Anderson, Secretary to Govt. Bombay, December 7, 1857, IOR/L/PS/6/461, Coll 25/13.

70. On the long shadow of surveillance and regulation of the pilgrimage that followed, see Michael Christopher Low, "Empire and the Hajj: Pilgrims, Plagues, and Pan-Islam under British Surveillance, 1865–1908," *IJMES* 40 (2008): 269–90. See also John Slight, *The British Empire and the Hajj: 1865–1956* (Cambridge, MA: Harvard University Press, 2015).

71. Coghlan to Pullen, October 21, 1858, in Brigadier W. M. Coghlan to T. Pycroft, Chief Secretary to Govt. Madras, October 25, 1858, IOR/L/PS/6/463, Coll 36/16.

72. Coghlan to Pullen, October 23?[*sic*], 1858, enclosed in Brigadier W. M. Coghlan to T. Pycroft, Chief Secretary to Govt. Madras, October 25, 1858, IOR/L/PS/6/463, Coll 36/16. This was a second letter after new information about Fadl was received in Aden.

73. Ibid.

74. Coghlan to Pycroft, November 8, 1858, as attachment to Bayley to Secretary to Govt. of India, December 2, 1858. Enclosed was a letter from Pullen in reply to the two from Coghlan noted above.

75. Pullen to Coghlan, n.d., in Coghlan to Pycroft, November 8, 1858, as attachment to Bayley to Secretary to Govt. of India, December 2, 1858.

76. This paragraph is based primarily on Ochsenwald, *Religion, Society, and the State in Arabia*, 143–51.

77. This event puts the call to jihad of *Al-Sayf al-Battar* in yet another light.

78. Such international commissions became an increasingly common feature in European dealings with the Ottoman Empire. After a massacre in the Syria region that was essentially a civil war, another commission was formed, which established the special administrative unit, the *mutasarrifiyya*, of Mt. Lebanon in 1861. See Caesar E. Farah, *The Politics of Interventionism in Ottoman Lebanon, 1830–61* (New York: I. B. Tauris, 2000); and Engin Akarli, *The Long Peace: Ottoman Lebanon, 1861–1920* (Berkeley: University of California Press, 1993).

79. See, e.g., Allan Sekula, "The Body and the Archive," *October* 39 (Winter 1986): 3–64; John Torpey, *The Invention of the Passport: Surveillance, Citizenship, and the State* (New York: Cambridge University Press, 2000); Simon A. Cole, *Suspect Identities: A History of Fingerprinting and Criminal Identification* (Cambridge, MA: Harvard University Press, 2001); Chandak Sengoopta, *Imprint of the Raj: How Fingerprinting Was Born in Colonial India* (New York: Macmillan, 2003); Khaled Fahmy, "Birth of the 'Secular' Individual: Medical and Legal Methods of Identification in Nineteenth-Century Egypt," in *Registration and Recognition: Documenting the Person in World History*, ed. Keith Breckenridge and Simon Szreter (OUP for

the British Academy, 2012), ch. 14; Simone Browne, *Dark Matters: On the Surveil-lance of Blackness* (Durham, NC: Duke University Press, 2015); and Michel Foucault, *Discipline and Punish: The Birth of the Prison*, trans. Alan Sheridan (New York: Pantheon, 1978).

80. Though it came out too late to be discussed here, for a global view of the penal architecture of the modern world order see the volume edited by Clare Anderson, *A Global History of Convicts and Penal Colonies* (New York: Oxford University Press, 2018).

81. The unevenness of power was of course patently clear when Ottoman gun bat-teries at Jedda fort did not return fire on the *Cyclops*. Ochsenwald, *Religion, Society, and the State in Arabia*, 148–49. However, it was perhaps the Ottoman payment of reparations for Christian losses while failing to secure any compensation for Muslim losses that highlighted the asymmetrical plane on which state sovereignty was being performed and internationalized.

82. Sayyid Fadl to Sayyid Turki Ibn Sayyid Said Ibn Sultan, 24 Muharram 1296 (January 18, 1879), Arabic original and English translation enclosed in Miles to Ross, March 18, 1879, IOR/R/15/6/12. Miles noted that Sayyid Turki, the sultan of Muscat, did not intend to reply to Fadl's letter, the purport of which was to seek aid from a closer power than the Ottomans after his ejection from Dhofar. The letter ended by invoking their geographical proximity as neighbors (*jiran*) and their shared genealogy: "We are each one limb" (*kulluna udw wahid*). The translator in Muscat rendered this freely as "We are both limbs of the same parent trunk," which captures the intent to link them as sayyid branches of the Prophet's family.

83. Pol. Dept. Bombay to multiple recipients (The Commissioner in Sind; The Resi-dent at Aden; The Commissioner of Customs, Bombay; The Police Commissioner, N.D.; The Police Commissioner, S.D.; The Political Agent, Kattywar; The Commissioner of Police, Bombay; The Political Agent, Cutch; The Political Agent, Colaba; The Agent, Governor General and Special Commissioner, Baroda; The Agent Governor General, Central India; The Government of India), February 1, 1876, IOR/R/2/653/62.

84. Schneider to Madras, October 12, 1875, and Schneider to Madras, September 6, 1875, IOR/R/2/653/62.

85. Indeed, the information on Fadl's movements in this section comes from an India Office file that belonged to a compilation on "outlawry," IOR/R/2/653/62.

86. Schneider to Madras, September 6, 1875, IOR/R/2/653/62.

87. See attachments in Carmichael Officiating Chief Secretary Judicial Department to Sec'y to Govt of Bombay, September 21, 1875, IOR/R/2/653/62.

88. IOR/R/2/653/62.

89. "Description Roll," January 10, 1876, IOR/R/2/653/62.

90. Ibid. That the table did not have a column for eye color was indicative of the novice effort at building a visual profile in words, a *portrait parlé*, as it would come to be known. The detail of Fadl's eyes was in fact volunteered by the native informants. The searching techniques of identification would by the end of the nineteenth century develop into an anthropometric science, become the major rival to the new technology

of fingerprinting, and take on the name of French police official Alphonse Bertillon. Cole, *Suspect Identities*.

91. The connections actually extended out much further. In an intriguing letter from the agent general of New South Wales, Saul Samuel, to the Colonial Office from February 1896, we are given a glimpse into the vast global reach of surveillance technologies and how they took on a market value. Saul was prepared to pay for any information that could be offered on the new anthropometric technique used across different jurisdictions—from India to the US—to identify habitual criminals. IOR/L/PJ/6/416, File 404.

Chapter 4

1. For another view, see, among others, Shahzad Bashir, *Sufi Bodies: Religion and Society in Medieval Islam* (New York: Columbia University Press, 2011); Scott Kugle, *Sufis and Saints' Bodies: Mysticism, Corporeality, and Sacred Power in Islam* (Chapel Hill: University of North Carolina Press, 2007); and Carl W. Ernst and Bruce B. Lawrence, *Sufi Martyrs of Love: The Chishti Order in South Asia and Beyond* (New York: Palgrave Macmillan, 2002). Following Bashir, "Sufism" is understood to mean an "analytical horizon" rather than a fixed system of thought and practice as implied in the secularized scholarly term—a sense Fadl grappled with in his last ruminations.

2. For radically other ways to read, see Michael Taussig, *Shamanism, Colonialism, and the Wild Man: A Study in Terror and Healing* (Chicago: University of Chicago Press, 1991); and Bruno Latour, *An Inquiry into Modes of Existence: An Anthropology of the Moderns*, trans. Catherine Porter (Cambridge, MA: Harvard University Press, 2013).

3. Malayamma and Panangangara, *Mampuram Thangal*, 326–27. This text is discussed in Chapter 5.

4. Bang, *Sufis and Scholars*.

5. Ibid., 204–5.

6. Ibid., 81.

7. Mattath, *Khuthubussamaan*, 14–16.

8. Ibid., 25.

9. The Wahhabi critiques of saints and shrine visitations (*ziyara*) did not go unanswered. The rough contemporary and possibly teacher of Fadl in Mecca, the highly influential Ahmad b. Zayni Dahlan (1817–86), wrote forcefully against Wahhabi excesses of interpretation and action. Freitag, *Indian Ocean Migrants*, 201–3. From the middle of the nineteenth century until his death, Dahlan, who became the Shafiʿi mufti of Mecca in 1871, was a key node in the vast network of Islamic knowledge transmission centered on Mecca and radiating in every direction. The al-Ahdals and Alawis had long been part of that network, their connection going back to the migration west from Basra in the tenth century. See Bang, *Sufis and Scholars*, 72–73, 220n24; and John Voll, "Linking Groups in the Networks of Eighteenth-Century Revivalist Scholars," in *Eighteenth-Century Renewal and Reform in Islam*, ed. Nehemiah Levtzion and John Voll (Syracuse, NY: Syracuse University Press, 1987), 69–92. On other linkages of this vast world of learning, see Bernard Haykel, *Revival and Reform in Islam: The Legacy of Muhammad Al-Shawkani* (New York: Cambridge

University Press, 2003); and Stefan Reichmuth, *The World of Murtada al-Zabidi (1732–91): Life, Networks, and Writings* (Cambridge, UK: Gibb Memorial Trust, 2009).

10. The notable works in English related to Fadl's life (Dale, Sathar, Alavi) offer valuable analyses of his entanglements with colonial rule and empire but do not treat his "Sufi" writings. Bang offers a good reading of one of his texts that I discuss later.

11. Arguably, even the legacy of Abduh, the Salafi reformer par excellence, is a contested one, ostensibly sanitized by successors, in particular Rashid Rida, to render insignificant or invisible his "conversion" to Sufism at an early age. Oliver Scharbrodt, "The Salafiyya and Sufism: Muhammad Abduh and His *Risalat al-Waridat* (Treatise on Mystical Inspiration)," *Bulletin of the School Oriental and African Studies* 70 (2007): 89–115.

12. Its newspaper of the same name was also the mouthpiece of a political consensus one might term conservative in a field that included as its opposite pole the liberal secular nationalists led by the youthful Mustafa Kamil.

13. Fadl, *Idah al-Asrar*, 100. As noted previously, our own usage of "Sufism" makes no assumption about its systematicity and treats it as an analytical horizon.

14. Bang, *Sufis and Scholars*, 87.

15. Ibid. Bang's characterization of Fadl is ambivalent, oscillating between man of religious conviction whose "outlook was broad" and political opportunist. The relation between the two is not drawn out and linked to sovereignty, so her reading of the *Idah* appears unmoored from the otherwise careful historicization of his career.

16. Fadl, *Idah al-Asrar*, 3.

17. In an earlier, admittedly hasty treatment I suggested that the references to canonical sources seemed to be an Egyptian editorial addition, "perhaps an index of the original's perceived deficiency as a pedagogical text." Jacob, "Of Angels and Men: Sayyid Fadl bin Alawi and Two Moments of Sovereignty," *Arab Studies Journal* 20, no. 1 (Spring 2012): 40–73, 51.

18. Fadl, *Idah al-Asrar*, 80.

19. Ibid., 2.

20. In *Lisan al-Arab*, Ibn Manzur glossed the word *qawadih* as rot or decay of the type that takes root in trees or teeth. Fadl seems to be using it in the sense of challenges that afflict the soul, hence I have translated it as "trials"; perhaps tribulations might be more apposite.

21. Fadl, *Idah al-Asrar*, 13–14.

22. Mitchell, *Colonising Egypt*, 131–50.

23. Fadl, *Idah al-Asrar*, 17.

24. Sahlins calls this "being-in-other-space," troubled by the designation of this power and these ontologies as supernatural: "The term supposes ethnocentric concepts of 'nature' and 'natural'—an autonomous world of soulless material things or Cartesian *res extensa*—ethnocentric concepts not pertinent to people who are engaged in a cosmic society of interacting subjects, including a variety of non-human beings with the consciousness, soul, intentionality and other qualities of human persons." Sahlins, "The Stranger-King," 184–85.

25. Fadl, *Idah al-Asrar*, 25.

26. Ibid., 31.

27. Ibid., 35.

28. On returns of divine sovereignty in Islamic political thought, often opposed to Sufism, see R. L. Euben, *Enemy in the Mirror: Islamic Fundamentalism and the Limits of Modern Rationalism* (Princeton, NJ: Princeton University Press, 1999); Sayed Khatab, *The Power of Sovereignty: The Political and Ideological Philosophy of Sayyid Qutb* (New York: Routledge, 2006); and Dragos Stoica, "In The Shade of God's Sovereignty: The Anti-Modern Political Theology of Sayyid Qutb in Cross-Cultural Perspective" (PhD diss., Concordia University, 2017).

29. On the codification of the legal order, see Avi Rubin, *Ottoman Nizamiye Courts: Law and Modernity* (New York: Palgrave Macmillan, 2011). For a revisionist view, see Muhammad Zubair Abbasi, "Islamic Law and Social Change: An Insight into the Making of Anglo-Muhammadan Law," *Journal of Islamic Studies* 25, no. 3 (September 2014): 325–49, https://doi.org/10.1093/jis/etu045.

30. Fadl, *Idah al-Asrar*, 38–39.

31. Ibid., 38–45.

32. Ibid., 55.

33. Ibid., 68. This calling is different from the "hailing" in Althusser. Here the law is in fact bracketed in the face of a subject's decision to live in its excess, and the call comes from a desire for life-as-other. Thereby even the Althusserian notion of belief as repeated performances of a ritual (related to Bourdieu's concept of habitus) is confounded by practices self-consciously directed at the paradoxical submission and transcendence of law's interpellations. Louis Althusser, "Ideology and Ideological State Apparatuses (Notes Toward an Investigation)," in *Lenin and Philosophy and Other Essays*, trans. Ben Brewster (New York: Monthly Review Press, 1971), 127–86. See Judith Butler's critique of his view of interpellation in "'Conscience Doth Make Subjects of Us All,'" *Yale French Studies* 88 (1995): 6–26.

34. Fadl, *Idah al-Asrar*, 70.

35. Ibid., 75–76. Scott Kugle traces a similar, earlier trajectory through the lens of "juridical sainthood" in *Rebel between Spirit and Law: Ahmad Zarruq, Sainthood, and Authority in Islam* (Bloomington: Indiana University Press, 2006).

36. Fadl, *Idah al-Asrar*, 77. On the significance of this genealogy in historical context, see Ho, *Graves of Tarim*, 37–41.

37. Elsewhere, it is mentioned that Alawi b. Ubaydallah died in Somalia in 383 AH (993 AD) and that the name means *ta'ir* (that which flies, godspeed). Fadl, *Hadhihi al-tariqa al-hanifa al-samha'* (Istanbul, 1317 [1899/1900]), 82.

38. Fadl, *Idah al-Asrar*, 78.

39. Ibid., 87.

40. Ibid.

41. Ibid., 79.

42. That in one of the only photos of Fadl he was wearing the regalia of an Ottoman pasha again raises questions of integrity, though it could just as well reveal the very same difficulty of inhabiting the life attuned to the soul that the text is intended to affirm.

43. Fadl, *Idah al-Asrar*, 80.

44. Ibid.

45. On a mid-twentieth-century psychoanalytic adaptation of Sufi categories, see Omnia El Shakry, *The Arabic Freud: Psychoanalysis and Islam in Modern Egypt* (Princeton, NJ: Princeton University Press, 2017).

46. Fadl, *Idah al-Asrar*, 127.

47. Ibid., 82. On the Sufi practice of loving the devotee and how gazing at the adolescent male became a source of social tensions and political conflict during the period of protracted crisis in the early modern Ottoman Empire, see Dror Ze'evi, *Producing Desire: Changing Sexual Discourse in the Ottoman Middle East, 1500–1900* (Berkeley: University of California Press, 2006), 77–98. That the physical beauty of the male form was an object of contemplation and more in this context is evinced by accusations of deviance launched by opponents of Sufism. There is no explicit statement in Fadl that male beauty is the key to this ecstatic practice.

48. Fadl, *Idah al-Asrar*, 82.

49. Ibid., 90.

50. Ibid., 91.

51. Ibid.

52. Fadl writes that simple empiricism is wrong in its neglect of knowledge obtained by other means than observation by the senses or instruments. This is the kind of knowledge/awareness that Sufism, particularly through the practice of *al-riyada*, materializes not through learning or even special insight but "by lifting the veil over the senses and forgetting/losing consciousness of the body completely." Ibid., 103–4.

53. There is an extensive discussion of this figure in the South Asian context, where the more common designation is *faqir*. Nile Green, *Islam and the Army in Colonial India: Sepoy Religion in The Service of Empire* (New York: Cambridge University Press, 2009), 18. See also Green, "Emerging Approaches to the Sufi Traditions of South Asia: Between Texts, Territories and the Transcendent," *South Asia Research* 24, no. 2 (2004): 123–48.

54. Fadl, *Idah al-Asrar*, 106.

55. Ibid., 107.

56. These were typically from among Sufi shaykhs who were recognized by others as having obtained the highest levels of learning and awareness and bore the title of *qutb* or *ghawth* (like Fadl's father). Fadl made a cryptic point that these highest of the pantheon of Sufis knew each other and "needed each other." Ibid., 113.

57. In Malay the word *keramat* signifies the gravesite and the person buried there. Sumit Mandal, "Popular Sites of Prayer, Transoceanic Migration, and Cultural Diversity: Exploring the Significance of *Keramat* in Southeast Asia," *Modern Asian Studies* 46, no. 2 (2012): 355–72.

58. Fadl, *Idah al-Asrar*, 113.

59. Ibid., 114.

60. India is regularly cited as a place rife with paranormal powers from evil sources and subsequent deviant behaviors. Ibid., 99, 103, 114.

61. Ibid., 115.

62. Ibid.

63. This trinity of *islam*, *iman*, and *ihsan* directed at a pious life and salvation resonates with Fred Donner's recent revisionist account of the religion's founding in *Muhammad and the Believers*.

64. This is clearly a Sufi rendering of *ihsan*, because in the standard Sunni definition it would mean *taqwa*, or piety and goodness as reflected in the practice of the mandated pillars of worship.

65. Fadl, *Idah al-Asrar*, 117.

66. Ibid., 132.

67. In their work on the changing urban household of Istanbul, Alan Duben and Cem Behar argue that the late nineteenth century's "communications revolution" was responsible for proliferating across the social body a new way of life, *alafranga*, which "was both the model of modernity as well as the focal point of a growing cultural alienation." Duben and Behar, *Istanbul Households: Marriage, Family and Fertility, 1880–1940* (New York: Cambridge University Press, 2002), 21. See also Jacob, *Working Out Egypt*.

68. Al-Muwaylihi's account was more substantial and hence will receive more attention in this chapter. The reference to Arslan was made in Malayamma and Panangangara, *Mampuram Thangal*, 460. They suggest a friendship was established between the two based on Arslan's contribution to *Hadir al-Alam al-Islami*, which will be discussed below.

69. Roger Allen, "'Hadith Isa Ibn Hisham' by Muhammad al Muwailihi: A Reconsideration," *Journal of Arabic Literature* 1 (1970): 88–108.

70. Jacob Landau, "An Insider's View of Istanbul: Ibrahim al-Muwaylihi's Ma Hunalika," *Die Welt des Islams*, new series, 27, no. 1/3 (1987): 70–81, 72–73.

71. Landau suggests they were given as "examples of the strange manner of appointments and promotions at the Court of Abdul Hamid II." Ibid., 76.

72. This sections draws from the version in Ibrahim al-Muwaylihi, *Al-Amal al-Kamila*, ed. Roger Allen (Cairo: Al-Majlis al-A'ala li-l-Thaqafa, 2007), 133. See also Bang, *Sufis and Scholars*, 84–85; and Freitag, *Indian Ocean Migrants*, 193–94, who references al-Muwaylihi.

73. For a view of where the modernist reformist trajectory led, at a cultural level, in postwar Ottoman/Turkish society and beyond, see M. Brett Wilson, "The Twilight of Ottoman Sufism: Antiquity, Immorality, and Nation in Yakup Kadri Karaosmanoglu's *Nur Baba*." *IJMES* 49 (2017): 233–53; Adeeb Khalid, "A Secular Islam: Nation, State, and Religion in Uzbekistan," *IJMES* 35, no. 4 (2003): 573–98; Natalie Clayer, *Religion et nation chez les Albanais: Xixe–Xxe Siècles* (Istanbul: Isis, 2002), and *Mystiques, État et société: Les Halvetis dans l'aire balkanique de la fin du XVe siècle à nos jours* (Leiden: Brill, 1994); and Friedhelm Hartwig, "Contemplation, Social Reform and the Recollection of Identity: Hadrami Migrants and Travellers between 1896 and 1972," *Die Welt des Islams* 41, no. 3 (November 2001): 311–47.

74. Al-Muwaylihi, *Al-Amal al-Kamila*, 133.

75. I borrow and adapt here Adrienne Rich's notion of compulsory heterosexuality: a normative psychosocial order that became like the air one breathes, in her case, "disguising and distorting of possible options" for women while advancing the power of men. Rich, "Compulsory Heterosexuality and Lesbian Existence" (1980), *Journal of Women's History* 15, no. 3 (Autumn 2003): 11–48.

76. For a historically informed anthropological account of that tectonic shift, which among other things produced the category of the minority, see Mahmood, *Religious Difference in a Secular Age.*

77. It is fascinating to speculate about his plans to spread Islam in the US, assuming he had such plans. Would he have gone himself or appointed a son as his delegate? Would they have established an Alawi-Qadiri cell as their base of expansion?

78. Al-Muwaylihi, either from a simple desire to report all the facts at his fingertips or from a more nuanced plan to underscore how counterproductive the measures pursued by these shaykhs were for the empire, noted that Kamal al-Din's Ottomanist efforts in India were discovered by the British and he was swiftly deported.

79. For a broader view, see Isabel Hofmeyr, Preben Kaarsholm, and Bodil Frederiksen, "Print Cultures, Nationalisms and Public Spheres in the Indian Ocean," *Africa* 81, no. 1 (2011): 1–22.

80. For a study of this transformation and its implications for the present from a comparative Islamic law perspective, see Iza Hussin, *The Politics of Islamic Law: Local Elites, Colonial Authority and the Making of the Muslim State* (Chicago: University of Chicago Press, 2015).

81. Works that stand out in this regard are Nico Kaptein, *Islam, Colonialism and the Modern Age in the Netherlands East Indies: A Biography of Sayyid Uthman, 1822–1914* (Leiden: Brill, 2014); Reese, "Shaykh Abdullahi al-Qutbi"; and Amal Ghazal, "Conservative Thought in the Liberal Age: Yusuf al-Nabhani, Dream-Stories and the Polemics against the Modern Era," in *Arabic Thought beyond the Liberal Age: Towards an Intellectual History of the Nahda,* ed. Jens Hanssen and Max Weiss (Cambridge: Cambridge University Press, 2016), 214–33.

82. As we will see in Chapter 6, Fadl's attempts to leave Istanbul were consistently foiled by both British and Ottoman design.

83. The other side of this story of the press, of course, is growing censorship during the Hamidian period. For an excellent view of the censorial state's formation and expansion, see Ipek K. Yosmaoğlu, "Chasing the Printed Word: Press Censorship in the Ottoman Empire, 1876-1913," *Turkish Studies Association Journal* 27, nos. 1/2 (2003): 15–49.

84. Lothrop Stoddard (1883–1950) held a PhD in history from Harvard and was a eugenicist fearful of the rise of the darker races after the weakening of his own race in the "White Civil War," as he saw World War I; see *The Rising Tide of Color against White World Supremacy* (New York: Charles Scribner's Sons, 1921). He discerned continuity in the revival of Islam that he located as beginning with Muhammad Ibn Abd al-Wahhab in the eighteenth century.

85. Arminius Vámbéry, *La Turquie d'aujourd'hui et d'avant Quarante Ans* (Paris:

P.-V. Stock, 1898), 71–72, quoted in Stoddard, *The New World of Islam* (New York: Charles Scribner's Sons, 1921), 79. On the next page, Stoddard went on to add weight to Vámbéry's analysis with numbers: "In 1900 there were in the whole Islamic world not more than 200 propagandist journals. By 1906 there were 500, while in 1914 there were well over 1,000."

86. Aydin, *Idea of the Muslim World*.

87. The translator was Ajaj Nuwayhad. I consulted the second Arabic edition published in 1933 (1352H) by a press in Cairo owned by Isa Effendi al-Babi al-Halabi. On Arslan, see W. Cleveland, *Islam against the West: Shakib Arslan and the Campaign for Islamic Nationalism* (Austin: University of Texas Press, 1985).

88. Aydin suggests that Arslan accepted Stoddard's clash of civilizations framework and contested only details. Aydin, *Idea of the Muslim World*, 78.

89. Sayyid Ismail Attas, "Al-Jaza'ir al-Hindiyya al-Sharqiyya al-Hulandiyya," *Hadir al-Alam al-Islami*, 1:364–75. On the history and prominence of the Attas family in Southeast Asia, see Arai, "Arabs Who Traversed the Indian Ocean."

90. Sayyid Muhammad Ibn Abd al-Rahman, "Tashih wa Tawdih by the pen of a Hadhrami Scholar," *Hadir al-Alam al-Islami*, 3:157–83; see 165 for the futuwwa reference. This intervention was appended to Arslan's "Al-Islam fi Madaghaskar wa Jaza'ir al-Qumur," 3:120–83. On futuwwa, see Jacob, *Working Out Egypt*, ch. 8; and Rizvi, *History of Sufism in India*, 1:293–95.

91. *Malumat* ran from 1895 to 1903. The masthead announced its related purpose and quality: "Pages [of the journal] with works of the pen that are serving, in every possible way, the glorious Islamic umma and the noble Ottoman nation, are always eloquent" (*ummet-i celile-i islamiyenin ve millet-i necibe-i osmaniyyenin her vecihle menafi'ine hadim asar-i kalemiyeye sahaif her zaman kushadedir*). I thank Veysel Simsek for alerting me to the value of this source and Zehra Gulbahar for again sharing her fine translation skills.

92. *Malumat* 261 (November 8, 1900): 416–21.

93. *Malumat* 269 (January 3, 1901): 584.

94. *Malumat* 270 (January 10, 1901): 601.

95. *Malumat* 280 (March 21, 1901): cover.

96. *Malumat* 272 (January 24, 1901): cover.

97. *Malumat* 232 (April 19, 1900): 816–17. For major coverage of the war including front cover illustrations, see *Malumat* nos. 225–28 (March).

98. *Malumat* 242 (June 28, 1900): 32–33.

99. This positioning of the Ottomans would lead to a search for other models outside the West; see Renée Worringer, *Ottomans Imagining Japan: East, Middle East, and Non-Western Modernity at the Turn of the Twentieth Century* (New York: Palgrave Macmillan, 2014). And in the other direction, see Selçuk Esenbel, "Japan's Global Claim to Asia and the World of Islam: Transnational Nationalism and World Power, 1900–1945," *AHR* 109, no. 4 (2004): 1140–70.

100. *Malumat* 364 (November 29, 1900): 489. In *Mampuram Thangal* (463), Malayamma and Panangangara give Fadl's death year as 1901 and mention the appearance

of the obituary in *Malumat*, citing K. K. Muhammad Abdul Karim, the authority in Malayalam on the Alawis.

101. The Ottoman daily *Ikdam* carried front-page announcements of his death and funeral on October 27 and 28, 1900. I thank Zozan Pehlivan for tracking these down.

102. Arslan, "Al-Sayyid Jamal al-Din al-Afghani: Hakim al-Sharq," *Hadir al-Alam al-Islami*, 2:289–303.

103. Al-Afghani's experience in Istanbul seemed set to replay. The first time he had gone was in 1869, when he was welcomed into Tanzimat reformist circles but expelled after being accused of heresy by the religious establishment in 1871. This could also explain his nervousness about returning to the Ottoman capital. In any case, he spent the last years of his life there, from 1892 until his death in 1897. This time, his relations with the sultan went south when allegations of his involvement in the assassination of the Qajar Shah Nasr al-Din surfaced in 1896. For the most thorough account of his career, see Nikki R. Keddie, *Sayyid Jamal al-Din "al-Afghani": A Political Biography* (Berkeley: University of California Press, 1972). On Arslan's relationship with him, see Cleveland, *Islam against the West*.

104. Arslan, "Al-Sayyid Jamal al-Din al-Afghani," 294.

105. Al-Afghani and Fadl both addressed letters to Abdulhamid virtually begging him to permit their departure from Istanbul. For the former's letter translated to English, see "Undated Turkish Letter from Jamal al-Din, Istanbul, to Sultan Abdulhamid, ca. 1895–96," in Keddie, *Sayyid Jamal al-Din*, app. 4, 444–47.

106. Ibid., 445.

107. Fadl's letter to Abdulhamid, dated October 22, 1897, requesting permission to leave for Medina will be discussed in Chapter 6.

108. Devji, *The Impossible Indian*.

109. Perhaps the most important category shift was in time and its measure. See On Barak, *On Time: Technology and Temporality in Modern Egypt* (Berkeley: University of California Press, 2013); and Avner Wishnitzer, *Reading Clocks, Alla Turca: Time and Society in the Late Ottoman Empire* (Chicago: University of Chicago Press, 2015).

110. Giorgio Agamben, *The Time That Remains: A Commentary on the Letter to the Romans*, trans. P. Dailey (Stanford, CA: Stanford University Press, 2005), 25. While the messianic per se is not apposite for Fadl's framework, the temporality—"the time of the now"—that Agamben wrests from the foundational myth of the church is.

Chapter 5

1. On Islamic reformism in Kerala, see Abraham, *Islamic Reform*; and Filippo Osella and Caroline Osella, "Muslim Entrepreneurs in Public Life between India and the Gulf: Making Good and Doing Good," special issue, *Journal of the Royal Anthropological Institute* 15, S1 (May 2009): S202–21, and "Islamism and Social Reform in Kerala, South India," *Modern Asian Studies* 42, no. 2/3, (2008): 317–46.

2. An insistence on context reveals very different kinds of social, religious, and political projects emerging at different times. Ahmad Dallal, "The Origins and Objectives of Islamic Revivalist Thought, 1750–1850," *Journal of the American Oriental Society*

113, no. 3 (July–September 1993): 341–59. For an example of how difficult it is in fact to contextualize more recent movements in light of transnational discourses on Islam, see Paul Dresch and Bernard Haykel, "Stereotypes and Political Styles: Islamists and Tribesfolk in Yemen," *IJMES* 24, no. 7 (November 1995): 405–31.

3. Samira Haj, *Reconfiguring Islamic Tradition: Reform, Rationality, and Modernity* (Stanford, CA: Stanford University Press, 2008). For a broader global view of the return of tradition, see Mark Sedgwick, *Against the Modern World: Traditionalism and the Secret Intellectual History of the Twentieth Century* (New York: Oxford University Press, 2004).

4. Ho, *Graves of Tarim*, 16. On the current situation in Pakistan, see, e.g., https://www.bbc.com/news/world-asia-38994318 (accessed December 28, 2018). See also Sarwat Viqar, "Sovereignty, Modernity and Urban Space: Everyday Socio-Spatial Practices in Karachi's Inner City Quarters" (PhD diss., Concordia University, 2016).

5. See http://www.alhabibali.com/en/ (accessed September 18, 2016).

6. http://assafir.com/Article/509810/Archive (accessed September 18, 2016).

7. Going back to the role of the smuggled cassette sermons of Ayatollah Khomeini in preparing the ground for the "Islamic" Iranian revolution, communication technologies and religious movements post–World War II have often been studied together. See, e.g., Annabelle Sreberny-Mohammadi and Ali Mohammadi, *Small Media Big Revolution: Communication, Culture and the Iranian Revolution* (Minneapolis: University of Minnesota Press, 1994); and for a more critical approach, see Charles Hirschkind, *The Ethical Soundscape: Cassette Sermons and Islamic Counterpublics* (New York: Columbia University Press, 2006), and "Experiments in Devotion Online: The Youtube *Khutba*," *IJMES* 44 (2012): 5–21. See also Peter Mandaville, *Transnational Muslim Politics: Reimagining the Umma* (New York: Routledge, 2001), 154; Arvind Rajagopal, *Politics after Television: Religious Nationalism and the Reshaping of the Indian Public* (New York: Cambridge University Press, 2001); Steven Barraclough, "Satellite Television in Iran: Prohibition, Imitation and Reform," *Middle Eastern Studies* 37, no. 3 (July 2001): 25–48; and Jon W. Anderson, "The Internet and Islam's New Interpreters," in *New Media in the Muslim World*, ed. Dale F. Eickelman and Anderson (Bloomington: Indiana University Press, 2003), 45–60.

8. The implications of cybermedia existing in a "smooth" space include being "nomadic," challenging if not overthrowing the capacity of older hierarchical structures to contain and arrest movements at will. The potentiality of this space was anticipated before its materialization by Deleuze and Guattari in *A Thousand Plateaus: Capitalism and Schizophrenia*, trans. Brian Massumi (Minneapolis: University of Minnesota Press, 1987), esp. 351–423.

9. This also seems prudent, given the number of media studies careers made by cannibalizing one of its firstborns for reveling in form; see Marshall McLuhan, *Understanding Media: The Extensions of Man* (New York: McGraw-Hill, 1964).

10. In Malabar itself there is heated debate in multiple forums (physical and virtual) on the proper interpretations of Islam, which would require another book to treat properly.

11. On the Saudi role in producing a "clean" cinema phenomenon in Egypt, see Karim Tartoussieh, "Cinema and the Islamic Revival in Egypt," *Arab Studies Journal* 15, no. 1 (Spring 2007): 30–43. For a creative analysis that looks at reality television, see Marwan M. Kraidy, "Saudi Arabia, Lebanon and the Changing Arab Information Order," *International Journal of Communication* 1 (2007): 139–56. Retrieved from http://repository.upenn.edu/asc_papers/198 (December 28, 2018). And on the possibility of resistance through a variety of media, see Mamoun Fendy, "CyberResistance: Saudi Opposition between Globalization and Localization," *CSSSH* 41, no. 1 (January 1999): 124–47.

12. Wisal (or Wesal) was shut down in 2014 by Saudi authorities after it was accused of fanning the flames of sectarianism in the country and in the region, leading to violence against Shi'a. See https://www.huffingtonpost.com/2014/11/05/saudi-arabia-wesal-tv-sectarian-tension_n_6105830.html (accessed December 28, 2018). However, after the minister of information who ordered the closure was removed from office, Wisal seems to have resumed operations and remain defiantly anti-Shi'a: http://tvwesal.com/about-us/ (accessed December 28, 2018).

13. *Fiqh* is the part of Islamic law encompassing the juristic tradition.

14. I found a playlist of fifty-eight episodes of *Kasr al-sanam* (Shattering the idol), which aired on Safa between 2012 and 2014, here: https://www.youtube.com/playlist?list=PLqxsrf-AmwqY3ZWqhx-rDuiFy_ryH4tWR (accessed August 25, 2014). It has since been deleted.

15. I lost the link to Umar al-Zayd's original article on al-Arabiyya.net when my computer was stolen and was unable to locate it again, but another piece quoted extensively from it, including the lines quoted here: Khalid al-Shay'ia, "Expert on Iranian Affairs Warns of Iran's Exploitation of the Hajj Season to Cause Unrest," October 18, 2011, https://www.alarabiya.net/articles/2011/10/18/172480.html (accessed September 3, 2017). The hajj dispute continued in 2016 (1437H) as Iran demanded an independent international Islamic commission to review Saudi preparations and conduct the world's largest annual pilgrimage after the previous year's trampling incident that left over four hundred Iranian pilgrims dead.

16. The version I viewed originally, https://www.youtube.com/watch?v=Slco3YMpxdo (accessed April 25, 2012), has since been removed. The popularity of this segment is evinced by its reposting in two parts: (1) https://www.youtube.com/watch?v=LEW8RdrhG9M&frags=pl%2Cwn, and (2) https://www.youtube.com/watch?v=uklqoaYzEEs&frags=pl%2Cwn (accessed December 28, 2018). The most relevant section begins in part 2 at time index 9:05/57:04.

17. https://www.youtube.com/watch?v=LEW8RdrhG9M&frags=pl%2Cwn; see time index 57:00/1:01:08.

18. Giorgio Agamben, "From the State of Control to a Praxis of Destituent Power" (lecture in Athens, November 16, 2013), https://roarmag.org/essays/agamben-destituent-power-democracy/ (accessed August 22, 2017). Examining Hajj management, John Willis has recently argued that biopolitics was a defining element in the formation of the Saudi state. "Governing the Living and the Dead: Mecca and the Emergence of the Saudi Biopolitical State," *AHR* 122, no. 2 (April 2017): 345–70.

19. In *Contesting the Saudi State: Islamic Voices from a New Generation* (New York: Cambridge University Press, 2007), Madawi al-Rasheed argues that Wahhabism is authoritarian; however, the rapid rise in Saudi wealth since the 1970s and the explosion in communications technology have together produced intellectual and political debate redeploying the very same terms of the eighteenth-century call to reform.

20. Pascal Ménoret, *The Saudi Enigma: A History*, trans. P. Camiller (New York: Zed Books, 2005), 47. Ménoret demonstrates that "Wahhabism" does not map onto any indigenous Saudi theology or political movement: "It involves a *passion* rather than a description, denotes an external fantasy rather than an actual reality, is part of a political strategy rather than a scientific approach" (58). See also Ménoret, *Joyriding in Riyadh: Oil, Urbanism, and Road Revolt* (New York: Cambridge University Press, 2014); and A. Knysh, "A Clear and Present Danger: 'Wahhabism' as a Rhetorical Foil," *Die Welt des Islams* 44, no. 1 (2004): 3–26.

21. The revision of the colonial history of race in India, for example, contrasts the global development of racial science in the eighteenth century with ostensibly older "civilizational" discourses that Indians themselves easily appropriated. However, beginning with a brilliant if macabre scene of skulls lined up on a surgeon's table in Calcutta, Shruti Kapila goes on to contrast the emergence of racial science and popular phrenology as part and parcel of colonial power with the local "insurgent knowledge and techniques" of *samudrikvidya*. The latter was also concerned with physical signs of difference but deployed its knowledge in a way that enabled a reconstitution of self at a highly individualized level. Kapila, "Race Matters: Orientalism and Religion, India and Beyond c.1770–1880," *Modern Asian Studies* 41, no. 3 (2007): 471–513.

22. *Qubur* (sing. *qabr*) simply means graves. The derivative *quburiyyun* is a neologism that literally translates as "grave-ists," analogous to *dusturiyun* (constitutionalists) derived from *dustur*. In the context of Wahhabi propaganda, the sought-after effect would be captured by "grave worshipper."

23. Such a critique did not have to emerge from outside, nor was it new; see Alexander Knysh, "The Cult of Saints and Religious Reformism in Hadhramaut," in Freitag and Clarence-Smith, *Hadhrami Traders, Scholars and Statesmen*, 199–216.

24. For a broader view, see Michael Farquhar, "Saudi Petrodollars, Spiritual Capital, and the Islamic University of Medina: A Wahhabi Missionary Project in Transnational Perspective," *IJMES* 47 (2015): 701–21, and *Circuits of Faith: Migration, Education, and the Wahhabi Mission* (Stanford, CA: Stanford University Press, 2016).

25. T. Hegghammer, *Jihad in Saudi Arabia: Violence and Pan-Islamism since 1979* (New York: Cambridge University Press, 2010).

26. These are *salat* (prayer), *sawm* (fasting), *zakat* (tithe), *hajj* (pilgrimage), and sometimes *jihad* (defined variously as spiritual struggle and defensive war).

27. Both quotes were tweets from May 17, 2014, https://twitter.com/d_omar55 (accessed August 19, 2014). A retweet from @abo_asseel on May 20 provides a link to al-Zayd's appearance on the satellite station al-Majd discussing "Esoteric Thought and Its Danger for Islam."

28. The comment appeared in the original version I viewed, https://www.youtube

.com/watch?v=Slco3YMpxdo (accessed April 25, 2012), which was removed, but only after the comments section had been disabled. The reposting of the al-Zayd DNA show is also accompanied by extensive comments.

29. Misrecognition of a Sufi as Wahhabi by the colonial state and the larger imperial bureaucracy may attest better than any other source to their moments of agreement. As late as 1925, the British were still assessing the legacy of Sayyid Fadl, which will be addressed later in relation to "returns." In one of the many reports from that period, Fadl was "remembered" as an "Arab priest" expelled from India for "the dissemination of violent Wahabi doctrines." C. H. Silver for Sec'y Economic and Commerce Department to Sec'y of State Colonial Office, December 15, 1925, IOR/L/PS/11/6, 648: 1912 Secret. Silver was merely repeating the view of the government of Madras, expressed in a letter to the Home Department of the government of India, September 3, 1925.

30. Mahmood, *Politics of Piety.*

31. Agrama, *Questioning Secularism.*

32. Medievalists have also made significant contributions concerning the creative uses of sources typically considered part of superstitious traditions. On using hagiographies to reveal the power of Sufis under the Seljuqs, see Omid Safi, *The Politics of Knowledge in Premodern Islam: Negotiating Ideology and Religious Inquiry* (Chapel Hill: University of North Carolina Press, 2006).

33. Malayamma and Panangangara, *Mampuram Thangal,* 25.

34. Ibid., 9–11.

35. Ibid., 98.

36. Ibid., 101–3.

37. Ibid., 104.

38. Ibid., 124.

39. Ibid., 126.

40. Ibid., 127.

41. Ibid., 129.

42. Ibid., 132. The term "discursive tradition," introduced in Chapter 2, references Tala Asad's famous reconceptualization of Islam as unfolding in a dynamic field of debate and argumentation rather than conventional views, which either presuppose an always already formed static entity or posit a thoroughly fragmented plurality of practices whose parts do not add up to a whole. In Asad's words: "What is a tradition? A tradition consists essentially of discourses, that seek to instruct practitioners regarding the correct form and purpose of a given practice that, precisely because it is established, has a history . . . An Islamic discursive tradition is simply a tradition of Muslim discourse that addresses itself to conceptions of the Islamic past and future, with reference to a particular Islamic practice in the present." Asad, "The Idea of an Anthropology of Islam" (occasional paper, Center for Contemporary Arab Studies, Georgetown University, Washington, DC, 1986): 1–22, 14.

43. On the gendered implications of conversion in relation to recognition and justice, see Wilson Chacko Jacob, "Conversion Trouble: The Alawis of Hadhramawt, Empire,

Gender and the Problem of Sovereignty in Nineteenth-Century South India," *Gender and History* 25, no. 3 (November 2013): 683–99.

44. Malayamma and Panangangara, *Mampuram Thangal*, 138, 141.

45. Ibid., 170–71.

46. While there is no room to consider this angle here, the Mappila public sphere in the present mirrors the Saudi one but with space for Sufi positions. See, e.g., the Malayalam Hidaya network's series *Mukhamukham* (Face-to-face), in which theological disputes are staged: https://www.youtube.com/watch?v=Enw8wTO13UU&frags=pl%2Cwn (accessed December 28, 2018).

47. Conolly to Pycroft, September 19, 1853, cited in Dale, *Islamic Society*, 166.

48. Cemil Aydin's recent revision of pan-Islamism as a shared discursive ground on which Ottoman-British diplomacy was enabled in new ways after the Russo-Turkish war and the major loss of Ottoman lands in Europe in 1878 recasts the Hamidian period as a whole. Aydin, "The Muslim World of the Queen and the Caliph: Illusions of Pan-Islamism from Imperial Peace to Jihad, 1873 to 1914" (paper presented at the UC Berkeley workshop *Between the World and the International: Thinking with Ottoman and Islamic Pasts*, November 11, 2016), and his *The Idea of the Muslim World*.

49. This section draws on the account given in *Madhribhumi*, June 5, 2005.

50. The quote is from a draft letter scribbled on a minute paper signed by J. P. Gibson in February 1925 and enclosed within a cover of the Political and Secret Department dating from 1912. The papers and attachments in this file number sixty pages and were absorbed by the Economic and Overseas Department into their records. IOR/L/PS/11/6, 648: 1912 Secret.

51. Of course, these are only attempts that sought British permission.

52. Report of Shakour Bey, March 5, 1895, enclosed in Cromer to Earl of Kimberley, March 5, 1895, FO 78-4790. Cromer noted that Shakour's position at the time was chief interpreter of the Intelligence Department of the Egyptian Army. A blog by Shakour's Irish great-granddaughter has some information about the family: http://anna-green.blogspot.in/2006/05/milhem-shakoor-bey.html. Samir Raafat, who writes about the life of Cairo's elite, mentions another Shakour involved in the suburban building projects of the early twentieth century: http://www.egy.com/landmarks/05-01-15.php (accessed August 30, 2017).

53. Cromer to Earl of Kimberley, March 3, 1895; and Draft of Earl of Kimberley to Cromer, April 5, 1895, FO 78-4790.

54. Cromer to Marquess of Salisbury, March 21, 1896, FO 78-4790.

55. Telegram draft of FO to Currie, March 27, 1896, FO 78-4790; relays information from political resident at Bushire.

56. India Office to Under Secretary of State FO, March 3, 1896, FO 78-4790.

57. FO to Currie, March 27, 1896.

58. Currie to FO, March 29, 1896, FO 78-4790.

59. Ultimately the Marquess of Salisbury, who was prime minister and foreign secretary, concurred with his ambassador at Istanbul, and it was decided to postpone any explicit warnings to the Turkish government. Draft of FO to IO, March 31, 1896, FO 78-4790.

60. Khalid Medani suggested an abiding affinity of noble families for one another as an explanation of the normality of such correspondence. He noted that to this day the British ambassador in Khartoum makes it a point to have dinner with the descendants of the mahdi of Sudan who led the movement in the 1880s that ended Egyptian administration and resulted in the death of General Charles Gordon, which in turn was met with horrific reprisals by British forces under General Kitchener. One can almost sense the macabre atmosphere of those dinners, recurring rituals to appease the spirits.

61. Confidential Chief Sec'y Govt. of Madras to Sec'y Govt. of India, Home Dept., September 3, 1925, IOR/L/PS/11/6, 648: 1912 Secret.

62. HH the Prince Seyed Ali Bey Hyder c/o H.D.H. Abdul Gaffoor Esq., Fort Colombo, July 20, 1925, IOR/L/PS/11/6, 648: 1912 Secret.

63. Ibid.

64. Home Dept to Madras, September 11, 1925, IOR/L/PS/11/6, 648: 1912 Secret. Before he could be detained, Sayyid Muhammad returned to Syria.

65. Judicial and Political Sec'y Minute, November 1919, IOR/L/PS/11/6, 648: 1912 Secret.

66. Each of these regional nation-states was to be prepared to lead an independent political future, and thus old transregional or new transnational movements had to be checked, even in the case of Zionism at times.

67. Political Department, Foreign Office Minute, November 8, 1911, IOR/L/PS/11/6, 648: 1912 Secret.

68. Cumberbatch to Lowther, October 18, 1911, IOR/L/PS/11/6, 648: 1912 Secret.

69. Sahl to Secretary of State for India, October 1, 1911, IOR/L/PS/11/6, 648: 1912 Secret.

70. History is irony: an Iowan town established in the wake of the ethnic cleansing of the indigenous population chose to name itself Elkader, in honor of the Algerian hero who led the resistance against French colonial violence (!): http://www.elkader-iowa.com/History.html (accessed September 26, 2016). See the interesting discussion of Abd al-Qadir's prison writing in John Chalcraft, *Popular Politics in the Making of the Modern Middle East* (Cambridge: Cambridge University Press, 2016), 102–11.

71. See Michael Provence, *The Great Syrian Revolt and the Rise of Arab Nationalism* (Austin: University of Texas, 2005), 104–5.

72. Minute by J. E. Shuckburgh, Secretary Judicial and Political Department, April 12, 1919, IOR/L/PS/11/6, 648: 1912 Secret. Shuckburgh suggested that by "Minister of Justice" Sahl probably meant the home secretary.

73. Sahl to King George V, enclosed in Gerald Spicer, Foreign Office to Under Secretary of State, India Office, February 21, 1919, IOR/L/PS/11/6, 648: 1912 Secret. This letter and another enclosed (Sahl to Minister of Justice) were undated translations from the Arabic originals. Interestingly, they were sent from Beirut via the chief political officer attached to the Egyptian Expeditionary Force, likely in late 1918.

74. Ibid.

75. Ibid. The English translations render the name as "Jufri."

76. Ibid.

77. Ibid.

78. Ibid.

79. Sayyid Sahl to King George (English trans.), 23 Dhu al-Hijja 1337 (September 20, 1919), enclosed in Foreign Office to India Office, November 11, 1919, IOR/L/PS/11/6, 648: 1912 Secret.

80. Ibid.

81. Though I did not find intense emotions of spiritual or cultural loss surrounding the end of the Ottoman caliphate—only intense fiscal concerns—they may nonetheless have been there; see Hassan, *Longing for the Lost Caliphate*, 142–54.

82. Sayyid Sahl to King George, 23 Dhu al-Hijja 1337.

83. The article initially described them as grandsons, but later, in recounting their genealogy, it is apparent they were Sahl's son's sons. See below and *Madhribhumi*, June 5, 2005, 25.

84. Ibid. The publisher of the pamphlet was given as the Shri Ram Jayam Press.

85. Ibid., 24.

86. This accords with the genealogy presented in al-Mashur's *Shams al-Zahira*, vol. 1.

87. *Madhribhumi*, June 5, 2005, 26.

88. Ibid., 27. The oral history version published by the magazine does not accord with the historical record.

89. Ibid. I am unsure if this refers to King Faisal's only son, Crown Prince Ghazi.

90. Ibid., 26.

Chapter 6

1. Darul Huda is a member of the Federation of the Universities of the Islamic World based in Morocco and the League of Islamic Universities based in Cairo, Egypt.

2. Sayed Haidar Ali Shihab Panakkad, Chancellor (Darul Huda Prospectus, n.d.). When Darul Huda was first established, it was as a small Islamic academy and did not achieve university status until 2009. Now it has campuses in Kerala, Andhra Pradesh, West Bengal, and Assam.

3. Haji, Darul Huda Prospectus, n.d.

4. "DHIU: A University with Difference," in Darul Huda Prospectus, n.d. Omitting the article in titling the mission statement, a common elision among Malayali speakers of English, recasts or widens the reach of the difference the institution hopes to make in the world.

5. Recognizing the much larger pool of students in the North, beginning in 1999 the Darul Huda began offering courses in Urdu in the framework of a "National Institute for Islamic and Contemporary Studies."

6. I am not the first to note this problem of memory. The mission statement of the Mappila Heritage Library, which is "unique of its kind in Malabar," also bills itself as "an attempt against forgetfulness." http://www.mappilaheritagelibrary.com.

7. Al-Ahdal, *The Sharpest Sword* (Muharram: At-Tibyan Publications, 1430 AH / January 2009 CE).

8. He was the first US citizen known to be targeted and assassinated in a drone attack, for which the Obama administration sought legal justification through the war on terror joint resolution (Public Law 107-40: Authorization for Use of Military Force) that Congress passed on September 18, 2001. https://www.congress.gov/107/plaws/publ40/PLAW-107publ40.pdf.

9. See, e.g., the chapters in the recent volume edited by Dyala Hamzah, *The Making of the Arab Intellectual: Empire, Public Sphere and the Colonial Coordinates of Selfhood* (New York: Routledge, 2013). Some interesting new perspectives on this moment are Johann Buessow, "Re-Imagining Islam in the Period of the First Modern Globalization: Muhammad Abduh and His *Theology of Unity*"; and Joachim Langner, "Religion in Motion and the Essence of Islam: Manifestations of the Global in Muhammad Abduh's Response to Farah Antun"; both in *A Global Middle East: Mobility, Materiality and Culture in the Modern Age, 1880–1950*, ed. Liat Kozma, Cyrus Schayegh, and Avner Wishnitzer (New York: I. B. Tauris, 2015), 273–320 and 356–64, respectively. See also Jens Hanssen and Max Weiss, eds., *Arabic Thought beyond the Liberal Age: Towards an Intellectual History of the Nahda* (New York: Cambridge University Press, 2016).

10. For a global view, see Nile Green, *Terrains of Exchange: Religious Economies of Global Islam* (New York: Oxford University Press, 2014).

11. These processes inform Kecia Ali's take on narrations of the life of Muhammad, tracing the modernization chronology to the conclusion that Islam was Protestantized. Ali, *The Lives of Muhammad* (Cambridge, MA: Harvard University Press, 2014).

12. Two recent works by Charles Maier speak to this point: *Once within Borders: Territories of Power, Wealth, and Belonging since 1500* (Cambridge, MA: The Belknap Press of Harvard University Press, 2016), and *Leviathan 2.0: Inventing Modern Statehood* (Cambridge, MA: Harvard University Press, 2012).

13. For a recent history of the Omani side of events that ultimately culminated in rebellion or revolution in Dhofar, see Abdel Razzaq Takriti, *Monsoon Revolution: Republicans, Sultans, and Empires in Oman, 1965–1976* (New York: Oxford University Press, 2013); on Fadl, see pp. 25–31. See also Calvin Allen, "Sayyids, Shets and Sultans: Politics and Trade in Masqat under the Al Bu Sa'id, 1785–1914" (PhD diss., University of Washington, 1978), and "The Indian Merchant Community of Masqat," *Bulletin of the School of Oriental and African Studies* 44, no. 1 (1981): 39–53.

14. Fadl to Turki, January 17, 1879, IOR/R/15/6/12 Dhofar.

15. It would be hard to distinguish Alavi's take from that of Brigadier-General Francis Loch, political resident at Aden, on whom she relies heavily. See, e.g., Enc. No. 5, Ltr. No. 3-9, Loch to C. Gonne Secretary to Govt of Bombay, Political Department, January 3, 1879; and Enc. No. 6, Ltr No. 42-208, Loch to Gonne, Pol Dept. February 4, 1879. These letters are in the series FO 78-3615, which she mines extensively for the truth of Fadl's life.

16. Alavi, *Muslim Cosmopolitanism in the Age of Empire*, Kindle loc. 2085 (p. 113) and loc. 3087 (p. 167). This flies in the face even of the British imperial records, which essentially support Fadl's account that he was invited to Dhofar to settle bloody tribal feuds. This does not mean that he had no political ambitions, only that an appreciation

of the political, not to mention the ethical, in terms of his conceptual universe, that is, not predetermined by empire-states, is lost in this reading.

17. It is not only colonial sources that can stand in the way of drawing a genuinely historical picture of individual sayyids; see Alexander Knysh, "The Sada in History: A Critical Essay on Hadrami Historiography," *Journal of the Royal Asiatic Society* 9, no. 2 (July 1999): 215–22.

18. Alavi's treatment of the other Muslim "outlaws" is more compelling, perhaps unsurprisingly since she offers extensive analyses of their writings in Urdu. Her assimilation of the Hadhramawt-Malabar transoceanic history of an Alawi like Fadl into what is essentially a land-based Delhi-Mutiny narrative frame does not agree in terms of the timeline. See her introduction to *Muslim Cosmopolitanism.*

19. Alavi, *Muslim Cosmopolitanism*, loc. 2915 (p. 158).

20. Although she does list some of his Arabic treatises, there are no attempts to read them. An unpublished biography ostensibly written by Fadl's son in Arabic (I was unable to locate it) is also cited, but other than mining the first few pages for widely available information this too is not analyzed as a text.

21. The first lines of the letter are also omitted, likely for their formulaic quality. One could say that all religious language was deemed extraneous to the real intent of the letter. This may explain the translator's logic, and though the intent may indeed be accurately captured, something very important is nonetheless lost in translation here.

22. To suggest as Alavi does that his activities in Dhofar were instances of Fadl playing the "sayyid card" is to assimilate him entirely into the very imperial grids she aims to problematize and to miss the histories of law, theology, politics, and mysticism as they intertwined with histories of port cities, tribes, and transregional migrations in the constitution of a "Muslim cosmopolis" with a distinct tradition of conceiving sovereignty. Alavi, *Muslim Cosmopolitanism*, loc. 2851 (p. 154) and loc. 2928 (p. 158).

23. His literal signature was translated loosely and placed at the beginning of the letter, "From Sayyed Fadhl, Governing at Dhofar under the protection of the Sublime Porte." Given the period and the Arabic terminology used, a more exact translation would be: "From the Government of Dhofar Protectorate (*al-tabiʿa*) of the Sublime State."

24. BOA, Yildiz, Petitions and reports Y. PRK. AZJ. Folder nr: 25. Document: 1/1. Date: 1310/1892. The report's contents suggests that it was written at an earlier time when Fadl was amir of Dhofar (1876–79) or shortly thereafter and translated into Turkish later, perhaps the year given on the folder.

25. BOA, Yildiz, Petitions and reports Y. PRK. AZJ. Folder nr: 40. Document: 1/2. Date: 1317/1899.

26. On the Ottoman-Qajar survey commissions established for the first time through the 1847 Treaty of Erzurum and continuing until 1914, see Sabri Ates, *The Ottoman-Iranian Borderlands: Making a Boundary, 1843–1914* (New York: Cambridge University Press, 2013). One of the more famous borders of the period was the Durand Line of 1896 delimiting the territories of British India and "the Afghans." (Durand was fully aware of the Moplah Outlaw case; see Richey to Durand, February 4, 1886, enclosed in Foreign Dept., Gov of India to Earl of Kimberly, Sec. of State for

India, March 16, 1886, BL IOR L/PS/7/46, 1089–99.) On the Egyptian-Libyan border, see Matthew Ellis, "Between Empire and Nation: The Emergence of Egypt's Libyan Borderland, 1841–1911 (PhD diss., Princeton University, 2012). See also Thongchai Winichakul, *Siam Mapped: A History of the Geo-Body of a Nation* (Honolulu: University of Hawai'i Press, 1994).

27. BOA, Yildiz, Petitions and reports Y. PRK. AZJ. Folder nr: 40. Document: 1/2. Date: 1317/1899.

28. Benton, *A Search for Sovereignty*, 243–50.

29. We saw in Chapter 3 Fadl's treatment of the pressing geopolitical concerns of Muslims in the Arab subcontinent in terms of state interests, masalih al-dawla. A number of works deal with this concept's reconfiguration to fit modern state practices: see Dyala Hamzah, "From *'Ilm* to *Sihafa* or the Politics of the Public Interest (*Maslaha*): Muhammad Rashîd Rida and His Journal *al-Manar* (1898–1935)," in *The Making of the Arab Intellectual: Empire, Public Sphere and the Colonial Coordinates of Selfhood*, ed. Hamzah (New York: Routledge, 2013), 90–127; Khaled Fahmy,"The Police and the People in Nineteenth-Century Egypt," *Die Welt des Islams* 39, no. 3 (November 1999): 340–77; and Aaron Jakes, "The Scales of Public Utility: Agricultural Roads and State Space in the Era of the British Occupation," in *The Long 1890s in Egypt: Colonial Quiescence, Subterranean Resistance*, ed. Marilyn Booth and Anthony Gorman (Edinburgh: Edinburgh University Press, 2014), 57–86. On the prior or classical evolution of *maslaha*, see Felicitas Opwis, *Maslahah and the Purpose of the Law: Islamic Discourse on Legal Change from the 4th/10th to 8th/14th Century* (Leiden: Brill, 2010). Also, for a cautionary tale on allowing the rupture in the nineteenth century to leave in its wake an idealized view of premodern legal transactions, see Ahmed F. Ibrahim, *Pragmatism in Islamic Law: A Social and Intellectual History* (Syracuse, NY: Syracuse University Press, 2015).

30. For the nineteenth-century colonial encounters that formed "the law," or modern law as such, see Esmeir, *Juridical Humanity*, for the Egyptian-British context; for the Algerian-French context, see Sarah Ghabrial, "The Traumas and Truths of the Body: Medical Evidence and Divorce in Colonial Algerian Courts, 1870–1930," *Journal of Middle East Women's Studies* 11, no. 3 (November 2015): 283–305.

31. Muhammad Ibn Ali al-Alawi migrated from Tarim to the coastal town of Mirbat in present-day Oman. His significance in genealogical terms is in the fact that "the lines of ascent of all Hadrami sayyids meet in him." Ho, *Graves of Tarim*, p. 40.

32. BOA, Yildiz, Petitions and reports Y. PRK. AZJ. Folder nr: 40. Document: 2/2. Date: 1317/1899.

33. On Barak, "Outsourcing: Energy and Empire in the Age of Coal, 1820–1911," *IJMES* 47 (2015): 425–45; see also chapter 1 in Timothy Mitchell, *Carbon Democracy: Political Power in the Age of Oil* (New York: Verso, 2011).

34. https://archive.org/stream/sirhenrymainebrioomain/sirhenrymainebrioomain_djvu.txt.

35. On Maine as the architect of colonial indirect rule, see Mantena, *Alibis of Empire*.

36. For this fascinating history, see Aimee M. Genell, "The Well-Defended Domains: Eurocentric International Law and the Making of the Ottoman Office of Legal Counsel" (paper presented at the workshop *Between the World and the International: Thinking with Ottoman and Islamic Pasts* convened by Samera Esmeir, UC Berkeley, November 10–11, 2016), and "Empire by Law: Ottoman Sovereignty and the British Occupation of Egypt, 1882–1923" (PhD diss., Columbia University, 2013).

37. On the insider-outsider status of the Ottomans in this family of nations, see Davide Rodogno, "European Legal Doctrines on Intervention and the Status of the Ottoman Empire within the 'Family of Nations' throughout the Nineteenth Century," *Journal of the History of International Law* 18 (2016): 5–41, doi: 10.1163/15718050-12340050. On the artificiality of 1856, see M. S. Palabiyik, "The Emergence of the Idea of 'International Law' in the Ottoman Empire before the Treaty of Paris (1856)," *Middle Eastern Studies* 50, no. 2 (2014): 233–51, doi: 10.1080/00263206.2013.870890; see also Palabiyik, "International Law for Survival: Teaching International Law in the Late Ottoman Empire (1859–1922)," *Bulletin of the School of Oriental and African Studies* (2014): 1–22, doi: 10.1017/S0041977X14001037. On one of the paradoxical ends of law developed in a context of empires yet with a nation-state horizon, see chapter 1, "The Ottoman Empire and the International Law of Minority Protection, 1815–1923," of Umut Ozsu, *Formalizing Displacement: International Law and Population Transfers* (New York: Oxford University Press, 2015).

38. BOA, Yildiz, Petitions and reports Y. PRK. AZJ. Folder nr: 40. Document: 2/2. Date: 1317/1899.

39. This is the general argument of my *Working Out Egypt*. See also M. C. Yildiz, "'What Is a Beautiful Body?': Late Ottoman 'Sportsman' Photographs and New Notions of Male Corporeal Beauty," *Middle East Journal of Culture and Communication* 8 (2015): 192–214; Lucie Ryzova, *The Age of the Efendiyya: Passages to Modernity in National-Colonial Egypt* (New York: Oxford University Press, 2014); and Keith Watenpaugh, *Being Modern in the Middle East: Revolution, Nationalism, Colonialism, and the Arab Middle Class* (Princeton, NJ: Princeton University Press, 2006).

40. Azyumardi Azra, *The Origins of Islamic Reformism in Southeast Asia: Networks of Malay-Indonesian and Middle Eastern "Ulama" in the Seventeenth and Eighteenth Centuries* (Honolulu: University of Hawai'i Press, 2004). See also Hussin, *Politics of Islamic Law.*

41. Horace Walpole, India Office to the Under Secretary of State, Foreign Affairs, August 24, 1893, FO 78-4790.

42. The linkages of Fadl to Zanzibar and Dhofar via the mediation of Hilal b. Amr and of the Sanusiyya movement to Muslims across Africa and South Asia are the subjects of the fascinating file BL IOR/R/20/E/198, Item 1, covering the year from December 1895 to December 1896. Also, it seems that upon leaving Dhofar in 1879, Fadl's initial plan was to sail to East Africa. Fadl to Nakib Saleh, 12 Safar 1296, enclosed in Saleh to Loch, February 5, 1879, Loch to Secy Govt Bombay Pol Dept, February 14, 1879, FO 78-3615. On North Africa, see Edmund Burke III, "Pan-Islam and Moroccan

Resistance to French Colonial Penetration, 1900–1912," *Journal of African History* 13, no. 1 (1972): 97–118.

43. Translated Copy of Fadl to Currie, August 2, 1896, enclosed in Herbert to FO, August 7, 1896, FO 78-4790.

44. Fadl had written directly to Gladstone before, in 1884, when he received an unfavorable reply from Madras regarding the government's handling of his property case in Malabar. He stated that his concern was the exercise of good and just government, which the queen and her officials were "always talking about," and not recuperating the value of the property even if it were big, which it was not. Fadl to Gladstone, 15 Rajab 1301 (May 10, 1884), enclosed in F. Clare-Ford Ambassador at Constantinople to India Office, October 12, 1893, FO 78-4790.

45. In that letter he made an opaque reference to the Ottoman red-crescent flag being raised in place of the Omani that suggested it was not appropriate; perhaps the real point was lost in translation. Nonetheless, it is interesting given our broader point about caring for a flock and sayyid sovereignty; he said: "As, however, I am totally unable to accept an alteration in the form of the administration of the Principality *or the substitution of a flag conveying a meaning which denotes a kind of connection* I beg to state that I am sending a special envoy thither for the purpose of restoring the affairs of the Principality to their original condition." What that "connection" might have been is left unclear, but it would seem that by 1896 Fadl was done with the Ottomans. Petition from Fadl to Currie, May 13, 1896, enclosed in Herbert (Istanbul) to FO, May 25, 1896, FO 78-4790.

46. Fadl to Currie, August 2, 1896, FO 78-4790.

47. Ibid.

48. Ibid.

49. These instructions were only sent on to London with Mr. Herbert's previously cited dispatch of August 7, 1896.

50. Translation of Fadl to Currie, May 13, 1896, enclosed in Herbert to FO, May 25, 1896, FO 78-4790.

51. BOA, Yıldız Tasnifi. Perakende Evrakı. Arzuhal ve Jurnaller. Y. PRK. AZJ. Dosya no. 35. Gömlek sıra no. 38. 1315 /1897.

52. Translation of Fadl to Currie, May 13, 1896, enclosed in Herbert to FO, May 25, 1896, FO 78-4790.

53. This account is drawn from a front-page report in the Ottoman daily *Ikdam*, October 28, 1900. An obituary also appeared on the front page the day before under the title "A Great Loss," stating the exact time of death as noon, Friday, October 26 / 2 Receb 1318.

54. The falling out between Sultan Abdulhamid and Sayyid Fadl might explain the former's absence from the funeral. However, the state honors granted to this Mappila-Arab sufi-sayyid hints at a more complex relationship.

55. Fadl, *Hadhihi al-tariqa al-hanifa al-samha'* (Istanbul, 1317 [1899/1900]); henceforth *This True and Merciful Way*.

56. Cover of *This True and Merciful Way*: "Maarif nezaretinin (181) numarali

ruhsatnamesiyle Kiztashi Caddesindeki Kirimi Abdullah Efendi'nin matbaasinda tab'
olunmushtur." I was unable to establish the date of the first printing.

57. Ibid., 2.

58. David Scott, *Conscripts of Modernity: The Tragedy of Colonial Enlightenment*
(Durham, NC: Duke University Press, 2004).

59. Fadl, *This True and Merciful Way*, 3.

60. Ibid.

61. Ibid., 4.

62. Earlier, in the section on the luminaries of the Alawiyya, Fadl made a marginal
insertion of his father's name into the genealogical chain with the exact day and date
of his death: Sunday, January 28, 1844. Ibid., 17.

63. See Ch. 4, n81.

64. The Prophet's life is where all speculation and related modeling begins. "Birth and
death inescapably bookend every human life, but not all life writing starts with the subject's
birth or ends with her death." Ali, *Lives of Muhammad*, 21 (quote), 25 (Sufi approach).
See also Annemarie Schimmel, *And Muhammad Is His Messenger: The Veneration of
the Prophet in Islamic Piety* (Chapel Hill: University of North Carolina Press, 1985). The
literature on shrines is now quite large; specific to the Alawis, see Bang, *Sufis and Scholars*;
and Ho, *Graves of Tarim*. On the general problem of making death and burial specifically
Islamic after the passing of the Prophet, see Leor Halevi, *Muhammad's Grave: Death Rites
and the Making of Islamic Society* (New York: Columbia University Press, 2007).

65. A "crore" is ten million and is usually used with Indian rupees but might also
be used in other contexts involving large numbers, such as population.

66. The adjacent house outside the gates that was displayed as Sayyid Alawi's and
had low ceilings was, according to Sayyid Jifri, a fake thrown up for tourists by man-
agers of the shrine complex.

67. In fact, descendants of Arab migrants, though not all necessarily sayyids of
the Ba Alawi, remain important political actors in Kerala today. During my summer
research trip in 2009, the most prominent Kerala Muslim leader, Shihab Thangal, an
Alawi sayyid, died. His passing was noted in every corner of the state. For more on this
figure, see http://www.shihabthangal.org/index.htm.

68. Abul Ala Maududi, hailed as one of the founders of political Islam and a Quran
translator, departs from the standard translations of *al-akhira* in this verse as "the hereafter"
by rendering it "Life to Come" (at least according to the English translation of his Urdu
original). See https://quran.com/17, go to "Settings," and select the Maududi translation.
In the context of the Night Journey and from Sayyid Fadl's usage in the *Idah* (see Ch. 4,
n24), "life-as-other" captures better the alterities of human life in relation to an unfolding
of the unity of life—wherein multiple times, places, and (non)beings are at play.

Conclusion

1. Tending to the grounds was a small army of laborers whose physical features
conveyed the diversity of South Asia.

2. My assumption that these men were elite was based on the luxury vehicle
from which each one of them alighted, leaving the driver to wait. Another sign was

the sublime scent imparted to the surroundings by what I suspected were their custom-made perfumes.

3. The sign-makers seem to believe that these are two different people.

4. Qaboos is the great-great grandson of Turki, from whom Fadl had sought aid in suppressing the rebellion in Dhofar.

5. See Chapter 2.

6. Arundhati Roy, *The Ministry of Utmost Happiness* (London: Hamish Hamilton, 2017), Kindle edition, loc. 164 of 6495 (p. 14).

7. For example, my first experience at the enormously popular and commercialized shrine of Nizamuddin (d. 1325) in Delhi was exactly the opposite of peace and quiet. My delicate constitution aside, the vast majority of visitors seemed nonplussed by the merchants and other representatives of money-making schemes and carried on with their individual quests.

8. An unusually varied set of views can be found in the recent volume edited by Zvi Ben-Dor Benite, Stefanos Geroulanos, and Nicole Jerr, *The Scaffolding of Sovereignty: Global and Aesthetic Perspectives on the History of a Concept* (New York: Columbia University Press, 2017).

9. Martti Koskenniemi, "Conclusion: Vocabularies of Sovereignty—Powers of a Paradox," in *Sovereignty in Fragments: The Past, Present and Future of a Contested Concept*, ed. Hent Kalmo and Quentin Skinner (New York: Cambridge University Press, 2010), 222–42; quote on 239. Remarkably for an edited volume, the concluding essay critiques nearly every contribution as lacking.

10. Giorgio Agamben, *The Kingdom and the Glory: For a Theological Genealogy of Economy and Government*, trans. Lorenzo Chiesa with Matteo Mandarini (Stanford, CA: Stanford University Press, 2011).

11. Hallaq, *Impossible State*.

12. Schmitt, *The "Nomos" of the Earth*; the German original was published in 1950, though according to Ulmen in his "Translator's Note," the majority of the manuscript was written between 1942 and 1945 (35). Schmitt uses the Greek *nomos* to signify much more than law; it is the entire order ensuing from the appropriation, division, and use of the earth.

13. Ibid., 100. The critical arc of Schmitt's argument is that US entry into World War I in 1917 (with Woodrow Wilson's move from isolation to intervention while newly claiming the impossibility of neutrality in a context when world peace and freedom were threatened) set the tone for the postwar shift away from the traditional Eurocentric, nondiscriminatory identification of belligerents—enabling the bracketing of war, that is, obviating annihilation—to a conception of just war and the criminal aggressor state. The death knell of the old order thus tolled.

14. Ibid., 252.

15. Lauren Benton, *Search for Sovereignty*, 282–83.

16. Schmitt's last lines in the foreword to *The "Nomos" of the Earth* are telling: "The earth has been promised to the peacemakers. The idea of a new *nomos* of the earth belongs only to them" (39).

17. Pedersen, *The Guardians*.

18. He was convinced that this *nomos*, which relegated the concrete legal-spatial

formation of European international law to history, would be as unsuccessful as its more hybrid interwar predecessor in securing peace. It was perhaps all the more remarkable that this critique of a US-dominated "free world" was launched from Germany in 1950 as the Cold War began.

19. Benton, *Search for Sovereignty*, 283.

20. Clare Anderson, *Convicts in the Indian Ocean: Transportation from South Asia to Mauritius, 1815–53* (New York: Palgrave Macmillan, 2000); Lakshmi Subramanian, "Of Pirates and Potentates: Maritime Jurisdiction and the Construction of Piracy in the Indian Ocean," *UTS Review* 6, no. 2 (November 2000): 14–23; Bose, *A Hundred Horizons*; Metcalf, *Imperial Connections*; Green, *Islam and the Army in Colonial India* and *Bombay Islam*; S. Layton, "Commerce, Authority and Piracy in the Indian Ocean World, c.1780–1850" (PhD diss., University of Cambridge, 2013); Matthew Hopper, *Slaves of One Master: Globalization and Slavery in Arabia in the Age of Empire* (New Haven, CT: Yale University Press, 2015); Mathew, *Margins of the Market*. See also the fascinating discussion of mutiny and sea voyages as "spaces for incubation and as vectors for diffusion of political radicalism," in N. Frykman, C. Anderson, L. Van Vos, and M. Rediker, "Mutiny and Maritime Radicalism in the Age of Revolution: An Introduction," *International Review of Social History*, special issue, 58 (2013): 1–14. For a different perspective on empires and agency, see Ho, *Graves of Tarim*; and Fahad A. Bishara, *A Sea of Debt: Law and Economic Life in the Western Indian Ocean, 1780–1950* (New York: Cambridge University Press, 2017).

21. On the mediation of divine sovereignty by human agents in the context of pilgrimage to the most sacred of Muslim shrines, see Juan Campo, "Authority, Ritual, and Spatial Order in Islam: The Pilgrimage to Mecca," *Journal of Ritual Studies* 5, no. 1 (Winter 1991): 65–91. Campo focuses on Islamic and modern "epistemes" of control and the potential for challenging them, while eliding the question of faith and its possibility of illuminating more than relationships between authority and obedience.

22. The numerous polls on diminishing religiosity measured in part by church attendance rely on the very concept of "religion" that is assumed to have receded in modernity. There is no way to know if people's desire for intimacy with a higher power, which may fade in and out during one's lifespan, has changed over time when religion is taken out of the equation as something already known. The closest one may get to such feelings statistically is represented in secular terms of "wonder about the universe," which a Pew study shows has in fact grown between 2007 and 2014: http://www.pewforum.org/religious-landscape-study/frequency-of-feeling-wonder-about-the-universe/.

23. I was often reminded of similarities and differences with his contemporary Lalla Zainab, who inherited the mantle of her father's spiritual and material power in the Algerian frontier and of whom Julia Clancy-Smith has written beautifully in *Rebel and Saint: Muslim Notables, Populist Protest, Colonial Encounters, Algeria and Tunisia, 1800–1904* (Berkeley: University of California Press, 1997), 214–53, and "The House of Zainab: Female Authority and Saintly Succession in Colonial Algeria," in *Women in Middle Eastern History*, ed. N. Keddie and B. Baron (New Haven, CT: Yale University Press, 1991).

Index

Made in the USA
Middletown, DE
25 July 2019